Second Edition

Learning and Memory

John Lutz

East Carolina University

Long Grove, Illinois

This book is dedicated to the future:
To John David and Chris

For information about this book, contact:
Waveland Press, Inc.
4180 IL Route 83, Suite 101
Long Grove, IL 60047-9580
(847) 634-0081
info@waveland.com
www.waveland.com

10-digit ISBN 1-57766-361-6
13-digit ISBN 978-1-57766-361-4

Printed in the United States of America

10 9 8 7 6 5 4

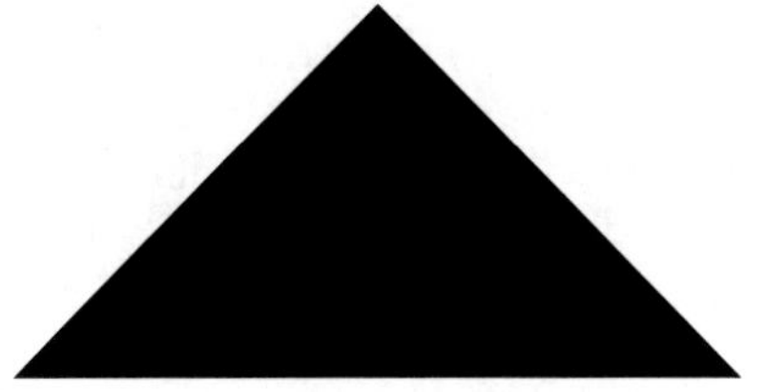

Preface to Students

My goal was to offer students a book that was easy to read and understand, yet still provided thorough coverage of the technical world of research and theory in learning and memory. First and foremost, I wanted the book to teach the concepts, not just list facts; therefore, the technical findings and theories are related to ordinary experiences. You will find many everyday examples. When you encounter an example, put yourself in it and remember details of your own experience that are relevant to the principles being illustrated. This will make the principles more meaningful for you. The exercises at the end of each chapter were designed to extend and elaborate on this approach by giving you practice in thinking about and using the concepts in analyzing realistic situations.

Read the book one section at a time. Try to summarize each section in a few sentences, at least mentally. You should be able to do at least two of the following three things with the key concepts at the beginning of each chapter: (1) define them, (2) group them into categories and subcategories, and (3) give an example of them. Your grouping of concepts might be helped by looking at the breakdown of chapter topics in the Contents. When you finish a chapter, try to answer the questions at the end.

If you have trouble comprehending technical writing, try reading the last half of chapter 13 right away. It provides many tips on how to understand and remember academic material. Although my goal was to write for students, I also had to write a book that would satisfy the teachers of this course, who demand scientific accuracy and documentation of every fact. I have included many references that indicate the basis for ideas, such as (Lutz, 2005). If you find these annotations distracting, just ignore them and focus on the discussion.

However, don't skip over the descriptions of the experiments. Experiments that are described in detail are meant to illustrate the concepts being discussed; you should try to relate each experiment to your own experiences. This can be done even with animal research! Students often tell me they can't relate to rat research. I never have been able to understand why; after all, each experiment is designed to discover something about how all creatures work, including humans, not just rats. If you use your imagination, you should be able to find similarities between your learning experiences and virtually every experiment cited in this book. If you can't do this, ask your teacher for assistance. That is what he or she is there for. If you make an honest intellectual effort to understand this material, you will be rewarded, not only with a better grade but also with a better understanding of your own world. Good luck.

Acknowledgments

There are many people who made it possible for me to write this book, and I wish to thank them all. I am especially grateful to all my teachers, but especially those at Florida State University and the University of Tennessee, and most especially William Calhoun and Howard Pollio and his wife, Marilyn, at Tennessee. I would also like to thank my colleagues and friends at East Carolina University, especially Robert Graham and Larry Means, and Darin Kaiser, now at IUPUI in Fort Wayne, Indiana; Michael Justice, now at Nova; and Michael Hoane, now at Southern Illinois University. This book represents my best effort at understanding the many ideas these people have presented to me. I must also acknowledge the help of reviewers who very diligently provided many detailed suggestions and helpful comments for the first edition: Stephen R. Coleman, Cleveland State University; Tom Gerstenberg, SUNY Potsdam; Mike Knight, University of Central Oklahoma; Roger Mellgren, University of Texas; and Gerald Mertens, St. Cloud State University. I would also like to thank Gayle Zawilla and all the people at Waveland Press who have helped me with this revision. Finally, and most especially, I would like to thank my wife and colleague, Marsha Ironsmith, and my sons, John David and Christopher, for their love, encouragement, and support during this project. I couldn't have done it without them, and they made it worth doing.

John Lutz

What Is Learning?

▲ Key Concepts ▲

behaviorism	maturation
cognitive neuroscience	memory
conditioning	operational definition
determinism	reductionism
hypothesis	reflex
information processing	reinforcement
innate	response
instinct	stimulus
learning	

Why do we do the things that we do? How are we able to do them? These are the fundamental questions that psychology attempts to answer. If the questions are put in these very general terms, psychologists would be in wide agreement about the answers: our hereditary backgrounds and the environments in which we live cause us to have certain abilities and desires and to do certain things. This is the classic nature (heredity) vs. nurture (the environment) distinction. Most people seem to have a general idea of what constitutes environmental or learning influences and what might be due to something else. However, many of us also find some situations difficult to understand and are only occasionally able to explain our decisions, and very few of us are able to give definitions that will truly capture the meaning of the words. Let's first address the question of why we do things by considering a few examples. Then we can try to work our way through the harder steps. Try to classify each of the following examples as the result of having been learned or of some other cause (like innate tendencies or instincts).

a. MJ has gotten very good at playing basketball.
b. Susan knows a lot about the poetry of e. e. cummings.
c. Edison Carter has a lot of trouble remembering any long number, such as his ten-digit school ID number.
d. Aphrodite, a two-year-old, is easily startled by sudden loud noises.
e. Aphrodite also knows to stay away from her big brother when their mother scolds him.
f. Prometheus the cat comes running to the kitchen at the sound of the can opener.
g. Prometheus arches his back and hisses at the sudden appearance of a dog.
h. Deep Blue, a computer program, beat the world champion in a chess game.

Make your decisions before reading further.

Most of us would consider MJ an example of learning because of the words "has gotten," which convey a sense of change. Few of us would suppose that he had come out of the womb shooting baskets, and the notion that he might have just "grown that way" doesn't seem too likely either—why him but not others? Similarly, Susan and her poetry, Aphrodite's caution around her brother, and Prometheus's fondness for the sound of can openers all suggest something that developed as a result of things that happened to them—practicing, reading, experiencing. So these seem likely to be examples of learning, and most people can recognize them as such.

Edison, however, can't seem to learn something well enough to remember it. While this example must involve learning, there's more to it than that. A built-in limit such as Edison's seems like an innate tendency, so after some thought some of us would come to that conclusion, although the limit is clearly on his ability to learn something new. Therefore, this is a complicated example that might involve bits of learning and other causes as well.

Since most children are easily startled by a sudden loud noise, and the tendency can be shown in most newborn babies, Aphrodite's reaction is fairly easily identified as a built-in or *innate* tendency. Developmental psychologists refer to it as the startle reflex, an innate behavior.

Many of us might suppose that Prometheus arching his back represents some innate tendency or instinct because cats and dogs often seem to react with hostility to each other. When we see this reaction in a cat, it usually seems to occur very quickly and automatically. On the other hand, sometimes cats and dogs live together, so it may be hard to decide for this one. Can some innate predispositions be changed through learning?

Finally, what is a computer doing in a book about learning? I have found that many students react to computers with what I call "protoplasm chauvinism"—computers aren't alive, therefore they can't think, and they can't learn. Deep Blue actually exists and has defeated the world chess champion, Garry Kasparov. Did it learn how to play, or was it just "programmed"? Programming seems analogous to an innate characteristic in a living creature, and thus not like learning at all. Perhaps the role of experience, or learning, was small in the case of Deep Blue, but other computer mechanisms have been designed to be capable of learning, and some computer scientists have studied the learning process in computers. These studies have had results directly comparable to studies of learning in living creatures, including human beings.

This book is fundamentally concerned with these questions about learning and will attempt to provide some partial answers from two perspectives that have turned out to be particularly informative and helpful. While psychologists often disagree on details, most would agree that the environment is an important shaper of our actions, and that learning is the mechanism by which the environment has its influence. Therefore, the study of the learning process is fundamentally important to an understanding of how and why we do things. One important perspective on how the learning process shapes us comes from a group of psychologists who emphasized the study of learning—**behaviorism**. The other, more recent perspective comes from *information-processing* research. Scientists from both backgrounds actually proceeded in their study of learning by following much the same path we just followed, but they started with carefully controlled experiments rather than natural examples. Only after years of exploring the characteristics of learning did they try to define what they were studying.

Behaviorist Views of Learning

The behaviorist view of learning was first proposed by John B. Watson almost a century ago. He suggested that our hereditary nature was relatively unimportant and that most of what we are and what we do is the result of learning. Watson suggested that the study of animals like dogs, cats, and rats in learning situations could tell us much about how people learn, and he believed that learning was the major influence on our behavior. He thought that our hereditary characteristics had only a small influence on our behavior, and he accepted the idea that learning was the result of experience and was the formation of an association between pieces of our experiences. He also felt that awareness was not necessary for learning to occur. Similarly, it may not be necessary for an individual to *want* to learn. Watson repeatedly argued against the use of such mentalistic terms as *awareness*, maintaining that they were unnecessary. He suggested that saying that an individual wanted something just begged the question with a mentalistic answer—why did the person want it to begin with? This was one of the primary principles of behaviorism, which advocated explanations based entirely on observable stimulus-and-response events without any reference to mental events such as thoughts, ideas, wants, awareness, or feelings, which are internal and therefore difficult to study. We often infer these internal events on the basis of our observations of someone's behavior and the events surrounding that behavior. Watson suggested that we should skip the inferred, intervening steps and try to connect the observable stimuli and responses directly. This behaviorist view of learning dominated much of psychology until the 1960s and still remains influential.

What exactly do we mean by the term *learning*? Although people routinely use the term to refer to acquiring a skill (e.g., basketball or tennis) or social awareness (e.g., Aphrodite avoiding her brother at crucial moments), they tend to restrict themselves to academic learning when asked to discuss the learning process or to define learning. However, the examples we have just considered make such a definition too restrictive; we believe that learning is the central factor determining most of our actions. Our habits, mannerisms, styles of personality, and even our likes and dislikes are all strongly influenced by learning. In addition, a great deal of the behavior of other creatures seems to be due to learning. Where, then, does learning start, and how do we distinguish it from other influences on behavior?

Unfortunately, the popular use of the term *learning* often differs from the technical use of the term by experimental psychologists. The examples of popular usage mentioned above generally conform to the usages by psychologists, but many other common usages mislead us about the nature of learning. Sometimes learned behaviors are labeled as *instincts* when the speaker clearly intends to use such terms as *reflexive* or *automatic*. For example, does the news editor truly mean that a reporter has "instincts" for a story? Does a sportscaster truly mean that an athlete has "instincts" for football? Generally, if pressed, these people would admit that what they mean is that the individuals in question have so much experience and practice at their tasks that they do things automatically or reflexively (in the case of the athlete's performance) or that this experience has led the reporter to make decisions automatically, without being able to clearly specify the exact reasons for the decisions. We must be more careful than this in our descriptions if we are to develop any understanding of these phenomena.

However, our examples do suggest some characteristics that seem to apply to all of the possible examples of learning:

1. *Learning involves a change in behavior.* This applies to MJ's basketball, Susan's poetry, Aphrodite's avoidance of her big brother, and Prometheus's coming to the kitchen.

2. *Learning happens because of experiences.* Again, its likely that the change suggested in each of these four examples was because of things that happened to the individuals.
3. *Learning leads to different behaviors, depending on the circumstances.* Not everyone plays basketball, and the players differ greatly in how they play; similarly, different folks have differing reactions to poetry, and different children learn to handle their big brothers differently.

In addition, our examples illustrate two other points:

4. *Other creatures besides people can learn.* Prometheus's learning might not look the same as Susan's, but it surely qualifies on the previous three characteristics.
5. *Skills and other things besides knowledge can be learned.* MJ's basketball skills and Aphrodite's fear are examples of learning things other than "facts" from books.

On the other hand, the cat's arching its back changes very little, is difficult to eliminate (few cats and dogs live in peaceful coexistence), and occurs in about the same way in every cat.

When we don't have any indication of change, then we might suspect that the behavior was caused by something other than learning, such as an instinct or innate tendency. Edison's memory limit might be genetically determined. Generally, however, psychologists have found that most human behavior does change and that there is little likelihood of instincts in people. The most commonly accepted idea is that the simpler a creature is, the more its behavior is governed by innate mechanisms, such as instincts, and more advanced or complex creatures depend more on learning. We often assume that humans are among the most advanced creatures. Although this general idea is widely believed, it has important qualifications and limitations; it's far from being a perfectly accurate analysis of the differences in species' behavior. We shall address these issues in chapter 9. Now let's consider some definitions of learning.

How Do We Define Learning?

Several psychologists have spent major portions of their careers in attempting to precisely define learning operationally. **Operational definitions** fit their examples properly—including all examples and excluding all nonexamples—and specify how someone would go about producing the phenomenon (specifying the activities or operations one has to go through to observe the thing defined). If an operational definition is properly worded, anyone can follow the procedures specified—the operations—and then reconstruct what is being defined. An operational definition, therefore, would tell you how to recognize examples of learning and how to recognize nonexamples when you see them.

Kimble's Operational Definition

One of the definitions of learning widely accepted by the behaviorists was formulated by Gregory Kimble. According to Kimble (1961), **learning** is "a relatively permanent change in behavioral potential as a result of [reinforced] practice" (p. 6). We can see that it fits our examples of Susan's poetry preference, the "street learning" of Aphrodite about her brother, and MJ's skill development.

Kimble's definition is one of the most widely respected and used, but it too has weaknesses. If we go through it word by word, discussing the strengths and weaknesses, we can discover a great deal about learning. The term *relatively permanent*, which sounds rather vague, was meant to refer to the fact that once something is learned, it stays with the learner until death or until something specific happens to eliminate it from the behavioral repertoire. Besides death, there are many ways in which a creature could "lose" a piece of learning, such as disease or brain injury, or (most importantly for us) through learning something else that is incompatible with the original learning and that either dominates (and therefore replaces) the original learning as an influence on behavior or just cancels it out. Most researchers feel that the new learning would not erase the old but would just cause the individual to make responses incompatible with the old so that the old learning would not be displayed. Thus, it has been generally believed that "forgetting" does not truly occur—the memories are still there, we just fail to retrieve them sometimes. Currently, several researchers in memory are investigating whether this is the case or whether the new learning actually modifies the old memory (Loftus, 1979). We will refer to some of this work in chapters 10 and 11.

Kimble used the word *change* to refer to the unfortunate fact that learning can result in losses as well as gains, or regression as well as improvement. In other words, we can learn bad habits, such as smoking or cursing, as well as good habits, such as reading or good manners; and we also can learn *not* to do something (often because we are punished for doing it). For example, suppose Aphrodite sees her big brother looking angry and decides *not* to go into the den to see what is on TV. In fact, learning itself has little to say about the goodness of what is learned in the way we usually think of such values. An evolutionary interpretation might presume that the learning process allows creatures to be better prepared to survive, but clearly sometimes the "wrong" things are learned. For example, smoking cigarettes is harmful to one's health, but many people still learn to do it.

Kimble originally referred to a *change in behavior* because it is a clearly observable event that fits the requirements of operational definitions nicely. Unfortunately, several psychologists have demonstrated that learning may occur in circumstances where there is no immediate change in behavior, so he had to change the term to *behavioral potential.* The classic demonstration was that of E. C. Tolman (Tolman & Honzik, 1930), who showed that rats left to wander around in a maze without receiving rewards at the end nevertheless were learning. When they did get rewarded, however, they quickly improved to the performance level of rats that had received rewards all along. Tolman suggested that it was unlikely that they had suddenly started learning faster; rather, he suggested that they had been learning all along but had no reason to display their learning. This is similar to classroom situations in which students don't express themselves. The teacher doesn't know how much they have learned until a test comes around; then the students have a reason to display what they have learned—getting a passing grade!

Thus, psychologists often make a distinction between learning and *performance*, a distinction that has been very useful for several reasons. This distinction allows psychologists to separate learning from *motivation*. Learning influences behavioral potential, and motivation influences the conversion of that potential into behavior; in other words, motivation can cause the learned potential to be realized or expressed. Learning represents part of the underlying reason for a behavior, whereas performance represents the observable consequence of learning.

What causes learning? Kimble's answer was "as a result of [reinforced] practice." Practice simply means that when the same experiences occur repeatedly, they will usually be learned better. Kimble chose the word *practice* rather than *experience* because at the time most psychologists felt that learning required more than one exposure to an experience (one "trial"). Usually several repetitions of an experience are necessary for learning, and additional practice almost always improves learning. However, since Kimble's day several important experiments have shown that, under certain circumstances, learning can occur as a result of just one exposure to a situation. The most important circumstance for one-trial learning is the impact of the stimuli used; for example, if we are training a dog to fear the sound of a bell by pairing the bell with an electric shock, then the stronger the shock, the fewer such pairings are needed to create the fear of the bell; at very high intensities, one pairing is often sufficient (Azrin & Holz, 1966; Church, 1969; Walters & Grusec, 1977).

In addition to practice, many other important characteristics of every experience influence how learning occurs. The study of these factors influencing learning is generally conducted by experiments on two forms of **conditioning**. Conditioning simply refers to two rather well specified learning situations, *classical* and *operant conditioning* (discussed in detail in chapters 3 and 4). Together they seem to describe many examples of learning; we shall see that they do apply at least somewhat to all the examples mentioned at the beginning of the chapter and many more. Chapters 2 through 7 present some of these studies of conditioning.

I have added brackets around the word *reinforced* in Kimble's definition; most texts don't bother, but earlier psychologists were about evenly divided over whether that word was necessary in the definition. Reinforcement is a very special and highly technical term when used in discussing learning, and we shall devote a great deal of discussion to it. **Reinforcement** means following a behavior with an especially powerful event, such as a reward or punisher. Sometimes in popular usage the term *reinforcement* refers to the mere fact that an experience has been repeated; this is not the way the term is used by psychologists.

Learning theorists have shown that one of the conditioning procedures mentioned above very clearly requires reinforcement, but in the other conditioning procedure the presence of reinforcement can be argued. For now, I take the position that reinforcement often makes learning easier and quicker, but it is not necessary—that is, learning can occur in the absence of rewards or punishments. I am a cognitive psychologist; I study memory, concept learning, and other topics in which reinforcement is difficult to find. Other psychologists, particularly those who emphasize operant conditioning (procedures such as behavior modification), often suggest that learning always involves reinforcement. We will discuss this question more fully in chapter 8. For now, we can at least state that reinforcement involves accompanying an experience with an important consequence, such as reward or punishment, which usually makes the learning occur more quickly (in fewer trials).

An Alternative Definition

Kimble's (1961) definition leaves a few situations unclear. For example, if you lose your leg in a car accident, your walking behavior will be different after the accident than it was before; however, we would probably not want to refer to this change as learning. However, it *is* a behavior change, and it was caused by an experience. Some psychologists have addressed this problem by excluding the troublesome cases. One such definition, by Hilgard and Bower (1966), refers to learning as "the process by which an activity originates or is changed through reacting to an encountered situation, provided that such change can't be explained on the basis of native response tendencies, maturation, or temporary states of the organism such as those caused by fatigue or drugs" (p. 2).

The first part of this definition (before the comma) says essentially the same thing as Kimble's in different words; activity refers to behavior, and encountered situations refers to experiences. It is the last part of the definition that adds something new. It suggests that some changes are not caused by learning and cites three examples. Native response tendencies refers primarily to instinctive behaviors, such as those of the cat arching its back. **Maturation**, another somewhat familiar term to most people that has several popular meanings, here refers to any change in behavior based on physical growth rather than experience. Many human infants' abilities, such as sitting upright, crawling, and walking, depend on muscle development and nervous system growth that proceed in more or less the same way, relatively unaffected by particular experiences (Dennis, 1940;

Hindley, Filliozat, Klackenberg, Nicolet-Meister, & Sand, 1966; Kagan & Klein, 1973). Because of this, we wish to exclude any behavior changes based on maturation from our definition of learning.

The last example—temporary states of the organism—fails to live up to the "relatively permanent" part of Kimble's definition; the effects of fatigue and drugs fade away with time. No specific experiences are necessary to eliminate their effects, whereas learned behaviors require other learning specifically tailored to their characteristics to be eliminated. In addition to being temporary, fatigue operates primarily on the muscles; on the other hand, learning operates on the nervous system in the higher creatures. (However, some simpler creatures such as jellyfish and protozoa seem capable of some learning, even though jellyfish possess such simple nervous systems that there is no "brain," and protozoa have neither nervous systems nor nerves [Corning, Dyal, & Willows, 1973]. This illustrates the kinds of problems that occur when you try to define something complex in a very precise way—exceptions and loopholes are always cropping up.)

Does learning occur in only one way, or are there several kinds of learning? This question has generated a great deal of debate among learning theorists. Some claim that there is only one form of learning, whereas others suggest a dozen or more forms (Gagne, 1965; Razran, 1971). The single-form theorists have generally argued that an association is formed in the nervous system during learning, and all associations are formed in basically the same way. They note that many of the most important influences on learning work essentially the same way in all learning situations. For example, we will see that more practice leads to better learning across many types of learning situations, and that the strength or intensity of the stimuli influences all types of learning.

On the other hand, theorists who suggest that there are several forms of learning point to differences in the training procedures and differences in many of the factors that influence each form. For example, in most skill-learning situations quite a lot of practice is necessary, whereas in some cognitive learning tasks much less practice is needed. A person may take a lot of swings at the tennis ball before she gets it over the net, whereas she may learn to spell a new word after one or two exposures to it. These two examples do not necessarily represent two forms of learning; psychologists specializing in behavior modification might classify both skill and knowledge learning as examples of operant conditioning. Thus, the amount of practice needed to learn is not an especially good characteristic to use in classifying learning tasks. We will postpone consideration of most of the detailed arguments about forms of learning until chapter 8. In the next few chapters we will discuss four widespread forms of learning: habituation, sensitization, classical conditioning, and operant conditioning. This discussion will illustrate the problems that advocates of each approach must explain in maintaining their positions.

Learning vs. Memory

One question about the definition of learning remains: What is the difference between learning and memory? Definitions of **memory** emphasize the idea that the individual must maintain an internal record of previous experiences (Gordon, 1983). Thus, every experience that could be called learning implies a memory for the learning that will be demonstrated when the situation arises again. So where does learning end and memory begin? A simple answer involves the subject matter of studies of learning and memory. An investigator who is interested in the process of acquisition is interested in *learning*; an investigator who is interested in how well or how long (or just how) this learning is retained is interested in *memory*. In recent research this conceptual difference is the only one that reliably works. Although it may seem a minor distinction, we shall see that the kinds of experiments done as a result of this theoretical focus can appear very different. Other criteria for separating learning and memory, especially on the basis of time intervals involved in experiments, fail because some memory experiments involve time intervals shorter than those in learning experiments.

Kimble's (1961) and Hilgard and Bower's (1966) definitions tell us how to identify cases of learning: When we see a change in the behavior of an individual, it might be caused by learning. Their definitions also tell us what causes learning: experiences. Psychologists often refer to a specific aspect of an experience as a *stimulus* and a specific behavior as a *response*. What is meant by these terms? Again, many psychologists have studied the ways in which humans and other creatures respond and the ways in which they can be stimulated. We will require only a general idea of what these terms represent; for more detailed discussions, refer to J. J. Gibson's (1950, 1966) pioneering work or to Frank Logan's (1970) text, on which the current discussion is based.

What Is a Stimulus?

Technically, any stimulus is some adequate change in energy that strikes an appropriate sensory receptor of a creature. Described in these terms, when you look at a person on the street, the stimulus that you receive is actually the pattern of light waves reflected from her face and the background striking the rods and cones in the retina of your eye. This kind of description will not usually be necessary for our purposes, but it does have some consequences that are important in understanding the learning process. For example, there are forms of energy that we are not built to notice, such as x-rays and other forms of radiation. We can't see or otherwise sense these energies; if we were carelessly walking around the Chernobyl nuclear energy plant, for example, we could receive a lethal dose of radiation and not know it until we got sick. We don't have appropriate sensory receptors for these kinds of energies. Also, the term *adequate change*, although it sounds ambiguous, is meant to suggest that sometimes energy levels can be too low to notice, such as a whisper from across the proverbial crowded room or a shout at a heavy metal rock concert. These points are captured in a more practical definition, which essentially states that a **stimulus** is any event that causes a noticeable reaction. If an individual shows some behavioral change that follows a certain event, we can assume that event is a stimulus. We do have to keep in mind that the reaction might not be the one we wanted, however (if the person at the aforementioned rock concert responds with "huh?," then we know that our shout was a stimulus—it just wasn't stimulating in the way we might have hoped).

Notice that the nature of the stimulus isn't spelled out completely; we haven't said how big or complex or long lasting stimuli are. This is actually on purpose: we are free to describe things as stimuli in any convenient way, as long as our description allows others to identify them. Sometimes we may need to describe a letter *q* as a stimulus; in other cases we might conveniently describe the word *queen* as the stimulus, rather than as five stimuli. This is not seen as contradictory, merely convenient. As long as we can show a reaction, we can assume we've got a stimulus; unfortunately, the reverse is not necessarily true. In other words, if our friend at the rock concert doesn't say "huh?," it may be because he just didn't feel like responding. Perhaps if we had him connected to some machines that measure heart rate, blood pressure, and brain wave activity, we could notice some pattern that suggested he had heard us. Basically, then, we can call anything that happens around an individual a stimulus if we can show that the person has reacted to it in some way and if we can describe it precisely enough for others to be able to recognize it. Stimuli typically used in the study of learning include lights, visual patterns (including printed words), sounds, and such things as electrical shocks and food. Although many other things could be used, these are usually easily controlled and therefore are most convenient.

Stimuli can be classified in a number of ways, but one way is especially useful to us. We should note that one type of stimulus seems to have a much greater influence on creatures than others, even from birth. These innately powerful stimuli (examples are food, drink, and painful events) will be referred to in chapter 2 as those that do not habituate but instead *sensitize*, in chapter 3 as *unconditioned stimuli*, and in chapter 4 as *reinforcers*. In each case we're talking about basically the same things, but we will discuss different ways in which they exert their power. The other category of stimuli includes many more things, but they are stimuli that generally seem to have less powerful effects. These weaker stimuli will be referred to in chapter 2 as those that *habituate* rather than sensitize, in chapter 3 as *conditioned stimuli*, and in chapter 4 as *discriminative stimuli*.

What Is a Response?

A **response**, or a specific behavior, is defined as "any glandular secretion, muscle action, or other objectively identifiable aspect of the behavior of an organism" (Logan, 1970, p. 25). Glandular secretions are things such as stomach acids, saliva, and tears. Muscular actions include most of what people usually think of as physical behavior: walking, picking things up and moving them, or movements in general. However, talking involves movement of the jaws, mouth, tongue, lips, and diaphragm and therefore also fits the definition of a response. These parts of the definition really serve to illustrate the term with some good examples, though. They actually could be included under the other part of the definition, "objectively identifiable aspect of the behavior of an organism." *Objectively identifiable* means that if you can describe a piece of behavior in such a way that anybody could recognize what you are referring to, you have defined that particular response operationally. Here again, responses are often described at different levels of magnitude or complexity in different studies; if the description is accurate, this is acceptable. The important consideration is that everybody can recognize whatever is being called the response. One complication is that responses can have stimulus properties. For example, if a fly is buzzing around you (a stimulus), and you try to swat it (a response), you are aware of whether you hit it or not, and getting this feedback about your response can act as a stimulus to generate other responses (such as swatting again). In most experiments, these complications are kept to a minimum by limiting the things presented and observed, but in real life, stimulation and responses to it are occurring rapidly, overlapping and interacting with each other.

The most important way of categorizing responses is on the basis of their origin. Responses can be learned or unlearned (innate). **Innate** responses can be described as instinctive, or reflexive, such as the cat's back arching. A **reflex** is usually much simpler than an instinct, involving fewer body parts and nerve connections; reflexes can be changed in that we can get them to be triggered by new stimuli through classical conditioning (see chapter 3); and people have a number of reflexes. On the other hand, **instincts** are generally much more complex, very hard to change in any fundamental way, and don't seem to occur in people (see chapter 9 for more discussion of this point).

Although stimuli and responses can be any size, we've found it much easier to deal with small, simple stimuli and responses. Finding learning principles that adequately explain the effects of complex stimuli, such as the decline of communism in Russia or the causes for voting responses in national elections, has proved to be very difficult; explaining why a rat will push on a lever to get food has been somewhat easier. Furthermore, once we've got the rat's behavior explained, similarities to human behavior emerge. Although there are striking differences between a rat working for food and an executive working for a paycheck, the obvious similarity of general form has allowed us to make some predictions, or **hypotheses**, about human behavior that have been supported by observation and experiment.

S–R Psychology

Our description of learning so far says that individuals learn by encountering stimulus situations that they must respond to in new ways; they remember these new ways of responding the next time they encounter those stimuli. This perspective has led to the study of conditioning by the behaviorists often being described as S–R (stimulus–response) psychology. This is a bit unfair for two reasons: First, every finding in any area of psychology ultimately could be described in terms of stimulus–response relationships, because every area of psychology assumes that behavior is predictable and follows some kind of rules; to believe otherwise would be to doubt that we could ever explain behavior. Thus, all psychology assumes that behaviors have causes; this assumption is referred to as **determinism.** Some areas of psychology follow a less strict or less specific kind of determinism, but all do so to some extent. Thus, for example, the clinical psychologist attempting to help an individual with an anxiety disorder must identify the things that make the person anxious. She may not label these causes this way, but they may be labeled the stimuli that generate anxiety responses. The learning psychologist uses these terms because he wishes to study these relationships in as precise a manner as possible. We will see indications of the deterministic nature of learning theories throughout this book, although probably the most obvious cases will occur during our discussion of the ideas of John B. Watson in chapter 3 and B. F. Skinner in chapters 4 and 5.

A second, less important weakness of the S–R label is that learning may not be limited strictly to simple pairings of one S followed by one R as the term S–R suggests. In real life many such connections or associations may be learned at the same time (S + S + S + R + R, etc.). Also, the individual could learn that a response generates a stimulus, which would be R–S learning (possibly, again, with multiple Rs and Ss), or that a stimulus is associated with another stimulus (S–S learning). All three of these ways (S–R, R–S, and S–S) of characterizing the conditioning process have been suggested for one or another form of learning. The one remaining pairing, R–R learning, has not received as much attention in learning, although it may well prove relevant some day. It does, however, describe the applied area of psychological testing (the responses the person makes on the test are supposed to predict the responses that person would make in some real-life situations).

Thus, we see that attempts to define learning are intimately related to attempts to study and understand learning as a process and a phenomenon. These attempts have many implications. Among the most important are that behavior is determined by environmental conditions; that there are rules that operate systematically and therefore specify how behavior is determined; and that these rules are rather general, applying to a wide variety of creatures and circumstances in basically the same ways. The rules governing learning are usually assumed to involve the formation of mental associations or connections; a connection is formed between mental representations of the stimuli and responses that the learner experiences. Most associational models describe connections between pairs of representations.

Laws of association were first suggested by Aristotle and later, around the 1700s, frequently discussed by philosophers like John Locke and James Mill who have come to be called the British empiricists. One British empiricist, David Hartley (1705–1757), created a whole psychology around them, and so might be called the founder of associationism, although not the inventor of the ideas (Boring, 1950). These principles suggested that ideas or thoughts were seen as related to each other, or connected to each other, because they were close together (the law of contiguity), because they occurred together often (the law of frequency), or because they were similar to each other (the law of similarity). These were among the most widely quoted principles; over a dozen were suggested by various philosophers.

Some associational models try to account for the connections and the rules governing them strictly at the level of observable events (stimuli and responses); other models attempt to explain these events at the level of neuron activity. Learning theories that try to explain behavior at the physiological or neurological level are called reductionistic. **Reductionism** is an attempt to explain phenomena at one level by using reasons based on a lower or more basic level; thus, a reductionist would attempt to explain psychological phenomena by resorting to physiological (biological) phenomena, and then explaining the biological events by using the principles of biochemistry. Ultimately, this approach would then explain chemical reactions on the basis of the laws of physics. Psychologists are divided over the degree of reduction most appropriate for psychological phenomena. A biochemical explanation of a person's behavior in a learning situation might be very convincing and detailed, but is it of any practical value? Often such an explanation is too unwieldy to be useful in dealing with the behavior itself. Many behaviorists, such as B. F. Skinner, are convinced that useful explanations of behavior can be obtained without reduction to the biological level. We will encounter both reductionistic and nonreductionistic theories in our discussion of learning and memory.

Learning from the Information Processing and Cognitive Neuroscience Viewpoints

Information processing became an important influence in psychology during the 1960s and in the last two decades has come to be a dominant view in experimental psychology. It begins with an analogy between human behavior and a computer, rather than comparing us with animals as the behaviorists did. The rationale for this was first proposed by the English computer scientist Alan Turing (1958) and has since become known as the Turing test. He proposed that if you had to identify who you were conversing with by asking questions, and had to read answers to your questions on tape fed through two slots in the wall, could you tell which slot had a person behind it and which had a computer behind it? If the computer can fool you, it passes the Turing test. During the 1990s, several actual competitions occurred, and a few computer programs have come close to passing. So sometimes a computer can display some human capacities.

More specifically, though, can computers learn? Early models of learning systems in computers such as Miller, Galanter, and Pribram's *Plans and the Structure of Behavior* (1960) have led to more recent powerful *connectionist* models of learning, such as McClelland and Rumelhart's parallel distributed processing computer program (1988), which truly seems capable of learning in that it can change the ways it represents things and the ways it responds to them. (The parallel distributed processing connectionist model of learning is described briefly in chapter 13.) This has led to an **information-processing** definition of learning as "a change in the output of a system as a result of input." The term *input* corresponds directly to the terms stimulus and experience in behavioral definitions, and the characteristics attributed to the term stimulus seem to apply to the term input. However, the term input includes keyboard activity as well as the stimuli described above. Similarly, the term *output* seems to translate directly to the term response, but also includes monitor displays and printouts. In addition, the word *change* is also used in the same way as the behaviorists used it. Finally, the term *system* is meant to include computers or even formal, structured systems like a set of mathematical propositions in addition to including humans and other animals. While it might seem bizarre to think of a list of mathematical formulas as being capable of change, that is really what goes on inside the processors in the PDP learning programs.

Furthermore, this definition allows the information processors and cognitive neuroscientists (defined below) to emphasize internal conditions much more than behavioral theorists; for the information processors, the fundamental question is how the system represents input, and they have concluded that different parts of a system may represent input or stimulation differently. This has led to a number of ideas which the behaviorists chose not to address. The information processors posed several questions that they considered crucial for understanding learning, such as: How can a system learn at all? That is, (1) what is the structure or arrangement of elements in the system which allows it to learn or change? They refer to this as the computational architecture of the system. (2) How are experiences or examples used? (3) What is the role of previous knowledge or learning in "interpreting" or "understanding" experiences? And (4) what is the role of the "critic," a rather whimsical name given to a component they felt necessary, a component that evaluates the learner's performance to determine if it is optimal—the best way of responding to the circumstances (Stillings, et al., 1995, p. 199). The information-processing view therefore places much more emphasis on the inner workings of the learner than the behaviorist position did.

Many information-processing researchers seem to have gradually evolved into scientists interested in the nervous system, describing the neural activity which supports learning and higher mental processes. These researchers call themselves **cognitive neuroscientists**, and they are an example of the reductionist approach mentioned earlier.

A Brief Overview

Now we have a general idea of what we will be discussing. Our next questions will be: What are the basic forms of learning, and what are they like? These two questions will require about eight chapters to answer. Chapter 2 presents two very simple forms of learning (habituation and sensitization), chapter 3 introduces a more complex form of learning (classical conditioning), and chapter 4 introduces another complex form of learning (operant conditioning). Chapter 5 describes the aversive methods of operant conditioning, and chapter 6 examines some of the theoretical issues involved in operant conditioning. Chapter 7 presents two phenomena common to all the previously described forms of learning (generalization and discrimination). These chapters represent the foundation on which more complex situations and questions may be considered.

Chapter 8 returns to our question about how many forms of learning exist, this time discussed from the point of view of similarities and differences between forms of learning. In chapter 9 we return to our introductory distinction, the difference between learning and instinct, and we attempt to bridge the gap between these two influences on behavior. The remaining chapters deal with memory. Chapter 10 discusses memory and complex learning from the traditional learning theory position, and chapters 11 and 12 discuss memory from the information-processing perspective. Chapter 13 presents alternative information-processing views and also presents some suggestions on how to improve memory based on this theoretical framework.

Summary

Learning was defined by behaviorists as a relatively permanent change in behavior or behavioral potential as a result of practice. This means that learning potentially lasts a lifetime, may lead to decreases or increases (improvements or losses) in particular behaviors, and is caused by repeated experiences. We distinguish between behaviors that have been learned and behaviors that are innate or instinctive. Instinctive behaviors show much less capacity for change and much less variability than learned behaviors, because they are determined by genetic factors. Learning allows for behavioral differences between individuals and variation within individuals over time because individuals encounter different environments. Changes in behavior due to maturation or temporary conditions, such as fatigue or drug states, are also distinguished from learning. It is believed that most human behavior is the result of learning and that we have few, if any, instinctive behaviors.

There are four basic forms of learning: habituation, sensitization, classical conditioning, and operant conditioning. Because learning involves behaviors, we analyze behavior into specific responses. Responses are objectively identifiable behavior segments. Experiences are broken down into pieces of experience called stimuli. The definition of a stimulus is at the experimenter's discretion, as long as it can be recognized and agreed upon by other observers, and as long as the event causes some change in the learner.

Information-processing definitions of learning emphasize the nature of the system doing the learning: How does the system represent the aspects of the environment in which it is learning, and how can it modify and use these representations?

Questions for Discussion, Thought, and Practice

1. Define and give examples of the key concepts at the beginning of this chapter. You may find it useful to rearrange the terms into groups based on similarity of meaning or topic or to make a chart or diagram using them.
2. What are some of the different causes of behaviors? We mentioned two in detail and several others briefly in chapter 1.
3. Is wagging its tail a behavior that is learned or instinctive in a dog? Consider this question from the same perspective as the discussion of the examples at the beginning of the chapter.
4. Where does learning come from (what causes it)?
5. How do we know that learning has occurred?

6. What are some characteristics of instinct? How do these differ from learning characteristics?
7. Would it be better if we didn't have to learn things? Consider the advantages and disadvantages of learning versus instinct for everyday human activities and for basic human characteristics, such as our extended childhood.
8. How do we know that something is a stimulus?
9. How do we know when a behavior is a response?

Habituation and Sensitization

Two Simple Forms of Learning

▲ KEY CONCEPTS ▲

fatigue	sensitization
habituation	sensory adaptation
intertrial interval	spinal animal
pseudoconditioning	spontaneous recovery

People who move to a home next to railroad tracks or an airport often find the noise of passing trains or planes annoying at first. But after a while, they often "get used to it" and sometimes don't even notice it. A similar sequence has happened to some of us in reaction to the TV station logos that some stations began putting in one corner of the screen a few years ago. At first these were annoying, but after a few months we barely noticed them. TV stations are apparently aware of this, because some of them now move a little when they first appear, and a few have even added sound! These examples are at least partly the result of a learning process called *habituation*.

In this chapter we will discuss habituation, along with *sensitization*, a pattern where responses become exaggerated rather than weakened. These are the simplest forms of learning; at one time they were not even considered to *be* learning, but merely evolutionary predecessors or precursors to it because of their simplicity. Early research on them was conducted primarily by physiological psychologists and generated relatively little interest among learning theorists. Although they are much simpler than other forms of learning, today they are usually included in the category of learning, primarily as a result of the work of Richard F. Thompson (Thompson & Spencer, 1966; Groves & Thompson, 1970). Thompson was a physiological psychologist interested in the biological mechanisms responsible for learning; he saw habituation as a good way of reducing learning to its physiological underpinnings (recall the discussion of reductionism in the last chapter).

What Is Habituation?

Habituation is usually defined as a decrease in the strength of a response as a result of repeated stimulation (Harris, 1943). Implicit in the definition is the idea that the repeated stimulation is very similar from one presentation to the next. In fact, that is one of the basic factors determining whether habituation occurs or not. Habituation therefore can, and usually does, consist of presenting one stimulus again and again until the response that usually occurs weakens and eventually disappears entirely (by "weaken" we mean that the response is not performed with as much vigor or energy, or as fully). Because only one stimulus and one response are involved, and the response just gets weaker, you can see that this is a very simple form of learning. This simplicity means that habituation can occur in many very simple creatures, and it is therefore the most widely found form of learning. Creatures that seem incapable of learning anything else may be habituated. Protozoa (one-celled animals) and coelenterates (also called cnideria; examples are jellyfish and sea anemones) are two phyla of animals that fit this description.

For example, the sea anemone has been habituated but seems unable to learn in other ways (Corning, Dyal, & Willows, 1973). The sea anemone is an animal that looks somewhat like a tiny, stumpy tree with a thick trunk and tentacles on top, which lives on the ocean floor in shallow water. It has relatively few responses; the ones of interest here are those involved in getting food. For some species of anemone, when a small fish brushes against some of the anemone's tentacles (thus acting as a stimulus for the anemone) the tentacles release a poison that paralyzes the fish. Then the tentacles begin moving in a rhythmic pattern that conveys the fish to the anemone's mouth so it can eat the fish. Habituation of these responses can be obtained simply by repeatedly touching the same tentacles with a pencil or short rod. After a dozen or so touches, the movement responses are noticeably weakened, and they usually have disappeared by the twentieth touch.

The skeptic may complain that those tentacles are simply too tired to respond, and that is true to some extent. But that is not habituation;

remember that fatigue is not considered a learning phenomenon, but habituation is. We must look at what is happening more carefully, because the great difficulty in studying habituation is isolating it from **fatigue** and from **sensory adaptation**, which is also a fatiguelike effect. If we change our pattern of stimulation, the anemone's response will reappear or recover some of its full force, demonstrating that habituation was occurring (probably in addition to fatigue and adaptation). We can change our pattern of stimulation by slowing down, speeding up, poking harder or more gently, or moving to a slightly different spot. All these changes will disrupt habituation (in other words, the response will return). Although some of these changes might allow the anemone to recover somewhat from fatigue or adaptation, it's doubtful that changing to a softer touch or speeding up the pace would do that. Therefore, these kinds of changes in stimulation allow the experimenter to tell whether she is observing habituation or just some fatiguelike effect.

Habituation can also be seen in more complex creatures, although its effects tend to be obscured by other forms of learning (especially classical conditioning). Also, because more complex creatures encounter more complex environments, which therefore change more, habituation will be disrupted more often or occur less completely. This is why habituation is usually thought of as a weak form of learning. In the higher animals, it is most easily observed when the animal's ability has been artificially limited, such as in **spinal animals** whose spinal cords have been severed just below the neck. Spinal frogs have been used in several experiments (Kimble & Ray, 1965). When these spinal frogs are stroked along the back, they make a wiping response with their hind legs; the leg on the stimulated side moves up and brushes the ribs with its flipper. This response can be habituated; it would be difficult with an intact frog because of all the messages the frog's brain would be sending down its spinal cord during normal activity, which might drown out the habituation effects. Similarly, habituation of reflexes such as the knee jerk can be shown in humans who have been paralyzed as a result of accidents.

Because habituation effects seem so weak and easily overcome, you may be wondering if it's really important in everyday life. The best examples of habituation in everyday human experience involve our sense of smell, which habituates more easily than most of our other senses. The person who gets ready for a date too early and puts on cologne or perfume a second time because he or she thinks it has "worn off" is an illustration of habituation. While some sensory adaptation probably is occurring (the chemical sensors in the nose becoming exhausted), we can show that habituation is involved by getting the person to inhale deeply or to smell something else. When the second smell is removed, that person is quite likely to have recovered the ability to smell the cologne or perfume for a while (because the new stimulus has disrupted the habituation). Habituation also occurs regularly to touch or tactile stimuli, to continuous sounds such as the hum of an air conditioner, and to recurring sounds that people who live near railroad tracks or airports encounter.

We have now illustrated several important factors that determine how effectively habituation will occur. Another factor, the most important factor (or *variable*, as experimenters refer to them), is the strength of the stimulus. Many experimenters have found that weak stimuli such as faint odors, slight touches, dim lights, or quiet sounds habituate fairly easily, whereas more intense stimuli such as strong odors, hard pokes, bright lights, or loud noises do not habituate at all or habituate very little. The major variables influencing habituation, then, are

1. *Intensity of the stimulus.* The weaker the stimulus, the more likely habituation is to occur.
2. *Timing of stimulus presentations.* The more rapidly we present the stimulus, the more effectively we habituate. In other words, the shorter the interval between stimulus presentations—the **intertrial interval** (ITI)—the fewer trials needed to obtain a given degree of habituation. However, longer intertrial intervals lead to more durable or longer-lasting effects. Long-interval ITIs are responsible for the habituation that occurs in people who live near railroad tracks or airports.
3. *Variation in the stimulus.* The less variation, or the greater the consistency of presentation of the stimulus, the more effectively habituation will occur. The stimulus should be presented at the same pace, the same intensity, and in the same location for maximum habituation.
4. *Presence of extraneous stimuli.* If the learner (the subject) encounters any other stimulus during the course of habituation, habituation may be disrupted.

One of the most valuable uses of habituation, which makes use of this last characteristic, has been in the study of newborn babies. An easily studied response in babies is the orienting response: When a noise or light is presented, the baby will look in the direction of the stimulus; this focusing of attention is accompanied by physiological changes, such as heart rate changes (Reese & Lipsett, 1970). This is a weak response and usually habituates easily, given variables 1 through 3 above. After the baby has habituated to the stimulus, a slightly different stimulus is substituted for it (for example, a noise of a slightly different pitch). If the baby remains habituated, we can assume it didn't notice the change; on the other hand, if habituation is disrupted and the orienting response reappears, the baby has noticed the change. By carefully changing stimuli this way, developmental psychologists have discovered a great deal about the sensory capacities of the newborn. In addition, they have demonstrated that humans are capable of a simple form of learning as soon as they are born and that their learning is influenced by the same variables that influence other learners.

A fifth variable influencing habituation is that responses differ in habituability. Some responses habituate easily, like the orienting response, whereas others do not habituate at all or do so poorly; an example is the response of the eyeblink to touching the eyelid. This characteristic may sometimes be predicted by noting the intensity of the stimulus used or by estimating the biological importance of the response, but it must often be determined by trial-and-error observation. Biologically important responses—that is, responses necessary or useful for a creature's survival—are usually difficult or impossible to habituate. Because we presume that most instincts have evolved because of their survival value, they should usually be impossible to habituate; the example of the cat arching its back in chapter 1 may illustrate this. Although it is often also true of reflexes, it is not always so, as the orienting reflex shows.

Learning theorists would describe the progression of habituation as showing fairly large decreases in responsiveness at first, with gradually diminishing changes as more and more presentations of the stimulus (more trials) occur, as is illustrated in figure 2.1. This figure is an ideal graph, as are many figures in this book—that is, it is smoother and more regular than actual data from experiments would be. The intention is to make the trends illustrated by the graph easier to see and understand. The graph indicates the amount of habituation by measuring the number of responses obtained with repeated presentations of the stimulus, but it could also measure the probability of responding (a closely related measurement) or the strength with which the response is made. Each of these provides an indication of how strongly the response is associated with the stimulus and therefore how much habituation has occurred.

Figure 2.1 The curve of habituation

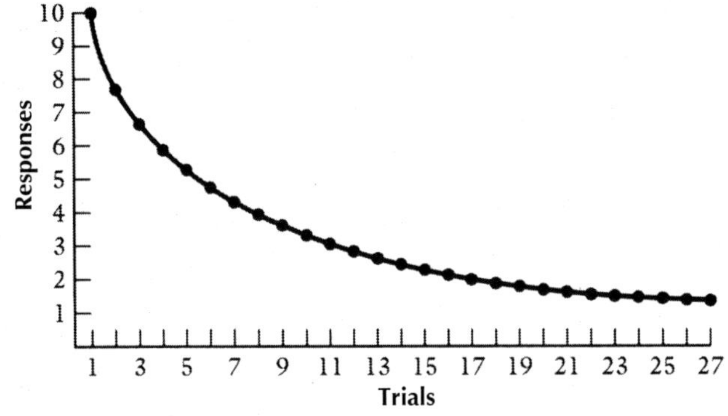

As can be seen, responding gradually approaches a minimum, which is often zero or no response at all. If there is a brief "time out" from the training, or a rest period, the response often regains some of its strength or likelihood of occurrence; this is illustrated in figure 2.2, which shows one such event after trial number 20. This phenomenon is called **spontaneous recovery**, and we will see it in our discussion of classical and operant conditioning as well. Whenever there is a delay in training, spontaneous recovery occurs; no extra training or change is necessary. The thoughtful reader may suggest that perhaps the rest period allows for a recovery from fatigue, and although the dissipation of fatigue does account for some of the observed response recovery, spontaneous recovery has been widely demonstrated and noted in situations in which fatigue could not have played a role. Spontaneous recovery is regarded as a phenomenon that is characteristic of learning.

Figure 2.3 shows actual data obtained by Thompson and Spencer (1966) for the habituation of the leg-jerk response in spinal cats to very brief (.01 to .03 millisecond) shocks at a rate of 10 per second. The data are reported as the average for groups of 10 trials in percentages of the response in comparison to a control condition, which is represented by the 100% line. We can see that habituation has reduced the responding by about half by the fourth block of 10 trials in the first series of trials. The graph levels off after this, suggesting that habituation has had its full effect in reducing responding by trial number 40. The graph also shows spontaneous recovery in the first three blocks of trials for the second series of trials, because there was a delay between the two series of trials. Also, the rate of stimulation was changed for this series from 10 per second to a much slower rate of 3 per minute. The average for the first block

Figure 2.2 Habituation and spontaneous recovery

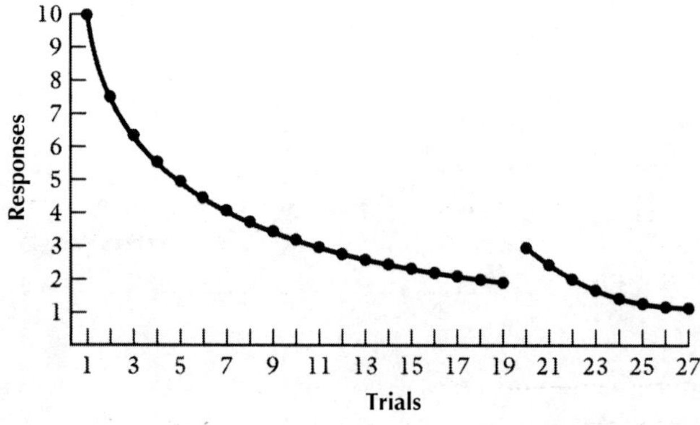

Figure 2.3 Habituation of the leg flexion responses of spinal cats

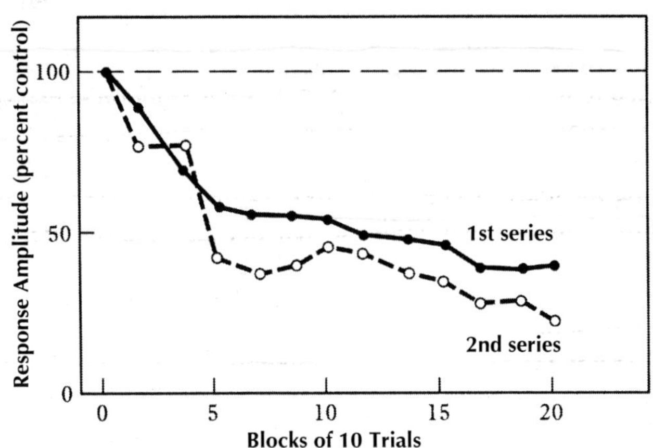

From "Habituation: A Model Phenomenon for the Study of Neuronal Substrates of Behavior," by R. F. Thompson & W. A. Spencer, 1966, *Psychological Review*, 93, p. 24. Copyright © 1966 by the American Psychological Association. Reprinted with permission.

of 10 trials for the second series has returned to the original control level. Thompson and Spencer (1966) found that the time required for this complete recovery averaged about 25 minutes. Because the shocks were presented 10 per second during the first series, habituation itself took only about 10 minutes.

What Is Sensitization?

Sensitization is practically the opposite of habituation: It is an increase in response as a result of repeated stimulation. At least four forms of sensitization have been distinguished (Razran, 1971), all on the basis of stimulus conditions. They are standard incremental, pseudoconditioning, alpha conditioning, and beta conditioning; we will consider only the first two forms. Several investigators have used the spinal frogs mentioned above to demonstrate sensitization (Corning & Lahue, 1971; Franzisket, 1963; and Kimble & Ray, 1965). Kimble and Ray (1965) showed that they could obtain either habituation or sensitization merely by changes in the variables mentioned above for habituation. In other words, if they stroked the frogs with more force, they got the wiping response to occur more forcefully (sensitization), but if they poked gently, habituation occurred. Similarly, changing the pattern of stimulation by poking slightly different spots or by slightly changing the force of the poke resulted in sensitization, but remaining constant in these characteristics led to habituation. Therefore, variables such as intensity and variation have the opposite effect for habituation and sensitization. Variables such as timing and the presence of other stimuli have similar effects, however. That is, the more rapidly the stimulation occurs, the more likely we are to obtain the change in question, but slower rates of presentation may lead to longer-lasting change, and both habituation and sensitization can be disrupted if some other stimulus intrudes during the training. The fifth variable could be stated in just the reverse way for sensitization: Some responses are easily habituated; these are usually very difficult to sensitize or may not be capable of being sensitized. On the other hand, responses that are easily sensitized often cannot be habituated.

To summarize the important variables in sensitization:

1. The stronger or more intense the stimulus, the more likely sensitization is to occur.
2. The more rapidly the stimulus is presented, the fewer presentations are necessary for sensitization to occur (recognizing that there is a limit to how quickly creatures can respond). Presentations at long intervals may result in longer-lasting change (Pinsker, Hening, Carew, & Kandel, 1973).
3. The greater the variation in intensity, position, or ITI (intertrial interval), the fewer trials needed to produce a given level of sensitization.
4. The presence of other stimuli can disrupt sensitization.
5. Some responses are easily sensitized; others apparently cannot be sensitized. Generally, the biologically useful responses are more likely to become sensitized.

The best illustration of sensitization in real life involves the infamous Chinese water torture supposedly used on prisoners of war during the Korean conflict. This involved strapping the prisoner in place so that he could not move his head. A bucket of water with a small hole in the bottom was hung over his head so that a drop of water hit him in the forehead repeatedly. This became very unpleasant after a while, in part because of sensitization. But drops of water are fairly mild stimuli; why didn't the prisoners habituate to them instead of becoming sensitized? A clue comes from research by Davis (1974). He used a 110 dB noise and recorded the startle response of rats. He also used a continuous background noise (an extraneous stimulus), which differed for different groups of rats. When the background noise was 60 dB, the rats habituated to the 110 dB tone; when the background noise was 70 dB, there was no change in the pattern of response; and when the background noise was 80 dB, the responses sensitized. Figure 2.4 shows his results for the 60 and 80 dB background conditions. If we imagine the prisoners of war thinking about their condition, we can realize that they were experiencing a great deal of general stress. High noise levels also generate stress; we can see a similarity between the prisoners' condition and that of rats in the noisy

Figure 2.4 Habituation (left-hand graph) and sensitization (right-hand graph) of the startle response to a 110-dB sound as a function of level of background noise

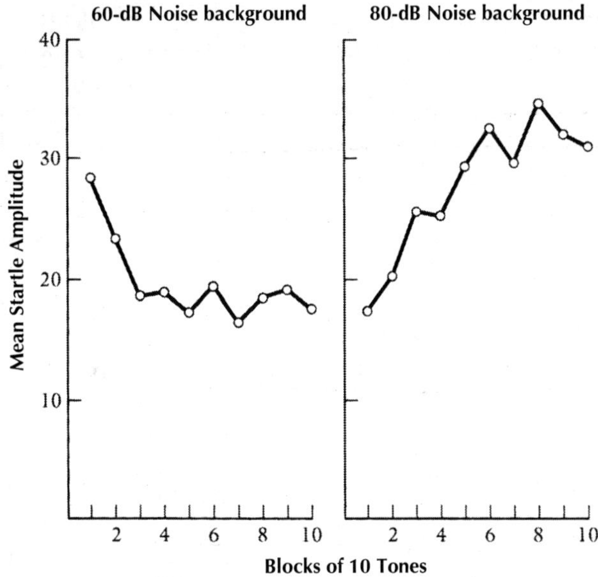

From "Sensitization of the Pet Startle Response by Noise," by M. Davis, 1974, Journal of Comparative and Physiological Psychology, 87, p. 572. Copyright © 1974 by the American Psychological Association. Reprinted with permission.

80-dB environment, which might explain why drops of water can become very unpleasant.

So far we have described a sensitization procedure that is similar to the habituation procedure in that the stimulus used is merely presented over and over. The other form we wish to describe involves using two stimuli. Usually the two stimuli have to be similar for this form to occur, such as a strong electrical shock and a mild shock or a loud noise and a softer noise. For example, if we use noises, then our subject would hear the loud noise repeatedly for a number of presentations (or trials). Then on one trial the less intense noise is presented instead of the loud noise. If sensitization has occurred, the response to the softer noise would be greater than it would have been normally. You might think of it as a situation in which the creature has come to "expect" the loud noise and is ready to react to it, and we "fool" it with the softer noise. That is not an explanation, nor is it a description that would satisfy many psychologists, but it should give some idea of what the procedure is like. This form of sensitization is often referred to as **pseudoconditioning**; in the next chapter we will refer to it again and the reason for calling it that will be clearer.

For now we should point out that, although we have used more than one stimulus, the two stimuli were never presented together—and that is why it's a form of sensitization rather than some other form of learning.

Pseudoconditioning therefore consists of the presentation of one strong stimulus for several trials immediately followed by the presentation of a weaker stimulus. The weaker stimulus then evokes (or generates) a response similar in strength to that which the stronger stimulus usually evokes. If we present the weak stimulus once more, we will see that this effect is not long lasting: we might get a slightly stronger response to the weak stimulus again, but probably not as strong as the first time, and upon a third presentation the effect usually will have disappeared.

The changes in response that occur during sensitization are illustrated by the idealized graph in figure 2.5. You might want to compare this to the right-hand graph of Davis's (1974) data in figure 2.4, which also shows sensitization. As with habituation, this curve suggests that the biggest changes occur during the first few trials and that the amount of change diminishes with continued presentations until the learner cannot respond any more strongly. Because responses increase in sensitization, the phenomenon of spontaneous recovery does not apply here.

One other characteristic of sensitization is that it seems to be a generalized increase in a creature's tendency to respond rather than a specific response change like habituation. Thus, sensitization has been described as a "state of the organism" change whereas habituation seems to be a change in a specific S–R pathway. This is easily noticed when testing for generalization; the ability of a different stimulus to cause responding after habituation of an original stimulus is not often mirrored in sensitization, which most often seems to cause the learner to become "jumpy" to a wide variety of stimuli.

Figure 2.5 The curve of sensitization

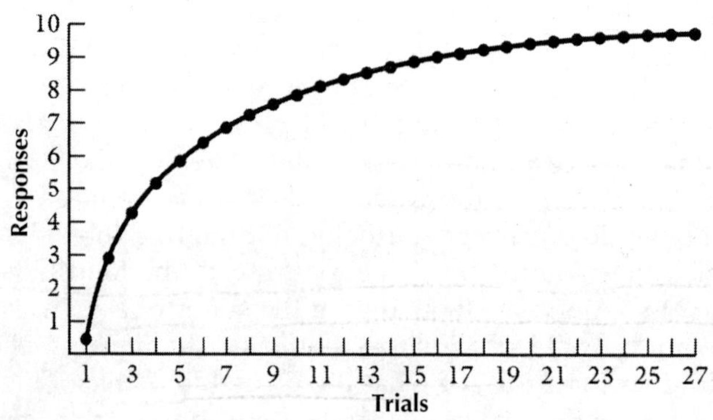

Habituation and Sensitization versus Other Forms of Learning

Why are habituation and sensitization now considered to be forms of learning, and why was there originally disagreement about including them? Remember our definition of learning: a relatively permanent change in behavior as a result of practice. The repeated presentations of one stimulus in habituation and sensitization make them the epitome of practice. In addition, both habituation and sensitization involve changing the strength of a response to a stimulus; in habituation, the response gets weaker, whereas in sensitization the response gets stronger. Changing the degree of responding certainly qualifies as a change in behavior. However, the change is also supposed to be relatively permanent, whereas the effects of habituation and sensitization are often temporary. Recall the Thompson and Spencer (1966) habituation data, which showed complete recovery of the response in about 25 minutes. Most other learning persists for much longer ("relatively permanent" in our definition was usually taken to be considerably longer than half an hour). The often temporary nature of the effects, especially in pseudoconditioning, led many early learning theorists to deny that habituation and sensitization were examples of learning. However, recent research has indicated that they may be longer lasting in some circumstances. Generally, slower rates of presentation (longer intertrial intervals) lead to more durable habituation effects, as Leaton (1976) demonstrated using rats. This would be like our slow but steady decrease in sensitivity to planes and trains when they regularly pass our house. In addition, Eric Kandel, in his work with the sea slug *Aplysia*, has shown that the slug given a series of 10 habituation trials on one day will almost completely recover by the next day. However, if the 10 trials are repeated for four days, this is sufficient to generate habituation effects that persist for several weeks (reviewed in Quinn, 1984).

Usually only one stimulus is used in habituation and sensitization studies, except in some cases of sensitization, and only one response occurs. Early learning theorists, who commonly studied the forms of learning described in the following chapters, emphasized the associations that must be learned when dealing with more than one stimulus. This emphasis on the associative nature of learning is still implicit in most discussions of learning today. The formation of an association is assumed to occur only when two previously unrelated stimuli (or two responses) are associated, or when a stimulus acquires the ability to generate a new response. None of these associational changes occur during habituation or sensitization. There is only a change in the strength of an already existing association. This nonassociative characterization made learning theorists reluctant to see habituation and sensitization as being anything other than primitive ancestors of learned behaviors, just slightly different from such phenomena as fatigue. However, the effects of the context on habituation and sensitization, like those found in Davis's previously mentioned 1974 study, suggest that associativelike effects may be seen in them. The importance of associations in these two forms of learning is currently uncertain. As more evidence about the effects of habituation and sensitization has been found, modern learning theorists have increasingly chosen to list both as forms of learning.

Because these forms of learning are so simple and limited, we might be tempted to dismiss their importance, especially for humans. However, imagine what your life would be like if you could never learn to ignore weak, repetitious stimulation. We are constantly bombarded by stimulation that is relatively unimportant to us. The ability to learn to ignore unimportant stimulation allows us to devote more of our limited attentional resources to more important stimulation (whether this description fits learning to ignore TV logos in the corner of the screen is for you to determine). The ability to habituate thus allows us to function more effectively. Sensitization gives us the opposite ability; when a stimulus is very important, we need to be able to respond to it vigorously and quickly. Which stimuli are unimportant? Generally, weak stimuli. Which stimuli are important? Usually, strong stimuli. These two forms of learning, although simple, provide us with important ways of reacting more effectively to the environment.

Generally, psychologists are agreed that these two forms of learning are precursors to the more complex forms. That is, these abilities of simple creatures to change their behaviors evolved first; as more advanced, complex organisms evolved, their more advanced abilities to learn evolved from habituation and sensitization. In particular, classical conditioning, the topic of the next chapter, shows many characteristics that suggest that it may have evolved from these early forms.

Neural Basis of Habituation and Sensitization

The nervous system mechanisms responsible for habituation and sensitization are not completely understood, but neuroscientists are generally agreed on several points. First, habituation seems to be more specific to the stimulus presented, and sensitization seems to be more of a generalized state of the organism.

Habituation has been shown to be the result of changes in sensory neurons in *Aplysia* (Kandel, 1979), a sea slug, as well as in rats (McIntosh & Gonzalez, 1991). That is, nerve cells responsible for detecting stimulation seem to reduce their output as a result of repeated stimulation. Thus, neurons responsible for generating responses (motor neurons) don't usually seem to be involved in habituation—they remain capable of generating the response in full, and this allows the creature to have the responses available for reaction to other stimuli. Kandel was able to carefully analyze the nature of habituation in the sea slug *Aplysia* because of several unique characteristics. *Aplysia* is a simple creature, with a relatively small number of neurons that are very large and easy to observe, and each *Aplysia* seems to be identical to its relatives in how those neurons are connected and function. Kandel found that the ability of the sensory neurons to conduct impulses along their axons was unaffected by habituation. However, the impulses caused less neurotransmitter release after habituation (Klein, Shapiro, & Kandel, 1980). Calcium ions cause synaptic vesicles at the end of axons to be pushed closer to the surface of the axon's cell walls, to connect to the cell walls, and to open, releasing the neurotransmitters they contain. Kandel discovered that a reduction in calcium ions after repeated stimulation led to a reduced ability of the sensory neuron to release neurotransmitters, thus reducing the input to interneurons and motor neurons (Castelluci & Kandel, 1974).

While this very localized mechanism describes the basic habituation process in simple creatures, in complex creatures such as mammals it seems to be just a part of the process. Rather than the first neurons in the sequence (the sensory neurons themselves) in complex creatures, it is the next set of neurons (interneurons in the sensory parts of the central nervous system) that seem to be involved. McIntosh and Gonzalez (1991) found that habituation caused changes in the sensory cortex of rats, and that long-term habituation involved more portions of the sensory cortex than short-term habituation.

These neurological studies indicate that the supposedly "simple" process of habituation is actually pretty complex and that there are at least two different types: short-term habituation following rapid presentations and long-term habituation following slower rates of presentation. These studies also verify the specificity of habituation: they suggest that habituation will occur only to the repeated stimulus (and others very similar to it) but not to other, different stimuli; and they indicate that the subject's ability to respond is not itself affected. Instead, it is sensitivity to that stimulus that is reduced during habituation.

In complex creatures, long-term habituation seems to involve changes in activity of the hippocampus and the appropriate areas of the sensory cortex (Honey & Good, 2000; Vinogradova, 2001). The hippocampus is involved in many learning and memory abilities. The left and right hippocampi are the size and shape of two-inch-long chili peppers "beneath" (interior to) our temporal lobes. They are connected to many cortical and subcortical portions of the brain. Reduced activity in the hippocampus is associated with reduced responsiveness (i.e., habituation). An intriguing suggestion by Sokolov (1960) is that the hippocampus serves to compare sensory input to existing representations (memories) of stimuli. These representations are stored in the sensory cortex. If there is a mismatch, the orienting reflex is generated. That is, the hippocampus is a comparator that serves to reduce our responsiveness to repeated stimuli, therefore allowing more potential for responding to other, possibly more important stimuli.

Sensitization in the sea slug *Aplysia* is almost the exact opposite of habituation: more neurotransmitters are released to stimulate motor neurons, which generate more responses. However, this increase seems to be due to cells called facilitatory interneurons that cause the sensory neurons to release more neurotransmitters. The interneurons release serotonin near the sensory synapses, which causes increases in calcium and changes the flow of potassium in the sensory axon. These two effects cause an increase in neurotransmitter release by the sensory neuron. In addition to these changes, long-term sensitization is caused by an increase in the number of sensory synapses.

Since sensitization involves a different chemical process than habituation, the two can occur independently of each other. In other words, repeated presentation of a stimulus may cause *both* processes to occur, and the degree of responding seen may be the result of the two tendencies combined (or the habituation tendency subtracted from the sensitization tendency). This is in fact the most widely held view, called the *opponent process theory*. The theory was originally proposed by Solomon and Corbit (1974) to describe emotional reactions. It is based on the fact that the two separate biochemical processes of habituation and sensitization occur at different rates; the excitatory process reaches a peak and declines more rapidly than the inhibitory process. They see the inhibitory process as a recovery reaction (a reaction to return the creature to its normal state) to the excitatory response. Solomon and Corbit also suggest that the inhibitory process is strengthened by repeated stimulation and weakened by disuse. Since they are influenced differently by the intensity and consistency of the stimulation, these processes will occur to differing degrees determined by the specific characteristics of the stimulation. Solomon and Corbit used their analysis to describe the changes in emotional responsiveness experienced by skydivers by suggesting that the "fear" response before and during the parachuting attempt may diminish with repeated jumps (habituate) and the "relief" following landing safely increases with repeated jumps until, after several jumps, the intense feeling of relief is perceived as excitement by the jumper, who then wishes to do it again. This maintains the behavior.

Summary

Habituation and sensitization are two very simple forms of learning. In them an already existing response is changed because of repeated stimulation. Habituation is a decrease in responding to a repeatedly presented stimulus. It occurs in a wide range of creatures, although it is often difficult to see in more complex animals, where its effects may be obscured by other types of learning. People show habituation most readily to constant stimuli such as the hum of an air conditioner. Habituation occurs most reliably with weak stimuli, rapidly presented in exactly the same way, and it is easily disrupted by extraneous stimuli. Some phylogenetically older responses or responses important for survival do not habituate. A rest period during habituation trials causes spontaneous recovery of the response. Although habituation is usually relatively temporary, sets of habituation trials over at least four days can lead to long-lasting habituation effects.

Essentially the opposite of habituation, sensitization is an increase in responding as a result of repeatedly presenting a stimulus. Stronger stimuli rapidly presented are more likely to sensitize; and varying the intensity, location, or timing of the stimulation is more likely to lead to sensitization. Extraneous stimuli also disrupt sensitization, and phylogenetically older or biologically more important responses are most likely to sensitize. The Chinese water torture is an example that involves sensitization. Pseudoconditioning is a type of sensitization procedure in which a strong stimulus is repeatedly presented for several trials with a weaker stimulus occasionally substituted for it. This causes the weaker stimulus to generate the stronger response associated with the other, stronger stimulus. Sensitization and habituation do not involve the formation of a new association. This and their usually temporary nature distinguishes them from the more complex forms of learning.

In habituation, sensory neurons release fewer neurotransmitters, therefore generating less activity in receiving cells such as motor neurons. In complex creatures this occurs primarily in the sensory cortex and hippocampus. Sensitization involves increases in neurotransmitters released in these same systems. These increases are the result of additional stimulation from facilitatory interneurons in the sensory systems.

QUESTIONS FOR DISCUSSION, THOUGHT, AND PRACTICE

1. Define and give an example of each of the key concepts. If you want a more challenging task, write a sentence for each term, then arrange the sentences into two or three meaningful paragraphs (you can add connecting sentences as needed). Now you have at least a partial summary of the chapter; compare it to the Summary section above.
2. At the movies, your date fondly caresses your arm while you are both holding hands. Describe how this could be made to lead to habituation or to sensitization. In other words, how could you be made less responsive to this or more responsive to it?
3. Think about the relationship between habituation and attention or concentration. How difficult would it be to study if we couldn't habituate? Can the factors influencing habituation be used to provide better study conditions?

4. Why does the intensity of a stimulus have such a powerful influence on a creature's reaction to that stimulus? Look for similarities between these forms of learning and the ones discussed in the following chapters in terms of the influence of stimulus intensity.
5. Timing also has important effects on all forms of learning. Why might timing be so important in habituation and sensitization?
6. Analyze the examples of trains and airports in terms of the variables that influence habituation. Timing was briefly discussed in the text, but what about consistency of presentation of the stimuli and their intensity?
7. Fill in the blanks: Veronica lived in a small apartment next to a fast-food restaurant with a sign that lit up every five seconds. At first she found this very annoying, but gradually she got used to it, and now she doesn't even notice it at all. One day her friend Betty asked Veronica if the sign didn't bother her. Veronica found that she began noticing the sign again for the next few days. This is referred to as ________________, and the variable that seems to have caused it is ________________. A month later, Veronica went home for Spring Break. When she returned to her apartment after a week, she found that she once again was uncomfortably aware of the flashing sign. This is an example of ________________.
8. Veronica's apartment is so small that her bed is pretty close to the refrigerator. Sometimes the clanking of ice cubes from the refrigerator's automatic ice maker, which seems to occur at random times and differently each time, keeps her from going to sleep, and occasionally a sudden burst from it will wake her up in the middle of the night. In fact, this seems to be happening more now than it used to. What is this an example of, and why (describe the variables operating here)?

Classical Conditioning

▲ Key Concepts ▲

acquisition training
anticipatory response
backward conditioning
blocking effect
classical conditioning
conditioned emotional response
conditioned response
conditioned stimulus
configural learning
contiguity
contingency
control group
counterconditioning
delayed conditioning
dependent variables
excitatory conditioning
extinction
higher-order conditioning
independent variables
inhibitory conditioning
interstimulus interval
latency
overshadowing
preexposure effect
preparatory response
reflex arc
salience
sensory preconditioning
simultaneous conditioning
stimulus substitution
systematic desensitization
temporal coding hypothesis
trace conditioning
unconditioned response
unconditioned stimulus

Each of us has our own peculiar likes and dislikes. I like basketball and science fiction, and I am a bit afraid of big dogs. You no doubt have a different set of likes and dislikes. Think of some favorite thing and something you really dislike. For my preferences, I can think of some experiences I had as a child that probably caused me to feel the way I do. If you try to remember some childhood experiences related to your likes and dislikes, you might be able to come up with some experiences which influenced your feelings about them.

In this chapter we will discuss a form of learning that is much more complex than either habituation or sensitization and that probably explains many of our emotional reactions to things: **classical conditioning.** It's more complex because it requires at least two stimuli, one weak or easily habituated and one usually strong or more easily sensitized. Because the learner associates these two stimuli with each other, and no such connection is necessary in either habituation or sensitization themselves, it is usually presumed that creatures had to evolve more complex nervous systems to be able to experience classical conditioning. Although this form of learning is usually referred to as classical conditioning (because it was the first form of learning to be systematically investigated), you may see references to it as *Pavlovian conditioning* (after its discoverer, Ivan Pavlov), *reflex conditioning* (which is what Pavlov called it), or *respondent learning* or *Type S learning* (terms suggested by B. F. Skinner when he distinguished it from operant conditioning in 1938).

Most of the important variables that influence classical conditioning were discovered by Pavlov and his students from the 1890s until the 1930s. Because their work was so thorough, we can get a good idea of how classical conditioning is done by a brief review of their experiments.

Pavlov's Experiments

Pavlov was a Russian medical researcher who became interested in the processes involved in the digestion of food. He focused on the role of stomach acid and other digestive juices in the breakdown of food. The experiments of interest to us involve his study of saliva as a digestive juice. To demonstrate that salivation was involved in digestion, he attempted to show that more saliva is produced when food is present in the mouth than when no food is present. To do this he surgically attached a small tube to the salivary glands of dogs. The tube went through the dogs' cheeks, where the saliva was collected in test tubes and the amount generated could be easily measured.

At first, things went well, as Pavlov found that much more saliva was produced when he put food (dried, ground-up meat) in the dogs' mouths than when their mouths were empty. However, as Pavlov and his students conducted more and more experiments, they began to find that the dogs were producing salivation and other digestive juices in huge amounts even when they were not given food. These levels were as high as the amount generated when food was present. They began to suspect that this was because the dogs were anticipating the food or expecting, upon seeing Pavlov, that food would soon be present. Pavlov felt that stimuli other than the food, such as his own appearance or the lab itself, were serving as signals to generate these secretions. A drawing of Pavlov's experimental equipment appears in figure 3.1.

Pavlov's classic experiments to test this hypothesis were to see whether he could cause the dogs to learn new signals for food. He wanted stimuli that were previously unrelated to food or salivation; he used various sounds such as bell tones, metronomes ticking, buzzers, and whistles, as well as visual and tactile stimuli (various touches). The particular sounds used didn't matter too much; the results were basically the same. Pavlov also often used a diluted mild acid to unconditionally generate salivation in place of the meat powder; these two stimuli worked about equally well for generating reflexive salivation. Pavlov would start the noise and then after a few seconds give the dogs the meat powder or acid solution. After several trials of the noise stimulus being followed by the food stimulus, he found that he could generate the salivation response by making the noise, even if he left out the meat. Because salivation is a reflex, he described this procedure as the training, or conditioning, of the reflex to a new stimulus, or *reflex conditioning*.

The food represents a type of stimulus referred to as an **unconditioned stimulus (US)**, because it generates the response automatically without any previous training. This is the way that Pavlov's writing was originally translated into English; however, modern scholars have noted that a better translation would have been *unconditional stimulus*, because

Figure 3.1 Pavlov's experimental apparatus

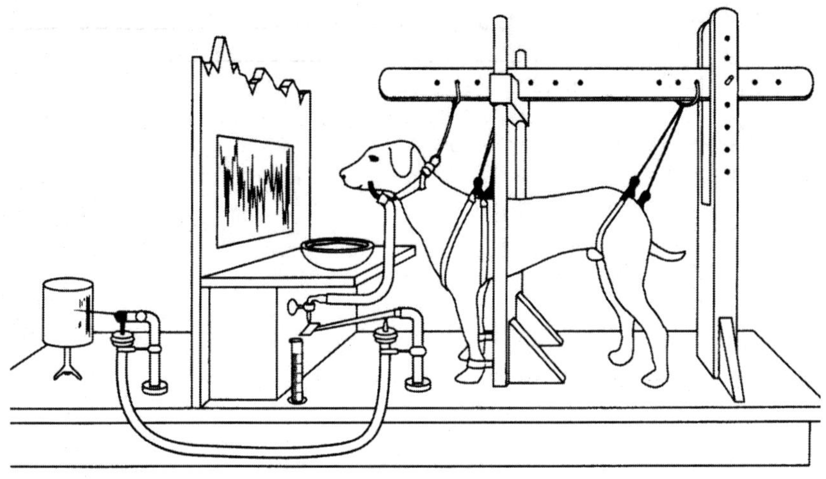

Adapted from "The Method of Pavlov in Animal Psychology," by R. M. Yerkes and S. Morgulis, 1909, *Psychological Bulletin*, 6, 257–273. American Psychological Association.

Pavlov felt that this stimulus generated a response that did not depend on anything else for its occurrence; it occurred unconditionally to the US. Unconditioned stimuli are usually strong and do not habituate easily; therefore we can count on their ability to generate a particular response over and over. The original response to the sound (basically the orienting response) habituates easily and is therefore not too important here (Dyal & Corning, 1973). The sound is an example of a *conditional stimulus*, because its ability to generate a salivary response is conditional on it having been paired with the US. Again, this was originally translated as **conditioned stimulus (CS)**. After training, the subject has been conditioned to respond to the CS in a new way, making the same response as to the US. When this reaction has occurred to the CS, it is referred to as the conditional or **conditioned response (CR)**, which allows us to distinguish between it and the response to the US; the response to the US is called (you might have guessed already) the unconditional or **unconditioned response (UR)**.

In Pavlov's experiment the response was salivation, whether it was to the US or the CS, so you may be wondering why we need to label it differently. In fact, there are three differences between the CR and the UR even in Pavlov's experiment. The first difference is that if the noise is made by itself (after the training, of course), we get salivation where we didn't before (that is the CR), whereas if the meat is given by itself, we will always get salivation (the UR); the stimulus generating the response is different in a fundamental way. The CS has a response-generating capacity it didn't have before. The second difference between the two responses is that the UR is usually stronger than the CR; that is, usually the dog will salivate more to the meat taste (US) than it will to the sound (CS). The third difference is that in Pavlov's experiment the sound was presented first, and then the dog was allowed to taste the food. We say that the sound (CS) *preceded* the food (US) in order of presentation. The consequence of this for the response is that the dog can respond to the sound before it responds to the food. Pavlov found as training went along that, indeed, the dogs came to salivate sooner and sooner (although these time differences were brief, they were quite consistent). So the CR is usually weaker and happens sooner than the UR because it is happening to a new type of stimulus, the CS. Differences in timing are important and are discussed further below.

Classical conditioning is often illustrated with the following diagram (with Pavlov's experiment used as an illustration):

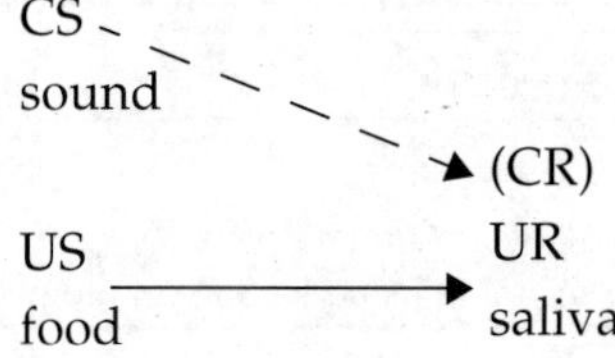

This simply shows that the unconditioned stimulus reliably generates an unconditioned response and that as a result of the US being preceded by the conditioned stimulus on a number of occasions, the conditioned stimulus eventually becomes capable of generating or eliciting the response also. Until fairly recently it was believed that there were three necessities for classical conditioning, all implied by the diagram above:

1. a neutral stimulus (the CS)
2. a stimulus that reliably elicits a response (the US)
3. **contiguity** (or nearness in time and space) of these two stimuli

The role of contiguity has been examined intensively and hotly debated over the last 30 years. We consider some of the questions about contiguity in the section "What Causes Learning?"

Extinction (or How Do I Get This Dog to Stop Slobbering?)

Once Pavlov had established the basic manner in which a classically conditioned response was acquired (**acquisition** is the training of a new CR), he then tried to figure out how to eliminate a conditioned response. To get rid of a conditioned response, an extinction procedure must be performed, because (according to our definition of learning) the CR will not just disappear with time. **Extinction** is, by definition, the elimination of a conditioned response as a result of repeated presentations of the conditioned stimulus without the unconditioned stimulus. In other words, we omit the US when we present the CS. Note that we don't say "take away" the US; that would imply that Pavlov rang the bell, gave food, and then removed it from the dog's mouth. We simply fail to present it. So Pavlov rang the bell many times without presenting any food and eventually eliminated the salivation to the bell. An idealized graph of the change in responding during these two procedures is shown in figure 3.2.

What Can Be Conditioned?

Pavlov felt that this form of learning could be demonstrated with any reflex, and later experimenters have in fact shown this for almost every reflex studied, including eyeblinks in rabbits and humans; limb flexions in many species including humans (the knee jerk is an example); startle responses; and physiological responses such as heart rate, blood pressure, and the galvanic skin response (GSR) (Hall, 1976). Reflexes have been extensively studied by physiological psychologists and learning psychologists because they represent a relatively simple link between behavior

Figure 3.2 The curve of classical conditioning and extinction

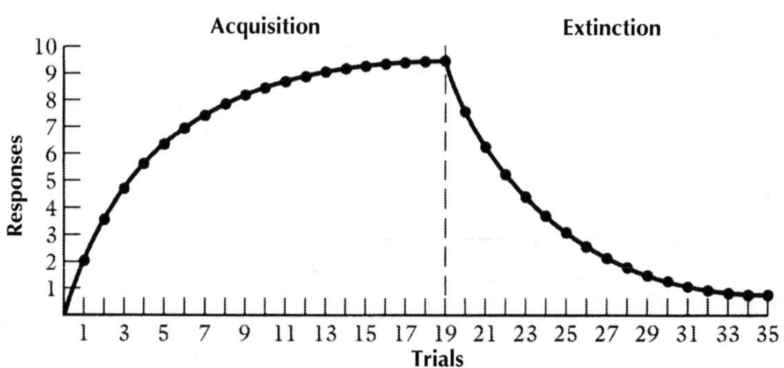

and physiological mechanisms. The nerve connections that allow reflexes to occur may consist of no more than three levels of nerve cells: sensory neurons, which receive stimulation from the senses; motor neurons, which send messages to muscles; and interneurons, which connect these two. A good example of this is the knee-jerk reflex in which a doctor taps the knee and the patient's leg kicks. The reaction is the result of a sensory neuron receiving messages from the sensory receptors around the knee-cap and sending them to the spinal cord. There interneurons send the message across the spinal cord to the motor neurons, which cause the leg muscles to act. Thus, the **reflex arc** provides a physiological model that explains how a simple response to a stimulus might be generated in a subject. Nevertheless, if classical conditioning only worked with reflexes, it might have remained a scientific laboratory curiosity of relatively minor importance in our everyday lives. John B. Watson demonstrated that classical conditioning was more important than that.

In a famous study, Watson (Watson & Rayner, 1920) showed that human emotions also could be classically conditioned. He used an infant, now referred to as Little Albert, so that the subject was relatively uninfluenced by previous learning. While Albert was playing with a furry white rat (the CS), Watson's assistant sneaked up behind him and banged on a large iron pipe with a hammer, producing a sudden loud noise (the US), scaring the daylights out of poor Albert and making him cry (the UR). After several repetitions of this procedure, just the appearance of the rat was enough to make Albert cry (the CR). His fear had become classically conditioned to a new stimulus. Watson argued that, in this way, all emotions could be conditioned. A child's love of its mother, for example, could be the result of her appearance being associated with the pleasure of nursing. Happiness, sadness, or any other emotions could be trained to new stimuli this way (Watson, 1924). As a consequence, we might be able to eliminate learned emotional reactions by extinction. Unfortunately for Albert, Watson was not allowed to extinguish this learned fear in him; Albert's mother discovered what was being done and took Albert away. Shortly thereafter, because of various personal and legal problems, Watson was forced to leave the academic institution where he conducted this research.

Can Fears Be Extinguished?

One of Watson's students, Mary Cover Jones (1924), eventually trained another child, Peter, in the same way and then proceeded to try to extinguish his fear. This was a noteworthy endeavor, because it turns out that emotional responses usually take much longer to extinguish than reflexes, partly because they involve more complex nervous system activity and partly because emotional responses are somewhat self-maintained. In other words, the fear response generated by the CS is noticed by the subject (or responder) and this awareness of one's own high arousal tends to maintain that state, even when the original US is not present. Learning psychologists would say that these emotional responses are functioning as stimuli as well as responses (response-produced stimuli).

To minimize this problem, once Peter had been conditioned to fear the furry pet, Jones waited until Peter was engaged in an activity that generated physical responses incompatible with fear. She waited until Peter was happily eating his baby food; presumably he was content and relaxed. Then she introduced the CS by placing it as far away from Peter as possible while still being visible to him on the other side of the room. When she did this over a number of relaxed eating sessions, she would gradually move the CS closer to him, being careful to note any signs of anxiety he might show. Over the course of many trials, she was able to gradually move the CS to the table on which Peter was eating, then next to his plate, then on his lap, without any signs of fear (the CR). At this point, Jones felt that she had eliminated the fear. However, we should notice that she had done more than just extinction; procedures of this type are referred to as **counterconditioning** or desensitization today.

The importance of this procedure was not really noticed for over 30 years until Joseph Wolpe (1958) modified it to develop **systematic desensitization,** a method of eliminating phobias and other neurotic fears. It's a bit unfortunate that Wolpe chose the name systematic desensitization, because the procedure really doesn't bear too much similarity to the sensitization procedures discussed in chapter 2. Wolpe first trained a person in relaxation techniques; then, when the person was able to become well relaxed easily, Wolpe began exposing the person to stimuli somewhat similar to the original feared CS. Wolpe asked the person which stimuli he reacted to most strongly and which he feared least, from which he constructed a list or hierarchy of stimuli from least to most feared. He started with the stimuli least feared, which were usually not very similar to the original stimulus, and gradually introduced stimuli more similar to the original CS, always making sure that no anxiety was generated. His technique has been successfully used with many different types of learned fears, including fear of heights, snakes, bugs, and cars.

Similar techniques have also been used in some cases of school phobia. These techniques involve extinction but usually also involve other procedures. In Wolpe's method, extinction was combined with principles of generalization (see chapter 7) and with training in relaxation, which was designed to produce a response incompatible with anxiety. Other counterconditioning techniques often involve explicitly pairing the feared CS with a US that elicits responses incompatible with fear in the hope that one response will essentially cancel out the other.

Remember that Watson founded the psychological position called *behaviorism*, which advocated learning principles as the explanation for all behavior. Watson felt that classical conditioning caused us all to be the way we are. He suggested that all creatures are born with a few basic likes (such as food and drink) and a basic dislike of pain, and that all the rest are classically conditioned tastes. Notice what we have discovered so far:

1. Many different kinds of creatures, including people, can be classically conditioned.
2. Responses other than reflexes can be conditioned, most especially emotional responses.
3. Emotional responses are much more difficult to extinguish than reflexive ones.
4. Awareness may not be necessary for the occurrence of conditioning.
5. The factors that influenced Pavlov's experiments also influenced other classical conditioning situations in the same way.

How Can We Tell that Conditioning Has Occurred?

We have now seen that classical conditioning can modify the occurrence of many reflexes and emotional responses. How can we tell when this has happened? As you recall from the definition of learning, a change in behavior is an indication that an individual may have experienced learning. So we have to see changes in behaviors to claim that classical conditioning has occurred. There are several kinds of changes we can look for, depending to some extent on what kind of US (and therefore, what kind of UR) we are studying. These are referred to as **dependent variables**. The major dependent variable studied in classical conditioning has often been (1) *strength, magnitude, or amplitude of response*. In Pavlov's experiment, this refers to the amount of salivation (how many drops of saliva occurred to the sound after training compared to before training). Many responses are fairly easy to measure in this way, for example, the strength of the knee jerk and several physiological responses such as blood pressure.

In addition, three other measures have been commonly used. Strength of response might be hard to estimate for Little Albert, but we might measure (2) the *percentage of occurrence of the CR*. In other words, for this US and UR, we could note how often the child shows the CR in the presence of the CS alone. Another common measure of amount of conditioning would be (3) **latency**, which refers to the time it takes the subject to make a response once the stimulus has been presented. You may recall that one of the differences between the CR and the UR is that the CR can happen earlier because it is happening (usually) to a stimulus that is being presented earlier. So any decrease in the time it takes to respond is an indication that conditioning has occurred.

The final measure is one suggested fairly recently for use in one type of experimental procedure, referred to as the **conditioned emotional response** (CER) procedure. The measure, called (4) the *suppression ratio*, has been especially employed when fearful or painful stimuli are used as the US. It is based on the fact that most creatures stop or slow down what they are doing when a CS associated with a painful US occurs. Thus, the usual CR that would closely follow the UR is not measured; the CER measure is usually considered to be a more indirect measure of learning. It requires that we observe our learner in a situation where it is freely responding fairly rapidly if possible. It is important to note that these frequent responses are not typically classical ones, such as reflexes or body state changes, but are usually voluntary responses, such as pressing levers to get food or other actions. When the CS is presented, the subject will slow its responding or stop altogether. For a given US, the amount of suppression or slowing of response is an indication of how well the CS is associated with that US, and hence how much learning has occurred. The ratio of responding when the CS is present divided by the total amount of responding (both with and without the CS) is the suppression ratio. *Conditioned suppression*, as it is also called, is especially important because of its implications; such a CS can affect ongoing behavior totally unrelated to the conditioning situation. In other words, an individual who has learned to associate some characteristic of the environment with unpleasantness may be inhibited by that stimulus even in circumstances irrelevant to the original situation or to unpleasantness. For example, many people are inhibited when they are around a police officer; for them the police uniform is a CS that has been associated with unpleasant experiences in the past, and the presence of the police officer "slows down" all of their behavior regardless of whether they were behaving legally or illegally.

Each measure has advantages and disadvantages. Amplitude or strength of response, percentage, and the CER measure each require that the CS be presented without the US, so that responding is influenced only by the CS. Thus each measure involves the use of an extinction trial. Latency avoids this problem but is difficult to use if the time interval between CS and US is extremely short (much less than half a second). Also, as suggested above, some conditioning procedures are more suited to one measure than to another.

Control Groups

To find out whether learning has occurred, we need to measure a response before the events that are supposed to cause learning and then after them. In addition, we have to show that the change was due to conditioning and not something else. Remember from chapter 2 that one form of sensitization was called pseudoconditioning; this could happen in our experiment, and we could mistake it for classical conditioning. To ensure that we don't make this mistake, we need a group of subjects that receives a pseudoconditioning procedure. Then we can compare this **control group** with the group we are training. If the training or experimental group shows a stronger response than the control group, the difference must be the amount of classical conditioning that has occurred. One control group for sensitization receives presentations of the US all by itself. We occasionally present the CS to see if it has acquired any ability to generate the UR. Because this is the pseudoconditioning procedure, any occurrences of the UR indicate pseudoconditioning and are subtracted from the measures for our experimental group. In addition to this control procedure, several other control groups must be studied. Typically, another group receives the CS alone to control for the occurrence of another form of sensitization, the possibility of sensitization of a response to a frequently presented CS. Finally, a traditional control group receives the CS at more or less random times and the US at more or less random times, but never experiences the two paired together. Again, if this results in any UR responding to the CS, the amount will be subtracted from the training group's score.

For example, if we were studying conditioning of the sucking reflex in babies, we might use the sound of a rattle as our CS and touch the baby's lips with a pacifier as the US. After presenting the rattle a few times by itself to show that it initially generates no sucking response, we present it followed immediately by a touch to the baby's lips for our experimental group, testing for occurrences of the sucking CR occasionally. Our pseudoconditioning control group receives the touch repeatedly by itself, and every once in a while we present the rattle by itself to see if it generates sucking. Our other sensitization control group receives the rattle sound (the CS) by itself as many times as the experimental group receives it, and we look for occurrences of a sucking response. Our final control group consists of semirandom presentations of rattle and touch without their ever being presented together.

Robert Rescorla (1967), in an extremely influential article, criticized this last control procedure. He suggested that it was actually leading to the development of an expectation that the CS would never be followed by the US (that is, our baby might learn that the rattle means it shouldn't bother sucking). This kind of conditioning is called **inhibitory conditioning** because the subject is learning not to make the response to the CS. In other words, our subject would learn that when it hears the rattle, it's not going to be touched, although it might be touched at other times. This is essentially the opposite of the other examples we have mentioned, which are usually described as **excitatory conditioning** because the subject learns to make the response in the presence of the CS.

Rescorla suggested that a more appropriate control would be what he called a "truly random" control group in which CS and US were presented in completely independent random patterns. Under this condition, by chance the two would occur together a small percentage of the time but would usually occur alone. Initial studies indicated that this condition usually results in slightly more CR responding than the traditional random but unpaired control procedure (Rescorla, 1967). However, in some conditioning procedures, such as eyeblink conditioning, the explicitly unpaired control has resulted in small amounts of excitatory responding rather than the inhibition that Rescorla predicted (Gormezano, Kehoe, & Marshall, 1983). Although there is some debate as to which is the most appropriate control, Rescorla's analysis of conditioning has generated a great deal of interest among researchers, and his "truly random" control is often employed.

What Influences Classical Conditioning?

Now let's consider how to make classical conditioning work more (or less) effectively. In other words, what could we do differently to make Pavlov's dogs, for example, learn to salivate with fewer practice trials? In scientific terms, we are interested in the major **independent variables** that affect conditioning. There are 10 major variables that we need to discuss, the two most important being the intensity or strength of the US and the timing of presentation of CS and US.

Intensity of the US

Also referred to as strength, amount, or magnitude of the US, the intensity of the US is probably the most obvious variable that could be manipulated. It works as you might anticipate. In Pavlov's experiments, this is equivalent to giving the dogs greater amounts of food. The greater the amount or intensity of the US, the fewer trials needed for a given level of conditioning (Pavlov, 1927; Wagner, Siegel, Thomas, & Ellison, 1964). If the US were an electric shock, then the stronger the shock, the more effective the procedure. For example, Wickens and Harding (1965) used mild (1.5 milliampere) shocks or stronger shocks (2.5 ma) paired for 20 trials with tones or lights. They measured the GSR or skin conductance (used in lie-detector tests; a measure of arousal or excitement) in their subjects (college students). Test trials during training and during extinction showed greater responding to the CS paired with the stronger shock. A good real-life illustration of this basic principle comes from the childhood experiences of running around outside barefoot. It takes fewer times stepping on a bee to learn to notice that bees are around than the number of times it takes to learn what "stickers" or sandspurs look like. This is partly because the intensity of the bee sting is greater than the intensity of the thorn.

Duration of the US

We could also change the time the subject is exposed to the US; for example, some subjects could be shocked for one second and others shocked for five seconds. Although you might think that this would be an important factor, it generally doesn't have much effect on degree of conditioning. This is probably because there are other important timing characteristics that obscure any US duration effect. Over a variety of procedures, some studies show shorter US durations to be more effective (Runquist & Spence, 1959), others show no difference (Wegner & Zeaman, 1958), and still others find longer durations more effective (Ashton, Bitgood, & Moore, 1969). Most researchers have concluded that US duration isn't too important.

Intensity and Duration of the CS

We could make our CS more noticeable by making it more intense or making it last longer, but these variables also usually have little effect on the ease of learning. Generally, early studies such as Pavlov's suggested that as long as the CS is bright enough, loud enough, powerful enough, and long lasting enough to be noticed against the background by the learner, it will be an effective CS. Further increases in CS intensity or duration will not show any improvement in performance. However, most early studies carefully controlled the amount of irrelevant stimulation, keeping distractions to a minimum. Modern experiments using several stimuli suggest that the stimulus generating the strongest orienting response will be easiest to associate with the US, all other things being equal. This is often the most intense stimulus, although it might most accurately be described as the most **salient** (most noticeable) stimulus. Creatures differ in what types of stimuli are most salient for them. Generally, however, the factor that best predicts salience is relative intensity rather than absolute intensity (Kamin, 1965). Thus, the stimulus that stands out or is most noticeable will generally be the most effective stimulus to use as a CS, but once we have such a stimulus, making it even more noticeable won't help much. Our barefoot child example above also illustrates CS salience in that the bee is more distinctive against a backyard background than stickers against the rest of the underbrush. In this case, however, greater salience of the bee is because of greater contrast plus the presence of movement and sound rather than being brighter or more colorful.

CS–US Interval

Interstimulus interval—the amount of time between occurrence of the CS and occurrence of the US—is one of the most important variables in classical conditioning. Four different variations in timing have been distinguished—delayed, trace, simultaneous, and backward conditioning. In **delayed conditioning**, the CS begins and then the US begins while the CS continues. In other words, the CS is presented first, but the US is presented while the learner is still experiencing the CS. For Pavlov's dog the bell began to ring, and then after it had been ringing for a second or so, the meat was placed in the dog's mouth while the bell continued ringing. Figure 3.3 diagrams the timing of the events in delayed conditioning. In our bee sting example, if the child doesn't see the bee but feels something moving under his foot and then feels the sting, we might have a wiggle CS shortly followed by a sting US, and we might suspect that the wiggling continued while the stinger was being applied, giving us a case of delayed conditioning.

Historically, psychologists found that the delayed procedure was the most effective, although **trace conditioning** could also be quite effective (Schneiderman, 1966). This is similar to delayed conditioning except that the CS does not overlap in time with the US. In other words, the CS comes on and goes off before the US comes on. Because the CS and US do not overlap, the only way learning could occur under these circumstances is if the learner had at least a brief "memory trace" of the CS that it could associate with the US (Gormezano & Kehoe, 1981; Pavlov, 1927). Hence the name, trace conditioning. Gormezano, Kehoe, and Marshall (1983) have argued convincingly that a memory trace is used to acquire a CR by showing that the greatest level of conditioned response (the peak CR) corresponds precisely to the trace interval, so that the creature is generating a maximal response at exactly the time that the US begins. Returning to our bee sting, what if the child sees the bee just before stepping on it? Once his foot is on top of the bee, he can't see it anymore: the sight of the bee is a CS in a trace conditioning situation, with the sting US occurring after the sight is gone. The sight of the bee may be a less effective CS in a trace conditioning situation than the feeling of it wiggling as a CS in a delayed conditioning situation.

Figure 3.3 The timing of events in delayed conditioning. A rise in the line representing the event indicates the onset of that event, and a fall in the line represents the end of the event. Time is progressing from left to right.

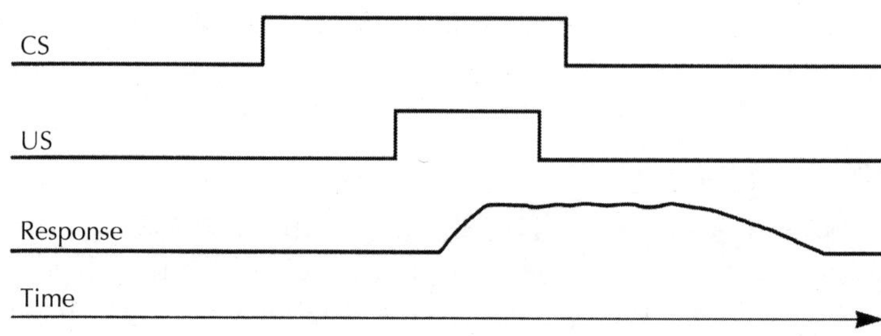

In addition to the advantage of delayed conditioning over trace conditioning in our bee sting example, the time interval between seeing the bee and getting stung is greater than the time between feeling the wiggle and getting stung. This could also make the visual CS less effective. For a large number of USs the most effective time interval is between a quarter second and two seconds, with half a second being fairly common; thus, a bell that starts ringing a half second before a puff of air to the eye will lead to eyeblinks to the bell alone in the fewest presentations. Smith, Coleman, and Gormezano (1969) used a trace conditioning procedure to study the effects of different interstimulus intervals (ISIs). They measured the eyeblink response in rabbits using a tone CS. Figure 3.4 shows their results for blocks of 21 trials. This figure shows that trace intervals of 200 and 400 msec (two-tenths and four-tenths of a second) produced much more rapid acquisition, led to higher final percentages of CR production, and took longer to extinguish than the other time intervals. The 800-msec group learned reasonably well, and the 100-msec group showed the gradual development of some responding to a final level of 60 percent. Finally, several conditions led to no learning at all; the very short ISIs (groups receiving 50 msec, zero msec, and –50 msec) are all along the bottom, generating a CR much less than 10 percent of the time, just like the control group, labeled C. You might also want to compare this figure to figure 3.2, noting how the ideal representation of conditioning and extinction actually occurs in experiments.

The third type of timing procedure, **simultaneous conditioning**, is the most intriguing in some ways. As you might expect, this consists of presenting the CS and the US at exactly the same time; that is, the CS and US start simultaneously. Because most psychologists believed until fairly recently that contiguity, or nearness, was the fundamental cause of classical conditioning, and because simultaneous is as contiguous as possible, one might expect that simultaneous conditioning would be the most effective timing arrangement. Unfortunately, in the early experiments it was very ineffective, leading most of the time to little or no learning (Heth & Rescorla, 1973), although there were some successful simultaneous conditioning demonstrations (Rescorla, 1980). More recent research using conditioned emotional response (CER) measures, however, clearly indicates that simultaneous conditioning can be as effective as delayed conditioning in causing an association to be formed (Barnet, Arnold, & Miller, 1991; Miller & Barnet, 1993). We will discuss the roles of contiguity and contingency in classical conditioning in more detail shortly. For now, probably the best description of simultaneous conditioning was suggested by R. R. Miller (Matzel, Held, & Miller, 1988): that it may lead to the creation of an association, but this association does not

Figure 3.4 Acquisition and extinction of the eyeblink response using eight CS–US intervals

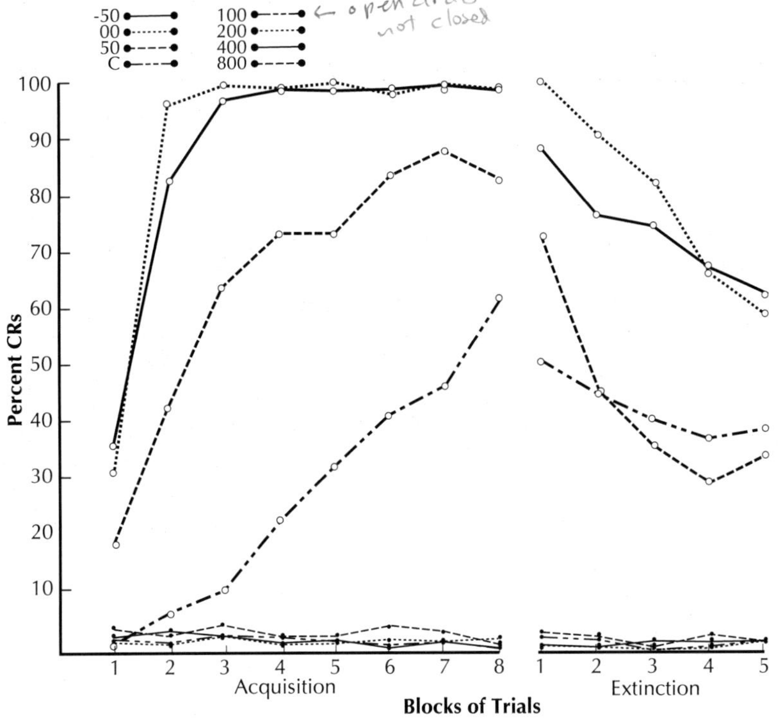

From "Classical Conditioning of the Rabbit's Nictitating Membrane Response at Backward, Simultaneous, and Forward CS–US Intervals," by M. C. Smith, S. R. Coleman, and I. Gormezano, 1969, *Journal of Comparative and Physiological Psychology, 69*, pp. 226–231.

generate the usual response. We will also return to this idea when we discuss the question of what is learned in classical conditioning.

The fourth type of timing procedure is called **backward conditioning**. In this procedure, the US is presented before the CS, although they may overlap in time. This has traditionally been regarded as the least effective procedure; only a few of the early Russian and American researchers reported evidence of successful backward conditioning, and the Russian procedures often required one thousand or more pairings of CS and US (Razran, 1965). Many studies using direct response measures have found that the backward procedure results in no better response rate than an unpaired control condition (Kamin, 1963). In fact, in some of these studies there was evidence that sometimes inhibitory conditioning occurred (Siegel & Domjan, 1971). That is, the subject comes to use the CS as a signal that the US is about to end; CS onset is actually coming before US offset and allows the learner to predict the end of the US. Although something is being learned, it's not really a "backward" association. Williams and Hurlburt (2000), however, using a conditioned emotional response measure, found that a CS that began immediately after a shock was as effective as one coming before the shock in suppressing response, but that if the CS started 3 seconds after the US ended, conditioning did not occur. Small changes in timing may determine the effectiveness of backward conditioning, but when indirect response measures are used, backward conditioning procedures do seem to be able to cause learning. Again, the suggestion made by Miller for simultaneous conditioning could be applied here: an association is formed, but it doesn't result in the response that we usually look at. The timing procedures for trace, simultaneous, and backward conditioning are diagrammed in figure 3.5.

When an indirect measure of learning is used, such as the conditioned suppression measure, the effect of ISI seems much less important (Furedy & Riley, 1987); that is, most of the procedures seem about equally able to create new associations. In early studies using the suppression ratio measure, Kamin (1965) was able to successfully condition rats using a trace conditioning procedure with an interval of one minute between termination of the CS and onset of the US. We will discuss a possible interpretation of this finding in the section on what causes learning. Short ISIs in the range of a second are generally best, but whether there is an optimal ISI depends on the type of response we are looking at and the intertrial interval as well (Hearst, 1988).

Intertrial Interval

Another time-dependent variable that may also be manipulated in classical conditioning procedures is the time between trials (remember that each presentation of the CS and US constitutes a trial). This variable generally works in roughly the opposite way from CS–US timing intervals. In other words, the longer the ITI the more effective the learning procedure (Prokasy, Grant, & Myers, 1956). It might be easier to understand

Figure 3.5 The timing of events in trace, simultaneous, and backward conditioning

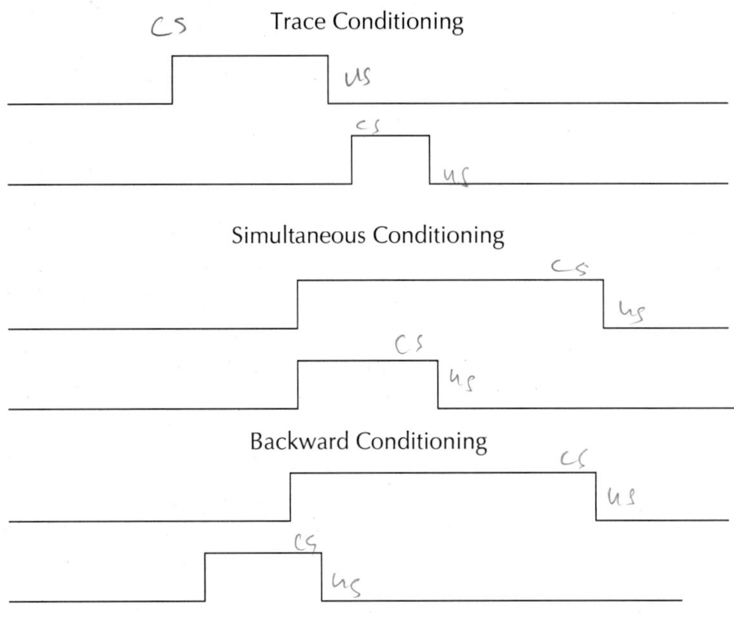

this variable by imagining what might happen with very short intervals; with an ITI of only a second or two, our learner might still be reacting to one presentation of the CS and US (still making a response) when the next presentation of CS and US occurs. One might imagine that this would not be a very good learning situation—too much happening at once to the learner. However, the advantage for longer ITIs applies over periods much longer than a few minutes; another possible reason why this might be so is that longer time intervals allow the stimuli that are to be associated to be experienced in more variable contexts. Why varied contexts may be helpful will be discussed in the section dealing with contiguity versus contingency. Recent research has suggested that the most effective interstimulus intervals (as discussed above) are not specific intervals such as a half second, but rather that there is a different most effective ISI for each different intertrial interval. Basically, the ISI must be small in comparison to the ITI; the smaller the ISI–ITI ratio, the more effectively conditioning proceeds (Hearst, 1988).

Practice

We could give our learner just a few trials or we could expose him to many trials; generally, the greater the amount of practice a subject receives, the better the learning. However, this statement needs to be qualified by referring to the learning-performance curve, which indicates great changes in performance on the first several trials and diminishing improvement with increasing numbers of trials until performance reaches an *asymptote* (or peak level) beyond which no change can be detected. Look again at the Smith, Coleman, and Gormezano (1969) eyeblink conditioning data presented in figure 3.4. Generally the eyeblink CR requires more practice than most classical conditioning procedures. These data show that a CR that appears to be learned very slowly, with much practice required, in one condition (the 100-msec delay condition) can be learned more quickly in other conditions (the 200- and 400-msec conditions), although even the most effective arrangements require more than 40 trials.

In addition to illustrating the importance of the interstimulus interval, the curves for the effective learning conditions also show the typical pattern of performance. These learning curves appear very similar to the curves presented in chapter 2 for sensitization. If you look back at those curves, you should be able to see the overall pattern of rapid increases that gradually taper off and recognize this trend in figure 3.4 as well. The curves also show that there is a maximum level of responding. In this study, the 100-msec group never reached this asymptotic level. This asymptote represents a limit on performance, but the subject may still be benefiting (learning) from the additional practice. The benefit of additional practice may be revealed by greater resistance to extinction, for example. If we examine the extinction portion of the graph carefully, we can see that the 400-msec conditioning interval group showed more resistance to extinction than the other groups; its level of responding after 100 extinction trials is even slightly higher than the 200-msec group.

Schedules

We have been discussing practice under the assumption that all trials are exactly the same; this is not the only way we could do it. We might have our US occur after every other presentation of the CS; in other words, half the time the CS is followed by the US and half the time it isn't. These conditions of 50% pairing do result in learning, but they are not as effective as 100% pairing. In fact, the percentage of pairing of CS and US is closely tied to effectiveness of conditioning; the closer to 100%, the better; the closer to 0%, the longer classical conditioning takes (Trapold & Spence, 1960). We will see quite different effects when we discuss this variable in operant conditioning in the section on schedules of reinforcement in chapter 4. → 100% better → 0%. longer

Novelty of the CS and US

A learner who has had previous experience with either the CS or the US will learn to associate them with each other more slowly. This is called the CS **preexposure effect** (Albert & Ayres, 1989) or *latent inhibition* (Lubow & Moore, 1959). It is usually explained by suggesting that the previous experience may have taught the learner that the CS is not relevant to any other stimulus and therefore may be safely ignored; it may well have become associated with the context (other sources of stimulation like the lab environment itself), and come to be "tuned out" along with those elements. Another explanation would be that the learner has habituated to this stimulus. Using such a stimulus as a CS will require that the learner dishabituates or unlearns that it was unimportant before learning its relevance to the US. Similarly, previous exposure to the US may have taught the learner that no other stimuli reliably occur before it and make the learner less sensitive to stimuli preceding it (Randich, 1981).

Similarity of the CS and US

If we were conducting an eyeblink conditioning experiment using a puff of air as the US, and we used a bright light as the CS, we might expect rapid learning. We might also be accused of cheating a little, because a light might generate blinking or squinting by itself, without the necessity of pairing with the airpuff. Traditionally, this kind of consideration was viewed as a condition to be avoided or controlled for and thus was not systematically investigated. CSs were supposed to be equally effective and therefore interchangeable, as Pavlov (1927) initially showed. However, recently researchers have been more concerned with this "belongingness" variable (so labeled by E. L. Thorndike [1932], who described some stimuli as belonging together whereas others were less related) and have begun to demonstrate ways of measuring the similarity of CS and US in some cases (Rozin & Kalat, 1971; Shapiro & LoLordo, 1982). We will simply state that generally a CS that bears some similarity or relationship to a US will be more easily associated with it in classical conditioning. We will return to this idea when we discuss the limits of learning (chapter 9).

Instructions

If we undertake to classically condition a person, we will generally have to explain something to that person about the experiment. In some cases this can affect the ease of conditioning. For example, in experiments where a mild shock is administered to the person's finger (US) and a tone signals the shock (CS), we can tell the learner this is going to happen and get our CR (finger twitching) in fewer trials than if the subject is not instructed. Further, we could mislead the subject by indicating that the tone signals times when shock will not follow, thereby slowing down the learning process (Brewer, 1974). Obviously this variable is only usable with verbal humans, and even then not with all conditioning procedures.

It is also much less important than many of the other variables mentioned above, because it usually has a less dramatic effect. However, some theorists have attached great significance to this type of finding, suggesting that it implies that subjects do not actually learn without awareness; in other words, many experiments have shown that people do not show nonverbal evidence of conditioning until they can verbally describe what is happening (Dawson & Schell, 1987).

Section Review

In classical conditioning, a fairly strong stimulus, the US, is paired with another stimulus, the conditioned stimulus, until the CS generates a response that it did not elicit before. The US can cause a reflex or an emotion, so that these kinds of responses may be classically conditioned. The number of pairings required to get a reliable, strong, conditioned response depends on:

1. The intensity of the US—the stronger the US the faster the learning occurs.
2. The exact timing and order of the two stimuli—when the CS begins and within a second or so later the US begins with the CS still present, learning is usually accomplished most effectively.
3. The percentage of times the CS is followed by the US—greater consistency leads to better learning.
4. Several other factors, such as previous exposure to the stimuli, their similarity to each other, the time interval between trials, and instructions; however, these are usually not as powerful as 1 through 3 above.

What Is Being Learned?

As can be seen, even in a basic classical conditioning experiment many things need to be carefully controlled and manipulated. Yet these represent only fairly simple conditioning procedures; things happening in the real world are often considerably more complex. We will now consider three of the more complex variations on the basic classical conditioning theme in the context of their theoretical implications.

Higher-Order Conditioning

Let's say that Pavlov pairs a bell (CS_1) with food for many trials, so that the bell becomes a good generator of the CR, salivation. He might then use the bell as if it were a US, pairing another stimulus with it, for example, turning on a light (CS_2) before ringing the bell. If this were done for several trials, Pavlov's dog might begin to salivate to the light as well as to the bell, even though the light itself was never paired with the food. This is referred to as *second-order conditioning;* often stimuli that can be used as unconditioned stimuli as a result of having been paired with a "true" US are called secondary reinforcers. A few researchers have gone on to create CRs even further removed from the original US by extending the process. That is, after the second-order conditioning procedure described above, we could use the light as a US and a third stimulus (perhaps a different sound from the first CS) as a new CS and obtain *third-order conditioning*. Higher orders than that have rarely been obtained. You may have already figured out why these higher-order procedures are so difficult to learn; each trial in later conditioning involves some extinction, because a "true" US is no longer present. As we get further removed from the US, extinction effects become more pronounced, the CR becomes weaker, and further conditioning becomes more unlikely and difficult.

Higher-order conditioning has had important theoretical implications for our understanding of the conditioning process, because it seems to suggest that a response, the CR, is necessary for learning. Many learning theorists have debated whether responding is necessary for learning. Recall our discussion in chapter 1 about S–R versus S–S learning. If a response is necessary for learning, then it might be that the learner is associating the response with the stimulus (learning to give the CR to the CS) and thus learning an S–R association. The alternative interpretation would be that the subject is learning that one stimulus (the CS) stands for or signals or represents in some way the other stimulus (the US). This S–S interpretation, often referred to as **stimulus substitution** (the CS substitutes for the US), does not require responding for learning. Because third- and higher-order conditioning procedures are very difficult, and because in them responding becomes progressively poorer, these results favor the S–R interpretations.

Variations on the higher-order conditioning procedure also seem to suggest an S–R interpretation. One interesting variation involves (1) training CS_1 (bell) to US (food); (2) pairing CS_2 (light) with CS_1 (bell) until salivation to CS_2 (light) also occurs; and (3) now pairing CS_1 (bell) with a new US_2 (shock). After a while, CS_1 (bell) will generate a fear response instead of salivation as a result of our third step. What will have happened to the response to the light (CS_2)? The S–S interpretation suggests that CS_1 and CS_2 should generate the same response because one stands for the other. However, the S-R interpretation says that CS_2 should still generate salivation; because it was never paired with the fear response, it should retain the salivation response even though CS_1 has developed a new CR. This is exactly what happens (Konorski, 1948). It might seem that we have resolved this question, then; S–R is what's happening. Unfortunately there is other contradictory evidence from a procedure called sensory preconditioning.

Sensory Preconditioning

If we change the order in which we do things just a little, we can perform a **sensory preconditioning** experiment (Brogden, 1939). This consists of first pairing two CSs with each other; for example, ringing a bell (CS_1), then turning on a light (CS_2) for a number of trials. Then we pair one of them, the light (CS_2), with a US (for example, shock) until it (the light) elicits a clear CR (in this case, a fear response). When we test CS_1 (the bell), we find that it also has acquired the potential to generate the fear CR. You may be thinking, so what—isn't this the same as the second-order conditioning already described? You must recall that the definition of a CS suggests that it is usually a weak stimulus, one that habituates easily. This means that in our first stage of pairing the two CSs, responses were becoming weaker with each pairing. Therefore, learning during that stage should have been very weak, if any even occurred, according to the S–R theory. Furthermore, the bell was never paired with the fear response. Yet learning did occur, strong enough for a CS never paired with the US directly to still elicit a CR. Sensory preconditioning and several other complex procedures (e.g., Rescorla, 1974) support the S–S or stimulus substitution explanation of learning.

So is it S–S or S–R connections that are being learned? More of the evidence seems to favor the S–S position, and today most of the researchers seem to be working on this basis. Clearly indirect measures such as the suppression ratio are more likely to suggest that S–S connections are occurring because they are a step removed from the customary UR at the outset. It may also be true that both types of association could be learned simultaneously in relatively complex creatures. If you are wondering why it matters, think of the implications of these many experiments. First, in higher-order conditioning and sensory preconditioning just one change in procedure leads to a totally different conclusion. Then note what these procedures suggest about the influence of classical conditioning; stimuli that are not directly paired with a US may still be associated with it by a learner because of indirect connections. The influence of conditioning is widened considerably.

As to the theoretical question, S–S versus S–R, the lack of an observable response makes learning an internal, inferred concept rather than a directly observable one. Behaviorally oriented psychologists (such as Watson) would clearly have preferred to treat learning as a directly observable phenomenon. Generally, psychologists interested in cognition (such as myself) prefer S–S interpretations. That is, considering internal events (thoughts and ideas) is very inconvenient if these events must always be followed by observable responses. For example, an early theory of word meaning that utilized classical conditioning suggested that meanings were learned as a result of the sounds of the word (CS) being paired with the object (US) (Osgood, 1954). Thus the word *tree* comes to generate the same internal events as encountering an actual tree as a result of conditioning. To describe this in terms of S–R connections would lead to the conclusion that the person hearing the word *tree* would have to make climbing motions to understand the word.

Similar problems exist in observing the kinds of fear reactions studied with the suppression ratio. In laboratory situations, the suppression ratio can be readily used; in real life, changes in ongoing activity due to the presence of a CS for fear may be obscured by the more variable nature of the ongoing activity. But the absence of changes in a suppression ratio measure in such circumstances would be poor evidence for concluding that no learning had occurred. In fact the very concept of indirect measurement by a suppression ratio implies that the response itself is not a fundamental element in the conditioning procedure; the suppression ratio assumes that we are measuring the strength of association between a CS and a US. Thus, an S–S interpretation proposes an analysis similar to the learning-performance distinction mentioned in chapter 1; if we see an obvious change in the response, then we can be pretty sure learning has occurred, but if we don't, we shouldn't conclude that the subject didn't learn. There may be new associations that will show up as indirect influences on behavior in some other circumstances.

Some researchers, especially Ralph Miller and his associates, have used sensory preconditioning procedures to evaluate the effectiveness of our four types of interstimulus intervals (Matzel, Held, & Miller, 1988; Barnet, Arnold, & Miller, 1991; Miller & Barnet, 1993; Barnet & Miller, 1996). In numerous experiments, Miller has shown that simultaneous and backward conditioning appear as effective as delayed or trace conditioning in creating an association. For example, in one set of studies they presented a five-second click followed by a five-second tone in the sensory preconditioning phase, thus using a trace conditioning presentation. Then, in phase two, they could present the tone before a shock for some animals (delayed conditioning), at the same time as the shock for some animals (simultaneous), or after the shock onset (backward) for some animals. The tone itself generated inhibition of a water-licking response only for the phase-two delayed subjects but not for the other two groups. However, the click generated inhibition equally for all three groups (Matzel, Held, & Miller, 1988). Thus (according to Miller and his colleagues), the response to the click indicated that an association had been formed in phase two for all the groups, but that association did not generate a response to the tone which they could observe directly in the backward and simultaneous groups. They suggest that all (brief) timing procedures lead to the formation of associations, but that some associations do not generate directly observable responses.

One important consequence of this interpretation is that the "simple" association of two stimuli must be understood as being more complicated than previously thought. That is, timing information must be a part of the association as well as information about the CS and US; this would allow for the differently occurring time sequences to differ in their response-generating ability. These researchers feel that not only is contiguity an important cause of classical conditioning, it is also a part of the learning that the creature acquires. Matzel, Held, and Miller (1988) referred to this as the **temporal coding hypothesis**—the relative timing of CS and US occurrences is encoded as well as the nature of the CS and the US. Thus, the temporal coding hypothesis suggests that (a) contiguity is sufficient for learning an association, (b) the timing relationship between CS and US is part of the association, (c) but responding is generated only if the CS predicts a US that starts after the CS starts, and (d) associations and their temporal characteristics can be combined or integrated (Williams & Hurlburt, 2000).

Configural Learning

Much of the recent research in classical conditioning has used several CSs simultaneously. For example, we could present a bell and a light at the same time and follow with a US like a shock, but present a buzzer and the light at the same time without the US. If we alternate these training trials, how will the learner respond to the light? One possibility is that the learner forms two "simple" associations during each type of trial, one between the light and the shock and one between the bell and the shock, but the light-shock association is being extinguished during the buzzer + light-no shock trials. So we might not see much response to the light. Another possibility, called **configural learning**, suggests that the learner forms an association between the bell and the light, and that this combination is treated as one complex stimulus configuration that becomes associated with the shock as a single unit (Pearce & Bouton, 2001). Meanwhile, the light also becomes associated with the buzzer as another unitary complex stimulus during the extinction trials. When the light is presented by itself, it then might generate a response because it has some similarity to the bell-light combination (this would then be an example of generalization, discussed in chapter 7). The light does indeed generate responses, supporting the combined stimuli interpretation. This research actually is investigating how creatures perceive patterns of stimulation: when several stimuli occur, are they each noticed independently, or are they combined into a single, complex stimulus pattern? Although there are some conflicting findings, the weight of the research seems to favor the single, complex stimulus interpretation (Pearce, 1987, 1994; Redhead & Pearce, 1995).

Pearce and Bouton (2001) have also used the idea that many associations can be formed between a possible CS and US and their context, along with Miller's idea of the temporal coding hypothesis, to explain spontaneous recovery. Remember that spontaneous recovery usually occurs when there is a longer than usual delay between trials during extinction. Pearce and Bouton suggest that the longer time interval causes the learner to perceive the next (extinction) trial as a different stimulus situation, since its timing properties are different from the other extinction trials. Therefore, it might not be seen as resembling the other extinction trials but may more closely resemble a training trial. This would cause it to generate a greater response than the previous extinction trials. Generally, any change in context may disrupt extinction somewhat, producing spontaneous recovery (Bouton & Nelson, 1998); or, if we rearrange the situation, a change in context can reduce spontaneous recovery (Brooks & Bouton, 1994). These findings support the Pearce and Bouton interpretation, which suggests that complex associations, including both details about the nature of the stimuli and about their timing characteristics, are formed between multiple stimulus elements during each learning or extinction trial.

What Causes Learning?

Our final theoretical question involves the fundamental cause of conditioning—is it contiguity or contingency? You might recall from our discussion of timing (CS–US intervals) that brief time intervals are usually crucial to the success of conditioning. Violation of the contiguity principle leads to poor learning except in one case, taste aversions, to be discussed in chapter 9 (The Context of Learning). As stated earlier, for many years this temporal nearness or contiguity was thought to be the necessary and sufficient condition for conditioning. However, this made the poor results of simultaneous conditioning, where contiguity is maximal, difficult to explain, as we saw. In 1968 Robert Rescorla suggested that contiguity was not the explanation (Rescorla, 1968, 1988; Rescorla & Holland, 1982) and proposed the notion of **contingency** instead.

Contingencies are "if-then" relationships; if the CS occurs, then the US will occur, and if the CS doesn't occur, then the US won't either. Rescorla and Wagner (1972; Wagner & Rescorla, 1972) suggested that this type of relationship leads to conditioning because it allows the learner to predict the occurrence of the US; whenever the CS occurs, it provides the information that the US will be coming soon. Their informational theory easily explains the poor results of early simultaneous conditioning studies; there the CS was of no value to the learner because it didn't provide any additional information about the US, because the US was already occurring. It also explains the effects of different schedules on conditioning. Recall that following the CS with the US every time (100%) is more effective than following the CS with the US three-fourths of the time (75%), which is better than 50% pairing, and so forth. Rescorla and Wagner suggested that 100% pairing provides the best information about the likelihood that the US will occur. In other words, 100% pairing makes the

CS a very reliable predictor of the US; but 50% makes the CS a much less reliable predictor, although it may still be the best predictor around. Thus, the stimulus that is best learned about in a complex situation is the one that is most consistently associated with the US.

Rescorla (1968) not only criticized the value of contiguity as an explanation for simultaneous conditioning and schedule effects, but he also showed that it was insufficient to explain several important experiments that described a phenomenon referred to as the **blocking effect** (Kamin, 1968). Some stimuli seem to be naturally more noticeable than others to creatures; for example, young children seem attracted to bright-colored things. Stimuli that seem to be more easily noticed by a species are said to **overshadow** the other stimuli. Thus for a rat, auditory stimuli are more noticeable than visual ones, because rats are often active in the dark when auditory stimuli are more available than visual ones. Pigeons and many other birds are usually the opposite; they rely more on vision than hearing. These overshadowing properties can be easily demonstrated: simply pair two stimuli—one of each type—with an unconditioned stimulus and note which one is more effective at eliciting the CR. The stimulus that is more effective is said to overshadow the less effective stimulus. This seems to be an innate characteristic of some creatures' sensory or response patterns.

The blocking effect is an experimental procedure that can artificially create such differences in stimulus sensitivity. In the original experiments, Kamin (1969) first paired a noise with a shock and obtained clear evidence (using the CER measure) of learning in rats after 16 trials. Then these rats were given eight trials with a compound CS consisting of the noise and a light together, paired with the same level of shock. When tested, these rats showed no evidence of conditioning to the light. The prior conditioning to the noise apparently blocked, or prevented, later conditioning to the light. Later experiments have shown that reversing the stimuli leads to the same results; that is, if the light is used in the initial trials, the noise is blocked. Rescorla and Wagner's (1972) interpretation of this result was that the second stimulus provided no new or additional information about the occurrence of the shock and therefore was not learned. Unfortunately, the original description of the contingency theory doesn't really work either, because the formulas described the contingency between a single CS and a single US in terms of the conditional probabilities of US given no CS versus US given the CS, and so on. There were no provisions for US given CS_1 but not CS_2.

Rescorla and Wagner (1972; Wagner & Rescorla, 1972) developed a theory that sidesteps somewhat the question of contingency versus contiguity but that builds on the ideas originally proposed by the contingency model. The informational value of a CS is still seen as important, but this value is seen as developing on a trial-by-trial basis in which the context of each trial and the results of previous trials must also be accounted for.

They presented a formula that can be used to describe the amount learned on each trial. The formula assumes that a maximum amount can be learned in any classical conditioning situation. This maximum level of learning can be estimated by noting the strength of the UR—the greater the unconditioned response, the greater the potential size of the CR. (Of course, the size of the UR is based to a great extent on the strength of the US.) The other factor used in the formula is the number of previous trials in which a stimulus has been paired with the US. Each trial in which a stimulus (or stimuli) is paired with the US "uses up" some of the potential amount learnable. Thus, the Rescorla and Wagner (1972) account of the blocking effect predicts that the more trials we have of phase one (with one stimulus), the less left over that can be associated with the second stimulus of phase two. This is exactly what has been found. In this fashion they have been able to make detailed predictions about a number of complex procedures, most of which have been verified.

The Rescorla-Wagner Formula

Rescorla and Wagner's (1972) formula for the amount learned is

$$\Delta V = K(L - Vsum)$$

The ΔV represents how much is learned on a given trial (the change in learning since the last trial). K is a constant that reflects how much of a complete association creatures are capable of learning on a given trial. The constant is usually given as a decimal fraction of totality, such as .2. This fraction may be influenced by the salience of the CS, the presence of competing stimuli, and the capacities of the learner. L is the total amount learnable and can be estimated by measuring the maximum performance of some highly trained subjects. Generally it depends on the intensity of the US—a 100-volt shock would lead to a final L value much greater than a 50-volt shock. Vsum is the amount of learning that has previously occurred to that US.

To illustrate, let's say we're shocking a rat with a shock intensity that causes an L of 100 units, and let's assume that we have determined from previous research that K in fact equals .2. Therefore, on the first trial ΔV = .2 (100 – 0); solving for ΔV, we get 20 units of learning. On the second trial, ΔV = .2(100 – 20), which works out to ΔV = .2(80) or 16 units learned. On the third trial, Vsum has become 36(20 + 16), so ΔV = .2(100 – 36) or V = .2(64), which equals 12.8, and our rat has learned 20 + 16 + 12.8 = 48.8 units of learning. Recognizing that L = 100 could be thought of as learning 100%, after three trials our rat has learned almost half of what it is capable of learning (48.8%). Figure 3.6 illustrates these calculations graphically.

If we apply this analysis to the blocking phenomenon, we can see that by trial 4 there's not much learning left to be associated with a second CS introduced at that point. The second CS will have to share the remaining 51.2% "learnability" with the original CS; consequently, it will not acquire much ability to generate a CR. If we assume that it has the same K as the original CS, .2, then it will have a maximum of about half of .2 × 51.2 = 10.24. At this rate, 5% for the most effective trial, this CS won't generate much of a CR even after many trials. Thus, the second CS has been "blocked" because there's not much learning left over for it. However, if there is a change in the intensity of the US when shifting from stage 1 to stage 2, the L value for the two stages would be different, and this might provide the potential for the second CS to be learned.

Further experiments by Kamin (1969) and others supported this idea by demonstrating that if the shock intensity is changed from stage 1 to stage 2, learning does occur to the second CS (which in those cases is no longer redundant). In other words, if Kamin used a 50-volt shock paired with one stimulus, then switched to 100 volts for the compound stimulus condition, both stimuli become good generators of the CR because each informs the subject about the US—the first stimulus predicts a shock and the second predicts a stronger shock. From the standpoint of the formula this is roughly equivalent to changing L from 100 for stage 1 to 200 for stage 2; the second CS has a value of 151.2 to share with the first CS, and we could easily calculate that each would acquire strong CR-generating capacities. Further, if the shock intensity is decreased—that is, the first stimulus predicts a 100-volt shock and the compound stimuli predict 50 volts—the second stimulus becomes capable of generating "relief" in the

Figure 3.6 Predictions of the amount learned on each trial using the Rescorla-Wagner formula

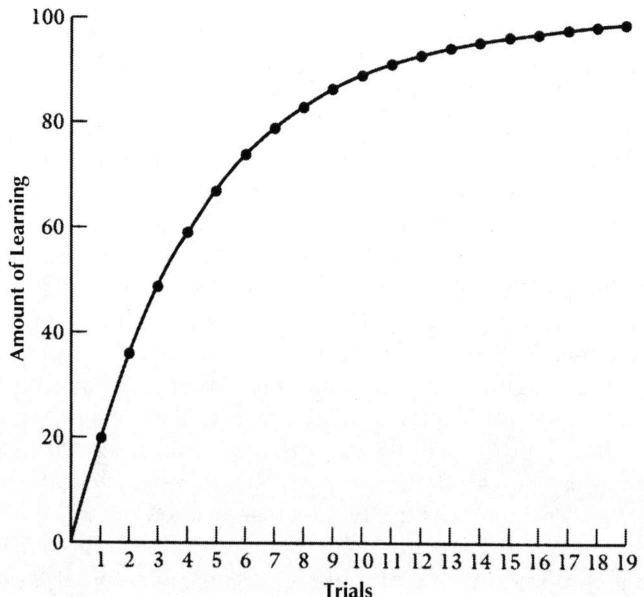

learner because she will come to associate it with the smaller shock. The formula was used to make just such predictions.

Of course, all of our given values have been hypothetical, and few attempts have been made to predict exactly how much is learned in a given situation. Rather, the formula has been useful in predicting the relative contributions of particular CSs and their context to the formation of classical associations in such situations as the blocking experiments. Thus, the formula provides a mechanism for making experiments more closely resemble real-life situations, where many stimuli come and go continuously.

The Rescorla-Wagner formula also suggests an explanation for the intertrial interval (ITI) variable described earlier. Remember that longer ITIs are more effective than brief intervals between training trials. If we use the idea just presented for the blocking experiment, we can describe the conditioning experiment as the occurrence of many stimuli along with the US. In addition to the intended CS, there are all the stimuli of the laboratory, the researchers in it, and the internal sensations of the subject. All of these occur along with the US during training trials. However, the other stimuli are also present between trials, when no US is occurring. Thus, they undergo extinction during the ITI. Long ITIs therefore allow the other stimuli to be more fully extinguished, leaving more of the "learnability" for the intended CS. This is a very appealing explanation and almost certainly is one reason why longer ITIs result in better learning. There is an additional explanation that also has merit, however. It is a cognitive explanation and will be discussed in the memory chapters where the relevant research on distribution of practice is presented.

Finally, another phenomenon that may be better understood from the informational perspective on classical conditioning involves the nature of the CR and its relationship to the UR. The CR has been interpreted in two ways: either as an anticipatory response or as a preparatory response. The difference is that the **anticipatory response** interpretation suggests that the reaction to the CS is essentially the UR occurring earlier because the CS is earlier than the US. The **preparatory response** explanation states that the CR prepares the organism for the US so that the US is more easily tolerated by the organism. Recall that in Pavlov's experiment both the CR and the UR were the same response, salivation, and in Watson's demonstration with Albert fear was both the UR and the CR. As noted, in these cases the only difference between CR and UR are intensity of the response, its timing, and which stimulus generates it. Both explanations fit these cases reasonably well. The dog could be anticipating the US and preparing to digest it with the same action.

However, in some cases, the CR and the UR are the opposite of each other. The initial example investigated involves the physiological reactions to electric shock. Typically, the reactions to shock include elevated heart rate and blood pressure. If the CR were also elevated heart rate and blood pressure as the anticipatory theory might allow, the result would be more systemic stress on the organism—a heart attack might be more likely. On the other hand, if the CR were the opposite of the UR, lowered heart rate and blood pressure, the UR would begin from a lowered base level; and the final result would be a less severe level of heart rate and blood pressure when a well-learned CS accompanies the US. Instead of the effects being added together, one would subtract from the other. The CR in effect counteracts the UR. This is exactly what occurs, a prediction more consistent with the preparatory interpretation and one also consistent with informational theories, which suggests that the value of a CS is in allowing the learner to predict the US. Predicting the US is useless unless it leads the learner to be better prepared for it.

A more dramatic example of this counteractive, preparatory characteristic of the CR involves the widely known phenomenon of drug tolerance. It has been suggested that tolerance is partly the result of classical conditioning (Siegel, 1979). The idea is that the circumstances surrounding the use of heroin, for example, become conditioned to the drug's chemical effects. Thus, the tying off of the arm and the feeling of the injection, along with the setting or context of the room, which friends are present, and so forth, act as CSs that generate an antagonistic or compensatory CR to the normal UR of the drug itself. After many trials, a strong CR develops that lessens the "high" experienced by the user, leading him to increase the dosage. However, this tolerance will only occur fully when all the usual CSs are present (or when that whole stimulus configuration, as Pearce and Bouton [2001] would describe it, is present). If the user receives the dosage he has become accustomed to having in the absence of some of the usual CSs, such as the usual room and social context, a smaller compensatory CR will occur and he could experience an overdose. Siegel (1979) interviewed drug users and their friends and found many overdose cases suggesting that this is exactly what happened.

When are CRs the opposite of the UR, and when are the two similar? One theory suggests that some responses consist of two physiological components that are the opposite of each other. These "opponent processes" (Solomon & Corbit, 1974) occur at different times after stimulation and are differently affected by experience. For example, one response to electrical shock is an elevated heart rate, but when the shock stops, reaction to this is a brief reduction in heart rate below the original level. Opponent process theory suggests that the first reaction does not change with experience but the second reaction, the "relief," becomes stronger and occurs earlier with training. This would cause the total increase in heart rate to be smaller with more experience. Currently, no good way of predicting which responses might be governed by opponent-process physiological mechanisms exists, other than the fact that some normal physical responses can occur below zero rate, nor is there a good way of explaining the physiology of the second component. However, the theory has generated considerable interest.

The information-based theories (Rescorla, 1967, 1982; Rescorla & Wagner, 1972) have not gone without criticism. The two major criticisms point out that (1) the formula describes CS salience strictly in terms of previous occurrences of the CS, and (2) there is no place for contiguity in the formula. At this point, both Wagner and Rescorla have acknowledged difficulties with the original strict contingency proposal (Papini & Bitterman, 1990). Wagner has attempted to incorporate considerations about the salience (noticeability) of various CSs in his accounts, as have others (Mackintosh, 1975; Pearce & Hall, 1980). Clear evidence that under some conditions some CSs are more effectively learned than others, even without previous differential exposure, does in fact exist. The overshadowing phenomenon previously described is one example. To better describe classical conditioning the learning process has been characterized by these theorists as one involving the surprisingness of the US; the best CS is one that can reduce the surprise of an unexpected US the most. Thus, CS salience is partly a consequence of the information value of the CS in reducing surprisingness. The ability to reduce surprisingness is due to the probability of the US following the CS in contrast to the probability of the US following other stimuli or not following the CS. However, salience is also partly due to the relative intensity of the CS.

The second criticism, the failure to allow for timing effects, has not resulted in a satisfactory alternative version of the formula but instead has led to other approaches. Proponents of these approaches have noted the fact that many of the experiments providing the strongest support for contingency theories use the CER procedure and the suppression ratio measure. The suppression ratio is usually relatively insensitive to timing differences, whereas direct measures of the CR such as response strength more often reveal the importance of contiguity. Contingency theorists would say that these direct response measures are not accurately estimating the underlying learning, and of course, all measures of learning are imperfect.

Others have suggested that contingency theory needs to be integrated with contiguity theory and other explanations, and all findings must be accommodated to have a complete theory. Although this has not been done to everyone's satisfaction, several theorists have made attempts. Most of these have suggested that classical conditioning is a multistage or multilevel process; generally, they suggest that conscious awareness of the contingency is critical at an early stage in learning, but later stages reflect different factors such as learning the physical and temporal properties of the stimuli, especially the contiguity indicated by the CS–US interval (Dawson & Schell, 1987; Maltzman, Weissbluth, & Wolff, 1978; and Prokasy, 1984 are examples). Thus, it is now recognized that both the contiguity of the stimuli and their interdependence, or the contingencies that exist between them, are important factors determining the effectiveness of classical conditioning procedures.

How do these theories interpret the question of S–S versus S–R associations? The emphasis on the role of the CS as a provider of information about the US places almost all current theories in the S–S camp. The use of response strength (how large a UR or CR is occurring) in the Rescorla-Wagner formula might suggest that it incorporates S–R associations, but this is merely the best practical way to measure the amount learnable and the amount learned; they reflect performance characteristics. An informational or contingency theory must be a type of S–S theory. Rescorla and Wagner's work has caused most modern interpretations of classical conditioning, such as the three mentioned in the previous paragraphs, to emphasize the S–S position and to incorporate contingencies and the learner's awareness of those contingencies. Thus, the "simple" associations suggested by Pavlov's early experiments turn out to be much more complex, potentially involving the combination of several CS elements, stimuli in the background or context, and information about timing relationships with the US to allow the learner to best anticipate the US and respond most effectively to it.

Classical Conditioning and the Nervous System

The neural mechanisms of classical conditioning are very complex, but several things are known about them. First, Kandel and his associates have found in their studies of the sea slug *Aplysia* (described in chapter 2) that similar chemical mechanisms are involved in classical conditioning and sensitization; namely, changes in calcium and potassium levels in sensory cells, which cause them to release more neurotransmitters. Further, they have shown that these changes are the result of strengthening already existing connections that were initially too weak to cause the receiving cell to fire. That is, in *Aplysia* they found a three-cell system in which neurons A and B each formed synapses with neuron C. However, before their training, the A neuron's connection was not sufficient to trigger a response in neuron C by itself, while the B neuron did cause C to fire. Repeated electrical stimulation of neuron A (treating it like a CS) followed by stimulation of neuron B (using it as the US) half a second later eventually led to a strengthening of the neuron A synapse so that it could also cause C to fire (Kandel & Tauc, 1964, 1965). These chemical mechanisms in *Aplysia* have also been found in eyeblink conditioning studies of rabbits (Usherwood, 1993). In addition to increased ability of the neurons representing CSs to stimulate their receiving cells, Glanzman (1995) found that the receiving cells, called postsynaptic neurons (the C neuron in our example), had increased sensitivity to neurotransmitters as a result of conditioning.

A second finding is that, as you might expect, each form of conditioning involves different pathways. That is, eyeblink conditioning involves different brain structures than fear conditioning, which involves different structures from heart-rate conditioning, and so forth. The eyeblink mechanisms are reasonably well described; it appears that there are two pathways of activity generated by the airpuff US in reflexive eyeblinks, a direct pathway through the brain stem, and a less direct pathway that also goes through the cerebellum. Classical conditioning of the eyeblink causes changes in this less direct pathway, which also mediates the conditioned stimulus (e.g., a tone); neurons in parts of the cerebellum become more likely to fire as a result of classical eyeblink conditioning (Canli & Donegan, 1995). This might explain why some conditioning procedures, like our heart-rate changes in shock conditioning or the drug tolerance findings of Siegel (1979), result in a CR with a different form from the UR; different pathways are being activated in the learned CS–CR condition than in the reflexive US–UR system (possibly with the US–UR system involving more pathways).

The hippocampus, while not involved in standard (delayed) eyelid conditioning, has been shown to be involved in trace conditioning of the eyelid and many other classical conditioning procedures. The hippocampus has several remarkable characteristics relevant to learning and memory. First, it has pathways which circle back upon themselves, forming a closed loop. This permits continued activity as a result of a stimulus, even if the stimulus itself stops, and therefore supports rehearsal of a stimulus. It serves this purpose in a "generic" fashion—that is, it doesn't receive input directly from the senses, but rather from areas of the sensory cortex. Presumably this input has already been analyzed (the stimuli have been recognized by the sensory cortex areas). It also sends output back to these areas via its specialized pyramidal cells. Second, these cells show most of the change in activity during learning, so they are the ones that in some sense "cause" the learning; pyramidal cells are capable of **long-term potentiation** (LTP), a long-lasting (days or even weeks) change in synaptic effectiveness as a result of shorter-lasting stimulation. This LTP occurs in the (postsynaptic) receptor sites in these cells and is specific to the synapses being stimulated. In other words, the synapses being stimulated become more sensitive to stimulation while other synapses on the same cell remain unchanged. Bliss and Gardner-Medwin (1973) found this phenomenon in hippocampal neurons when these cells were repeatedly stimulated. Larson and Lynch (1986) found this change was more pronounced when the animal was actively exploring its environment at the time of stimulation, suggesting that an animal in a relatively unfamiliar environment may be more prepared to learn new associations.

Berger and Thompson (1978), using a rabbit eyeblink conditioning procedure and monitoring hippocampal activity, found increased activity in the hippocampus after just eight trials, although a CR did not appear until after more than 50 trials. They interpreted the early hippocampal activity as indicating that the creature had detected the contingency between CS and US; later, the pattern of activity of the hippocampus was mirrored in the pattern of responding. Many researchers have attributed this duplication of patterning to the hippocampus developing a "model" of the learning procedure, and this represents a third remarkable characteristic of the hippocampus. Hippocampal damage interferes with the ability to learn in many of the procedures we have described in this chapter, including trace conditioning, sensory preconditioning, and the blocking effect (Macphail, 1993).

Finally, many more brain systems are involved than just those mentioned, and they may vary for different creatures. For example, the hippocampus has been found to be necessary for the blocking effect to occur in rabbits (Solomon, 1977) but not in pigeons, where it is necessary for the CS preexposure effect (Good & Macphail, 1994). Thus, it seems likely that many brain systems are involved in classical conditioning, with somewhat different subsets responsible for different conditioning phenomena, depending on the kind of creature studied.

How to Analyze Examples

In many classes on learning, students are asked to demonstrate their understanding of the basics of the classical conditioning process by labeling the components in an example. Often they have difficultly, especially in distinguishing the CS from the US. A method suggested by Dr. Robert Graham (personal communication) seems helpful to some. First, identify a response that shows some change as a result of the situation described. Once the response has been recognized, search the example for a stimulus that occurred before it that would "naturally" have caused that response—that is, some stimulus that would have generated that response automatically or innately, without learning, or at least would have been able to cause it before the event in question. This is the US. Now look for another stimulus before the response that appears to have been unable to cause the response before the event described, but that has now become capable of generating the response as a result of the event described. This is the CS. Labeling the CR distinctly from the UR is then just recognizing that the CR is in reaction to the CS, and the UR is in reaction to the US. Here is a practice example:

> Bertie's parents decide to train him to pucker more because they think he looks cute that way. Every time they shake a rattle, they immediately follow it by touching his lips with the nipple of an empty baby bottle. Pretty soon Bertie is puckering up and sucking every time he hears a rattle.

In this example, the response we're interested in is clearly puckering and sucking because it changes. The stimulus that comes before the puckering and that probably generated puckering before Bertie's parents got their clever idea is the stimulation with the nipple; this is the US. The other stimulus that occurs before his puckering is the sound of the rattle—it probably didn't generate puckering before the parents' conditioning efforts, but because of their training it is now able to generate puckering; it is the CS. Bertie's puckering to the nipple is his UR, and his puckering to the rattle is the CR. We could wonder what type of conditioning this is; from the description several are possible. If Daddy shakes the rattle and a fraction of a second later Mommy stimulates Bertie's lips while Daddy is still shaking, it would be delayed conditioning. Or Daddy might shake for a few seconds, then stop, and Mommy starts stimulating after he stops. This would be trace conditioning.

Summary

Classical conditioning was first described by the Russian medical researcher Ivan Pavlov when he showed that a sound could be paired with food to generate the salivation that the food originally reflexively generated. The sound was labeled a conditioned stimulus and the food an unconditioned stimulus; the response to the food was an unconditioned response and the salivation in response to the sound was a conditioned response. Watson later showed that emotions as well as reflexes could be classically conditioned in his demonstration with Little Albert. The important influences on classical conditioning are the strength or intensity of the US, the relative intensity of the CS, the amount of practice or number of pairings, the schedule of pairings, and the CS–US interval. Four types of interstimulus intervals have been used; the most effective for generating the usual CR is delayed conditioning, followed by trace, with simultaneous being relatively ineffective and backward very ineffective. However, complex experiments using several training stages suggest that all of these can lead to the development of an association.

Higher-order conditioning experiments involve using a trained CS as if it were a US. These experiments usually suggest that the learner must respond in order to learn. However, sensory preconditioning experiments, which involve pairing two potential CSs before using one of them in a classical conditioning procedure, suggest that responding is not necessary for learning. Configural learning experiments using several CSs indicate that the learner develops an association between them and may treat them as a single unitary stimulus complex, which then may be associated with the US.

Originally, contiguity was thought to be the necessary and sufficient cause of classical learning. However, research by Rescorla and Wagner suggested that the existence of a contingency, or dependency of US on

CS, was the crucial cause of classical conditioning. Currently, both explanations are thought to be crucial for learning, probably at different periods during the learning process and at different levels in the nervous system. Rescorla and Wagner also developed a formula for predicting the amount learned on each trial.

Classical conditioning involves neurochemical changes similar to those found in sensitization, namely, increases in neurotransmitters released by sensory neurons. When two neurons repeatedly stimulate a third neuron at the same time, the neuron that releases the smaller amount of neurotransmitter increases the amount it releases during classical conditioning. Changes in neurons in the hippocampus support the formation of classical associations in higher brain regions in the cortex.

Questions for Discussion, Thought, and Practice

1. Define and give an example of each of the key concepts. Then rearrange the list by grouping the terms dealing with similar topics together. Finally, arrange the groups into related combinations of groups.
2. Matilda's aunt always chews the breath freshener Perts. Ever since her aunt scolded her and spanked her one day when she was eight, Matilda has hated the smell of Perts.
   a. Analyze this example of classical conditioning, labeling the CS, US, CR, and UR. Describe the temporal pattern—what is the CS–US timing arrangement that is occurring?
   b. How would we extinguish Matilda's hatred? Be sure to describe extinction rather than some form of counterconditioning.
3. Easy Ed always studies in his favorite armchair right by the front door. During the winter, after a while, he starts shivering when he hears the door opening, even before the cold air hits him.
   a. Analyze this example, labeling the CS, US, CR, and UR, and determine what temporal pattern is occurring here.
   b. How could we have made Easy Ed shiver in fewer training trials? Describe at least two important changes we could make in this situation (in other words, describe two changes in the independent variables).
4. Phyllis Ann is playing jacks on the sidewalk when the ball bounces toward a storm drain. She quickly dives and catches it but skins both elbows and bruises her hip in the process. She cries so much that Mommy has to put Casper the Friendly Ghost band-aids on all her boo-boos. Now she gets very upset just at the sight of the storm drain. Analyze this example as you did for question 3.

5. Durward is showering in the dorm when he hears a toilet flush. Seconds later, he experiences a sudden, unpleasant change in the water temperature. From then on, whenever he hears any flushing sound while showering, he flinches and cringes. Analyze this example as you did for question 3.
6. Several of the variables that influence classical conditioning also affect habituation and sensitization. Which variables? Why might they operate similarly for the simple forms of learning as well as for classical conditioning? Conversely, why don't the others affect habituation and sensitization as well?
7. We're using bites of lemon meringue pie as our US. Our subject normally generates 10 drops of saliva per bite. Before each bite we show the subject a red flag. After the first trial, the red flag generates 3 drops of saliva, so we know that $K = .3$ in Rescorla and Wagner's formula. Using their formula, calculate how much is learned on each of the next two trials, and what the total would be for the three trials.

Operant Conditioning

▲ Key Concepts ▲

behavior modification
contingency management
continuous reinforcement
cumulative recorder
depression effect
deprivation
discriminative stimulus
elation effect
fixed interval
fixed ratio
instrumental conditioning
law of effect
maintenance
matching law
negative reinforcement
operant conditioning
partial reinforcement extinction effect
positive reinforcement
positive reinforcer
post-reinforcement pause
punisher
punishment
rate of response
satiation
schedule
shaping
trial-and-error learning
variable interval
variable ratio

Thus far we have considered several basic forms of learning. However, many students view these forms as playing a relatively minor role in their everyday lives. Students are generally more concerned with questions of why some people work harder in school or at their jobs than others, or why they find it hard to study two weeks before a test but enjoy learning to play bridge or tennis during that time. These are activities like our chapter 1 examples of MJ playing basketball, Aphrodite avoiding her big brother, and Prometheus the cat running to the kitchen when he hears the can opener. Each of these activities involves several important characteristics that differentiate them from the forms of learning described previously. First, they all seem to be the result of choices made by the learner, deliberate actions rather than reflexive reactions. The *why* question indicates the voluntary nature of the activities. Learning psychologists have generally tried to answer the why question by examining the relationship between each activity and the events immediately following it; they suggest that the apparent choice is predictable if they can specify the nature of these consequences or reinforcers. For example, they would point to the obvious reward of food for Prometheus, and they might suggest that potentially there are several powerful and immediate positive consequences that would encourage someone to want to play bridge or tennis or basketball. The excitement of competition, especially when we win, is fairly obvious; but the pleasure of the social interactions with friends also may be rewarding aspects of these games. On the other hand, the reinforcers for studying or working hard at a job may also be powerful; good grades lead to good jobs, which lead to big paychecks, which lead to having lots of food and other material "rewards," and so forth. Here the trouble may be that these rewards occur too long after the responses to be effective. Thus, the choice that a person makes may be the result of either the size or value of a reward or the delay involved in obtaining it.

In addition to involving voluntary actions rather than automatic reactions, these kinds of behaviors also seem more complex; for many of them the individual must learn several kinds of things. In playing bridge or basketball, we must learn coordinated movements such as shuffling and dealing cards or shooting the ball accurately; but we must also learn when to do these things and in what order. We learn to coordinate our movements, direct them at the appropriate objects, and arrange them in useful sequences. That is, we try to shoot the ball into the basket while keeping it away from our opponents, but we try to deal the cards where our opponents can pick them up easily. And we also learn to "know" that after we deal, we pick up our own cards and then arrange them in suits, or that after we make a basket, we move back to our defensive position. All of these considerations seem characteristic of our school and work activities as well; in all these cases the activities are complex and done by a choice that is heavily influenced by the consequences of the activities. The study of how the consequences of voluntary actions influence those actions is called instrumental learning or **operant conditioning.**

Thorndike's Experiments

The experiments generally acknowledged to be the first in operant conditioning were conducted by Edward L. Thorndike at about the same time as Pavlov did his original work. Thorndike used several different tasks; the two most famous are the maze (illustrated in figure 4.1) and the puzzle box (figure 4.2). Thorndike would put a rat or chicken at the beginning of the maze (*start* in figure 4.1) and watch it wander through the maze until it reached the end (the *goal*), where it would receive a piece of food. Thorndike would note how long it took and how many dead ends (blind alleys or errors) the animal had entered. He noted that with each practice trial, the animal would make fewer errors and would run through the maze faster. He referred to this gradual, bit-by-bit improvement as **trial-and-error learning**, a description that is still quite appropriate (Thorndike, 1911, 1932).

The other task, the puzzle box, consisted of a cage made from a fruit crate. The cage was constructed with several latch mechanisms on the door, all of which could be operated from the inside. Thorndike would put a cat in the puzzle box and observe what it did and how long it took the cat to operate the latch and escape. Again, what he saw over repeated occasions was that initially the cat would engage in many behaviors and take a long time to escape, but that with additional trials the ineffective behaviors such as grooming, biting the bars, sniffing in corners, or defecating (the "errors") would gradually drop out of the cat's activities. Eventually, the only behavior left was the cat's attempts to operate the relevant latch, and it would escape fairly quickly.

Figure 4.1 A maze

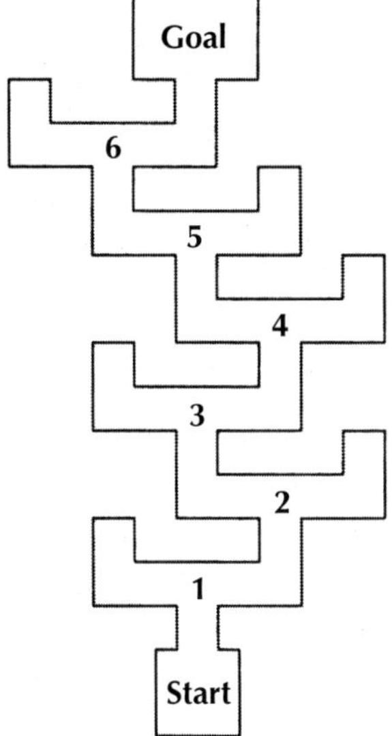

From Catania, A. Charles, *Learning*, Fourth Edition, © 1998. Reprinted by permission of Pearson Education, Inc., Upper Saddle River, New Jersey.

Figure 4.2 Thorndike's puzzle box

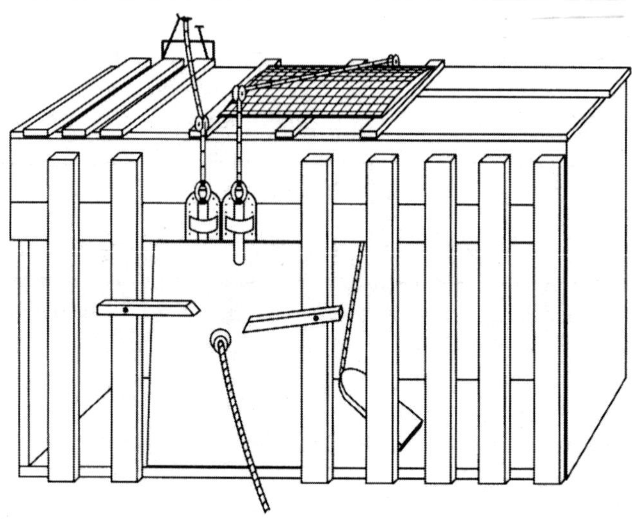

From Thorndike, 1898.

Again, trial-and-error learning fit. The same pattern of trying many responses at first and gradually becoming more proficient occurs when we learn to play bridge or basketball; the more effective behaviors are more likely to be followed by the reward (success, i.e., winning the hand or making the basket), and so they persist. The effect of rewards on the animal behaviors in Thorndike's experiments is the same as the effect of rewards on our bridge or basketball playing or work activities. The cats and people become more coordinated and efficient in their actions and also come to "choose" some actions more often than others.

Thorndike suggested that the stimulus of the maze was connected to the responses of accurate running by the action of the reward; he suggested that this S–R connection was "stamped in" by the reward. Thorndike called this strengthening of an S–R connection the **law of effect.** His attempt to focus on events before responses that could cause them led him to emphasize the relationship between the response and the stimulus before it. This is an important idea, because the learner needs to know not only that a response can get a reward, but also when that relationship is in effect. Trying to deal cards on the basketball court would not often lead to reward; neither would pawing at the maze. However, emphasizing this relationship causes us to neglect the powerful relationship between the action and its consequences.

B. F. Skinner (1938) proposed a better solution. He suggested that Thorndike had come up with a different form of learning from Pavlovian classical conditioning. He labeled Thorndike's type of learning *operant conditioning* because he suggested that in operant conditioning the creature's response had an effect on, or operated on, its environment. Therefore, he said, the cat operated on the puzzle box in such a way that it was opened; such responses are operants, as distinguished from the classical responses, which he labeled respondents. The differences between these two forms of learning will be discussed more fully in chapter 8. For now, we need to recognize that operants are quite different kinds of responses that involve voluntary actions rather than reflexes and reactions, and that operants are much more influenced by their consequences (such as getting out of the puzzle box) than are respondents. A diagram of operant conditioning based on Skinner's description would look like this:

$$S_D - - - R \rightarrow S_{r+}$$

The S_D refers to a **discriminative stimulus** (often just called the "ess-dee"), a signal to the learner that now is a good time to respond. In Thorndike's experiments, the stimuli that the animals experienced in the maze and the puzzle box were the S_Ds. R is the response, running or escaping. The S_{r+} is a stimulus that is reinforcing, in a positive or appetitive way, the reward or reinforcer. The dotted line between S_D and R is meant to suggest that this connection is much less important than the one indicated by the arrow, between R and reinforcer. Thus, Skinner emphasized the relationship between a response and its consequences and maintained that this kind of association was different from that described in Pavlovian conditioning. For our bridge-playing example, the deck of cards, card table, and three other people might be S_Ds for the responses of shuffling and then dealing, which might eventually be reinforced by winning the hand (the S_{r+}). The basketball court, classroom, and workplace represent discriminative stimuli for the other examples we mentioned. Take a moment to review what responses and reinforcers might be involved in our examples.

How Many Ways Can You Reinforce? Four Paradigms

Skinner described four basic types of response-reinforcer relationships: positive reinforcement, illustrated by the experiments and most of the examples described above; punishment type I; punishment type II; and negative reinforcement. **Positive reinforcement** occurs when a desirable or appetitive reinforcer is obtained as a consequence of a response; this usually causes the response to *increase* in frequency or probability of being made. The **punishment** procedures, on the other hand, cause behaviors to *decrease* in probability or become less likely. There are two ways to do this: deliver an unpleasant or aversive consequence, or remove an appetitive reinforcer, contingent on the response. Spanking or scolding a child for misbehavior, getting a ticket for speeding, or shocking a rat for a response are examples of the delivery of an unpleasant consequence, usually called a negative reinforcer or **punisher.** These are called punishment type I and might be diagrammed this way:

S_D ········	R ——→	S_{r-}
open road	speeding	ticket

Punishment type II, often called omission training, consists of the removal of some **positive reinforcer** as a result of a response. Sending a child to his room, "grounding" a teenager, and "time-out" situations are examples of punishment type II; in each case the individual loses out on something. Being sent to one's room or being grounded or timed out means loss of the opportunity to interact with friends, loss of personal attention, and loss of freedom to travel around. Punishment type II might be diagrammed this way:

		remove
S_D ········	R ——→	S_{r+}
date	stays out late	grounded

Negative reinforcement is the process of removing an aversive stimulus or negative reinforcer contingent upon some response. Because a negative thing is being taken away, the behavior is going to *increase* in probability; if you talk your way out of a speeding ticket, you're more likely to try to talk your way out if you get stopped by a police officer again. Similarly, in our Aphrodite example from chapter 1, she will be very likely to avoid her big brother by going somewhere else if it keeps him from harassing her. Negative reinforcement might be diagrammed this way:

		remove
S_D ········	R ——→	S_{r-}
officer	excuse	ticket torn up

Note that negative reinforcement causes behaviors to increase; this makes it quite different from the punishment procedures, which make behaviors decrease or stop. The results of negative reinforcement are the same as those of positive reinforcement; in both cases, behavior increases. This distinction is a fundamental one but is often misunderstood by new students of learning. It might help to focus on the terms *appetitive reinforcer* and *punisher* as opposed to *positive reinforcer* and *negative reinforcer*; currently, operant conditioners are trying to use the appetitive and aversive terminology to refer to the stimuli employed, but the older positive and negative terminology is very common and will be found regularly. The student must learn to distinguish between these "things" and the terms that are used to refer to how the things are applied, positive reinforce*ment*, punish*ment*, and negative reinforce*ment*.

Thus, all four procedures involve a contingency between a response and a reinforcer; remember that in classical conditioning we spoke of contingencies, but they involved relationships between stimuli, CS and US. In operant conditioning the contingencies are between *responses* and stimuli following them. Positive reinforcement involves a reward occurring as a result of a response; if the response happens, the individual gets the reward, but if she doesn't make the response, she doesn't get the reward. Each procedure can be described this way. In effect, it might be said that the individual determines her own fate by her pattern of responding. Skinner has discussed this point in several debates on the nature of "free will" and determinism (Skinner, 1956) and in a book and an article (Skinner, 1950, 1971). His main point has been that the relationship works both ways; the learner controls her environment, and the environment also controls her. What looks like her "free will" or "choice" is just her responding to reinforcement contingencies. Because we don't know everything about all of her past experiences, we aren't always aware of how she is being controlled by those contingencies. If we did, Skinner claimed that we would see that all of her behavior is determined by those contingencies.

The relationships among the four procedures are often described by using a diagram like figure 4.3. It illustrates that we have two types of stimuli that may be manipulated, appetitive or positive reinforcers and punishers or negative reinforcers. We also have two ways to manipulate them: We can deliver them or take them away. This leads to a 2 × 2 matrix with four possible reinforcement procedures, two that increase behaviors and two that decrease behaviors. Something desirable or positive being delivered or something negative or aversive being taken away increases behaviors, whereas something negative delivered or something positive removed decreases behaviors.

Figure 4.3 The four possible reinforcement procedures

	Types of Reinforcers	
	Positive (Pleasant)	Negative (Unpleasant)
Present	Positive reinforcement (Behavior increases)	Punishment *Type I* (Behavior decreases)
Remove	Punishment *Type II* (Behavior decreases)	Negative reinforcement (Behavior increases)

These four procedures represent acquisition procedures, because in each case the learner acquires a contingency. Extinction procedures also exist so that any contingency can be extinguished. Note that technically it is the contingency that is eliminated, causing extinction of what was learned, not necessarily elimination of the response. In many casual discussions, this distinction is ignored, and often it doesn't matter; however, there are occasions when it is important. Extinction of a learned positive reinforcement contingency means that the reinforcer is omitted. The rat presses the bar but receives no food, or the child says "please" but doesn't receive a cookie. Extinction of a negative reinforcement contingency means that the punisher is omitted. In this case, if the rat is being shocked and has learned to press the bar to stop the shock, during extinction pressing the bar no longer stops the shock. In both of these cases, the result is that the response decreases or disappears entirely as a result of extinction; extinguishing the contingency means that we are getting rid of the response also. In these two cases, then, describing the procedure as extinguishing the response is reasonably appropriate. However, if we are extinguishing learning that resulted from either of the punishment procedures, in fact we are removing the contingency between a response and an unpleasant outcome—the unpleasant outcome no longer occurs when the response is made. This means that if we have been shocking a rat every time it presses the bar, during extinction we would no longer shock for bar presses. The response will return to its previous level of being performed, which usually means it will happen more often.

Many students have a difficult time appreciating this circumstance because of their preconceptions about how things are "supposed to be." We punish or extinguish "wrong" responses—why would we punish a wrong response and then stop punishing it so that it could reappear? Probably in real life such situations might seem implausible, yet they do occur if we search for them correctly. For example, imagine the parent who punishes a child for cursing. The child stops cursing around the parent because cursing is followed by something unpleasant when the parent is around. However, if the child curses when the parent is not around, it might not get punished. Now we have an extinction trial that will weaken the suppressing effect of the punishment. In other words, now the child may go back to cursing, at least when the parent isn't around. Our definitions of punishment and extinction allow us to properly study and understand these complex events. We discuss the punishment procedures and negative reinforcement in chapter 5. The remainder of this chapter deals with positive reinforcement.

In addition to distinguishing among these forms of learning, Skinner invented a very convenient device for studying operant conditioning. He called it an operant chamber, but it is almost universally referred to as a Skinner box (figure 4.4). It consists of a small cage for a rat or pigeon with a food trough in one wall. Near the food opening is a lever or bar (for the

Figure 4.4 Skinner's operant chamber for the study of rat behavior

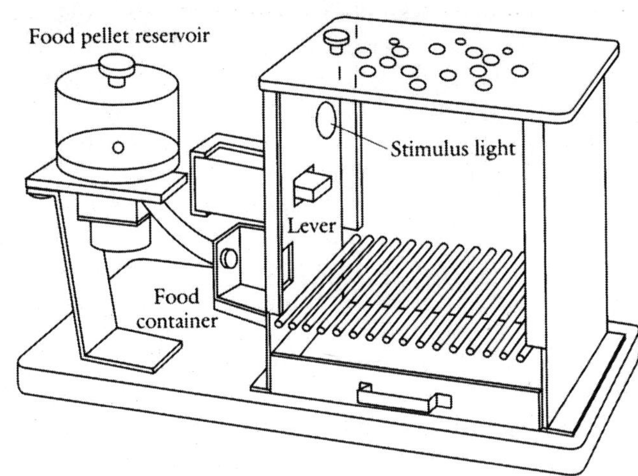

rat version) or a pressure-sensitive plastic panel (for the pigeon version). The rat must push the bar down to respond; the pigeon must peck at the panel. A light just above the bar can serve as an S_D; if the light is on, the animal may respond and get a piece of food, but if the light is not on (a condition labeled SΔ, called "essdelta"), nothing happens when the rat presses the bar. In addition, the "floor" of the Skinner box usually consists of a set of metal rods on which the animal stands. These rods can be electrified, so that the rat can be shocked every time it responds (allowing the study of punishment type I) or so that the rat can turn off the shock by pressing the bar (allowing the study of negative reinforcement). The Skinner box differs from mazes and puzzle boxes in that it allows the subject to respond when it wants, as often as it wants. In contrast to this free-response situation, the maze is a discrete-trials device that allows only one performance of the response at a time. After each response the subject must be restarted in a maze; this is not necessary in the operant chamber.

Shaping

Pigeons obviously do lots of pecking, especially for food—but do rats push down on things in real life? Actually, they aren't especially likely to do so. One of Skinner's notable discoveries was a technique for getting new behaviors from a subject. He called the process **shaping**, and it consists of taking advantage of the variations that naturally occur in any repeated behavior (Skinner, 1938). When the rat is first placed in the Skinner box, it may do any of its normal behaviors—grooming, exploring, or just sitting there—just like Thorndike's cats in the puzzle box. Skinner would wait until the rat's activity brought it near and facing the food opening. Then he would drop a piece of food into the trough. After a number of repetitions of this, the rat would be spending all its time near the food opening. Skinner would then wait until the rat leaned toward the bar before rewarding it. Then he would reward the rat only when it was closer to the bar until the rat was actually touching it. Variations in touching from one time to the next would mean that sometimes the rat would push on the bar. Skinner could reinforce the weaker presses, but quite often the rat would push hard enough to operate the mechanism and reward itself. Thus, shaping consists of rewarding *successive approximations* to the desired response. Because all behaviors vary, rewarding variations in a specific direction will eventually result in what looks like a "new" behavior; for Skinner, there were no new behaviors, just new variations of old behaviors.

Shaping is an important tool for obtaining desired behaviors in animals, but it's not the only tool available. In some cases "new" behaviors for an individual may be created by having another individual demonstrate them; this is called modeling, imitation, or observational learning. One other technique exists for humans: We can be verbally instructed (or taught) to make some response. These are useful alternatives to shaping in that they are usually much quicker; however, shaping will work in circumstances where modeling or verbal instruction are not possible. For example, the severely mentally handicapped occasionally have to be shaped to do self-help behaviors because they have insufficient vocabularies to understand all the instructions. Probably a combination of shaping, modeling, and instruction are involved in most of the everyday examples we have mentioned. We can easily imagine the shaping aspects of learning skills such as shuffling cards or shooting a basketball; the feeling of having accomplished the activity effectively and successfully reinforces our "good" efforts but does not follow our mistakes. We see the ball going the right way or not, or we experience the satisfaction of having the cards go where we want them; we also get reinforcement from others who praise those efforts. On the other hand, we inevitably learn many of the basic aspects of performing these activities by observing others or receiving instructions.

Positive Reinforcement

How Can You Tell It's Been Done? Rates and Other Measures

When we reward someone for doing something, how do we know that we have indeed rewarded him? We have to see the behavior changing in some way. In Thorndike's maze, the changes are that the animal runs faster from start to finish (latency of response) and that it makes fewer errors with increased practice. In the puzzle box situation it's sometimes hard to record errors, so latency is the best measure. As noted above, these tasks are often called discrete-trial or **instrumental conditioning** procedures, because the subject must be returned to the situation after each complete response. In many discrete-trial tasks, errors or latency measures are easily obtained. Latency requires a discriminative stimulus that occurs before each response but stops once the response is made; the time interval between S_D onset and response is the latency.

However, in the Skinner box neither of these measures are practical. In the Skinner box the S_D often remains present while the animal makes many responses. The response measure most often used is the **rate of response** (number of responses per unit of time) because the subject is free to respond as often as it likes. In any such free-response or operant situation, rate is a very convenient measure, because it only requires that you have a timing device and are able to count responses for each time interval. However, in many laboratory studies a device called a **cumulative recorder** is used to record responses automatically across time. This device allows a continuous, long sheet of paper to roll along under a pen. The pen moves up a notch every time the animal responds; when it reaches the top of the page, it automatically resets to the bottom. Because the paper moves at a constant rate, the rate of responding is easily noted as a change in the angle or steepness of the line that the pen traces. In addition, stops or pauses in the pattern of responses are easily noted as horizontal portions of the line. In a cumulative recording, the current response is always added to the previous total, so the curve never goes downhill; extinction results in a flat horizontal line because no more responses are added. We will see several examples of cumulative recordings when we discuss schedules of reinforcement. Figure 4.5 diagrams the basic cumulative recording procedure.

Figure 4.5 A diagram of a cumulative recorder

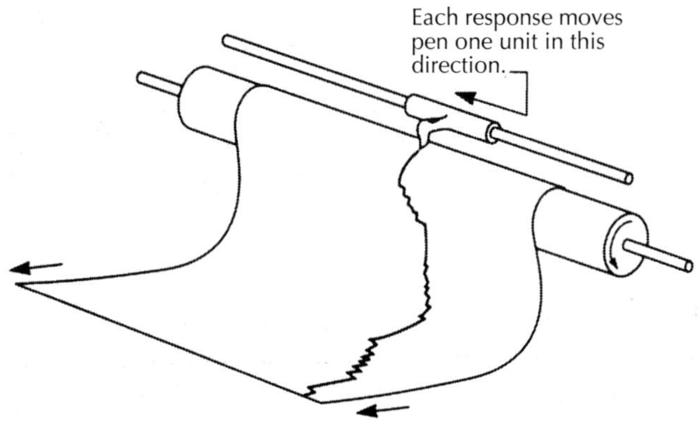
Each response moves
pen one unit in this
direction.

It might be useful here for us to distinguish between the acquisition and the maintenance of responses. **Acquisition** refers to the *initial learning of the response;* **maintenance** refers to how often a *previously learned* response is performed. Learning to read and write in elementary school illustrates acquisition; writing letters to friends or reading magazines while sitting in a waiting room are examples of these behaviors being maintained after acquisition. Think how difficult reading and writing are for the elementary schoolchild, and think about why the child is trying to acquire these skills. Then think of the relative ease that we display in reading magazines or writing letters, and think of why we do these things as adults. These situations and the ways the behaviors are performed may be different enough to make this distinction useful. The cumulative recorder is especially handy for observing how behaviors are maintained once they are learned, because it can show us a continuous graph of the subject's current level of responding.

Note that with errors and latency, smaller numbers indicate better performance, but with rate, higher numbers indicate better performance. Also notice that the measure of learning used depends on what kind of response we're interested in changing and how we want that response to change. If we are trying to modify responses that are emitted rapidly and repeatedly, such as a youngster's tendency to say bad words, rate of response might be ideal for measuring our effectiveness. However, it might be less useful for measuring such responses as reading or hitting a baseball. Reading might be measured best by noting the amount of time spent (percentage of the time the response occurs) if we were interested in keeping an individual on task, or by measuring errors if we were concerned with a young reader's proficiency. Hitting a baseball is usually measured by number of successful hits out of total chances, a percentage.

If we had some standard or criterion, we could measure length of acquisition or trials to criterion. This measure is not often used because of the necessity of specifying a clear criterion. Also, strength or magnitude of response is rarely used. Strength is obviously irrelevant in most of the examples we have mentioned, and this is usually the case.

Control Groups. We need to be able to show that these measures are changing due to the operant learning procedures we are using and not due to something else. Control groups in operant conditioning studies are usually fewer in number than in classical conditioning studies; usually only one group not receiving the treatment is necessary. So, if we were studying the effect of a food reinforcement on rats running through a maze, we might have several groups of rats, each of which might get a different amount of food upon reaching the goal in the maze. We would probably need only one control group consisting of rats that receive no food in the maze.

Skinner, who emphasized data from individual subjects, commonly employed no separate control group. Instead, he would use an *abab* design (Sidman, 1961), which consists of recording a baseline measure of performance before any reinforcing had been done (the first *a*), then recording performance during the learning phase (the first *b*), then recording performance during a return to baseline conditions (the second *a*), and finally recording when the learning conditions were reintroduced (the second *b*). Thus each subject's performance during the learning stage is compared to its own typical performance; each subject serves as its own control. For example, in a positive reinforcement study a subject's behavior should change consistently, so that the responding during the two *a* phases is low and the responding during the two *b* phases is high. The introduction of the return to baseline and back to reinforcing again ensures that any rise in response rate is seen to change as a function of the reinforcement contingency and not some artifact or quirk of chance. This design is frequently employed in behavior modification applications; it is also an example of a within-subjects experimental design.

How Can You Do It?

Reinforcement as an Independent Variable

Now that we can measure how much operant learning is happening, how can we get it to happen? Skinner's emphasis on reinforcement suggests that the major independent variables in operant conditioning are the ways we can change the reinforcer. There are several important ways we can do this.

Size of the Reward and Deprivation. If we are rewarding a rat for pressing a bar by giving it food, we could give it big chunks of food or small chunks. Changing the size or amount of reinforcer (or incentive) in this way leads to a fairly obvious result—the larger the reinforcer, the better the performance (Crespi, 1942; Guttman, 1953; Roberts, 1969). This straightforward result must be qualified, however, by noting that our rat will get full sooner on big chunks; as it gets full, it's likely that it will not perform as well. In fact, once satiated, the rat will stop performing entirely. The rat did not stop learning or forget how to respond, though; it merely was no longer motivated to demonstrate that learning. Similarly, a person working at a job will generally work harder for a larger paycheck. However, a chief executive officer earning a salary and nontaxable incentives of a million dollars a year may be so satiated on financial rewards that any increases in her work as a result of a substantial pay raise would be difficult to determine. This **satiation** effect is one of several indications that amount of reinforcement has an important influence on performance, but probably a weaker or indirect influence on the underlying learning itself.

Why was the rat motivated to begin with? Because we kept it from having food for a while. Standard procedures often involve keeping food from the rat for 12 to 24 hours; this is called **deprivation**. We can objectively describe the deprivation state of a subject this way, and avoid complications arising from trying to describe hunger sensations inside the individual. Such internal conditions are called drive states; a great deal of study of drive states has resulted in a great deal of confusion about their exact operation (there is some discussion of these issues in chapter 6). To effectively use a reinforcer, the experimenter must always be in control of the learner's access to that reinforcer. An individual who can obtain a reinforcer without performing the desired response probably won't bother making the desired response. Deprivation state works in a straightforward way; the longer an individual has been without a particular reinforcer, the more effective that reinforcer is in controlling that individual's behavior (Pavlik & Reynolds, 1963). A person who hasn't eaten in six hours may or may not be willing to dig a ditch for a hamburger, but a person who hasn't eaten in two days will grab the shovel from your hands and run to the ditch for that same hamburger. In addition, there is some indication that the motivating influence of deprivation extends beyond performance to affect the underlying learning. That is, the individual who is deprived longer actually learns more effectively (Logan, 1956; Miller, 1961). This evidence is presented in the section dealing with contrast effects.

Delay of Reinforcer. The individual could receive the reinforcer immediately after responding or after some delay. As you might expect, the sooner the reinforcer is delivered the more effectively the individual learns, as numerous studies have demonstrated (Perin, 1943; Tarpy & Sawabini, 1974); however, this variable is not so crucial as in classical conditioning. In many everyday-life situations reinforcement is delayed for very long times, as when people get paid for a week's work at the end of the week. What allows learning to occur or performance to be maintained, even with long delays of reward? Two important factors have been identified: the nature and background of the learner, and the events happening during the delay. An intelligent, good learner such as a human being, especially one old enough to understand language, might be capable of learning with fairly long delays. Often, the linguistic skills can serve as mediators to bridge the gap. Also, as people get older they are often shaped to tolerate longer and longer delays for some reinforcers. Some nonhuman learners can tolerate delays of a few minutes (primates, for example), but most animals' performance deteriorates severely with delays longer than 10 seconds.

The other factor is what happens during the delay. The more intervening events, the less likely it is that the learner will come to associate the desired response with the reinforcer. The most important events are other responses made by the learner; creatures naturally tend to associate responses and reinforcers that occur closest together in time (Spence, 1956). Thus, even a creature such as a rat might be able to learn with a long delay if we could prevent it from making any other responses in that situation during the delay. In fact, research conducted by Lett (1975) using a simple T-maze demonstrated that rats could learn with delays of up to 60 minutes. Her method for accomplishing this was to remove the rat from the maze immediately after it had made its response (whether it had chosen correctly or not). It was placed in its home cage until the delay interval was over (Lett gave three groups of subjects different delay intervals: 1, 20, or 60 minutes). Then the rat was placed in the start-box and rewarded if it had chosen correctly; if it had chosen incorrectly, it was just confined in the start-box for 1 minute. Only one trial was given per day, so after that second time in the start-box the animal was returned to its home cage. Thus, Lett took great care to prevent the animals from experiencing anything relevant to the learning situation or making any other responses in it during the delay; in addition, she chose a very simple task. The three groups of rats all learned, and learned about equally well.

Thus, delays in reinforcing operant behaviors can be overcome, but only if circumstances are just right. We can allow a long delay in reinforcing a person if (1) we remove him from the learning situation so that he will not perform any other responses or associate anything else with the reinforcer; (2) we verbally state the reinforcement contingency, reminding him of the relationship between his response and the reinforcer; and (3) we're lucky enough that nothing happens to disrupt this connection over a long time interval. Generally, however, shorter intervals between the response and the reward make for much more efficient learning and performance: think back to our examples of studying versus playing games. If you have ever succumbed to the temptations that distract you from studying, you can appreciate that the activity you chose was heavily influenced by the immediacy of the reward.

Contrast Effects. All the experiments described so far deal with comparing several groups. For example, in examining the effect of amount of reinforcer, we give one group two pieces of food for each response and give another group only one piece per response. What if we gave an individual an experience with each condition? Would she perform just like the two-piece group when she got two pieces and just like the one-piece group when she got one piece? Not quite. When these studies are done, they reveal that the subject's responding is exaggerated; these results are called *contrast effects*. The classic study was done exactly as described (Crespi, 1942; Zeaman, 1949). In the first experiment that provided proper control groups, Zeaman used four groups of rats. Two groups received large amounts of food for running through a maze, and two groups received smaller amounts. After the four groups had reached a stable level of performance, it was clear that the larger-reward groups were consistently faster. Then Zeaman switched one of the larger-reward groups to the smaller amount of reward and one of the smaller-reward groups to the larger amount. The group that was switched from larger to smaller rewards immediately declined in performance to a point even below that of the small-amount control group. Crespi and Zeaman had labeled this extreme decline a **depression effect**, but more recent researchers have called it a *negative contrast effect*. It was as if the rats were so depressed by getting the smaller reward all of a sudden that they ran more slowly than if they had gotten the similar amount all along. For the group switched from a small to a larger reward the opposite result occurred. Their performance soared to above that shown by the rats getting the large amount all along. Crespi labeled this the **elation effect**; modern researchers have termed it a *positive contrast effect*. Figure 4.6 presents an idealized illustration of how the four groups performed. As it suggests, neither effect is permanent. As more trials using the new amount occur, the elation and depression effects get smaller and smaller until the animals are performing at the level of their counterparts who had always received that amount. Several investigators have demonstrated these effects with different subjects and different tasks.

However, the elation effect does not always show up. It can reliably be found when the shift is a large one (a big difference between the two amounts of reinforcement), when it is sudden rather than gradual, and when the learner has had prior experience with shifts in reward (Flaherty, 1982). Bower (1981) suggested that the elation effect was harder to find because in many cases the comparison group was performing at the maximum level. If this were the case, that maximum level couldn't be beaten,

Figure 4.6 An illustration of the reinforcement contrast effects. The small–large group shows the elation effect, and the large–small group shows the depression effect.

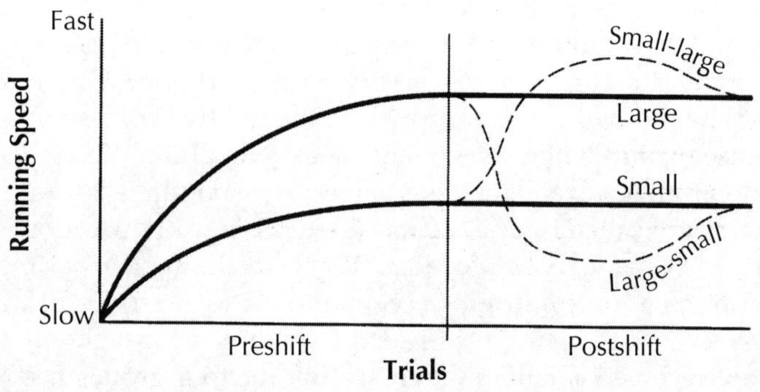

merely tied, and we wouldn't be able to see an elation effect. We can observe contrast effects routinely in work situations; the initial burst of renewed activity after a pay raise illustrates the elation effect, and a depression effect can be observed when economic conditions require pay cuts for workers.

Contrast effects have also been studied with delay of reinforcement. Subjects switched from short delays to long delays sometimes show a depression effect, performing more poorly than they would have if they had been on the longer delay for all trials. However, this effect has not often been found, and a positive-delay contrast effect is even harder to obtain. Thus, usually shifts in delay have no effect (Beery, 1968; Flaherty, 1982; McHose & Tauber, 1972).

These experiments all involved a successive shift; the learner experiences one condition and then is shifted to another. It is also possible to study simultaneous contrast effects; here the subject is trained on two tasks simultaneously, and the two resulting levels of performance are compared. For example, Bower (1961) trained rats using a large reward in a black runway and a small reward in a white runway. He found that these rats ran more slowly in the white, small-reward runway than rats that had only received the small-reward training, a depression effect in a simultaneous contrast situation. Generally, these results are similar to those for successive contrast studies but somewhat less consistent (Flaherty, 1982).

An important implication of these studies is that changing the nature of the reinforcement influences the performance of the response but not necessarily how well it's actually learned (Pubols, 1960). That is, it seems unlikely that subjects showing the depression effect are forgetting how to make the response or unlearning it. The level of responding changes too quickly for that to be the explanation. It's more likely that they are just less motivated to demonstrate their learning. This implies that such variables as amount of reinforcer are more influential on performance than on the underlying learning itself.

Contrast effects in deprivation states have also been studied, although less intensively (Hillman, Hunter, & Kimble, 1953; Miller, 1961). These studies were designed somewhat differently, and the results suggest a different conclusion. For example, let's say that experimenters train some subjects under 16 hours of food deprivation and others under 8 hours of deprivation until they reach a stable level of performance. Then both groups are switched to 12 hours of deprivation and tested. We don't see any crossing over (which would have indicated elation or depression). In fact, the two switched groups don't even reach an equal level. The group originally trained on 16 hours of food deprivation retains an advantage over the 8-hour group, even when they both are changed to 12 hours of deprivation. Why would they perform better? The most plausible explanation is that they must have been learning better when they were deprived for 16 hours, and this extra learning gave them a "competitive edge" when placed on an equal footing. Therefore, some theorists suggest that deprivation states affect the underlying learning, but that the amount of reinforcer affects only the performance of the learning. Figure 4.7 illustrates how these deprivation contrast effects would appear. Deprivation contrast effects also tend to disappear with increasing numbers of trials.

Schedules of Reinforcement. As we noted above, animals in a free-responding situation will respond rapidly for a larger reinforcer until they are satiated. This means that the experimenter is limited to a testing session of a certain length, which is determined by the subject's "stomach capacity." In addition, the responses just before satiation might not be trustworthy because they are from a partially satiated subject. One of Skinner's most important discoveries was a procedure that solved this problem. He decided to try rewarding his already trained subjects on an intermittent basis, or **schedule**—instead of rewarding every response, why not reward every other response? He referred to the reinforcement of every response as **continuous reinforcement**, and the rewarding of every other response as an example of a **fixed ratio** (FR) schedule of intermittent reinforcement (Ferster & Skinner, 1957; Skinner, 1961). In a fixed ratio schedule, subjects are rewarded on the basis of one reinforcement for every X responses, X being the size of the schedule determined by the experimenter. Reinforcing every other response would be an FR:2 (a 2 to 1 ratio; because the 1 is always the same, it's usually not written out).

Skinner was able to gradually move from an FR:2 to an FR:10 (one reinforcement after every 10 responses) with his rats while still maintaining a high rate of response. The rat on such a schedule would be reinforced on making its tenth response, then after its twentieth, thirtieth, and

Figure 4.7 The deprivation contrast effect. The effect of changing the degree of food deprivation on performance.

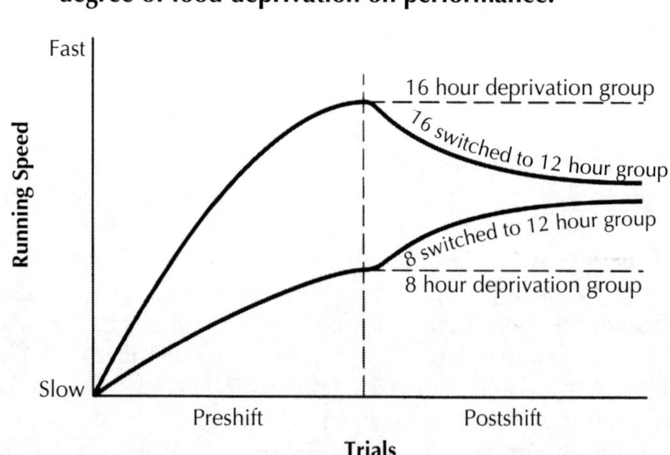

so on. However, although Skinner was able to obtain many more responses at high rates with his fixed ratio schedule, he also noticed that the animals' performance was rather erratic; they would respond rapidly until rewarded, but immediately after reinforcement the rats would usually stop responding entirely for a short time (now referred to as the **post-reinforcement pause**). Other subjects such as pigeons showed this same pattern: high overall rates of responding on fixed ratios, but brief periods of nonresponding immediately after reinforcement (Ferster & Skinner, 1957). Figure 4.8 shows idealized response patterns for a well-trained subject maintained on continuous reinforcement (CRF) and another subject maintained on an FR schedule.

Skinner wished to eliminate the postreinforcement pause. He eventually discovered that if he just gave the reward for a random number of responses for each set, the erratic performance would disappear and he would be left with a subject that was performing very rapidly and steadily. In such a schedule, which he called a **variable ratio** (VR), the subject is still rewarded on the basis of one reward for every X responses, but the reward is not delivered at any predictable point. So the rat on a VR:10 schedule would be rewarded an average of once for each ten responses, but the reward might come after its fifth response, and then not until its twentieth response. The ratio would average ten responses per reward, but the rat could not learn to predict what happens after a rewarded response or which response will be rewarded. Eventually, by chance an animal will receive a reward after the tenth response for one set

Figure 4.8 Rate of responding as a function of continuous reinforcement (CRF) and a fixed ratio schedule

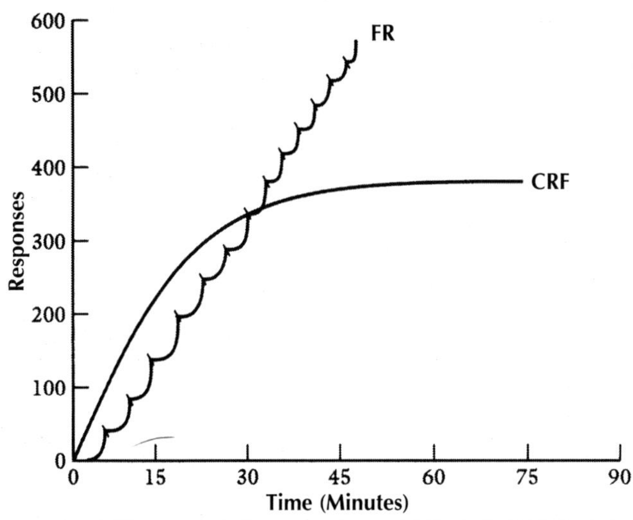

and after the first response for the next set; thus, it would receive rewards back to back that time.

Because of these occurrences and the general lack of predictability of exactly when a reward is going to be delivered, variable ratio schedules minimize the post-reinforcement pauses and lead to more stable rates of responding. In both fixed ratio and variable ratio schedules, the subject that responds the most often (the fastest) gets the most rewards—the faster one works, the more one gets during a given work period. Thus, both types of ratio schedules lead to high overall rates of responding, but FR schedules lead to more variability in rate (ranging from responding quickly to not responding), and VR schedules lead to nice, stable rates of responding. Generally, the higher the demand of the schedule (the bigger the ratio, with VR:8 being bigger than VR:3), the faster the subject will respond. However, eventually every subject reaches a limit, especially on fixed-ratio schedules. At some point in FR schedules the post-reinforcement pause begins to get longer, and extending the ratio higher just leads to the post-reinforcement pause canceling out the gain of increasing or even exceeding the working speed so that the overall rate drops (Felton & Lyon, 1966).

In addition to continuous reinforcement and fixed and variable ratio schedules, Skinner identified two other basic schedules, fixed and variable interval schedules. **Fixed interval** (FI) schedules are based on time intervals so that the learner is required to make a response after each period of, for example, 60 seconds, in order to receive a reward. The machinery of the Skinner box is programmed so that a response that delivers a reinforcer also turns off the reward-delivery device for 60 seconds. After that interval the machinery is turned on so that a reward is again available for a response. This would be an FI:1, where the number indicates the length of the interval in minutes. In such a schedule, the learner can only obtain one reinforcement per interval, so there's no need to work very fast; one response per interval is fine, if it's at the right time. Thus, well-trained subjects on FI schedules don't do much for the first part of the interval. However, as more time passes since the last reward, the subject becomes more likely to respond and gradually begins to work faster until the reinforcement occurs. The learner who has had some experience with this schedule displays a wavelike or scalloped pattern of responding at a relatively low rate, with a relatively long post-reinforcement pause (Ferster & Skinner, 1957).

To eliminate the post-reinforcement pause and produce a steady (but slow) rate of responding, Skinner devised a **variable interval** (VI) schedule. This consisted of allowing the subject to obtain reinforcement once per interval, but the length of the interval varies randomly around some specific average. Because the subject doesn't know when a reinforcement is obtainable, it must continue to respond throughout each interval if it wishes to receive a reinforcement. Because a reinforcer may occur just after another (back-to-back intervals occasionally occur in which the first is a long interval and the next is very short), the subject can never take a "time out" or post-reinforcement pause. On the other hand, the subject doesn't have to respond really quickly; slow but steady is fine. Subjects maintained on VI schedules respond slowly but persistently (Ferster & Skinner, 1957). Figure 4.9 shows an idealized graph of responding on these three schedules.

These partial schedules seem to have dramatic effects on how a subject performs. Once the subject has acquired a response pattern through shaping and a period of continuous reinforcement, its responding may be maintained at some desired level with the right partial schedule. If we want fast work, we would use a ratio schedule; if we want slow but steady work, a variable interval schedule should be introduced. Skinner in fact suggested that most everyday situations caused reinforcements to be delivered on a partial schedule of some kind and that this led to the patterns of performance that we see. People who work for a commission, such as car salespeople, are on a ratio schedule and can be expected to work fast—over the long term, the more customers they talk to, the more sales they have. In fact, they are on a variable ratio schedule because they never know which customer will be a "live one." People who are paid a weekly salary are on a fixed interval schedule and can be expected to show a post-reinforcement pause—Monday morning sluggishness. Of course, many work situations involve several sources of reinforcement. People who obtain social reinforcement such as the friendship of their colleagues, or their praise and admiration, receive these rewards on different schedules from their salaries. It would therefore be harder to detect a post-reinforcement pause on the day after payday in their behavior.

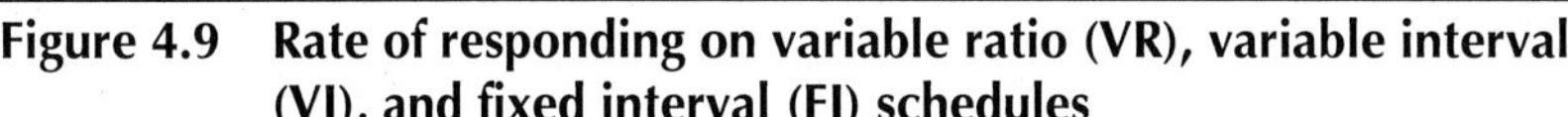

Figure 4.9 Rate of responding on variable ratio (VR), variable interval (VI), and fixed interval (FI) schedules

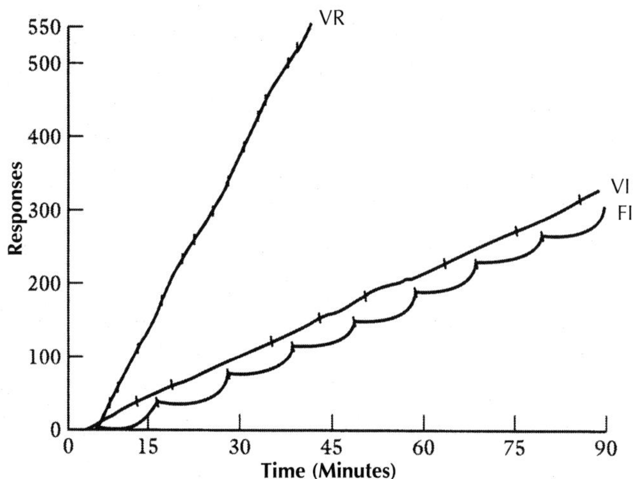

If one wishes to generate a particular pattern of performance, one needs to create the proper schedule. For example, an oft-noticed classroom phenomenon involves teachers making reading assignments during class. If the teacher says, "You have 20 minutes to read the section on the geography of North Africa," he has introduced a fixed interval schedule; the students are likely to waste most of the early portions of the time. This is not their "fault"; it is merely because the FI schedule causes a pause. If he wished to eliminate this pause, the teacher could create a variable interval reward situation. Skinner suggested that this may be done with a kitchen timer; one simply gives it a random twist. When the timer buzzes, everyone attending to the assignment gets a small reward (a check mark, smiley face, or gold star) and the timer is given another random twist. Interval schedules should be good for establishing slow but persistent work patterns; these are desirable when teachers want concentration or comprehension. If a lot of practice is desired, a ratio schedule should be used. Perhaps learning the multiplication tables or practicing handwriting or the alphabet would be tasks that would benefit from ratio schedules.

Schedules and People. One qualification must be made regarding the examples in the previous paragraph. Several experimenters have shown that people are less consistent than animals in their behavior on partial reinforcement. Considerable variability exists from one person to the next, particularly on fixed interval schedules (Davey, 1981). Some people work rapidly on FI schedules and others work slowly. Weiner (1969, 1972) has suggested that the person's previous experience with other reinforcement contingencies is a major influence in determining whether a rapid or slow response rate is seen. A person who is accustomed to ratio schedules is likely to work faster on an FI schedule. In addition, the wording of instructions can also affect the individual's response on an FI schedule (Kaufman, Baron, & Kopp, 1966). If we examine the classroom situation described above, we can see this. When students are given 20 minutes to read an assignment, there are always some who start right in and finish early. Others behave as described in the previous paragraph, waiting until the end of the interval to begin reading. It is reasonable to expect that these students previously have had different experiences with deadlines and reinforcement.

Schedules and Extinction. Partial schedules also exhibit another characteristic. Given the findings on amount and delay of reinforcement that we have discussed, you might think that partial schedules might extinguish more easily than continuously reinforced responses. Surprisingly, they are much more resistant to extinction than continuously reinforced responses. The subject on a ratio schedule makes many more responses during extinction than a continuously reinforced subject, and subjects on interval schedules persist far longer than continuously reinforced subjects. At first, this might seem illogical—these subjects are usually "getting less" than a continuously reinforced subject for the same number of responses; shouldn't they extinguish more easily? But the reverse is true, and explaining this **partial reinforcement extinction effect** (PREE) has been difficult. One possibility suggested by Mowrer and Jones (1945) is that perhaps the subject on a partial schedule can't distinguish between the schedule and extinction. This seems initially plausible; however, it is almost certainly wrong. If the subject can't tell the difference between a VR:5 and extinction, it shouldn't be able to tell the difference between a VR:5 and a VR:10 either. However, even a rat can tell this difference; it responds faster on the VR:10.

Another possible explanation of the PREE involves the emotional reaction to partial schedules. It is called the frustration tolerance explanation, and it examines what happens when the subject makes a response that is not rewarded. When the subject encounters the partial schedule for the first time, it goes from getting a reward for each response to only getting rewarded for some responses. The subject may feel frustrated on the nonreinforced trials. If it responds again anyway and gets reinforced, we have rewarded it for persisting in spite of feeling frustrated. As we give it more such practice, it builds up a tendency to respond in spite of feeling frustrated—a *frustration tolerance.* This shows up in extinction as the same tendency to persist in spite of nonreinforcement, which is the partial reinforcement extinction effect. Because subjects on continuous reinforcement have not built up any tolerance to frustration, they extinguish more easily.

Although emotional effects can be seen in high demand partial reinforcement situations, matching them up with the operant responses being observed has not provided very strong support for this theory. Nevertheless, it remains a very appealing possibility. A third possible explanation takes some of the elements of frustration tolerance to create the most widely accepted explanation of the PREE. Proposed by Capaldi (1966), this sequential theory leaves out the emotional component and simply suggests that a nonreinforced trial followed by a reinforced trial teaches the subject to continue responding in spite of not getting reinforced. Capaldi suggested that the number of times such pairs occur (the number of NR pairs, where N means "not reinforced" and R means "reinforced") predicts the resistance to extinction of a schedule. He designed sequences of FR:2 schedules that differed in the number of NR pairs. Three such patterns were:

1. NRNR
2. RNRN
3. RRNN

Although all three schedules deliver reinforcements half the time, pattern 1 has two NR sequences, pattern 2 has only one, and pattern 3 has none. Capaldi was able to show that resistance to extinction was greatest for pattern 1 and poorest for pattern 3; in one experiment these effects were strong enough to lead to significant differences after just 10 responses on the schedule for each group (Spivey, 1967). In addition, because Capaldi's theory requires a memory trace of the previous nonreinforced trial to be associated with the current rewarded trial, the effect of partial reinforcement is influenced by the time between trials. If the intertrial interval is fairly long, our subject will not remember that previous trial as well, and the resistance of partial reinforcement to extinction should be reduced. Because much of the research on the PREE was conducted in discrete-response situations, such as runway alleys or mazes, the ITI could be easily controlled; generally, longer intertrial intervals reduce the PREE (Capaldi, 1971). Capaldi's sequential theory has proved to be a successful predictor of resistance to extinction in numerous studies and is currently the most widely accepted explanation for the PREE.

Concurrent Schedules and the Matching Law. In recent years a great deal of research has focused on subjects' performance when two interval schedules are in effect simultaneously. Although technically this is an example of a simultaneous contrast design, in studies using Skinner boxes it is more often referred to as a *concurrent schedule*. The researchers usually interpret their results from a somewhat different perspective than researchers studying contrast effects. A typical study of concurrent schedule behavior might be accomplished in the following way. A rat is trained to press a bar on a variable interval schedule of 1 minute using a green light as an S_D. The same rat is also trained to pull a chain for reinforcement on a VI schedule of 3 minutes with a red light S_D; usually these two training procedures are carried out in the same Skinner box and are alternated. If we turn on both lights, how will the rat behave?

We observe how often the rat makes each response. (Actually, bar presses and chain pulls might not be equally easy to make; most experiments have used two bars to eliminate the possibility of this problem. I used two different responses to make the discussion easier to follow.) In effect, we are observing how the rat chooses to reinforce itself when allowed the choice. In a given amount of time (for example, 3 minutes), the rat can get three reinforcements for pressing the bar but only one for pulling the chain. One might think that the rat would only make the response that led to the most frequent reinforcement, but this is not what happens. Instead the rat produces a pattern of responding that matches the pattern of reinforcement. In our example, the rat can receive reinforcement three times more often for pressing the bar than for pulling the chain, so it would make three times as many bar presses as chain pulls. This kind of result has been obtained with several species, including people, and is called the *matching law* (Herrnstein, 1961). Herrnstein expressed the relationship with the following formula:

$$\frac{Ra}{Ra + Rb} = \frac{S_{r+}a}{(S_{r+}a) + (S_{r+}b)}$$

In this formula, Ra stands for the number of responses of type a, bar presses in our example, and Rb stands for the number of the other type of responses, chain pulling. $S_{r+}a$ stands for the number of reinforcers obtainable for making response a, and $S_{r+}b$ refers to the number of reinforcers obtainable for response b. In our example, for any given amount of time, three reinforcers are obtainable for bar pressing for each chain-pulling reinforcer, so the reinforcer ratio is 3/(3 + 1), or ¾ for bar pressing and ¼ for chain pulling. The matching law predicts that about ¾ of the rat's responses will be bar presses and ¼ will be chain pulls, and that's what happens.

In addition, we can manipulate the amount of reinforcement differently for our two responses and discover the same kind of relationship. The formula has exactly the same form, but we would use the S_{r+} to refer to the size of the reinforcers rather than their frequency. Finally, the delay in delivering the reinforcement can also be manipulated; in this case, the formula would use the reciprocal of the delay (1/Delay) for each part in the right-hand term of the formula. These three factors could even be combined in one formula, where each factor is multiplied by the others. This leads to precise predictions of the comparative effectiveness of two very different interval reinforcement procedures. For example, the formula suggests that a small immediate reward will often be preferred to a larger reward that is delayed. This is because a reward of four pieces of food is only twice as much as a reward of two pieces of food, but a delay of an hour is 60 times as long as a delay of a minute. In other words, we would have to have differences in amount or frequency of unbelievable magnitude to have differences comparable to commonly occurring differences in delay intervals.

Putting actual values into the formula in this way leads to predictions that often fit behavioral choices well. Our examples of students playing bridge or tennis rather than studying illustrate how immediate rewards may outweigh potentially greater rewards of getting good grades when the tests are several days off. This leads to cramming the night before the test. However, if the immediate rewards were not so immediate, they might not exert so much control. One suggestion that has been shown to help would be to make the decision very early in the day instead of on the spur of the moment. Deciding at noon to study rather than play bridge that evening is a much easier decision if one can stick to it (it might be helpful to also determine when a good alternative time to play might be). Several researchers have demonstrated that the impact of this "early commitment" on choice behavior is to make it easier to choose the larger reward in spite of the greater delay and to stick with that choice (Mischel, 1966, 1974).

We noted the similarity between the matching law research and the research on contrast effects described earlier. In fact, several recent studies have employed the essentials of contrast studies in the matching law context. For example, imagine we train a pigeon on two variable interval schedules, pecking a red key on a VI 2-minute schedule and pecking a green key on a VI 3-minute schedule. The matching law predicts that the pigeon will spend more time pecking the red key. We could consider this a simultaneous contrast situation. Now suppose we change the VI 3-minute schedule to VI 4 minutes, adding a successive contrast effect for that schedule. Our prediction, based on both the matching law and our discussion of simultaneous contrast effects, would be that the pigeon will peck the green key even less frequently than before, because it leads to even less frequent rewards than before.

The interesting aspect of applying the matching law to this experiment is what it predicts about responding on the red key. Even though we didn't alter the schedule for the red key, the matching law predicts that the pigeon will increase its rate of pecking it. In other words, the matching law predicts that changing one schedule will cause a corresponding change in responding on that schedule and a change in the opposite direction for responding on another, accompanying schedule, even though there has been no change in the accompanying schedule. This prediction has been verified in several experiments (Nevin, 1992; Williams, 1988). Here is another case of the context of a learning situation having an influence on the individual's performance in that learning situation.

This type of experiment illustrates the great appeal of the matching law; it allows us to make predictions about the more complex world outside the laboratory. We can apply the principles of the matching law to more realistic life experiences. The office worker performs daily tasks under the influence not only of a salary (perhaps an FI-1 month) but also of various social reinforcers such as pleasant coffee breaks (probably another FI schedule), affection from colleagues for being a good coworker, or praise for finishing an important project. The matching law might allow us to predict changes in the worker's performance if we could accurately identify all of the reinforcement contingencies and the changes in them. Although it's unlikely that we will be able to identify all the contingencies influencing an individual anytime soon, we at least have a tool for comparing the effects of several types of reinforcers. With the matching law we might be able to compare schedules even though they involve different amounts, delays, or rates of reinforcement. A great deal of research has been devoted to just these questions over the last 30 years.

Limitations of Matching Law Formula. Most learners behave like our example pigeons, which made 75% of their responses bar presses and 25% chain pulls in proportion to the reinforcement ratios for that example. However, a few individuals respond more than they should to the preferred schedule—they overmatch, for example making 90% of their responses bar presses. Also, a few individuals undermatch—for example, we might have a bird that responds with bar presses only 60% of the time. A modification of the original formula by Baum (1974, 1979) allows for more accurate description of learner performance and includes cases such as these. Baum's changes introduce two correction factors. One correction is to introduce a variable term *S*, which stands for the sensitivity of the learner's behavior to the reinforcer ratio, and the other correction factor he labeled *B*, which represented any bias towards one choice that the learner had which was not due to the ratio. The *sensitivity measure* multiplies (or divides) the reinforcement ratio and the *bias measure* is added to it. Unfortunately, these measures must be obtained after the fact for each individual, making true predictions difficult.

Additional problems with the matching law are that so far virtually all of the research using it has been done by employing interval schedules; the applicability of matching law principles to behavior on ratio or other schedules has not yet been firmly established (the few matching studies using ratio schedules are consistent with those using interval schedules; see Williams, 1988), and all studies use positive reinforcement. How the matching law might apply to punishment procedures or to negative reinforcement is not yet known. Another problem is that if animals are trained on the two schedules separately so that they never learn to switch between them, they tend to respond only to the richer choice and not match at all. This has been called *extreme overmatching* (Donahoe & Palmer, 1994). Furthermore, if there is no "empty" time between the interval schedules (called a "changeover delay"), sometimes the animals just respond to each choice about equally (*extreme undermatching*, Shull & Pliskoff, 1967).

Finally, the matching law is descriptive, not explanatory: it describes how creatures respond under two schedules of reinforcement, but it doesn't explain why they do so. Attempts to explain matching behavior have either emphasized the learner's sensitivity to the total overall pattern (optimization), or the learner's sensitivity to the immediate current situation (momentary maximization), with several theories competing and no clearly preferred choice. These limitations make application of matching law principles to everyday life somewhat risky; we must examine such situations carefully, and then verify that they occur according to the predictions. Nevertheless, some researchers have used the matching law to make predictions about complex real-life situations involving self-control and economic behavior with some success.

Matching Law and Self-Control Studies. The self-control studies began with an experiment by Rachlin and Green (1972). They trained pigeons using two key lights, green and red. The animals were rewarded with two seconds of access to food (as much as they could gulp down in two seconds) immediately when they pecked the red key 25 times, or they could receive four seconds of food access when they pecked the green key, but they had to wait four seconds to get access. Thus pecking the red key gave a small, immediate reward and pecking the green key gave a larger, delayed reward. Rachlin and Green noted that many previous studies involving rats as well as pigeons had shown that these creatures would show a definite preference for the smaller immediate reward.

However, Rachlin and Green made their pigeons choose ahead of time which key they would work at; they added an extra stage before the pigeon could peck the colored keys. The keys were both lit with white light in this "initial link" stage (as they called it); pecking the left one would cause the keys to be darkened for a few seconds and then light up one red and one green. Pecking the right key when both were white would result in both keys being darkened and then one would be lit up green. Thus, in the first, initial link stage, the pigeon could choose which type of reinforcement situation it would work under, or "commit" to, as Rachlin and Green described it. This added step caused the animals to show a shift in preference: whereas before they preferred the immediate reward even though it was smaller, now they selected the greater reward (the green key), which was delayed. Many studies using both humans and other animals following this general design have shown similar results (Logue, 1995, 1998). Thus, making a decision ("committing") and then having to experience a delay before actually responding on the basis of that decision leads the learner to choosing the best course of action in the long run rather than the immediate reward.

In addition, several studies have shown that delay has an accelerating effect; if a five-second delay generates 20 responses, a ten-second delay might generate only 5 responses instead of the 10 (half of the 5-second level) we might expect. Green, Fischer, Perlow, and Sherman (1981) showed another way to overcome this: they trained pigeons to peck a red key for 2 seconds of food delayed 2 seconds or to peck a green key for 6 seconds of food delayed 6 seconds. In this condition, the pigeons chose the immediate reinforcer almost exclusively. However, when Green and his colleagues (1981) added 18 seconds to the delay time for each condition (making the birds wait 20 seconds for the 2 seconds of food for the red key and 24 seconds for the 6 seconds of food for the green key) the birds chose the greater amount (pecked the green key) more than 80% of the time. The added interval caused the birds to switch from the "impulsive" immediate reward to the delayed reward, which represented more self-control.

Once someone has made a commitment to one choice over another, will she be able to stick to it? One factor that has been shown to influence this aspect of self-control is the actual presence of the reinforcers. Mischel and Ebbesen (1970) gave preschool children their choice of waiting 15 minutes for a treat they preferred or getting a less preferred treat immediately. If they chose to wait for their favorite, the children could change their mind and take the less desired treat at any time during the 15-minute wait. In one condition the treats were visible to the children, and in another condition they were not visible. As you might suspect, the preschoolers had a harder time waiting with the treats visible. Mischel has also found that giving children an activity (like playing with a Slinky) increased their ability to wait for the preferred treat (Mischel, Ebbesen, &

Zeiss, 1972). Several kinds of people have self-control problems that might be influenced this way; in addition to children, drug addicts (Madden, Petry, Badger, & Bickel, 1997) and people who overeat (Stuart, 1967) have been studied from this perspective.

Fixed Interval Schedules and Timing. Another major research topic using schedules has involved the ability of creatures to keep track of the passage of time. Our description of fixed interval schedules noted that creatures pause right after reinforcement but begin to respond after this pause and gradually increase their response rate until reinforced, when they pause again. This indicates that these creatures have some way of at least approximately keeping track of the passage of time. How good are other animals at timing events? Most of us know that we can approximate how much time passed by using the trick of counting, "one thousand and one, one thousand and two," etc., to pace ourselves. But this makes use of our language and our counting abilities, something we don't expect from animals. Yet both pigeons and rats show remarkable timing abilities—about as good as our own—in fixed interval studies.

What would happen to the animal's responding if we skipped a reinforcement during a fixed interval maintenance period? This is essentially what is done in a "gap" experiment (Roberts, 1981). Roberts showed that when he introduced a "gap" interval with no reinforcement, animals would increase their responding until the time when reinforcement was due; but then, rather than continuing to respond until reinforced (for a later interval), they would decrease their responding until they were essentially pausing near the middle of what would have been the next interval. In other words, they showed a peak in responding when reinforcement was due, a tent-shaped pattern with the downslope (after the time the reinforcer was due) about the same shape as the upslope just before the reward. His animals peaked within a few seconds of the interval duration on which they were trained. This pattern of responding suggests that pigeons, rats, and many other advanced creatures besides ourselves have some way of keeping track of the passage of time—an "internal clock"—and that creatures can use this clock to determine when to respond, when things are due to happen, and even when they are overdue and thus perhaps unlikely to occur that particular time. This pacemaker can be used by other animals about as accurately as we use our counting method.

Studies have shown that the pacemaker can be "speeded up" by the use of amphetamines or other stimulants, so that the animal responds in less than the interval (Maricq, Roberts, & Church, 1981; Kraemer, Randall, Dose, & Brown, 1997), and the pacemaker can be slowed down by atropine (Meck & Church, 1987). Clever experiments using two fixed interval schedules have shown that the timer "counts up" like a stopwatch ("one, two, three . . .") rather than "counting down" like a kitchen timer ("ten, nine, eight . . ."). For example, Roberts (1981) trained animals on an FI:20 schedule signaled by a light and an FI:40 schedule using a tone as an S_D. After they were well trained on both schedules, he tested them by starting a trial with the light, signaling the 20-second interval, then switching to the tone signaling the 40-second interval. He switched after waiting 5 seconds for some test trials, 10 for some, and 15 for some. If the animals were counting down like a kitchen timer, they might have continued and started responding after 20 seconds, when they reached zero; in other words, the switch would show no visible effect. If they "reset" their counter when the switch occurred, and counted up, then they should begin responding after 45, 50, or 60 seconds for the respective conditions. If they just kept counting up from where they were, then they should show peak responding at 40 seconds no matter when the switch happened. This last pattern was what Roberts (1981) obtained, indicating that animals' internal pacemakers counted up starting from zero without resetting in his experimental conditions.

In addition, more recent research has indicated that animals can stop counting and pick up where they left off if signaled to do so. In one series of experiments, FI: 30 training intervals were signaled by a light S_D while the room was lighted, but during 90 second test intervals (with no reinforcement) the S_D was sometimes presented with the room lit but other times with the room darkened. When the animals received test trials in the darkened condition, they showed a different shift in their response times than they did in the lighted room. This change in context caused the animals in the darkened condition to essentially stop counting and hold where they were until the signal indicating the return of the 30-second interval reappeared, at which time they resumed counting (Kaiser, Zentall, & Neiman, 2002). The change in ambient conditions caused the animals to take a "time out" from their time monitoring.

So it seems that many animals are quite effective at estimating how much time has passed, and that they may be able to use this ability in complex ways, timing when conditions indicate they should, stopping their count when conditions signal a need to pause, and resuming the count. Theories attempting to explain such ability have generally assumed that a creature would have to have a pacemaker, or a mechanism that produces a regular pulse (at least a "cursor" ticking away); a temporary memory-storage component ("how many pulses so far?"); a more permanent memory ("how many pulses are required for this?"); and a comparator mechanism (an example of the "critic" mentioned in the information-processing definition of learning in chapter 1) for determining whether the required count has been obtained. Therefore, such explanations are examples of the information-processing approach. The most widely accepted such theory is Gibbon's *scalar expectancy theory* (Gibbon & Church, 1984).

The Modification and Management of Behavior

Clearly, operant conditioning is a form of learning that exerts a tremendous influence on our everyday behavior. We can see the impact of positive reinforcement, punishment, and negative reinforcement around us daily. All we need to do is observe a behavior and look for its consequences. If we see a behavior happening often, we should expect to see positive reinforcement following it. If we see a behavior not happening very much, then we should expect to see punishment following it, or we should see other behaviors getting positively reinforced in its place. This type of analysis has been successfully undertaken in several types of settings. **Behavior modification** and **contingency management** programs have been used in many institutional settings, from classrooms to residential centers for the emotionally disturbed or mentally disabled. Behavior therapy programs are successfully employed by many individual clinical psychologists in the treatment of a wide variety of complaints. In all of these areas the approach is similar: once the reinforcement contingencies have been identified, the behavior therapist tries to introduce new, more appropriate reinforcement contingencies and eliminate undesirable contingencies.

To apply principles of operant conditioning to everyday life, one must focus on specific behaviors and then look for some indication of the direction of the behavior change. If the behavior is increasing or occurring very frequently, then positive reinforcement or negative reinforcement is occurring. To determine which one it is, observe whether a stimulus is being presented or removed as a consequence of the behavior. If a stimulus is being presented and the behavior is increasing, then positive reinforcement is occurring. If a stimulus is being removed because of a response, then negative reinforcement is occurring. Similarly, if the behavior is decreasing, then punishment is occurring. A decrease in behavior followed by the occurrence of a stimulus is punishment type I, and a decrease followed by the removal of a stimulus is punishment type II or omission.

In the following examples, try to determine the response, the reinforcer, and the type of reinforcement procedure. Also try to identify the type of schedule—continuous, ratio, or interval—and any discriminative stimuli. Partial schedules are best recognized by noting whether the subject can respond more and receive more; such a relationship represents a ratio schedule. If the subject can receive only a fixed amount per time interval no matter how quickly she works, we are observing an interval schedule. **Discriminative stimuli** are distinctive characteristics of the situation that warn the subject ahead of time that a contingency is in effect. To identify them, look for a stimulus before the response that distinguishes the situation from others. Let's apply this analysis to the following example:

> Mr. Placed said, "Okay, Kathy, it's your turn to read." Kathy picked up right where Billy left off. The teacher smiled and said "very good" when she finished.

In this example, the behavior that is changing (the response) is Kathy's reading. Because this behavior seems to be more likely to occur in the future, this must be positive or negative reinforcement. The reinforcer is probably the teacher smiling and saying "very good." Because something is being given that causes the behavior to increase, this must be positive reinforcement. Two things tell Kathy when and what to do. These discriminative stimuli are "Okay, Kathy, it's your turn" and Billy leaving off at a certain spot. Because this situation is described as a single event, we can't really determine a schedule of reinforcement, although we might suspect that the teacher goes down the rows in some typical order most days. In that case, we would be observing an interval schedule in operation. Here's another example.

> Snively stopped going to the water cooler because his boss gave him a hard stare and a frown when she walked by and noticed it.

Here the response that changes is Snively going to the cooler. Because this behavior is happening less often, this must be a form of punishment. What follows the response that seems to be affecting it is the hard stare and frown, which is the reinforcer. Because this is being given to Snively as a result of his behavior, this must be punishment type I. Possible S_Ds might be the fact that he's at work or is thirsty, or the sight of the water cooler. Finally, because Snively's boss stares and frowns only when she walks by and notices, Snively is on a partial schedule. If he goes to the cooler more often, he will likely get caught more often, so this must be a ratio schedule. Because there's no way of knowing when the boss is likely to be walking by, it's a variable ratio.

Summary

Thorndike conducted the first experiments on operant conditioning around the turn of the century. He observed animals running through mazes or escaping from his puzzle box and described their behavior as trial-and-error learning. Skinner distinguished between the kinds of learning studied by Thorndike and Pavlov, classifying Thorndike's as operant conditioning. He suggested that in operant conditioning the learner associates its voluntary responses with their consequences.

Skinner described four types of operant contingencies: positive reinforcement, negative reinforcement, and two forms of punishment. Positive reinforcement occurs when a response is followed by the delivery of a desirable or appetitive reinforcer. This leads to responses occurring more frequently. Negative reinforcement occurs when a response leads to the removal or prevention of an unpleasant or aversive stimulus. This also leads to that response happening more frequently. Punishment type I occurs when an unpleasant or aversive reinforcer is delivered contingent on a response, making the response less likely. Punishment type II or omission training occurs when a positive reinforcer is removed contingent on a response, which also causes that response to occur less frequently.

Skinner also invented a device for the convenient study of operant behavior, the Skinner box. He devised a process of shaping in order to train rats to make the desired response. Shaping involves the reinforcement of successively closer approximations to the desired response. In the Skinner box, responses are most commonly measured using the rate of responding, whereas latency of response is most easily used in Thorndike's puzzle box and latency or errors most easily used in a maze.

The important variables that influence amount of operant learning are (1) size or strength of reinforcer, with greater amounts leading to faster learning; (2) length of deprivation, with longer times without the reinforcer leading to faster learning; (3) delay of reinforcer, with longer delays leading to poorer learning; (4) contrast effects involving changes in these variables; and (5) schedules of reinforcement. Skinner identified five basic schedules of reinforcement. Continuous reinforcement involved reinforcing every response; this was effective for initial acquisition but eventually leads to a decline in responding due to satiation. Fixed ratio schedules (rewarding every fifth response, for example) maintain a fast response rate, but there is a pause just after the delivery of the reward. Variable ratio schedules eliminate this post-reinforcement pause by rewarding at a random point in the ratio sequence; they therefore produce high and stable levels of responding. Fixed interval schedules reward one response per time interval and therefore produce slow rates of responding with long post-reinforcement pauses. Variable interval schedules eliminate the post-reinforcement pause, thus producing slow but steady and very persistent patterns of responding.

The four partial reinforcement schedules are much more resistant to extinction than continuously reinforced responses, probably because they train the learner to persist in responding in spite of not receiving a reward. Capaldi suggested that they do this through the occurrence of NR pairings—a nonreinforced response being followed by a reinforced response. If we train an individual to make two responses under two different interval schedules, we are employing concurrent schedules. We would find that the individual's responding is proportional to the relative amount of reinforcement that each schedule delivers. This is known as the matching law, and it has come to be useful in studying the relative importance of different reward conditions.

Questions for Discussion, Thought, and Practice

1. Define and give an example of each key concept. Because there are so many, grouping them into related categories and subcategories can also be a useful study exercise.
2. Analyze the following example, identifying the response, reinforcer, type of reinforcement, schedule, and discriminative stimulus: The Divine Miss P. was in a hurry to get into the movies one night, so she cut into the line near the front. A lot of people were milling around, so no one noticed and she ended up getting a great seat. The next time she went to an Ungrateful Wretch concert there was also a long line, so she tried it again and it worked again. She is doing it more and more frequently.
3. Analyze this example (be careful about the type of reinforcement): Young Bertram discovered that if he always had a textbook open when he sat at his desk on school nights, his parents would leave him alone. If he didn't have a book open, they would nag him whenever they checked on him.
4. Analyze this example: The coach makes his star quarterback, Gipper, sit out the first quarter of a game when he hears that Gipper was downtown partying the night before a game. Gipper has since cut way down on his Friday night partying.
5. Analyze this example (be careful about discriminative stimuli): Every Wednesday Millie's PE class featured social dancing. But none of the guys wanted to dance with Millie and usually said unkind things about her appearance. One Wednesday Millie had a bad headache and was excused from PE. For the rest of the semester Millie complained of headaches every Wednesday, and she got out of PE most of those times.
6. Identify some of the positive reinforcing contingencies influencing your daily behavior at college. Try to describe these contingencies in terms of the amount, delay, and schedule of reinforcement involved in each. Then try to estimate their relative impact on your behavior by using the matching law.
7. Consider some of the choice situations you have encountered (without renewing any heavy emotional strains). Can you analyze your eventual decision in terms of the sizes and delays involved for the possible choices? How did these factors influence your final behavior? Can you see a pattern to any repeated choices that might be an example of the matching law?

Punishment and Negative Reinforcement

▲ KEY CONCEPTS ▲

alternative responses
avoidance
consistency of punishment
contingency theory
delay of punishment
escape
intensity of punisher
learned helplessness
negative reinforcement
objections to punishment
omission training
punishment type I
punishment type II
shuttle box
species-specific defensive reaction
time out
two-factor theory

Punishment

Punishment is actually two techniques for eliminating behaviors, as was noted in chapter 4. One punishment technique is to deliver some aversive stimulus contingent on a response. This is the most familiar form, **punishment type I**, and is illustrated by procedures such as scolding or spanking a child for misbehaving, or the abuse that occurs in governmental punishment situations such as prison. Punishment type I or "positive punishment" has been used by parents, teachers, and leaders all too frequently throughout human history. Many societies today still have an institutional preference for this method of behavior reduction.

To us, such punitive methods seem especially common in third world countries, which we believe to be less advanced and "enlightened" than we are, but it's easy enough to find examples in America as well. Although we don't cut off the hand of the thief for stealing, we do often turn to other methods of punishment type I as our first choice for getting rid of undesired behaviors. On the other hand, most psychologists would place punishment as the least preferred method of eliminating behavior (e.g., Alberto & Troutman, 1982). A great deal of research has been directed at determining whether punishment is effective, what conditions make it effective, and how effective it is relative to other, more "humane" alternatives.

Punishment type I can be readily studied in an operant conditioning experiment. For example, if we were to use rats in a Skinner box, we would first train them using positive reinforcement to make a response, which we can study carefully. That is, we train the rat to press the bar for food. Once the rat is doing this at a good, steady rate (usually on a VR schedule), we can observe the effects of our punishment procedure on its bar-pressing behavior. Typically, this would mean that we would begin delivering an electric shock to the rat whenever it presses the bar. We can study various characteristics of our shock procedure and relate them to how quickly the bar pressing is suppressed. As you might recall from chapter 4, punishment type I can be diagrammed this way:

S_D	- - - - - - - -	R	⟶	S_{r-}
cue light		bar press		shock

The other form of punishment, **punishment type II** (also called **omission training**), consists of removing some pleasant or desirable stimulus as a consequence of a behavior. This technique has become increasingly popular during the last two decades and is illustrated by the familiar procedures of sending the child to his room for misbehavior, removing privileges, or "grounding" the teenager. Although the technique has been widely promoted by applied psychologists as a more humane method of behavior management, it has received very little experimental study in nonapplied settings. This is basically because, although it's fairly easy to remove privileges from human beings, such opportunities rarely occur when studying animals. Unfortunately, studies using humans rarely have the controls necessary for firm conclusions about the effectiveness of this procedure under different circumstances. Most of our understanding of the punishment process comes from the study of type I. However, the principles learned from the study of type I do seem to apply to type II as well. Punishment type II can be diagrammed as follows:

S_D	- - - - - - -	R	⟶	remove S_{r+}
parent present		fighting		loses time with friends

Measuring Punishment

The effectiveness of punishment type I can be studied in several ways. As mentioned, we could train some response through positive reinforcement and then begin to punish it. When we begin the punishment, we might continue to deliver the positive reinforcer. We might expect that the response would continue to be made in this circumstance, but at a much lower rate than that of a control group that was not punished. Another approach would be to omit the positive reinforcement as soon as we begin punishing. In this case, because we are combining the effects of extinction of the positive reinforcement contingency with the punishment effects, we would compare this group to a control group that was merely extinguished. We would expect that our punished group would slow down faster and stop responding sooner than the control group. An interesting variation of this procedure is to stop punishing after a number of trials and observe the effect on further extinction trials. Do these succeeding trials show a consistent pattern of less responding than an extinction group that received no punishment? If not, then the punishment effects have only been temporary. This is a possibility that Skinner (1938) and Estes (1944) examined carefully; their conclusions are discussed in the section dealing with Skinner's objections to punishment.

Independent Variables Influencing Punishment

Many of the same variables that we discussed under positive reinforcement also influence punishment, often in a comparable way. For example, two of the most important influences on the effectiveness of positive reinforcement are amount and delay of reinforcer. In a similar way, the effectiveness of a punisher is directly related to its **intensity** and **delay**. A strong shock to a rat, or a hard spanking to a child, will suppress the response more effectively than a weaker shock or spanking. (Azrin & Holz, 1966; Church, 1969; Walters & Grusec, 1977 are reviews of the extensive literature.) In addition, the effect of a longer-lasting punisher is comparable to the effect of a stronger one; shocking a rat for three seconds suppresses its behavior more effectively than shocking it for one second (Church, Raymond, & Beauchamp, 1967), just as giving the child ten whacks to the posterior is more effective than giving five.

The punisher is also much more effective if delivered immediately than if it is delayed. In one study, the effectiveness of the punisher in suppressing bar pressing with a 30-second delay was only one-half of its effectiveness with no delay (Camp, Raymond, & Church, 1967). Such drastic decreases over short intervals are routinely noted with animals and, as with positive reinforcement, are usually attributed to the events that might occur during the delay. Delay of punishment will reduce the effectiveness of the punishment unless nothing occurs during the delay, or unless the learner is capable of bridging the gap in spite of these distractions. A young child who must "Wait till your father gets home" may have a very difficult time associating the punisher with the behavior to be eliminated. Unfortunately, this procedure still occurs; many parents feel that explaining to children why they are being punished will bridge the gap. However, if one realizes that children are being exposed to very stressful events while also being lectured on their misbehavior, one might wonder how much the children would get out of the lecture. Generally, delays greatly reduce the effectiveness of punishment; to be effective, punishment should be immediate.

In addition to these straightforward variables influencing punishment, there are several others that are more subtle and are not of concern in positive reinforcement. One of the most important is the *gradualness* of the introduction of punishment. It has been shown in several circumstances that initial use of weak or mild punishers lessens the effectiveness of later punishers. In a classic study, Miller (1960) trained two groups of rats to run down an alley for food. He then introduced a mild electric shock to one group, which was gradually increased over the next 750 trials. By trial 750, these rats were continuing to run despite the shock, which had increased to 335 volts by then. The other group received no shocks until trial 750, at which point they received the final intensity delivered to group I, 335 volts. Their running was significantly inhibited on trial 751, but the gradual group continued at their usual speed.

This gradual introduction of the punisher is something that many parents do, beginning with a mild "warning" and progressing through more violent verbal threats, culminating with physical action such as a spanking. Merely noting that the misbehavior was still being performed, up through the spanking, should point out the ineffectiveness of such procedures. The likelihood would be that several spankings would have to be administered before the misbehavior was suppressed. In most cases, the introduction of a mild punisher does not disrupt the individual's ongoing behavior very much; the individual learns to keep responding in spite of the presence of a mildly unpleasant stimulus. As the intensity is gradually increased, this learning to persist is generalized to increasingly more intense punishers.

Other variables that influence the effectiveness of punishment have nothing to do with the punisher itself, but rather the original learning of the response itself. A well-learned response is more resistant to punishment than a poorly learned one. Miller (1961) found that responses learned after just a few training trials were more effectively suppressed than responses learned with more training, even though the same intensity of shock was used for both conditions. If a response has been maintained on a partial schedule of reinforcement, its resistance to punishment seems to depend on the frequency of reinforcement, with frequently reinforced responses (those on small ratios or short intervals) being harder to suppress with punishment (Church & Raymond, 1967).

Taken together, these findings suggest that the *number of reinforcements* received for a response is an important variable influencing the effectiveness of a punishment procedure on that response. In addition, a response learned under conditions of high reward or high deprivation level will be more difficult to suppress than responses that have received small rewards or that have been learned under low levels of deprivation.

Finally, the availability of **alternative responses** influences the effectiveness of the punisher. Consider our rat pressing the bar for food. When we begin to shock it for pressing, the rat is confronted with the dilemma of being hungry and having only one way to get food, which also leads to shock. What is it to do? If we provide it with another choice (a second lever), we may see much more rapid and complete suppression of the punished response, because the subject can quit doing the punished response and obtain its reinforcer by making the alternative response. This result has been found in several studies using humans (e.g., Herman & Azrin, 1964) and points to the need for a clear understanding of the origin of the behavior to be punished. Any behavior that is to be punished is occurring at some baseline rate that is higher than we desire. Why is the behavior occurring too frequently? Observation of the baseline conditions might identify positive reinforcers that could be eliminated, making punishment unnecessary by using extinction instead. Observation also might lead to the introduction of training the individual to make other, more desirable responses, which might obtain the same reinforcer and again lead to the elimination of the undesired behavior without the use of punishment.

One variable that has been extensively studied in positive reinforcement situations is the *schedule of reinforcement*. This can be applied to the use of punishment also; however, the results are very different. If we punish every occurrence of the response, using continuous reinforcement (CRF), we get much more suppression of responding than if we use any of the partial schedules in punishing. In other words, spanking every single occurrence of a misbehavior is much more effective than spanking every other occurrence (which would be an FR:2) or once every 5 minutes if the misbehavior occurs (an FI:5 minutes). Most experimenters agree that the suppressing effects of punishment depend on the strong association of the response with the punishing event. This association is most strongly learned when the pairing of these two events is 100%. Continuous punishment represents this condition; in contrast, our FR:2 schedule represents only 50% pairing. Thus, an FR:2 schedule is about half as effective as continuous punishment, and an FR:4 schedule is one-fourth as effective as continuous punishment. This is the general pattern of results (Azrin, Holz, & Hake, 1963). The best way to appreciate these results is to recognize that **consistency of punishment** is very important. Inconsistency leads to ineffective punishment. However, if we extinguish the punishment contingency—that is, we stop punishing—we find that responses recover or return to baseline levels more quickly after continuous punishment than after partial schedules of punishment. In other words, the effects of intermittent or partial schedules of punishment are more resistant to extinction than those of continuous punishment. This is the same partial reinforcement extinction effect (PREE) discussed in the previous chapter and therefore works in the same way for punishment type I and positive reinforcement.

Should I Punish? Skinner's Objections

Our discussion of the independent variables affecting punishment clearly shows how to punish. To punish effectively, we must use an intense level of punishment, deliver it immediately every time the response is made, do this from the outset, and provide an alternative to the punished response. We can illustrate the effectiveness of punishment when done correctly by describing an experiment by O. I. Lovaas (Bucher & Lovaas, 1968; Lovaas & Simmons, 1969). Lovaas is one of the few researchers who have used significant punishers on humans. For obvious ethical reasons, punishment studies involving human subjects are rare; ones using a truly unpleasant punisher are rarer still. In his debate on the effectiveness of punishment, for example, Thorndike used a word-learning task, and the punisher was the word "wrong" for incorrect responses.

Lovaas was able to justify the use of shock on humans because of the peculiar nature of the situation. The subjects involved were extremely retarded or severely disturbed autistic children. These particular children would often engage in self-injurious behavior such as biting themselves or banging their heads against a wall unless restrained with straitjackets or protected with crash helmets. The behaviors are severe enough that these children sometimes break bones or get infections from open gashes. Lovaas used a foot-long rod that delivered a shock for about one second, which Lovaas described as being similar to a dentist's drill without Novocaine. For 15 one-hour sessions, frequency of self-destructive behaviors and other nonsocial behaviors were simply recorded; on session 16, each self-destructive act was immediately followed by an electrical shock strong enough to be considered painful, accompanied by the word "No."

The results for one retarded child, Linda, are presented in figure 5.1. As you can see, she averaged over 200 self-destructive behaviors per session during the 15 baseline sessions. However, as soon as the punishment procedure was used, self-destructive behavior dropped to zero. Lovaas used one shock to her leg paired with "No" on days 16, 17, 19, and 21, and just the word "No" on days 18 and 22. "No" became an effective way of suppressing her self-hitting, not only in the experimental room but in other areas of the building and when used by other experimenters. Interestingly, her whining behavior also dropped significantly. In all, the child received only four shocks, but these were sufficient to totally eliminate a behavior that she had done hundreds of times a day for several years.

Figure 5.1 Frequency of one child's self-destructive, avoiding adults, and whining behaviors during baseline, shock (S), and "No" (N) days

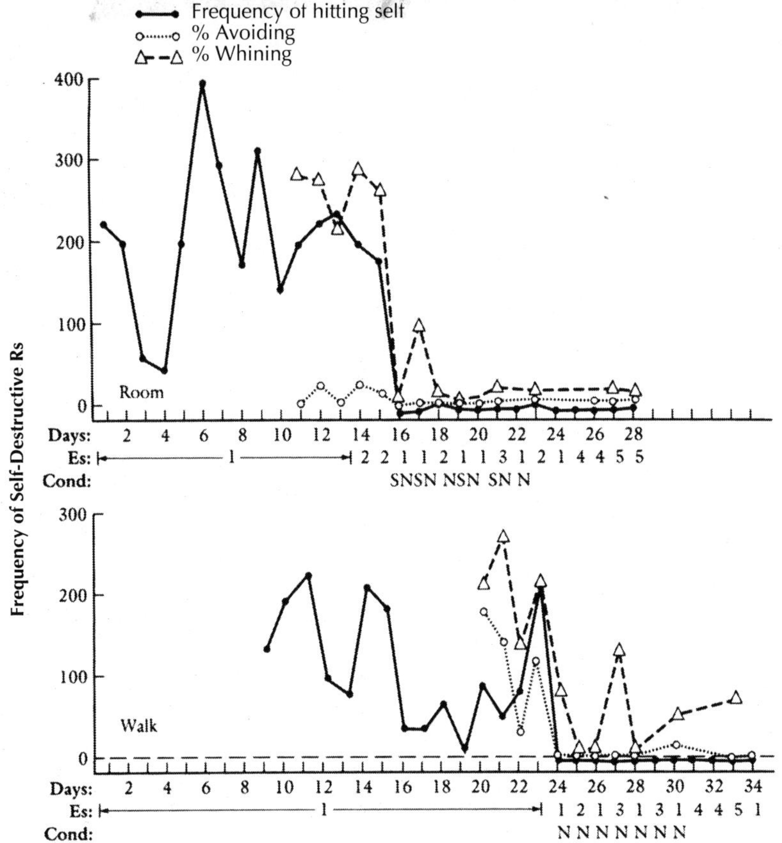

From "Manipulation of Self-Destruction in Three Retarded Children," by O. I. Lovaas and J. Q. Simmons, 1969, *Journal of Applied Behavior Analysis*, 2. Copyright © 1969 by the Journal of Applied Behavior Analysis. Reprinted by permission.

When punishment is immediate and intense, and delivered at its final intensity to begin with, it can be extremely effective.

If this experiment seems harsh or cruel, then perhaps you should examine your reactions. Was it not crueler to allow the child to continue injuring herself? If you still have problems with this kind of study, then you must look at your reactions to punishment itself, rather than just to this experiment. Perhaps you are in agreement with B. F. Skinner, who was strongly opposed to the use of punishment. He felt that if you arranged positive contingencies properly, you wouldn't need to use punishment at all. He felt that the use of punishment diverts our efforts away from the use of positive reinforcement, which he felt was far preferable. In 1953 Skinner detailed his **objections to punishment**; he listed over a dozen objections in all. Some of his objections revolve around moral issues and can only be noted. Each individual must evaluate them for himself or herself. Other objections involve the effectiveness of punishment, and therefore we can evaluate their importance through research. We will consider several of each type of Skinner's criticisms.

Skinner's first objection to punishment was that it does not permanently eliminate a behavior, it merely temporarily suppresses it. This is an empirical question and there is a great deal of evidence. In 1944 Estes, one of Skinner's most important students, demonstrated that punished responses would reappear when the punishment was withheld. However, since that time there have been other experiments with contradictory results. We can understand these contradictory findings by remembering our discussion of the independent variables influencing punishment. The response might reappear after punishment if (1) it was punished with a weak punisher, (2) it was punished inconsistently, (3) it was the only response the individual had for obtaining some reinforcer, or (4) it was a response that was very strongly learned. On the other hand, the response is much less likely to recur if it was severely and consistently punished, if there were alternative responses available, or if it was not a highly practiced or heavily rewarded response initially (Azrin & Holz, 1966). The fact that punished responses do sometimes reappear argues against theories such as Thorndike's, which suggest that the subject has "unlearned" the punished response. If responses are unlearned, they should never reappear unless relearned again. However, this does not mean that the effects of punishment are only temporary; the effects of a positive reinforcement procedure and a later punishment procedure may both be permanent. These two opposing tendencies would have to "compete" for expression in the individual's behavior; one would have to win out, but that doesn't mean that the other is no longer remembered. When the punishment procedure is carried out correctly, it can be as durable as the other forms of learning (ibid.).

Skinner's second objection was that punishment causes unfortunate emotional by-products. Here, too, there is clear evidence that punishment also causes emotional reactions, primarily fear and anger. These effects are so routinely observed that they are important components of several of the theoretical explanations of punishment (which we describe shortly). Most of us would call these emotional reactions unfortunate, although this is a moral decision and there may be some alternative ways of evaluating this fact. Along with this objection, Skinner also noted that punishment generates aggression in the learner toward the agent delivering the punishment. This aggression in the learner often can also be easily observed. Many clinical practitioners have noted that when individuals are unable to express the aggressive tendencies toward the punishing agent directly (as in the case of an authoritarian parent), they may vent these feelings on other people or even objects. This is known as *displaced aggression*.

Although many studies have shown that punishment often leads to aggressive behavior by the punished individual (Azrin & Holz, 1966), several studies of the use of punishment on emotionally disturbed and mentally handicapped humans indicate that there are more positive social and emotional side effects than negative ones for these people. Often these individuals display more prosocial behaviors such as affection, attention seeking, and cooperation as a result of the punishment, and actual increases in aggressive behavior do not regularly occur (Carr & Lovaas, 1983). The negative emotional side effects of shock used as a punishing agent seem to be very temporary for these individuals, in contrast to randomly delivered (noncontingent) shocks (Van Houten, 1983). Thus, the emotional side effects of punishment are varied and difficult to predict accurately. For example, these effects may depend on the type of punishing agent; the pain of a shock apparently stops when the shock stops, but the pain of a spanking may persist somewhat longer. The difference in duration may influence the individual's reaction to the punishment. The differences between the special populations used in most human punishment studies and normal humans may also influence the likelihood of undesired emotional side effects.

Another objection was that punishment indicates to a learner what she should *not* do, but does not provide any indication by itself of what the individual *should* do. In addition to this, Skinner also objected that punishment often causes one undesirable behavior to be replaced by another. There are numerous illustrations of these problems in everyday life. The child scolded for saying "naughty" words goes back outside and instead sticks her tongue out at others out of spite—anger, the unfortunate emotional by-product, leads to one undesirable behavior replacing another, because the child was not rewarded for a more appropriate response. These problems have not appeared very often in studies such as those cited by Carr and Lovaas (1983), but that is because these studies routinely have well-trained researchers on hand to reward more desired behaviors. Thus, the parent using punishment should be prepared to follow the punishment with monitoring of the child's behavior in order to positively reinforce more desirable behavior.

Skinner objected that punishment justifies inflicting pain on others. This is strictly a moral objection, but it has very powerful implications for anyone concerned about the attitudes and ideas of the individuals being punished. When we spank a child, we teach him that there are times when it's all right to hurt someone. We often assume that the child recognizes the conditions that make it all right to punish, and this can be a very shaky assumption. If the child is young, how will he come to understand such a lesson? Will he realize that it's all right to punish only when the individual has done something "wrong"? Or will he learn that it's all right to punish when you are bigger and more powerful than the other person? It's difficult to ensure that the right lessons are learned with punishment.

Another of Skinner's objections was that being in a situation where a previously punished response could be made without punishment may lead an individual to do so. In other words, a child may learn that if a response is made around an authority figure such as a parent, teacher, or police officer, she will be punished, but if none of these people are around, she can make the response. The child learns the discriminative stimuli for punishment and may make the response in their absence. An everyday example of learning the S_Ds for punishment can be observed on any highway; if a police car is around, people drive the speed limit, but they go much faster when no police car is visible.

Several researchers have suggested ways of varying the punishment procedure to promote greater generalization. For example, if several people administer the punishment, it will be less likely to generate suppression specific only to one person (Carr & Lovaas, 1983). Another procedure used to eliminate discriminating authority presence from absence was used by Corte, Wolf, and Locke (1971): they had the adult therapist hide from the subject but observe him. When the subject engaged in self-injury, the therapist came out of hiding and delivered a shock. The punishment generalized to situations in which the adult was absent.

The final objection of Skinner's that we will note is his observation that punishment causes the individual to drift from escape to avoidance behavior. The differences between these two will be discussed shortly in more detail. For now, it is sufficient to note that avoidance responses are much more rigid and more difficult to eliminate than escape behaviors. What we are describing here are the passive avoidance responses mentioned above. This drifting would make the learner much less able to learn new responses to the situation in the future.

All these objections are important considerations for anyone who wishes to use punishment type I. Because of them, many psychologists advocate punishment type II as the preferred, more humane method. This has led to an increasing use of "**time out**" and response cost procedures. However, careful consideration will lead to the conclusion that many of Skinner's objections also apply to this form of punishment. For type II to be effective, desirable outcomes must be withdrawn. The more desirable something is, the more effectively we can punish by removing it. But the more desirable it is, the more upset the individual will be at having it withheld. Unfortunate emotional by-products, the possibility that the behavior will not be permanently eliminated or will be replaced with other undesirable behaviors, and the failure to provide a better alternative response may all occur with the use of this form of punishment as well. The primary advantages to the use of punishment type II are that we are less likely to convey the message that it's all right to hurt others sometimes, and we are less likely to generate aggressive tendencies in the individual. However, many of us might well agree with Skinner, at least in principle, and conclude that we should use punishment as little as possible. Positive reinforcement of more desirable behavior and extinction of undesirable behavior were Skinner's preferred methods for modifying behavior.

What Makes Punishment Work?

What makes punishment work? Why does it have its suppressive effects? Several different proposals have been made to explain what's going on in punishment. One possibility is that punishment just suppresses all activity because of the presence of an unpleasant stimulus. The punished response is suppressed the most because it occurs most often before the unpleasant event. The overall suppressive effects of unpleasant stimuli are well documented; the conditioned emotional response procedure mentioned in chapter 3 is one example of this. However, punishment does more than this; a punisher contingent on a particular response suppresses that response significantly more than it suppresses other responses. Schuster and Rachlin (1968) and Goodall (1984) have shown that contingent shocks suppress the response more than randomly delivered (noncontingent) shocks, even when there are an equal number of shocks delivered for both conditions.

Another type of theory suggests that the circumstances surrounding punishment (the S_Ds) become classically conditioned to the punisher. They serve as CSs that generate a fear response. The fear response (often freezing in place or running) is incompatible with the response we are trying to punish and therefore interferes with its occurrence (Guthrie, 1934). This incompatible response idea implies that the punished response may reappear when the signals associated with punishment are absent, and this does sometimes occur. Further, it suggests that the nature of the punished response is a factor influencing the effectiveness of punishment. In other words, if the response can be easily performed while the subject is experiencing its fear reactions to the punishment, then punishment will be ineffective.

A classic study by Fowler and Miller (1963) demonstrated this idea. Rats were trained to run down an alley for food. Then one group was shocked on its hind feet just before the goal, and the other group was shocked on its front paws. Shocking the front paws makes the rat cringe or flinch back, which is incompatible with entering the goal. The rats shocked on their rear paws lurched forward, which got them into the goal faster. The reaction to the punishment could either interfere with the running response or facilitate it—the effectiveness of punishment is influenced by the relationship between the response and the reactions to punishment. However, this is not the whole answer. In another important study, Boe and Church (1967) demonstrated that this response competition alone is not sufficient. They showed that a contingency between the shock and the response significantly increases the effectiveness of the shock compared to a group that receives noncontingent shock. If both groups receive an equal number of shocks, response competition should be equal. Because there was a difference between them, competition alone is not the answer.

Two-factor theories of punishment are related to the incompatible response idea. Originally proposed by Mowrer (1947) and modified later by Dinsmoor (1954, 1977), such theories suggest that the individual learns cues (which may be internal sensations) that are associated with the punishment. Mowrer suggested that these cues generate a motivational state (fear), which then causes the individual to make responses other than the punished response to reduce the fear. For Mowrer, the punished response generates internal sensations that the individual associates with fear; by not making the response the individual avoids feeling those sensations that lead to fear. Dinsmoor proposed a theory of similar form but omitted the internal fear concept by suggesting that the cues themselves become aversive. Punishment causes the circumstances surrounding the punishing event to become aversive. The subject stops making the punished response to prevent these unpleasant cues from occurring. In both theories, the cues themselves may be the internal sensations or feedback resulting from making the punished response. These theories are often referred to as *passive avoidance* theories of punishment, because they suggest that the passive behavior of failing to make a response may be what is learned through punishment. By failing to respond, the subject avoids the punishment. At this point, these theories seem reasonable, although they do have limitations such as the fact that the internal cues, by definition, cannot be observed. Thus, they are relatively difficult to prove or disprove. In addition, as with other competition theories, the problem is that often no actual responses are seen that are incompatible with the punished response.

The final theoretical approach we will mention minimizes the classical aspects of the situation and emphasizes the effect of the contingency between response and aversive event. Azrin (1956) and Church (1969) have suggested that the subject learns to associate its response with a punishing event so that it learns, "If I do this, I get hurt; but if I don't do this, I won't get hurt." The learning of this contingency causes the response to be suppressed. Although this approach is not really incompatible with the explanations offered by Mowrer and Dinsmoor, its emphasis on the connection between what the learner does and what happens to the learner probably allows for the most effective use of punishment. Such effective use ought to emphasize that the learner must recognize that her actions result in an undesirable outcome; for most people, this knowledge of a contingency would lead them to stop making the punished response.

Negative Reinforcement

Almost every day for over ten years I have spent an hour in the morning doing exercises for my back. They are a chore, but they really help me avoid having back pain, and when I do strain my back, they help me recover more quickly and less painfully. This is an example of **negative reinforcement**, which consists of eliminating an unpleasant stimulus contingent on a response being made. As a consequence the response becomes more likely, whereas in punishment the response becomes less likely. Our example in chapter 1 of Aphrodite avoiding her big brother when their mother scolds him is another example of negative reinforcement. In fact, many of our routine daily activities can be seen as examples of responding under negative reinforcement conditions. We clean house to avoid the embarrassment of friends raising their eyebrows in scorn; we drive the speed limit to avoid getting a ticket; we apologize for wrongdoings to escape the punishment being delivered; students duck their heads in class to avoid being called on when they don't know the answer. Finally, many of our social customs, such as waiting our turn, saying "please" and "thank you," the rules of driving, and the rules of courtesy, are simply mechanisms that allow us to avoid or escape conflict in crowded environments.

As these examples suggest, there are actually two types of negative reinforcement procedures: escape and avoidance conditioning. **Escape conditioning** means that an individual is exposed to the unpleasant stimulus and then makes a response that causes the unpleasantness to stop. When I was first shown the back exercises I do, I did them because they reduced the pain a little, so I was escaping some of it. **Avoidance conditioning** means that the individual may, after learning, make the response in anticipation of the unpleasantness and therefore prevent it from happening. In avoidance conditioning, it is possible for the learner to perform so that it no longer ever experiences the unpleasant event. Most of the time now I am continuing to exercise to *avoid* back pain, rather than just *escape* it after it happens. Although this may seem like a small difference, it makes explanations of avoidance much more complex than explanations of escape and has thus led to a great deal of research aimed at understanding the mechanisms of avoidance behavior. Both types of negative reinforcement would be diagrammed the same way, however, as shown below.

$$S_D \text{ - - - - - - - } R \longrightarrow \overset{\text{remove}}{S_{r-}}$$

Often the procedural difference between escape and avoidance conditioning consists only of arranging the situation so that the learner is able to respond in advance of the aversive event. In other words, in escape conditioning we might place a rat in a Skinner box and begin shocking it until it presses the bar. Pressing the bar would stop the shock for some time. After that time, the shock would come back on and continue until the rat pressed the bar again. In each escape trial, pressing the bar is ineffective until the shock actually begins. Often the shock itself can be seen as the discriminative stimulus, and its removal is the reinforcing event.

On the other hand, an avoidance procedure would provide a signal indicating that shock would start within (for example) 10 seconds. If the rat pressed the bar before the 10 seconds were up, it would receive no shock for that trial. Typically, this arrangement would blur the difference between trials so that in actuality, pressing the bar would postpone the shock. In other words, if the signal indicated shock in 10 seconds, pressing the bar might postpone the shock for 30 seconds. Twenty seconds after the bar press, the signal would come on again, indicating shock in 10 seconds unless the bar is pressed. In this way, the well-trained rat in the avoidance procedure could keep responding effectively and never receive a shock again.

In addition to studying rats and pigeons in Skinner boxes, many investigators have studied dogs or rats in a device called a **shuttle box**. This is simply two compartments large enough for the subject and sharing one wall. Typically, one compartment is painted black and the other is white. They are separated by a barrier that the animal can cross with some moderate effort. It may be a half-door that a dog just has to jump over, or it may be a door that a rat has to open by turning a wheel. We place the animal in one compartment and turn on the shock. Using the shuttle box in a one-way procedure would mean that if the animal crossed the barrier, it would always be safe on the other side. In other words, the one-way shuttle makes one side always shocked (for example, the white side), and the other (black) side always safe. We would always have to put the animal back in the white side to start another trial. In a two-way shuttle box arrangement the subject is shocked in both compartments. In other words, once the learner jumps over the barrier, it is only safe from the shock for a while (for example, 30 seconds). After that time, the shock comes on in that compartment as well and the subject must go back to the first compartment, where it will be safe from shock for another 30 seconds. The animal must keep jumping back and forth over the barrier. We can use one-way and two-way shuttle box procedures to study avoidance by arranging the contingency to provide an advance warning signal and allowing a response to be made before the shock. We can also use either one to study escape by making effective responses impossible until the shock starts. Figure 5.2 illustrates a shuttle box.

The one-way shuttle box probably resembles real-life examples more closely than the two-way procedure, but the two-way procedure is more convenient to use experimentally. We can more easily see the similarity between the one-way procedure and such situations as the child who is

Figure 5.2 A shuttle box for dogs

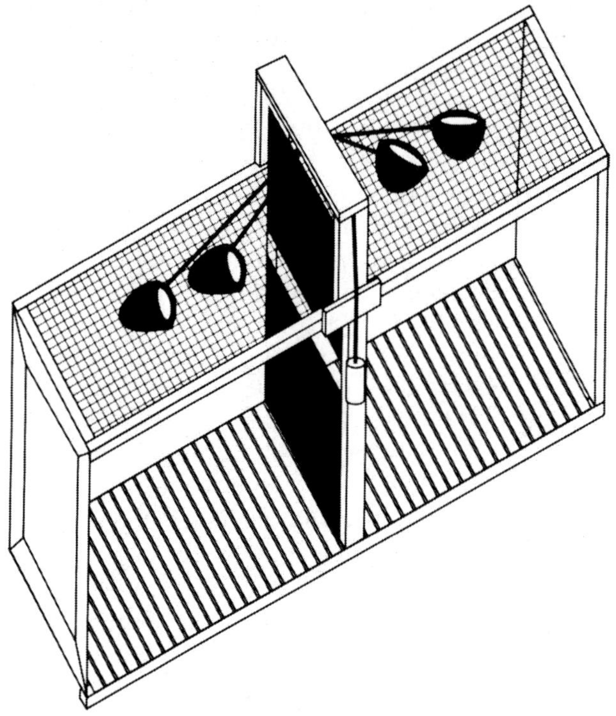

From "Traumatic Avoidance Learning: Acquisition in Normal Dogs," by R. L. Solomon and L. C. Wynne, 1953, *Psychological Monographs, 67* (Whole No. 354).

losing a fight with another child and runs away. He is escaping the aversive stimuli. If he runs away the next time he sees the other child, he would be avoiding. Escape behavior often evolves into avoidance behavior if an avoidance response is possible: that is, if an advance signal occurs and if the response will prevent the unpleasant outcome.

We will focus on one major independent variable in negative reinforcement, intensity of the reinforcer. Other variables have been less thoroughly studied, sometimes because their role seems well understood from the other forms of operant conditioning. Some variables used in other operant procedures simply do not apply to negative reinforcement. For example, deprivation state, which is important in using positive reinforcement, is essentially a meaningless term in negative reinforcement. The opportunity for alternative responses, important in the use of punishment, is also much less important in using negative reinforcement. Two variables that need brief mention are schedules and delay. Schedules of reinforcement seem to function in a similar fashion as in punishment, with better performance when continuous schedules are used and poorer performance with increasingly demanding partial schedules (Hineline & Rachlin, 1969). That is, a dog that escapes shock with every jump learns much more effectively than a dog whose jumps lead to escape from the shock only half the time. Delay of reinforcement (the shock does not stop immediately after the response) leads to poorer learning, probably for the same reasons discussed for the other operant procedures (Fowler & Trapold, 1962).

In positive reinforcement, stronger reinforcement generally leads to better learning. Negative reinforcement shows a similar pattern: the strength of reinforcement is determined by how much shock is used before the response is made and how much it is reduced by making the response. For example, if we shock a rat with 50 volts and its response stops the shock, it will not learn to avoid as quickly as another rat that reduces the intensity from 100 volts to zero with its response. However, a rat whose response reduces the shock from 100 volts to 50 volts will learn about as quickly as a rat reducing the shock from 50 volts to zero. Thus, the amount of shock reduction is a better determinant of escape or avoidance performance than the absolute level of the shock (Campbell & Kraeling, 1953).

In Skinner boxes or in one-way shuttle box situations, the greater the reduction in amount of shock, the better the performance. However, in the two-way shuttle box, greater shocks lead to more difficulty in learning. To understand why, think of what is being required of the dog in the two-way shuttle box. We shock it and it jumps to the other side, where it will soon be shocked again. Eventually, it must learn to escape or avoid shock by jumping toward a place where it has gotten shocked before, and where it may get shocked again. This is not a very appealing outcome, and the stronger the shock, the less attractive the other chamber appears to the dog, because it has received that same strong shock there. This theory suggests that the dog is caught in a situation that generates fear of where it is and fear of where it must go as well. In this case, the greater the shock, the greater the fear and the harder it is for the dog to persuade itself to jump (Olton, 1973).

Black, Nadel, and O'Keefe (1977) found that rats with hippocampal damage performed somewhat poorer on one-way avoidance tasks but actually learned two-way avoidance more quickly. They explained this result as indicating that the hippocampus was involved in matching location with emotional consequences; when it was damaged, the animals no longer feared both sides of the two-way shuttle, so that their performance could actually improve over that of normal rats. Thus, they provide support for Olton's idea. Many experimenters have noted that two-way avoidance is a very peculiar circumstance. There are relatively few conditions comparable to it in everyday life. However, it illustrates the possible role of a classically conditioned fear in negative reinforcement. The role of fear has been an especially important question for investigators of negative reinforcement, and although the theoretical explanation given for the effect of shock intensity is not accepted by all researchers, it is a fairly widely accepted idea.

Why Is Avoidance So Complex?

Theories of Avoidance

Escape conditioning has not been especially difficult for learning theorists to explain. The individual who is experiencing something unpleasant makes a response that reduces or eliminates this unpleasantness. The change in the stimulus conditions is clearly observable by both learner and objective observer. This is not the case for avoidance responses. In avoidance responding, the learner makes a response and no external change can be seen, because the response came before the unpleasantness occurred. Objectively, the situation in the environment is the same with regard to the unpleasantness before and after the response. There is no change in the amount of shock as a result of the response. So why does the response persist? At this point you are probably thinking, what a dumb question—the dog keeps jumping over the hurdle because it "knows" that if it jumps, it won't get shocked. You must remember that learning theorists since Watson's time are not fond of explanations based on such internal events as thoughts, ideas, or expectations. The only evidence we have that the animal knows something is its behavior; if we say it "knows" to jump, our proof of that is the fact that it jumps. Unfortunately, this is not very good proof, because it could jump for several other reasons; perhaps it has an innate tendency to jump whenever it encounters something associated with pain, for example. Surely we can do better than that.

The fundamental problem for learning theorists is that in each of the other operant procedures, an observable stimulus is present after the response that wasn't there before the response, or a stimulus that was present is removed (in omission punishment or escape); this isn't true of avoidance conditioning. This very difficult problem is often expressed as the question, How can a nonevent maintain behavior? The power of avoidance conditioning in maintaining behavior is easily demonstrated; a classic experiment by Solomon and Wynne (1953) showed that dogs persisted in responding very quickly for hundreds of trials after less than 10 shocks. A graph of responding for one typical dog during acquisition only is shown in figure 5.3. Notice that the first seven responses were slow; the dog received shocks on these trials. After trial 7, the dog responded very quickly (well under the 10-second time requirement) for all the remaining trials.

Figure 5.3 One typical dog's pattern of responding in a shuttle box using negative reinforcement. The short horizontal line at 10 seconds indicates that faster responses (above the line) allow the dog to avoid, whereas slower responses (the first six below the line) are escape responses.

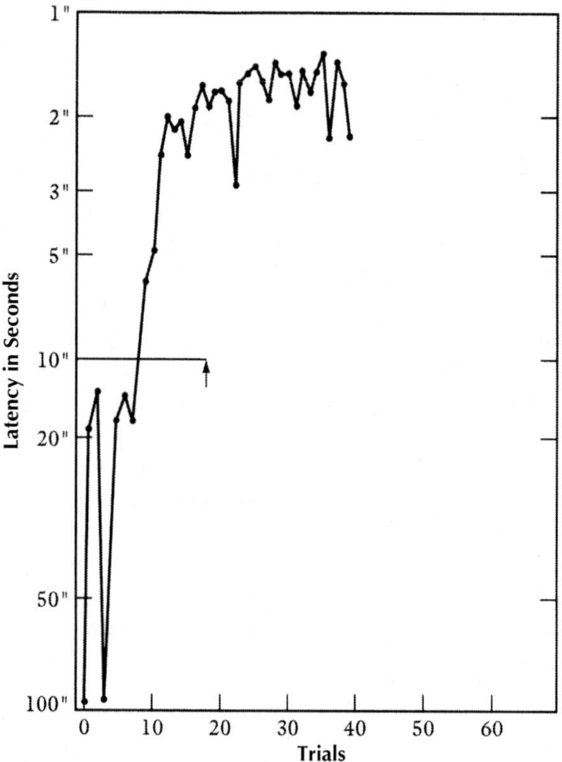

From "Traumatic Avoidance Learning: Acquisition in Normal Dogs," by R. L. Solomon and L. C. Wynne, 1953, *Psychological Monographs, 67* (Whole No. 354).

The problem of the nonevent becomes clearer when we discuss the extinction process for escape and avoidance. This would consist of turning off the shock in an escape situation. The animal will soon stop making the escape response—there's no need to do it. However, in avoidance conditioning, the well-trained animal keeps making the response even when the shock mechanism is disconnected. The reason is basically that the learner has no opportunity to discover that the shock will not occur even without its response; it responds before the shock is due, so it cannot experience the situation of the shock not happening without its responding. We must force the creature to learn that its response is no longer necessary. This can be done in two ways. One is to prevent the response while eliminating the shock. If we fix the barrier so that the dog can't jump over it while at the same time omitting the shock, eventually the dog learns that the response is no longer necessary, and it is extinguished. The other way is to show that the response is ineffective—the dog jumps and is immediately shocked anyway. Soon it gives up jumping. This is often referred to as flooding. Both flooding and response prevention are accompanied by a great deal of fear during the early stages. The fear is especially noticeable in contrast to the animal that is allowed to perform normally. The well-trained dog jumps back and forth so routinely that it resembles the executive commuting back and forth to work, making the name "shuttle box" symbolic of businesslike efficiency. There is little evidence of fear in the well-trained avoider (Kamin, Brimer, & Black, 1963; Solomon, Kamin, & Wynne, 1953). Extinction procedures severely disrupt the animal's composure. Similarly, a child who runs away from the bully may laugh along the way—unless he encounters the bully's pal who holds him up.

The similarity between escape responses and reflexes suggested to some that this situation was simply a case of classical conditioning. The escape response was just a reflexive reaction that could be conditioned to signals in advance of the shock. These conditioned stimuli would suppress responding in a punishment situation but would enhance responding in escape situations. In other words, responses that would be easily punished would be difficult to negatively reinforce. This explanation would focus on innate reactions to stimuli; a withdrawal reaction would be incompatible with whatever response is being punished but would be perfectly appropriate for escaping or avoiding. Unfortunately, jumping over the barrier doesn't especially look like a reflex. Furthermore, the successful avoider is responding before the shock. When it does this, it causes any CS to occur without the US of shock, so the conditioning should be extinguished after some successful avoiding.

Two-Factor Theory

Both classical and operant explanations of avoidance seem inadequate by themselves. O. H. Mowrer (1939) suggested that they had to be combined to explain avoidance. His explanation is called the **two-factor theory** of avoidance, and it represented a breakthrough in our understanding of avoidance and of all operant behavior. Mowrer suggested that in an avoidance situation, the learner becomes classically conditioned to fear the signals that are present before the shock occurs. These signals are therefore both discriminative stimuli and conditioned stimuli. This occurs during the early trials, when the learner hasn't learned well enough to avoid and is just escaping the shock. Once the learner is fast enough at responding to avoid, Mowrer suggested that the fear generated by these conditioned stimuli is aversive in and of itself. The response reduces this fear, because it removes the learner from the conditioned stimuli that generate the fear. Therefore, the dog that is avoiding successfully is really behaving to reduce its fear. Because we can't observe the fear very easily, it appears to us as if the dog is avoiding shock when in fact it is just escaping fear. We might diagram the situation as follows. Early in training, during the phase that is clearly escape, the dog's responding appears this way:

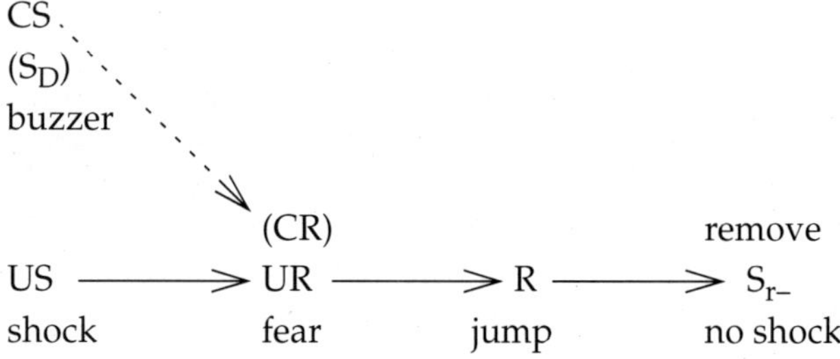

After training, when the dog is avoiding successfully, the situation might be diagrammed this way:

			remove	remove
CS ⟶	CR ⟶	R ⟶	CS ⟶	S_{r-}
buzzer	fear	jump	no buzzer	no fear

The two-factor theory generated a great deal of interest and research after it was proposed. Although some of the research supported the theory, some did not. For example, we have already noted that the well-trained avoider doesn't appear to be especially fearful; the dog appears very businesslike. Yet the theory depends on fear. Research has shown that the signals used in avoidance tasks (the buzzer above) become somewhat aversive; they often suppress responding if presented during other operant tasks, such as the conditioned emotional response measure described in chapter 3 (Kamin, Brimer, & Black, 1963). However, Kamin et al. found that the amount of suppression leveled off and then declined with increasing amounts of training, but the avoidance response remained strong. This lack of consistency of correspondence between fear measures and operant responding has been the routine finding. The learner will make responses to stop the CS in other circumstances; however, it won't make responses to avoid the CS itself (Dinsmoor, 1962; Miller, 1948). Perhaps the strongest support for a role for classical conditioning in avoidance is that the termination of the CS is related to performance. In the early experiments, as soon as the dog jumped over the barrier, both the CS (signal) and the US (shock) stopped. When researchers began to deliberately control the termination of the signal independently of the response, they found that if the CS continues for a brief time, for example, 5 seconds after the response, the dog takes much longer to learn to avoid. However, this could be an indication that the buzzer is providing feedback that the learner has made the response correctly (D'Amato, Fazzaro, & Etkin, 1968).

Now we know that some classical conditioning is involved in avoidance. Although evidence for a CR of fear is poor, there is clear evidence that the signals preceding the shock are learned: this is a CS–US relationship. Why don't we see better evidence of fear, and why isn't the conditioning extinguished when the dog is successfully avoiding?

One answer to the problem of extinction was suggested by R. L. Solomon and L. C. Wynne (1953). They noted that the CS is typically present for a relatively long time during the early escape trials, usually more than 10 seconds. In other words, the buzzer starts buzzing and continues until the animal has escaped the shock. This may take as long as 30 seconds. Later on in training, the dog jumps within a few seconds of hearing the buzzer. It not only avoids the shock, but also escapes the buzzer after only a few seconds of exposure to it. This may not be enough time for very much extinction of the fear of the buzzer. In fact, Solomon and Wynne (1953) suggested that the learner may distinguish between buzzers on the basis of duration; it learns to fear a long buzzer, and this fear is not extinguished by exposure to a short buzzer. Buzzers of different duration may be perceived differently by the learner. The response of jumping keeps the buzzer brief and prevents extinction. When the buzzer starts, the animal has no way of knowing how long it will last, so it performs as it has learned to in the presence of the long buzzer. Solomon and Wynne suggested that the dog is escaping a long-lasting buzzer.

Contingency Theory

The problems with demonstrating fear have led to an alternative theory that is similar to Mowrer's theory but leaves out the fear component (Seligman & Johnston, 1973). This alternative simply suggests that the animal in avoidance conditioning has learned two contingencies, one classical and one operant. The classical contingency is that if the CS occurs the US will occur—the buzzer will be followed by shock, and no buzzer means no shock. This is learned during the early escape trials. The operant contingency is that the subject learns that if it jumps, it will not be shocked; but if it doesn't jump, it will be shocked. This contingency is learned later, and once it is well learned, the theory suggests that it is triggered by the CS generating the expectation of shock. The dog jumps in response to this expectation and the expectation that it will get shocked if it doesn't jump.

The **contingency theory** fits most of the data described above. Because it doesn't rely on fear as a motivational factor, it predicts that the avoidance response will occur at a stable level once the operant contingency is learned. In contrast, the two-factor theory predicts some vacillation of responding because the fear is extinguished somewhat by successful avoidance responses. It predicts that a CS not terminated by the response would slow learning; here the classical contingency would influence the performance of the operant response (essentially, the dog might think it had performed incorrectly because the signal didn't consistently change with the shock). Usually, though, the classical components are only relevant to the initial escape behavior and play little role in the later avoidance responding.

The contingency theory predicts that there would be two ways to properly extinguish an avoidance response. We could teach the dog that either half of the operant contingency was false and extinguish it. In other words, we could shock it in spite of jumping and use flooding to disprove one part of the contingency, or prevent its response while not shocking it to disprove the other part of the contingency. Unfortunately, the description of these expectancies based on learning contingencies seems very much like the mentalistic explanations that behaviorists were trying so hard to keep from using. Mowrer's two-factor theory still has many advocates and actually has much to offer. For example, the clinical psychologist treating people with avoidance problems must consider the emotional components of avoidance behavior as carefully as the actual avoidance itself.

Species-Specific Defensive Reaction Theory

There is one other alternative to these theories. Bolles (1970) argued that they were all inadequate to explain avoidance in natural circumstances, because they all depend on escape evolving into avoidance and on cues signaling danger. If an antelope had to escape the claws and teeth of a predator before it could learn to avoid that predator, it wouldn't be a very long-lived antelope. Once the truly unpleasant stimuli are occurring, the learner is usually doomed. The antelope population would be very small if they had to learn by this trial-and-error method. Further, a predator that always provided signals before it attacked or that allowed its prey to escape once it had it in its claws would be a pretty inept predator. Bolles proposed that many creatures have innate response tendencies that are triggered automatically by certain stimuli the first time the animal encounters them. He labeled these responses **species-specific defensive reactions** (SSDRs) and suggested that each type of creature would have its own set of preferred SSDRs.

Bolles identified three types of defensive responses: fighting, fleeing, and freezing in place. He further noted that each species seems to have its own order of preference for them, and the most preferred response will be attempted until exhaustion or until it is no longer possible or effective. Then the second choice will be attempted if the creature is still alive. There is overwhelming evidence for this idea; antelope always try to run first, turtles flee inside their shells, opossums freeze by playing dead, wild boar fight back. Each species has a defensive response tailored to its physical nature; this is the most preferred response. Only when all the built-in responses are impossible or ineffective will the creature be forced to learn an alternative response in the ways suggested by two-factor theorists. Bolles notes that teaching a dog to jump to avoid is easy because jumping is near the top of the defense hierarchy for dogs; however, teaching a rat to press a bar is much harder because pressing is unrelated to the rat's normal defensive reactions. Bolles therefore suggests that learning to avoid is not a typical occurrence in nature.

The two-factor theory and its relatives seem to be more appropriate to human behavior than Bolles's SSDR theory. Unlike many other animal species, all humans do not show the same stereotyped response to danger. In the same circumstances different people do different things. If we are mugged in an alley, some of us fight back, some try to run away, and some hand over their wallets. Although the boy running away may seem like a plausible example of an SSDR reaction, we can easily see different responses to bullies on any playground. Most of us show enough variability in our responding that it is difficult to identify which kind of response might be an SSDR. Perhaps the laboratory analysis of avoidance bears more relevance to our behavior, and SSDR theory more often fits other animals' behavior. This is not to suggest that other animals do not learn to avoid, just that many of them may have built-in avoidance mechanisms for certain kinds of threats. New kinds of threats would require learning an avoidance response for them as well. Thus, the deer may have an SSDR for running when certain stimuli associated with its natural predators occur, but these stimuli don't always occur when a human hunter is preparing to shoot. The deer may have to react with an escape response to the sound of the gun. The task for psychologists is to determine for which species and which defensive behaviors SSDRs are more appropriate and which species, under which circumstances, are more likely to rely on complex learning of avoidance responses.

Learned Helplessness

After Mowrer proposed the two-factor theory of avoidance, many experimenters tried to separate the two forms of conditioning to study them independently of each other. We noted several of this type of study in our discussion; manipulating the termination of the CS warning represents one experiment of this type. Another attempt was the **learned helplessness** experiments of Seligman and his associates (Maier & Seligman, 1976; Overmeier & Seligman, 1967). Essentially, they tried to classically condition their dogs before placing them in the avoidance situation. They gave their dogs intense shocks for up to five seconds in a separate apparatus that restrained the dogs. The day after this inescapable shock session, the dogs were placed in a shuttle box. According to our understanding of the two-factor theory, we might expect that the dogs would learn to avoid faster because they have already learned to fear the shock and any cues associated with it, and this fear would be capable of motivating the dog to avoid effectively. However, just the opposite occurred; this group of Seligman's dogs was much poorer than average at learning to avoid in a two-way shuttle box. They often just lay in the compartment taking the shock and whimpering. Seligman suggested that the previous exposure to inescapable, unavoidable shock had taught the dogs that they couldn't escape or avoid shock. This learning blocked or prevented the dogs from learning how to avoid in later situations. The dogs had learned to be helpless in this situation.

Seligman's results generated a great deal of interest both inside and outside the laboratory. Psychologists interested in clinical problems found the learned helplessness phenomenon especially relevant to many human situations. Clinicians often must help people who have become passive in the face of adversity, from schoolchildren who don't do their homework or raise their hands in class to employees who just go through the motions at work. When a person won't ask the boss for a raise "because it won't do any good," that person has learned to be helpless. To illustrate the applicability to human situations, Hiroto (1974) and Hiroto and Seligman (1975) subjected humans to uncontrollable conditions (insoluble problems or inescapable noise) and found that their performance afterward was poorer in both cognitive and instrumental tasks than subjects exposed to solvable problems or controllable noise. In people the results are less dramatic than in animal studies, but this is probably because the aversive situations are much more unpleasant in the animal research. Questionnaires administered to subjects in studies of this type routinely find subjects reporting increased feelings of helplessness, incompetence, frustration, and depression (Roth & Kubal, 1975). Understanding this phenomenon and how it could be changed seemed to be a very worthwhile goal.

In numerous studies researchers have been able to rule out strictly biochemical interpretations (Weiss, Stone, & Harrel, 1970), emotional exhaustion (Seligman & Groves, 1970), and competing responses (Overmeier & Seligman, 1967). The most plausible explanation involves the associative process described above in which the dogs learned that they were going to be shocked and there was nothing they could do about it. Strong evidence in support of this interpretation also comes from the fact that the previous experience of the dog strongly influences its susceptibility to the learned helplessness procedure. Dogs that are laboratory raised, and therefore lacking experience with influencing their environment, are much more susceptible than more experienced dogs. Also, if a dog is given some escape training before it receives the inescapable shock, the helplessness effect does not occur in the avoidance situation (Seligman & Groves, 1970; Seligman, Rosellini, & Kozak, 1975).

Thus, previous experience in which the individual is able to influence the outcome or nature of the events "immunizes" her from the effects of learned helplessness.

Seligman, Maier, and Geer (1968) found that the most effective way to eliminate the helplessness was to literally drag the dogs back and forth in the shuttle box. After several experiences of being dragged away from the shock, the dog begins to walk away after a tug on the leash, and soon it doesn't even need this prompt to respond. The analogy to human situations is clear: to eliminate helplessness, the person must be forced to make a response. Once the person has made responses and seen that they are effective, he will be much less passive and helpless. However, arranging situations so that the individual must make an active response is often very difficult. In addition, therapy aimed at reducing the cognitive and emotional side effects of helplessness is also necessary. Current research with humans has emphasized the cognitive consequences of the helplessness situation. It seems that the attributions that people make about why they fail influence whether they become depressed or helpless. These attributions involve variables such as locus of control (attributing failure to internal reasons such as lack of ability rather than to external reasons such as task difficulty) and the specificity of the situation (is this a general indication of how things are or just one incident?). Abramson, Seligman, and Teasdale (1978) have used the learned helplessness research and these variables to develop a complex attributional model of depression to explain the differences between people in their reaction to inescapable situations.

Summary

There are two forms of punishment: Type I involves an individual receiving an unpleasant stimulus as a result of a response, such as being spanked for misbehavior. Type II, often called omission training, involves losing a pleasant stimulus as a result of a response; an example is the "time out" procedure used in schools. Both forms lead to a decrease in responding. Type I is the most commonly used and most widely studied in the laboratory. More intense punishers suppress responses more effectively, and delaying the punisher lessens its effectiveness. Starting with a mild punisher and gradually increasing its intensity is very ineffective, and partial schedules of punishment are less effective than continuously delivered punishment. Well-learned responses are harder to eliminate with punishment, and the availability of alternative responses influences the effectiveness of punishment. B. F. Skinner presented many ethical and practical objections to punishment, some of which have been supported by research. He felt that punishment effects were temporary; modern researchers have shown the conditions under which it will be relatively permanent (for example, the presence of alternative responses). Punishment also causes unfortunate emotional by-products that may become classically conditioned to the punishing agent or other surroundings, does not provide positive alternatives to the punished response, and may lead the learner to discriminate between circumstances where the punishment contingency is in effect and other times when he may "get away with it."

Negative reinforcement is an entirely different procedure from punishment because it causes a behavior to occur more frequently. It consists of removing an unpleasant stimulus contingent on a response. One negative reinforcement procedure is escape, where a subject receives a shock (for example) and makes a response that stops the shock. The other is avoidance, where a learner can make a response in anticipation of the unpleasant event and prevent its occurrence altogether. Escape conditioning has been relatively easy to explain, but avoidance is extremely complex, because an effectively learned response does not cause an observable change in the external environment. A two-factor theory of avoidance suggests that a classically conditioned "fear" is reduced by the learner's response, and this fear reduction is what maintains the operant response. An alternative theory suggests that defensive responses are not always learned, but instead are innate and are tailored to the creature's natural habitat and physical characteristics. The study of two-factor theory led to the discovery of learned helplessness, in which prior exposure to classical inescapable shock prevents the individual from learning an avoidance response.

Questions for Discussion, Thought, and Practice

1. Define and give an example of each key concept. Group the concepts into two categories, terms related to punishment and terms related to negative reinforcement. Then try to divide each group into subgroups.
2. Analyze the following examples, identifying the response, reinforcer, discriminative stimulus, and type of reinforcement. Refer to the end of chapter 4 for how to analyze examples if you need review.
   a. Everyone at school was wearing baseball caps, so Luann thought she would too. But all the other kids laughed at her, so Luann stopped wearing a cap after just two days.
   b. Young Bill Mountebank often parks illegally in no-parking zones, except on Thursdays, when "Eagle Eye" Cauldron is on duty. "Eagle Eye" has ticketed Bill three times, all on Thursdays.
   c. In supermarkets, Mr. and Ms. Mollycoddle give their children candy in order to stop embarrassing crying episodes. Analyze the parents' behavior: what is reinforcing it?

3. What are the implications of example c. above? Are parents the only ones who can reinforce in parent–child interactions? Do you have to understand how to reinforce to be able to use reinforcement?
4. One night somebody tried to break into Alan's house. Although the burglar was unsuccessful, Alan subsequently installed dead-bolt locks and motion sensor lights. Every night without fail, he goes around and checks the locks before going to bed. Is Alan's behavior an example of punishment or negative reinforcement? Analyze Alan's behavior. Also, what would Alan's emotional state be like when he is locking up (think Solomon and Wynne here), compared to what his emotional state might be when the power fails or he wakes up realizing that he forgot to lock up?
5. What are the differences among punishment, extinction, and negative reinforcement?
6. What is the difference between escape and avoidance? Why is this difference so important?
7. Determine whether each example below involves primarily punishment type I, punishment type II, negative reinforcement, or extinction. Remember to estimate whether the response is increasing or decreasing in frequency of occurrence.
   a. A student works all weekend on a library report but is disappointed when she gets only a C grade for her efforts.
   b. A juvenile delinquent is assigned work duties without pay after starting a fight.
   c. A carpenter suffers pain from numerous small bruises, cuts, and slivers on her hands.
   d. Billy has learned to keep his mouth shut when his cousin starts to brag about how good he is at football.
   e. Eddie's mom takes his treat away if he doesn't say "thank you."

Theories of Reinforcement

▲ KEY CONCEPTS ▲

central theory	primary reinforcer
drive-reduction theory	response hierarchy
homeostasis	secondary reinforcer
hypothalamus	three-term contingency
local theory	token economy
Premack principle	transsituationality

In this chapter we consider two important questions about operant conditioning. First, we briefly discuss the question: What is being learned in operant conditioning? Our second question is: Why does reinforcement work? These questions not only have important theoretical consequences but also have important practical implications for our understanding of learning.

What Is Being Learned in Operant Conditioning?

Our description of operant conditioning has three elements in it: a signaling stimulus, a response, and a reinforcing stimulus. Each of these may be connected to each of the other two, making three possible pairs of connections. Although a three-way association might be possible, operant conditioners generally have described three associations between pairs of elements in the operant situation, because paired relationships are much easier to understand. Is the individual learning to do something in response to a particular situation (an S–R association), or learning to make a response to get a reinforcer (an R–S association), or learning that in a particular situation a reward may occur (an S–S association)? In other words, we conceive of these three possibilities: S_D – R, R – S_{r+}, and S_D – S_{r+}. This last association is basically a classical conditioning connection, and yet it does describe a part of the operant situation. In other words, it suggests that our subject is learning, "In this situation a reward may occur." This will be noted in our comparison of classical and operant conditioning in chapter 8; it basically means that there are no pure examples of operant conditioning. All operant conditioning involves some classical conditioning as well.

To illustrate the differences in understanding the learning situation, imagine a child raising her hand to answer a question in school (and being called on and praised) and an executive writing reports to earn her salary. Each may connect the discriminative stimuli (the classroom and the office) with the response (raising her hand and writing reports) as an S–R association. This seems like a mechanical reaction to the situation: "I should do this now." Or each person might connect her response to the reward, the R–S association of "If I do this, I'll get this." This association could make for a more enthusiastic response, because a better response could lead to an increased reward. Finally, the S–S association suggests that our learners would associate classrooms with praise and the office with salaries. Such associations might make for happy individuals who didn't necessarily recognize the value of their responses. The combination of associations we assume to be operating can influence the performance of our learner, how the learner feels, and our interpretation and evaluation of the situation.

Thorndike originally described his early experiments as the result of rewards "stamping in" an association between a stimulus (which we now call an S_D) and a response. This makes him one of the few true S–R psychologists. For Thorndike, the important association that was learned was between the stimulus events before a response and the response itself. He felt that reinforcement or reward strengthened the already existing connections between signaling stimuli and responses. Thorndike felt that in any given stimulus situation, the learner has a large set of responses available. These responses are all potentially available, presumably because the learner has made them in the past in those circumstances for some reason (either because they are innate or because they had been previously reinforced). The potential responses are not equally likely to occur, however. They are arranged in a hierarchy of probability of occurrence. Reinforcement has its effect because it shows the learner which response in the situation is best. In a sense, Thorndike was an early advocate of the feedback value of reward. The reward teaches the subject which response is most effective in that situation—it causes that response to be selected because its connection to the stimulus situation becomes strengthened. The strengthened connection causes that response to move closer to the top of the **response hierarchy**—it becomes more likely than the responses that were originally ahead of it. Possible hierarchies of responses for Thorndike's cat in the puzzle box on the first trial and after several trials are illustrated in table 6.1.

Table 6.1 Possible Response Hierarchies for Thorndike's Cat

Before Conditioning	After Conditioning
R1 Grooming	R1 Pawing Latch
R2 Sleeping	R2 Pawing Cage
R3 Sniffing	R3 Walking Around
R4 Urinating	R4 Sniffing
R5 Walking Around	R5 Grooming
R6 Pawing Cage Parts	

Analyzing our examples in this way suggests that the child has a number of responses she makes in school, such as smiling at classmates, drawing, writing, reading, talking, primping, and so forth, along with raising her hand. We could notice how frequently each occurred in the class; her teacher's praise causes the hand raising to be more strongly associated with class and therefore to move up in the hierarchy. We can imagine another hierarchy being rearranged for the executive, and in both cases responding can be characterized as, "Well, I guess this is the best thing to do in these circumstances; I should choose this response now."

Another interesting S–R analysis of operant conditioning was that proposed by Edwin Guthrie (1935). Guthrie believed that each piece of learning took only one trial. Whatever the learner was doing just before reinforcement would be repeated the next time he was in that situation. If we remember Thorndike's puzzle box experiments, we can appreciate how Guthrie's theory worked. He noted that the last response made, operating the latch mechanism, caused the cat to be removed from the puzzle box. This reinforcement prevents any other responses from being made in the puzzle box, and therefore, the next time the cat is in the puzzle box, it is likely to try to operate the latch—it essentially starts up where it left off. After a number of reinforced trials, the response has become associated with all the possible stimulus cues in the puzzle box. It thus becomes the only response made. For Guthrie, reinforcement itself is only important as an element which, by being added to the situation, changes the situation. If the original starting conditions occur again, the learner repeats that last response. Our student and our executive might think, "This worked the last time, so I might as well try it again."

There are two problems with an S–R description of operant conditioning. One is that it doesn't provide for the creature learning anything about the reinforcement itself. In other words, it shouldn't matter whether we train the pigeon in a Skinner box with food or water; it is still learning to peck in the box. In our examples, the child and the executive will respond the same whether we use food, money, or just praise to change their responding. In such a view, the pigeon isn't learning to "expect" the food; however, several experimenters have shown that the pigeon gradually develops different pecking responses for food and water (Moore, 1973). Other experiments have shown that although changing from one reinforcer to another can be done, sometimes this leads to a temporary disruption of behavior, as if the learner is searching for its usual reward. So the learner is certainly learning something about the reinforcement, as well as about the discriminative stimulus and the response. Reinforcing the child with money rather than praise could lead to several kinds of change in the way she raises her hand, depending on her age and sophistication about cultural norms. On the other hand, few executives are likely to show changes in their response hierarchies for praise as dramatic as the changes they show for raises.

The second problem with the S–R interpretation of operant conditioning is that in a strict interpretation, it suggests that the learner is just making a reflexive reaction to the discriminative stimulus as it does in classical conditioning. This is not especially likely. If we train a rat to run through a maze for food, then flood the maze and make the rat swim through it to get food, the rat shows good transfer of learning (MacFarlane, 1930). In this case it's clear our rat hasn't learned a particular reflexive reaction to the situation but has instead learned that it has to somehow get to the end of the maze to get food.

Thus, both the S–R and S–S accounts of operant conditioning have strong elements of classical conditioning as their main ingredients. S–S accounts describe operant conditioning as the acquisition of a learned incentive. To understand this idea we must not focus on the usual discriminative stimulus presented by the experimenter, but on the stimulus last encountered by the learner, as Guthrie suggested. In other words, our rat in the Skinner box is touching the bar just before being rewarded. Perhaps it learns to associate the bar with food (the S–S association). This idea, best presented by Bindra (1974), suggests that reinforcers have two motivational effects. They generate an increase in activity level, and they elicit reactions of approach toward positive reinforcers and withdrawal away from negative reinforcers. These approach or withdrawal reactions become conditioned to the stimulus closest to the reinforcer itself. Thus, the bar basically becomes a CS that elicits approach because it is immediately followed by the food. Pressing the bar is just one way to be close to it. This type of analysis has actually received some experimental support by combining a CS learned in one procedure with a separate operant situation. The two-factor theory of avoidance is an example of this type of analysis. The results are compatible with this S–S theory except when a positive CS (which should generate approach) is combined with a positive reinforcement procedure. This procedure should lead to faster responding when the two positive elements are combined, but it rarely does.

The major problem for this type of analysis is the same as the problem with S–R explanations: The exact form of the response is either immaterial or determined by classical considerations to be reflexive. However, the rat doesn't just stay near the bar, it usually ends up pressing it. A response that could be of any form should show more variability of form. And to describe bar pressing, raising one's hand, or writing reports as reflexes is stretching the definition of reflexes quite a bit. Williams (1965) has shown that reflexive salivation and operant responding to food are often poorly correlated. This means that the operant response does not occur to stimuli in the very regular fashion that reflexes do. However, these ideas do point out that the learner in an operant situation is learning some classical associations as well, and that these associations may affect the operant performance.

Skinner argued that in many cases it was very difficult to specify the antecedent discriminative stimuli. Furthermore, these stimuli often don't seem to be especially unique in generating a response hierarchy set. In other words, in any given situation many responses could be made, and these same responses could be made in many other situations as well. Although not totally ignoring the stimuli that precede a response, Skinner did reduce their importance drastically. He preferred to focus on the establishment of an R–S association in which the learner is taught, "If I make this response, I get this reward." He felt that the subject learns a contingency between its efforts and environmental consequences. The contingency actually has two parts to it, because the individual learns a differential pair of relationships: "If I write this report, I'll get a raise; but if I don't finish it on time, I won't get the raise."

Skinner recognized that we could add the discriminating function of preceding stimuli to the contingency description if we wished. That is, our learner could be acquiring the following contingency: "When I see this signal, if I make this response I get a reward, and if I don't I won't; but when I see that other signal, whether I make this response or not, nothing will happen." However, this last type of contingency is awkward; we really had to create a complicated description to fit in all three pieces of the contingency. Furthermore, Skinner felt that it added little to our understanding of the situation; by far the most important aspect of the situation is the R–S contingency. He showed that manipulation of this contingency has dramatic effects on performance with his descriptions of the schedules of reinforcement. Changes in the scheduling of reinforcement produced precisely corresponding changes in the pattern of responding.

Skinner's argument emphasizes the power of reinforcers in manipulating responses. As we noted in chapter 4, in addition to changing schedules, we can change the amount or delay of the reinforcement and show dramatic effects on responding. Changing a discriminative stimulus in these ways has a much different effect. If we train a subject to press a bar when a red light comes on, is it likely to press more if we use a brighter light? Of course not, nor would it help to make the light a different shade of red, or move it to a different spot, or make the light come from a larger area. The specific nature of the discriminative stimulus is irrelevant to the learner's performance. Skinner was not very interested in theoretical issues, so although he recognized that the subject might be learning what he called a **three-term contingency,** he felt that we need only be concerned with the nature of the two-term contingency relating response and reinforcer.

The trouble with a strict R–S_{r+} account is that it works fine in explaining things while the subject is making the response, but it doesn't say anything about why the response would be made in the first place. That is, what happens before the response that results in the response occurring? An R–S_{r+} description requires another association that includes signals before the response indicating that it's time to make the response.

Rescorla (1987; Rescorla & Holland, 1982) proposed a cognitive model that emphasizes not only the R–S_{r+} association, but also the interaction of this association with the S–S_{r+} classical contingency present in operant conditioning. Several experiments, summarized by Colwill and Rescorla (1986), show the importance of these two associations. The R–S_{r+} association is supported by research that trains two responses, each for a different reward. Then one reward is devalued in some fashion, and we notice what happens to the response associated with it. This is commonly done by associating that reinforcer with illness. For example, if food and water are the two reinforcers, after the subject has learned to push a lever for food, pull a chain for water, and responds at a stable rate, we pair the food with lithium chloride (which causes nausea when consumed) and then find that our rat keeps on pulling the chain a lot but slows way down in lever pushes.

In the clearest demonstration, Colwill and Rescorla (1986) trained rats to push the same manipulandum to the left for one reinforcer and to the right for another. There are no differences in the discriminative stimuli for the two contingencies, so S–S and S–R associations can have little effect on performance. The only difference is in the response; two different responses to associate with two different reinforcers. As the experimenters expected, the pushes in the direction that obtained the devalued reinforcer declined dramatically, and the pushes in the other direction increased slightly (because of the matching law, described in chapter 4). These subjects had clearly associated one response with one reinforcer and another response with the other reinforcer.

Rescorla (1987) extended the R–S_{r+} account by incorporating a classical S–S_{r+} association. He felt that the classical association could influence the likelihood of the R–S_{r+} association being formed. He felt that some discriminative stimuli will function more effectively in prompting the response. These occasion-setting stimuli are those that are more likely to generate the response; this can be predicted from a knowledge of the way they function as classical conditioned stimuli. For example, knowledge of any CS overshadowing or blocking effects, and knowledge of the nature of the CR and its relation to the operant response, may be necessary to understand the operant situation. Some of our discussion of two-factor theories of avoidance conditioning in chapter 5 shows the same kind of analysis. Although the $R–S_{r+}$ is the crucial association formed, it cannot stand alone; some classical conditioning must occur in operant conditioning for operant responding to occur.

Why Does Reinforcement Work?

The remainder of this chapter will address a question that has perplexed learning psychologists since Thorndike's time: Why do reinforcers work? Why will rats, pigeons, and people work to obtain food, water, and other rewards and work to eliminate painful or unpleasant stimuli? This may seem a trivial question; to most of us, it's obvious why creatures work for food and water and work to avoid pain. Our bodies need food and water to survive, and our bodies suffer when exposed to pain, and that's why reinforcers work the way they do. However, it turns out that even these "obvious" cases are more complicated than they seem. Let us first deal with this "obvious" answer.

Drive-Reduction Theories

The idea that food and water are reinforcing because they satisfy bodily needs is known as **drive-reduction theory**. It was described most thoroughly by Clark Hull and Kenneth Spence, and our presentation of this theory will basically follow their description (Hull, 1943). Simply put, they proposed the following formula to describe the process of reinforcement:

$$N \rightarrow D \rightarrow R \rightarrow S_{r+}$$

N stands for physical needs; in the case of food, this means that our body tissues require nutrients to survive. D stands for the psychological drive, in this case, hunger. R is the response, and S_{r+} is the reinforcer of food. The physical need for nutrients causes a psychological drive—the hunger drive—which makes us more active and directs our activity to seeking out food. The response that obtains food is reinforced by the food because food satisfies the physical need for nutrients. When the need is satisfied and therefore reduced, so is the drive, and therefore the behavior stops. This seemingly obvious description led to a large number of experiments of many types designed to discover the details of this drive-reduction system and to verify it. Unfortunately, as more was learned about the nature of hunger, the obvious drive-reduction theory looked poorer and poorer as an explanation.

Local Theory. The key to drive-reduction theories is connecting the physical needs to the psychological drives. Many experiments over the years have shown that this connection is so complex that verification of the drive-reduction theory is extremely difficult. Early research established that *local* stimulation played a role in initiating drives but were not crucial. Local means the sensations outside the central nervous system that are specific to the drive. In other words, the empty feelings in your stomach may cause hunger, or the dryness in the mouth may cause thirst. W. B. Cannon showed that stomach contractions were accompanied by reports of feeling hungry (Cannon & Washburn, 1912). However, reports of feeling hungry peak at one's customary mealtime and gradually decline, even if the person has not eaten. Furthermore, when Hull surgically diverted a dog's esophagus, he showed that the dog ate a normal amount, stopping after it had swallowed a typical meal, even though no food reached its stomach (Hull, Livingston, Rouse, & Barker, 1951). The dog persisted in this sham eating for eight nights. Local sensations alone are not sufficient to explain the need–drive relationship.

Central Theory. Research next examined the role of *central* factors in hunger and thirst and indicated that areas in the **hypothalamus** of the brain are sensitive to the composition of the blood flowing through the arteries and veins. For hunger, these hypothalamic centers measure the concentration of glucose, or blood sugar. If the blood in the arteries contains about as much glucose as the blood in the veins, then body tissues are not receiving any more glucose than they are excreting. This basically represents a state of hunger, whereas a high concentration of glucose in the arteries relative to the veins indicates lots of food going to body tissues, so that the creature has no need for food (Mayer, 1955). Experiments on animals indicated that when these "start eating" areas were stimulated with implanted electrodes, the animal would eat (Miller, 1958), while destroying them made the animal abstain from eating (Teitelbaum & Stellar, 1954). Furthermore, there was another area of the hypothalamus that seemed to be a "stop eating" center; when stimulated, it caused the animal to stop eating, and if it was damaged, the animal ate as long as food was available. Destruction of the "stop eating" area of the hypothalamus led to rats that weighed three times the weight of normal rats (Hetherington & Ranson, 1940).

However, in addition to glucose sensitivity, hunger is also influenced by lipid (fat) levels in the body (Carpenter & Grossman, 1983; Kennedy, 1953). The mechanism for lipid sensitivity has not been fully determined and may be in the hypothalamus or through a local detector in the liver (Friedman & Stricker, 1976). For a "stop eating" center to act, the food consumed must be converted to glucose and sent into the circulatory system. The activity of the "stop eating" center begins long before the digestion of the food has produced enough glucose to activate the center.

Regions of the hypothalamus also have been identified as thirst-regulating centers that also seem to work in an opposing "check and balance" fashion (Teitelbaum & Epstein, 1962). These "start drinking" and "stop drinking" centers are sensitive to the saltiness of the blood. A high concentration of salt in the bloodstream indicates that the salt is dissolved in a relatively small amount of water, meaning the creature is thirsty. Here again, several other factors are involved in thirst and in water retention, but clearly the hypothalamus and the regions connected to it are involved. More recent research has demonstrated that the hypothalamus plays a role in locomotor approach, or the tendency of the creature to move forward and explore the environment (reviewed by Glickman & Schiff, 1967; also see Glickman, 1973). Thus, it seems that the hypothalamus and the brain centers connected to it are the mechanisms that convert bodily needs to psychological drives.

Unfortunately, several experiments reveal weaknesses in this central drive-reduction theory. One problem is that the system apparently can be fooled by artificial sweeteners such as saccharin. In several classic experiments, Sheffield demonstrated that a saccharine solution would not only reinforce learning a simple maze, but would do so more effectively than a nutritive but less sweet dextrose solution (Sheffield & Roby, 1950; Sheffield, Roby, & Campbell, 1954). The problem here is that saccharin, like all of the artificial sweeteners, was created for the express purpose of providing no food value. Why would a psychological drive be reduced by a nonnutritive substance (one that does not reduce the physical need)? Furthermore, an experiment by Miller and Kessen (1952) revealed that milk was more reinforcing when consumed by mouth than when it was pumped directly into the stomach. What difference should it make to the hypothalamus how the glucose gets there? Drive-reduction theory doesn't have much to say about this kind of problem.

Thus, we see that the seemingly very straightforward idea of reinforcement being caused by the action of food on body systems had to evolve into a complex theory with many details still missing. Hunger and thirst represent the two drives that fit a drive-reduction model best, and even for them the theory is complex and has difficulty with some findings. Drive-reduction explanations of fear or pain avoidance have been proposed with slightly less success than the hunger and thirst descriptions. However, the drive-reduction idea has a great deal of commonsense appeal to it and has received some support. Two important consequences of the attempt to salvage something out of drive-reduction theories are the ideas of secondary reinforcement and homeostatic motivation. Both of these concepts attempt to explain reinforcers that drive-reduction theory doesn't explain well.

Homeostatic Theory. Homeostatic theories follow the basic form of drive-reduction theory except that they provide for cases where the learner responds to *increase* the level of the drive or need as well as decrease it. The clearest example of such a situation would be body temperature regulation. Mammals maintain an optimum (best or most desirable) body temperature—the familiar 98.6 degrees for humans. If our bodies get heated above this level, our nervous systems cause us to try to get rid of the excess heat by sweating and becoming less active. This is consistent with a drive-reduction interpretation. However, our nervous systems also try to increase our activity level when our body temperature falls much below 98.6 by making us more active, making us shiver, and so forth. Such attempts are the exact opposite of drive reduction.

The attempt to maintain an intermediate body condition is referred to as **homeostasis**, and the notion that some drives may act to either increase or decrease body levels depending on the current status of the body seems to fit a number of drives very well. In particular, the sex drive, rest and activity cycles, and stimulation-seeking behavior such as curiosity and exploration seem to be fairly well explained by homeostatic mechanisms. That is, in each case the organism sometimes works to reduce the level of tension or arousal and sometimes works to increase the level of arousal or tension. For example, after being at a wild party with a large, energetic crowd, the peace and quiet of one's own bed seem welcome. On the other hand, a few hours of sitting in front of a textbook in a quiet room can make one wish for some noise and activity. We can view these as our attempts to maintain a homeostatic balance of amount of stimulation. Unfortunately, the appeal of the homeostatic idea is lessened when we try to find physical reasons and mechanisms behind these drives. Why do creatures need some optimum level of stimulation or activity? So far the answer to this question has eluded us.

More recent physiological research, reviewed by Rolls (2000) indicates possible homeostatic mechanisms in the lower part of the frontal lobe and also suggest solutions to some of the drive reduction problems. This research mostly involved monitoring the nervous system activity of monkeys in positive reinforcement situations using food rewards, although there are some studies of human hospital patients. Rolls describes two centers, a primary sensory cortex where the taste is represented and a secondary cortical area, the orbitofrontal cortex (approximately the lower frontal lobe area), which seems to represent the reward value of the taste. The activity of this secondary area decreases as the reward value of the stimulus decreases (in other words, this region stops reacting when the creature becomes full, which leads to decreased activity—the creature stops eating). This pattern helps make sense out of the "stop eating" problem; Rolls states that it is likely that habituation in this region reduces the desire for additional amounts of the reward. He states that this allows the primary cortex to remain active even when the creature is not hungry. This allows for these representations to be involved in activities other than those involving reward, such as recalling memories or forming them. Thus, an animal may still learn where a food source is even when not hungry—if you are driving around in the afternoon and you smell doughnuts, you can resolve to go by that same corner and stop for some the next morning.

Rolls (2000) indicates that this frontal lobe region allows for both taste and smell characteristics to be combined and also is involved in touch and pain responsiveness. It seems to be a center that allows reinforcers and punishers to become more general in their function; instead of a reinforcer being strictly associated with one response, it may be treated as a goal that may be obtained by several kinds of action as a result of the way it is represented there. Rolls suggests that this center essentially evaluates whether a reward is expected and generates mismatch messages when a reward is not obtained when expected; thus, this center allows for many of the phenomena discussed in chapters 4 and 5; for example, patterns of responding during extinction and on schedules of reinforcement may be the result of activity here. Damage to this area in humans may result in socially inappropriate behavior, inability to modify one's behavior to minimize negative consequences, and inability to appreciate emotional expressions on human faces. (A smiling face is often associated with the delivery of a reward, but a frowning or angry face is usually associated with punishers.) The major neurotransmitter involved in learning about both rewarding and punishing events seems to be dopamine.

The orbitofrontal cortex is connected to many brain areas, including the hypothalamus (which we have already learned is a key mechanism involved in hunger, thirst, and other drives) and the amygdala, another part of the limbic system. The amygdala also receives input from several sensory systems and sends output to these systems, to the hypothalamus, and to centers that influence motor output (the motor cortex and/or the corpus striatum) and is thus well suited to combining several inputs. Rolls (2000) describes research indicating that changes in the amygdala occur during the learning of reinforcement relationships, including the development of secondary reinforcers, and suggests that the amygdala is the brain center that supports the development of operant associations, especially information relevant to approaching or avoiding. Rolls suggests that the frontal lobe–amygdala system allows for the development of generalized emotional states that often serve as motivational forces.

Secondary Reinforcement

Thus far, even a combination of drive-reduction explanations for some reinforcers and homeostatic explanations for others leaves us with some problem reinforcers. There are some reinforcers, particularly with humans, that don't fit either explanation well. It seems unlikely that the reinforcing abilities of money, grades in school, and such social reinforcers as attention and smiles are due to physical needs. Attempts to explain these reinforcers led to the concept of secondary reinforcement, which suggests that they are learned reinforcers. That is, money, smiles, and attention acquire their ability to reinforce through being paired with primary reinforcers. Thus we have two classes of reinforcers: **primary reinforcers**, which are based on innate physical needs, and **secondary reinforcers**, which are learned. Drive-reduction and homeostatic theories represent the mechanisms of the primary drives. The secondary drives are learned through their association with primary drives.

Traditionally, secondary reinforcement has been presented as involving the operation of classical conditioning during operant reinforcement. Imagine our rat in the standard Skinner box situation, learning to press the bar for food when a signal light comes on. Because the signal is always present when the rat gets food, it is also a CS associated with food. As a CS it becomes capable of eliciting the responses normally elicited by the US. For food, these responses include the internal events that serve as reinforcers. Therefore, the rat will press the bar whenever the light comes on. However, in this example the light may not be acquiring reinforcing properties but merely the ability of a discriminative stimulus to signal that a response–primary reinforcer contingency is in effect—the occasion-setting function discussed in the previous section. To alleviate this problem we can wait for the bar-pressing response to occur, then turn on the light, and then deliver the food reward. Many experimenters have followed this design and demonstrated that the light acquires the ability to reinforce bar pressing under these circumstances (reviewed by Longstreth, 1971).

With such a design, the influence of standard classical conditioning variables becomes clear. The strength or amount of the primary reinforcement (US) influences the effectiveness of a secondary reinforcer paired with it (D'Amato, 1955). In addition, Bersh (1951) showed that timing and number of pairings were important influences on the effectiveness of a secondary reinforcer. He found that a stimulus that preceded the food by a half second or one second became a much more effective secondary reinforcer than stimuli that occurred simultaneously with the food or that preceded it by longer intervals. Note that these are the results often found for the standard delayed classical conditioning procedure.

Bersh (1951) also found that increasing the number of such pairings from 20 to 120 increased the effectiveness of the light as a secondary reinforcer. The effectiveness of secondary reinforcers typically has been examined by using them by themselves to reinforce a response, often the same one initially used during training. This kind of test is basically an examination of the resistance of the secondary reinforcer to extinction; in fact, most laboratory studies have shown that the usefulness of secondary reinforcers is relatively temporary. This seems in marked contrast to the influence of secondary reinforcers in real life. Money, praise, and congratulations seem to be relatively durable reinforcers for most of us.

To explain the greater durability of secondary reinforcers in real life, Miller (1961; Eggar & Miller, 1963) suggested that the basis for secondary reinforcers was their informational value—that is, the secondary reinforcer tells us that a primary reinforcer is on the way. During extinction, this informational value is eliminated because the contingency is not in effect. Thus, the effectiveness of money as a secondary reinforcer is a result of its continuing ability to predict the occurrence of primary reinforcement. It is not so much the initial classical pairing of stimuli that is important but rather the continued existence of the contingency between them. But is this contingency a classical one or an operant one? In other words, we can distinguish between our learner being aware that money and food occur together (a classical contingency between two stimuli) and our learner being aware that the money can be used to obtain food (an operant contingency between a response and a stimulus). Several experimenters have shown that this second contingency exists and is extremely important in determining the effectiveness of token economies.

Token economies are applications of secondary reinforcement principles, primarily in institutional settings such as schools (Ayllon & Azrin, 1968). Tokens are easily manipulated objects given to individuals such as students, as rewards for good work or behavior. Their convenient form means they can be given immediately after the desired response. After the learner has accumulated a sufficient number of tokens, she can turn them in for some reward of her own choosing. Token economies have proved effective in a wide variety of settings (Kazdin, 1994) and have remained popular for several decades. Often in token economy applications the contingent relationship between the tokens and the ultimate reinforcers is merely explained to the learner at the outset. In such cases, the classical contingency may not be directly experienced by the learner until she has earned sufficient tokens to "buy" a reinforcer. Therefore, one can easily argue that the learner is in fact learning an operant contingency in which, if she responds by turning in a certain number of tokens, she will receive the reinforcer. The secondary nature of such an arrangement may be that the response of buying, or turning in tokens, is reinforcing other responses. Currently, the exact nature of secondary reinforcement is not well understood, with several theories equally plausible as explanations (Williams, 1988).

The concept of secondary reinforcement is extremely important because it greatly broadens the range of influence that operant conditioning may have. Because token economies have been successfully created artificially, the interpretation of money as a secondary reinforcer seems quite plausible. We may further extend this concept to the explanation of the social reinforcers as well. Receiving attention or a smile is an experience that is often followed by further positive stimulation, especially in the experience of children. This type of explanation was originally proposed by Watson (1919), illustrated by his conditioning of emotion in Little Albert.

Responding as Reinforcement

The problems with the concept of primary reinforcement illustrated in our discussion of drive reduction and homeostasis have led some learning theorists to an entirely different reaction to the question of why things are reinforcing. The ultimate pragmatic reaction to the question "Why do reinforcers work?" was that proposed by B. F. Skinner. Because of the difficulties encountered by drive-reduction theories, he suggested that the question was not worth answering in the traditional way they proposed. Instead, Skinner answered the question with the definition of positive reinforcers: any stimulus that, when delivered contingent on a response, increases the probability of that response. A reinforcer is reinforcing because it works that way.

Before you reject this approach as begging the question, consider the practical consequence of it. Skinner pointed out that few if any of the things we call reinforcers always work as reinforcers. Food won't reinforce an individual who has just eaten, and if we use too little food and/or require too much work, we may not increase the desired response. By definition, in such cases food is not functioning as a reinforcer. Skinner suggested that the only way we can identify reinforcers is by trying them out and seeing what happens. If the behavior changes in the predicted way, then we have a positive reinforcer; if not, then we don't. This use of an operational definition avoids the problems sometimes encountered in applied settings when the user complains that reinforcement doesn't work. Often in such cases, the thing used as a reinforcer simply isn't functioning as one. This approach may at first appear circular: we define things as reinforcers when they reinforce. One of Skinner's colleagues, P. E. Meehl (1950), proposed a solution to this circularity problem by suggesting that, once we have identified a reinforcer, we may use it to reinforce other responses besides the one used to identify it. In other words, we can show that it works as a reinforcer in many other situations. Meehl called this the principle of **transsituationality**.

One of Skinner's students, David Premack, took his operational idea in another direction. He combined it with the idea mentioned in our discussion of secondary reinforcement—that responding may be reinforcing. He assumed that it is not objects that are reinforcing, but activities. It is not food that is reinforcing, but the act of eating. Food just provides the opportunity for eating behavior to occur. Certainly the experiments of Hull and his colleagues (1951) and Miller and Kessen (1952) described earlier in this chapter show that eating behaviors still occur even in the absence of their usual need-reducing consequences. Premack suggested that the best way to identify reinforcers was to look for frequent behaviors. After all, why would a creature do something frequently unless it was reinforcing? If we allow an individual to behave freely, we can assume that the things in which it engages the most are positively reinforcing. However, Premack also suggested that these reinforcers would only work as reinforcers for less frequent activities—by this definition, responses capable of being reinforced must occur less often than the reinforcing activities. This has come to be known as the **Premack principle**, and he illustrated it with two classic experiments, one in the lab and one in an applied setting.

In the laboratory experiment, Premack (1962) showed that things may not be inherently reinforcing. He did this by showing that a thing we normally assume is a reinforcer, water, may be interchanged with a thing we normally assume is a reinforceable response, running. He allowed rats free access to an activity wheel and a drinking trough and observed their operant levels of running and drinking. On the basis of their relative amounts of running and drinking he divided the rats into two groups. One group consisted of rats that spent more time running than drinking, and the other group spent more time drinking than running. Then Premack instituted a reinforcement contingency based on his principle. For the group of rats that spent more time running, he made access to the running wheel contingent on drinking; the other group, which drank more than they ran, had to run in order to receive access to the water. Each activity defined as a response in this way increased in frequency as a result of requiring it for the rat to obtain the activity defined as a reinforcer. In other words, the rats who initially ran more increased their drinking when running was contingent on drinking, and the rats who initially drank more increased their running when drinking was contingent on running.

In his applied demonstration, Premack (1959) observed children with free access to two activities, playing a pinball machine and eating candy. The pinball machine and the candy dispenser were placed next to each other, and the pinball machine was rewired to operate continuously. Some children displayed a higher rate of candy eating than pinball playing, and others showed more pinball playing than candy eating. Premack was able to increase the level of their less frequent activity by making their more frequent activity contingent on it. The "eaters" played more pinball and the "players" ate more candy.

The Premack principle was somewhat radical when initially proposed. First, it contradicted Meehl's (1950) principle of transsituationality; it suggested that a thing determined to be a reinforcer might not always work as one. Second, it contradicted the notion that there was a special class of things or events that were reinforcing. Reinforcers were not necessarily things that were pleasant, reduced drives, led to consummatory behavior, changed arousal level, or activated specific neural centers. Instead, Premack's principle suggested that there were no special objects, that reinforcement was a temporary property determined by the relationship of the contingent activity to the response. Because of its radical approach, the Premack principle received a great deal of attention, both in support and in criticism. The support emphasized the ease of its application, its apparent simplicity, and its ability to make accurate predictions. The criticisms focused on shortcomings: the principle didn't always seem to work; it didn't seem easy to apply it to the reinforcement of behaviors more tedious than exercise, games, and consumption; and there was no corresponding version of it to explain punishment. However, Premack (1965) demonstrated a punishment version of the principle that simply reversed the order of the contingency; if a less probable behavior is made contingent on a more probable behavior, then the more probable behavior will be suppressed.

The ease and simplicity of the principle turned out to be somewhat deceptive. Although it appears very easy to employ (you just count the number of each of two activities during the individual's free time), in practice such measurement can be tricky. What constitutes one drink from the water trough? Premack attempted to avoid this problem by recording time spent on the activity, but several researchers showed that accurate measurement of time was somewhat dependent on how one defined a drink (Allison, 1989). Does one count the time in between sips, while the individual is swallowing? Because chewing is more time consuming, might we conclude that eating is a more probable behavior than drinking, and establish a contingency on that basis? These measurement problems, although not serious, make the principle somewhat less easy to use than at first appearance.

A more important criticism is that the principle didn't always work. Premack's (1965) analysis of the failures of his principle was that in each case the contingency was arranged so that the creature could perform its normal amount of the most probable (reinforcing) activity without increasing its level of performing the less probable (response) behavior. In other words, in each case, he suggested that the contingency requirement had been too lenient. However, other analyses, particularly those of Allison and Timberlake (1973, 1974), suggested that the action of reinforcement was less dependent on the probabilities of behaviors relative to each other; instead, the current frequency of a behavior relative to its usual frequency was the important factor.

Timberlake and Allison suggested that the usual effect of operant conditioning experiments was to restrict the learner's access to an intended reinforcer. In other words, if we wished to use food as a reinforcer, we keep the rat hungry for the day before the experiment. If the animal's normal baseline level of eating was 45 minutes a day, and we decrease its opportunity to eat to zero, we can effectively use food (or more properly, the opportunity to eat) as a reinforcer. This opportunity to eat will function as a reinforcer until the rat has been able to perform it as frequently as usual. Timberlake and Allison (1974) modified Premack's original experiment by simply creating contingencies that reduced the rat's rate of performing the response used as a reinforcer. In other words, if they wished to use running in the running wheel as a reinforcer, the contingency they devised required lots of drinking for access to a little bit of running. On the other hand, if they wished to use drinking as the reinforcer, the animal had to run a lot for access to a little water. The important aspect of the schedule was not that lots of responding was demanded, however; instead, it was that the reinforcing activity was restricted. If the animal failed to make the required response, it got much less of the reinforcing activity than normal, which motivated it to respond more in order to get closer to the baseline level of the reinforcing activity.

Timberlake and Allison interpret the effect of reinforcement as being a mechanism that regulates behavior. They suggest that the learner has a hierarchy of preferred responses (as Thorndike suggested) that is the optimum arrangement for her; that particular arrangement of frequency of responding leads to the best results for her. This is easy enough to imagine for the executive and student examples we described earlier. Each learner makes many responses, arranged so that she obtains the greatest total of rewards. The executive does some report writing, some phone calling, some meeting attending, and so forth, and overall is regarded as a good worker, thus getting her raise. The exact proportions of each activity are determined by the relationship between that activity and the accessibility of the reinforcer associated with it relative to the accessibility of other reinforcers. (Accessibility implies that the individual may not have had as much of a reinforcer as she wants during a particular interval.) The function of reinforcers is to adjust the relative occurrence of responses and their sequence so as to maximize the overall amount of reinforcement. In addition, the effectiveness of a reinforcer is influenced by the particular response chosen and the alternatives to that response. If our executive is especially good at writing reports but does not like to give presentations orally, she may try to spend more time obtaining reinforcement through report writing than through giving talks.

We can appreciate the ideas suggested by Premack and by Timberlake and Allison by noting our reactions to various tasks and chores we encounter regularly. For example, most college students have had occasions where chores such as cleaning their room or washing their car became less unpleasant or even mildly enjoyable. If you remember such an incident, think about the surrounding events. Often these tasks become somewhat preferred in comparison to other difficult tasks that we have had to do frequently for an extended period, such as studying for tests or writing papers. Timberlake and Allison would say that our opportunity to engage in cleaning behavior had been artificially suppressed below baseline by school requirements. Our satisfaction at completing cleaning chores at these times would suggest to them that the opportunity to clean could be used as a reinforcer for us for a while. You might also notice the high rate of car washing in the spring, after opportunities to engage in this activity have been restricted by cold weather all winter. Furthermore, once we have "caught up" in our car-washing activity (during the summer), we find it less rewarding.

The most important implication of the Premack principle is that we must observe naturally occurring baseline behaviors to determine what will function as reinforcers. We can't just assume that something we think is pleasant (or unpleasant) will function as a reward (or punisher), or even that a proven reinforcer will always function as one. As a consequence, if we wish to reinforce an activity, we must find another activity through observing the learner that is more probable for him. Then we must arrange a contingency that restricts that activity unless the desired response is performed more often. Timberlake and Allison would suggest that we wouldn't have to compare the rates of the two activities, just suppress the rate of the activity we wish to use as the reinforcer. However, they might also suggest that the effectiveness of our procedure would depend on our subject's opportunities for performing similar activities or substitute activities. Premack, as well as Timberlake and Allison, would suggest that any reinforcer we found would not be permanent. Premack would say this because he would claim that the effectiveness of the reinforcer would depend on what response we choose to modify. Timberlake and Allison would claim that the effectiveness of the reinforcer would depend on how much access to it was restricted and how much restriction occurred.

Learning theorists have come to favor this approach to explaining reinforcement because it focuses our attention on aspects of the learning situation that we might be able to change. Although understanding the physiological mechanisms of common reinforcers is important, and although much progress has been made in this type of research, it has not led to very many ideas about how to reinforce better. The more pragmatic approach initiated by Skinner has proved more useful thus far, because it has led to new suggestions for arranging reinforcement contingencies. The emphasis on careful observation and recording of the learner's activities as a guide to choosing reinforcers has proved to be a very useful technique in behavior modification programs (Alberto & Troutman, 1982).

Summary

There are three possible associations between pairs of elements in the operant conditioning procedure. The initial idea of an S–R connection, favored by Thorndike, suffers from its emphasis on reflexlike responses. The idea emphasized by Skinner—of R–S_{r+} associations—is generally assumed to be the key association in operant conditioning. However, even the supporters of this approach, such as Rescorla, have recognized that learners need some association between these events and an event that comes before them both. Rescorla has combined the R–S_{r+} association with a classical S–S_{r+} association to provide the most promising account so far of what is learned in operant conditioning.

The mechanisms of reinforcement have proved even more difficult to pin down. The idea that reinforcers satisfy bodily needs, as proposed by drive-reduction theories, has some shortcomings and has been difficult to describe precisely at the physiological level, although some progress has been made. Skinner proposed that we avoid this kind of explanation and focus instead on the practical approach of defining under what conditions a particular reinforcer works. Premack suggested that the value of a reinforcer was not absolute, but rather a function of the immediate frequency of occurrence of that reinforcing activity relative to the frequency of occurrence of other activities. He suggested that reinforcement was relative: his principle was that behaviors engaged in frequently would function as reinforcers for behaviors less frequently engaged in. Timberlake and Allison suggested that a better description would compare the immediate rate of an activity to its usual rate. They indicated that any behavior occurring less frequently than usual could function as a reinforcer.

Questions for Discussion, Thought, and Practice

1. Define and give an example of each of the key concepts. Use each concept in a sentence, then see if you can arrange the sentences into a few meaningful paragraphs, adding transitional sentences if necessary.
2. List at least five or six typical activities you do in a morning. Then try to identify how they have been reinforced. Has the reinforcement caused you to arrange them in particular sequences or to devote more or less time to them? For example, why do you brush your teeth when you do?
3. Different kinds of creatures may learn different kinds of associations in operant conditioning. Which creatures might be more likely to learn S–R associations, and which might learn R–S_{r+} associations?
4. Natasha calls her Uncle Boris every day but only calls Grandma Badinov once a week. How could we use the Premack principle to get her to talk to Granny more often?

seven

Generalization and Discrimination

▲ KEY CONCEPTS ▲

algebraic summation theory
asymmetrical
behavioral contrast
continuity theory
discrimination
generalization
gradient
Lashley-Wade hypothesis
noncontinuity theory
peak shift
relational theory
S+ and S–
semantic generalization
simultaneous discrimination
stimulus dimension
successive discrimination
symmetrical
transposition

Generalization is the tendency to apply what you have learned to new, similar situations. When Pavlov trained a dog to salivate when it heard a bell ring, he could show that the dog would also salivate to other sounds. In fact, the amount that the dog salivated to a new sound depended on how much that new sound resembled the original sound. Generalization can be shown not only in classical conditioning but also in operant conditioning and in our two primitive forms of learning, habituation and sensitization. All forms of learning exhibit generalization tendencies, and it's a good thing. Learning would be virtually useless without the tendency to apply that learning in new, related situations.

For example, imagine a mother teaching her child to look both ways before crossing the street outside her house. She begins with a combination of verbal instruction, modeling, and shaping. She holds onto him and says, "Now look to the left," and turns him that way. Then she turns him to the right and says, "Now look to the right, and if no cars are coming, you can cross the street." After doing this a few times, she watches him do it himself and rewards him with "Very good" if he does it right. If the child didn't generalize at all, he would carefully look both ways in front of his own house, but not at the corner intersection a few houses away, or downtown on the busy streets, or anywhere else. All these situations differ somewhat from the original situation. The differences may seem trivial to you, but that is probably because you have been generalizing your learning all your life and have come to easily recognize that such small differences are unimportant and can be safely ignored.

Discrimination is the technical term for the opposite of generalization; it is the tendency to distinguish between a new situation and the original learning situation when they must be distinguished. For example, it usually isn't necessary to look both ways when crossing from one side of the living room to another in your house, or to look both ways before crossing the hall at the mall. We discriminate between these situations and the street situation; that is, we probably respond differently to them because we have learned that it's useful to discriminate that way. Discrimination can also be easily demonstrated in all the forms of learning we have discussed. Because these phenomena are so universal, an understanding of how and why they work is essential for understanding learning. We will begin with generalization and then discuss discrimination.

Generalization

In our Pavlovian example, we mentioned that the amount of generalization could be predicted by noting the similarity of the new stimulus to the training stimulus. This is the fundamental principle determining the amount of generalization that a stimulus will produce. It is typically represented by a curve called the **gradient** of generalization, shown in figure 7.1. The horizontal axis of this graph represents some measure of physical similarity of the stimuli, with the training stimulus usually put in the middle and called an **S+**. Thus, stimuli similar to it are also near the middle, and as we move away from the middle to the left or right, we are showing that the stimuli we are testing are more and more different from the training stimulus. The vertical axis indicates amount of responding. At the middle, above S+, the curve is at its highest, indicating that the most responding occurs to our training stimulus, S+. The curve drops down on either side of the S+, getting lower the further we go in either direction, indicating less and less responding the further we get from the S+. The curve looks like this whether we are doing a classical conditioning study where S+ is a conditioned stimulus, such as our bell example,

Figure 7.1 The curve of generalization for colors when the subject has been trained with an S+ light of 550 nm

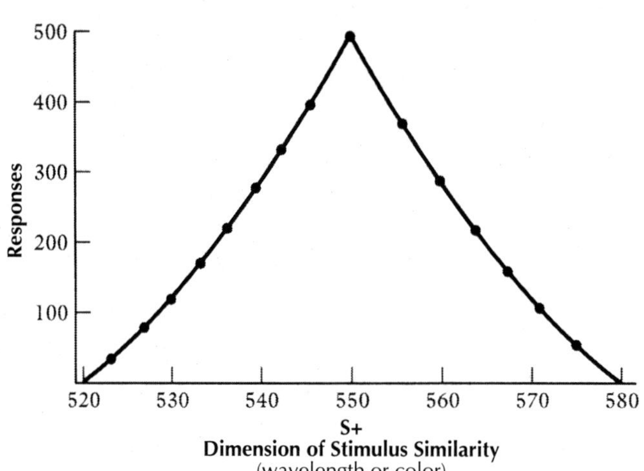

or an operant study. In an operant conditioning study, the S+ is a discriminative stimulus, such as a red cue light that tells the rat that it can receive a reward if it presses the bar while the light is on. In both cases, the amount of responding is predictable by noting the physical similarity of other stimuli to the training stimulus.

Notice that the curve is **symmetrical**—the left and right halves are mirror images of each other. In a classic experiment, Guttman and Kalish (1956) studied pigeons and obtained curves very much like this using a particular color as the S+ and food reinforcement and testing for generalization to other colors. They used four groups, each trained on a different color. They measured responding in their subjects during extinction, testing each subject on 11 other colors in a random order. After one series of all 11 colors, the subject was tested on all 11 again in a different random order. Twelve different series of the 11 colors were used. In this way they controlled for the effects of extinction, because these effects should have been about equal for each color. They obtained the four curves represented in figure 7.2. As you can see, each curve resembles our idealized graph fairly closely. Furthermore, this is generally what is found for any dimension we examine; for our classical bell example, we might find such a curve for pitch or frequency, loudness, duration, or complexity of the sounds. For the operant example studied by Guttman and Kalish, we would probably again find such a curve for color, brightness, size, position, orientation characteristics, or any other **stimulus dimension** on which we could measure a visual stimulus. Generalization is thus usually predictable on the basis of the physical similarity of the stimuli—the greater the physical similarity, the greater the generalization.

Figure 7.2 Generalization curves from four groups of subjects each trained with a different wavelength of light

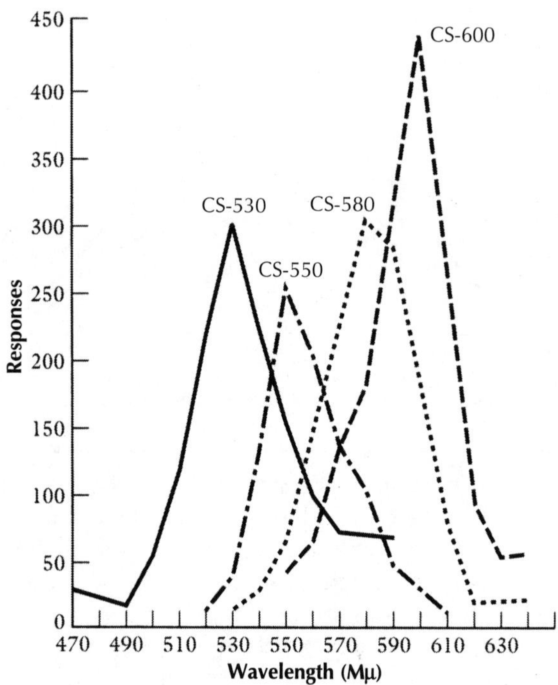

From "Discriminability and Stimulus Generalization," by N. Guttman & H. I. Kalish, 1956, *Journal of Experimental Psychology, 51*, 79–88.

There is one exception to the principle of physical similarity. If we study human beings and use a verbal stimulus as our S+, generalization will be based on the meaning of the word rather than on its appearance. Imagine that we classically condition a person using a mild electric shock and measuring his "fear" reaction with the GSR (galvanic skin response, one of the measures used in lie-detector tests). We show him a list of words, and every time the words *Chicago* or *Dallas* show up on the list, he receives the mild shock to his fingers. When we test for generalization, we find a strong GSR reaction to these cities and also a pretty strong response to other cities, such as Miami or Pittsburgh. However, we find much less response to *chicken* or *palace*, words that look and sound like the training words (Corteen & Wood, 1972). On the other hand, we would be unlikely to find this pattern of results if we used an infant in this study, because the infant has not acquired many word meanings. Thus, **semantic generalization** indicates that generalization tendencies are highly influenced by experience. Apparently, with a great deal of experience, people can learn a new dimension for generalizing, in this case a meaning dimension. In addition, this type of experiment suggests that some aspects of word meanings are acquired through a classical conditioning process. Semantic generalization is, of course, specific to humans and to the use of verbal stimuli. When actual objects are used, people generalize on the basis of the objects' physical characteristics.

The curves shown in figures 7.1 and 7.2 are often called excitatory generalization curves because they are the result of training the subject to make a response. On the other hand, recall that habituation involves training a subject not to respond; such a tendency is called an inhibitory response tendency. Habituation training also generalizes, producing an inhibitory generalization curve as shown in figure 7.3. Basically, this curve looks like the first curve upside down. It merely indicates that the tendency to not respond would be greatest for the training stimulus (here labeled S–) and decrease as we got further away from the training stimulus. Thus, a baby who has been habituated to a soft hum from a fan so that she no longer orients to it will also show little response to similar sounds, such as that of an electric razor, but may show some orientation to different sounds, such as a hair dryer, and will probably show the normal full orienting response to a bell.

Inhibitory response tendencies may also be generated in classical conditioning and operant conditioning procedures and would show these generalization tendencies. That is, in classical conditioning, for example, we might always ring a bell CS when no shock occurred but never when the shock US did occur. We would create an inhibitory CS; the bell signals safety and generates relief from fear in our subject. This inhibition of the

Figure 7.3 An inhibitory curve of generalization in which an S– of a 500 Hz tone has been habituated or extinguished

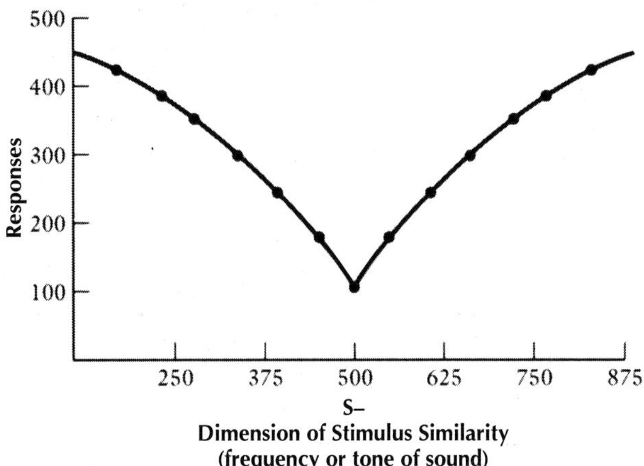

fear response would generalize around the bell (Weisman & Palmer, 1969). Finally, we could also extinguish some classically or operantly learned response in the presence of a particular stimulus. Extinction would also generate an inhibitory response tendency that would generalize in the same fashion as our generalization curve for habituation.

Control Procedures in Generalization Studies

Because the generalization gradient is obtained by noting the change in a subject's responding when different stimuli are presented, each subject is in a sense serving under both control and experimental conditions. However, generalization studies still require careful attention to details of procedure. First, the subject must be trained in the standard way, and it must be responding at a stable level. Then we may begin presenting other stimuli to test for generalization. However, we must remember that each presentation of a test stimulus is an extinction trial for that stimulus, because the only way to test is to present stimuli unaccompanied by any US or reinforcer. As we just noted, extinction or inhibitory tendencies generalize, so these test trials will also inhibit responding to neighboring stimuli, including the training stimulus. If we were to systematically move away from the training stimulus in our testing, these inhibitory tendencies would distort the generalization curve more and more as we went along. So testing must proceed by randomly picking stimuli from along the dimension we're studying and using a different random order for each subject. This should lead to all these little bits of extinction canceling each other out and thus having no systematic effect on the final curve. However, the problem of an overall decline in responding remains. Often this is controlled by interspersing the test trials among sets of training trials and regularly checking to ensure that responding to the S+ is maintained at a constant level.

Independent Variables that Influence Generalization

As we noted, the amount of responding to a particular test stimulus depends on its similarity to the training stimulus, as described by the generalization gradient. But what influences the shape of the gradient itself? Why is it not broader and flatter, indicating more generalization, or narrower and steeper, indicating less generalization (or more discrimination)? Only a few variables influence the slope of the generalization curve; one of the most important is the amount of practice (Hearst & Koresko, 1968). If we test our subject for generalization early, after only a few training trials, we see very low levels of responding to the S+ and also low levels of responding to most of our test stimuli. The result is a curve that looks very broad or flat, which indicates a great deal of generalization (the curve labeled a in figure 7.4). After more training trials, the response to the S+ is greater, and responding to test stimuli near it is also higher, although testing stimuli further away still reveals low levels of responding. This results in a steeper generalization curve, such as the curve labeled b in figure 7.4. Continuing training until performance to the S+ has reached a stable level generates the typical curve labeled c in figure 7.4. Extended training beyond this point sometimes results in an even steeper curve, but not always (Blough & Blough, 1977).

In addition to the total amount of practice, the schedule of reinforcement used during training, the variability in the training stimulus, and the delay between training and testing can influence the shape of the generalization gradient. Usually, a partial reinforcement schedule produces a steeper generalization curve than continuous reinforcement. Schedules that are relatively dense—that is, that allow the subject to obtain quite a lot of reinforcers—lead to the steepest generalization gradients (Haber & Kalish, 1963). For example, a variable ratio 3 schedule would lead to a steeper curve than a VR25, and a variable interval of 30 seconds would show steeper generalization gradients than a VI 2 minutes. These two variables illustrate that the amount of training and the type of training influence the degree of generalization. If we need to have a thoroughly trained individual, or we train her on a partial schedule, we will probably obtain less generalization. But if we wish this individual to generalize more, we would have to take steps to counteract these effects.

Varying the training stimulus is one way to give a lot of training while still obtaining a high degree of generalization. Varying the stimuli used during training has the effect of broadening the generalization curve. This might be best understood by thinking of variations in the S+ as actually being perceived by the learner as different stimuli. Thus, each stimulus would have a generalization curve about it that would be added

Figure 7.4 Curves of generalization after little (a), moderate (b), and thorough (c) training

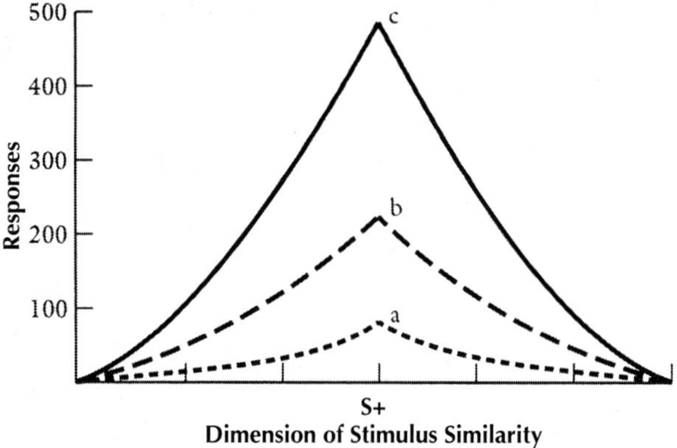

to the others, making for a broader overall curve. Remember our example of the mother training her child to cross the street. She certainly wants her child to generalize this training broadly—the child should look both ways anytime he is around moving cars. But most of the training will take place at the most convenient location, in front of the child's home. This might result in fairly narrow generalization unless Mommy makes a deliberate effort to include training at other places; taking the child to the grocery store or downtown a few times, or even to Grandma's house to practice, should help lead to broad generalization. We don't often conceive of our everyday learning experiences as requiring greater generalization, but sometimes we should.

The longer we delay our testing for generalization, the flatter or broader the curve of generalization will be (Burr & Thomas, 1972; Perkins & Weyant, 1958; Thomas, Windell, Bakke, Kreye, Kimose, & Aposhyan, 1985). Overall responding generally is decreased with increased delays, which has the effect of flattening the curve. This also could be used to counteract the effects of extended training or partial schedules, although it might be a less practical method.

What Causes Generalization?

The question generating the most interest among psychologists studying generalization is: Why does it work the way it does? What causes the gradient to have its characteristic shape? The fact that it is so universal suggests to many that the curve is the result of innate characteristics of the nervous systems of creatures. We are born with nervous and perceptual systems that are arranged or "wired" to work in this way. Pavlov himself suggested this when he described the phenomenon. The alternative is to note that the world consists of stimuli that are infinitely variable in their similarities to each other. This view suggests that creatures generalize because of experience with variations in stimuli and was best expressed by the physiological psychologist Karl Lashley (1929; Krechevsky, 1932; Lashley & Wade, 1946). Lashley suggested that the learner is trained to make a response in a given situation and will attempt to make that response in any situation unless it has learned to distinguish the training situation from others. In other words, Lashley felt that a totally naive learner would generalize totally—an inexperienced creature would respond equally to all stimuli as if they were the training stimulus. It is experience with other stimuli that causes the learner to distinguish between different stimuli. In particular, Lashley suggested that minimal experience with a stimulus dimension was necessary for a creature to be able to make discriminations along that dimension. Minimal experience means at least one other time the creature has been exposed to another value of that dimension. If a creature has no experience with color, it should generalize training on a red signal to all other colors equally and respond no matter what color it sees.

Several studies have examined the **Lashley-Wade hypothesis** in this manner. In one study (Peterson, 1962), ducklings were raised from birth in an environment illuminated solely by one wavelength of light (589 nm, a yellow color). Thus everything the baby ducks saw was in shades of yellow. After several weeks, the ducks were trained to make an operant response when a specific yellow light was illuminated. When tested, the ducks had a very flat, broad generalization gradient, suggesting that in fact they generalized to all colors equally (see figure 7.5). Raising a creature in a restricted sensory environment may cause some deterioration in that creature's ability to detect the changes in stimuli. The visual system will degenerate when an animal is raised in darkness; perhaps these ducks became colorblind. However, in other studies the subjects were trained to discriminate along the required dimension later as a follow-up to examine this possibility. This training has usually been successful, arguing against a permanent impairment in ability to discriminate. Other investigators have used visual patterns such as vertical stripes in the same way. Blakemore and Cooper (1970) used kittens reared in vertically striped environments, trained with vertical stripes as the S_D, and tested for generalization to other angles of the stripes. Their results suggested a deterioration in the ability to perceive horizontal stripes.

In addition, there have been several exceptions to Peterson's (1962) findings that have been difficult to explain (Rudolph & Honig, 1972; Tracy, 1970). Tracy (1970) showed that ducks have a perceptual preference

Figure 7.5 The curve of generalization for subjects raised on a light of only one wavelength (589 nm) and trained using that wavelength

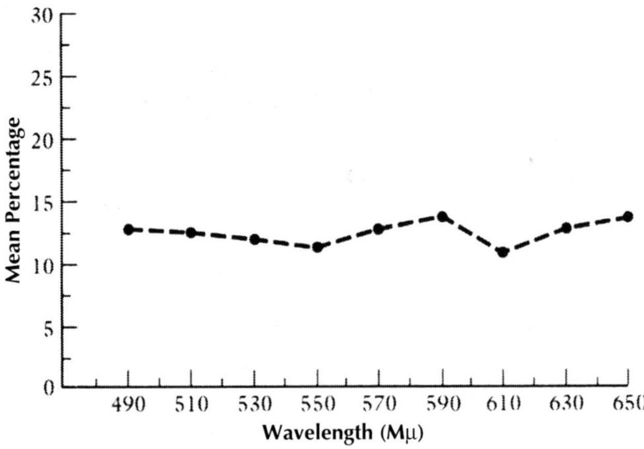

Adapted with permission from "Effect of Monochromatic Rearing on the Control of Responding by Wavelength," by N. Peterson, 1962, *Science*, 136, 774–775. Copyright © 1962 by the AAAS.

for greenish light, which may distort experimental results based on these animals. Thus, the results from experiments of this type are inconclusive. Often the subjects show a very broad curve of generalization, but not always; and the possibility exists that the animals that do show broad generalization may have some sensory impairment. Finally, even in the "flat" data there is usually a slight peak at the training stimulus, and some have pointed out that this illustrates an innate tendency to respond more to the training stimulus. Thus, although creatures inexperienced with a stimulus dimension generally show flatter generalization curves, this evidence is relatively weak and we cannot say that the Lashley-Wade hypothesis is proven. Although it seems to have some support, it may be that the alternative hypothesis of innate generalization mechanisms is also correct. In other words, the standard generalization gradient may be the result of both innate tendencies and naturally occurring differential experience.

In addition to studies of this kind, recall that one of the variables that influences the shape of the generalization curve is amount of training. More training leads to a steeper generalization gradient, exactly as the Lashley-Wade hypothesis would predict. An individual usually needs exposure to at least one other value of a dimension to compare with a training stimulus in order to show the normal generalization gradient. This additional experience teaches the learner to pay attention to that dimension. Lashley felt that until this differential experience occurs, the dimension does not exist for the learner—the learner isn't aware that it's a dimension that can vary. The idea that a learner must learn to attend to a dimension, and that this learning may be independent of the other learning going on, has led to Lashley's theory being called a **noncontinuity theory**. His noncontinuity theory emphasizes that each piece of learning may be independent of all the other pieces, and that the different pieces could be learned in different orders or ways by different learners. The learner in a noncontinuity theory first learns to attend to a particular dimension or property (for example, color), and then learns which kind of color is good (is associated with reinforcement) and which is not.

In contrast, a **continuity theory** (such as the one proposed by Hull, 1943, and Spence, 1937) requires that all the properties are learned simultaneously on each trial, each a little bit at a time. On each trial, the learner would learn that the size, shape, color, and other properties of the stimulus are associated with the reinforcement. Therefore, as the learner experiences more trials, he automatically becomes more likely to generalize in the usual way along all dimensions. However, the little evidence we have seems to support the noncontinuity position better. It does seem that only some of the components of a stimulus are learned about on a trial, with the rest learned on later trials. So, for example, on one trial the rat may learn that the stimulus is red and a few inches in diameter, on the next it learns that the stimulus is 50 watts bright and at eye level, and so on. Reynolds (1961) provided the best support for this interpretation using an operant conditioning procedure on pigeons. Some of his pigeons learned to respond to the color of a stimulus whereas others learned about the shape of the stimulus. It seems that, during training, a learner comes to pay attention to some aspects of a stimulus but may learn to ignore other aspects of that stimulus. The training may well force the learner to do this.

The noncontinuity theory requires a training experience and one other experience for normal generalization to occur. Think what this one other experience is like. What Lashley was really saying was that all experiences involve discrimination—we are reinforced in the presence of some stimuli but not reinforced in the presence of others. Lashley was simply saying that one of each type of occurrence is necessary for us to be able to generalize the way we do. To fully understand generalization we must also understand its opposite, discrimination.

Discrimination

Normally, although the generalization curve also reflects tendencies to distinguish between stimuli (to discriminate), psychologists do not focus on those aspects of the curve. It is only when the curve is much steeper that psychologists discuss discrimination. We say the learner discriminates when she responds solely or primarily to the training stimulus. This is usually the result of a specific set of training procedures. Basically, discrimination training involves alternating at least two experiences: one that causes a response to be acquired, and one or more that cause the same response to be extinguished. These two types of experiences teach the learner that she should make the responses in some circumstances but not in others.

In a classical conditioning discrimination study, we would have a stimulus paired with the US, called the **S+**, and at least one stimulus not paired with the US, called the **S–**. In an operant conditioning discrimination study, one stimulus would signal that the response could obtain reinforcement; this would be called the S_D or discriminative stimulus. Another stimulus would signal that the response would lead to no consequence; this is called the SΔ, or S delta. These two stimuli would be randomly alternated during training. This is called a **successive discrimination** procedure. We could also train our subject using two levers or keys that are both always present. If we always reward responses on one but never reward responses to the other, we are using a **simultaneous discrimination** procedure. As a result of this training, our learner would respond to the S_D but not to the SΔ. In addition, the learner would also respond to things like the S_D, and not respond to things like the SΔ. The resulting tendencies to respond to different stimuli would look like the solid curve in figure 7.6, similar to data obtained by several experimenters (Hanson, 1959; Jenkins & Harrison, 1962).

Figure 7.6 An idealized curve of generalization after discrimination training using a 100-watt light as S+ and a 75-watt light as S–

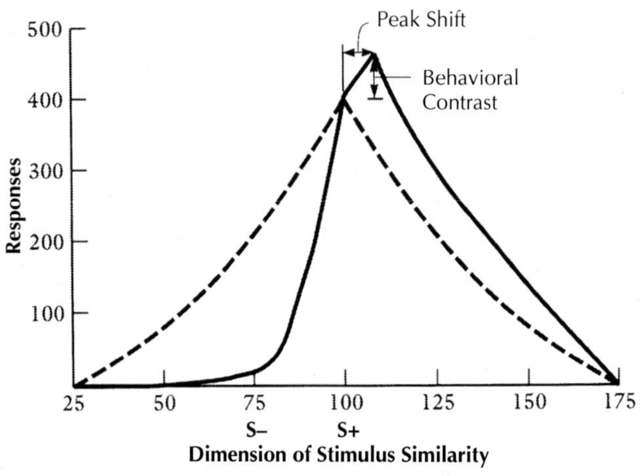

Notice how this figure appears lopsided compared to the typical generalization curve, which is also shown in the figure as a dotted line. The two halves of the discrimination curve are quite different, or **asymmetrical**, but the generalization curve is symmetrical. Also notice that the discrimination curve has a higher peak than the generalization curve, and that this peak is not above the S_D. The peak in discrimination training is shifted away from the SΔ. This is called the **peak shift**. The fact that the peak is also exaggerated—higher than it would normally be—is called **behavioral contrast**. Thus, the curve of generalization tendencies that results from discrimination training has three possible characteristics: (1) responding near the SΔ is suppressed, making the curve asymmetrical; (2) the greatest amount of responding is not to the S_D, but to a stimulus near it on the opposite side from the SΔ (the peak shift); and (3) the greatest amount of responding to a single stimulus is more than if no discrimination training is given (behavioral contrast).

Imagine that we are training a rat to press a bar when we light up a 100-watt light bulb. This is the S_D. Whenever the 100-watt bulb is lit, the rat can press the bar and get food. On randomly alternating trials, though, we light up a 75-watt bulb. This is our SΔ, and when it is lit, nothing happens when the rat presses the bar. The rat will learn to press a lot when the 100-watt bulb is lit, and to not press when the 75-watt bulb is lit. But it will also learn to not press much when any light resembling the 75-watt bulb is lit and to press pretty often when any bulb close to 100 watts is lit. So our rat will probably not press much when a 60-watt bulb or lower is lit, or when an 80-watt bulb is lit, because these are all pretty similar to the

75-watt bulb. On the other hand, our rat should press pretty much to a 110-watt bulb, because it is similar to the 100-watt bulb. The rat should also press the bar some when a 90-watt bulb is lit, because that also is like the 100-watt bulb, although it's also a little like the 75-watt bulb. Its response to an 85-watt bulb should be in between the responses for the 75-watt and the 100-watt bulbs, because 85 is about midway between them. This is what figure 7.6 describes. In these cases, responding can be predicted just by doing simple subtraction of the measured values of the stimuli—this tells us that the amount of responding is predicted by the amount of similarity of the test stimulus to the training stimuli. The training stimulus that is most similar will have the most influence on responding to any test stimulus.

What about responding to a 105-watt bulb? Our discrimination curve suggests that the rat will respond more to this bulb than to the original training stimulus of 100 watts! How can we understand such a strange prediction? Because this is what happens, we had better try. Imagine yourself in this situation instead of the rat. Every time you see a 100-watt bulb lit and respond, the experimenter says, "Good," "That's right," or something like that. When you respond to the 75-watt bulb, he says nothing. Of course, you probably don't know that they are 100 and 75 watts, but you can easily see that they are different. You probably will come to understand the situation and describe it to yourself this way: "When I see the brighter one, I should respond." "Brighter" describes the relationship between the two stimuli, and it doesn't require knowledge of their actual absolute characteristics, just an ability to compare them and evaluate the difference. In fact, this represents one of the important analyses of the discrimination curve. Think what it predicts. If you and the rat have learned a relationship, you should apply that principle or relationship to future experiences. If you are given a choice between two lights, the principle says, "Pick the brighter one."

This **relational theory**, first proposed by the Gestalt psychologist Wolfgang Kohler (1939), predicts that you would pick a 105-watt bulb over the original 100-watt training bulb, because the 105-watt bulb is brighter. You respond according to your "understanding" of the relationship that you have been taught. In fact, this is what Kohler found in his experiments using a simultaneous discrimination procedure. Because we are describing the results in terms of understanding and relationships, Kohler's relational theory is a cognitive explanation. It predicts that you and the rat will always choose the brighter of two lights after this training. Kohler noted that the subjects in his experiments seemed to have applied the principle to new pairs of stimuli; he said that they had transposed the relationship to new stimuli. For this reason, the peak shift was originally discovered as an example of what was called **transposition**. In his original experiments, Kohler presented stimuli in pairs, not only during the simultaneous training procedure but also during testing, and the transposition was easily noticed. The successive discrimination experiment, which presented only one stimulus at a time, suggests a slightly different pattern in which a brighter light generates more responding only up to a point. However, even with one-at-a-time presentation, the peak shift occurs.

Because the relational theory is a cognitive explanation, behavioristic learning theorists found it unsatisfactory. After all, our lightbulb example seems plausible enough when used to describe a person's reaction to the situation, but it's hard to imagine the rat or pigeon saying to itself, "Pick the brighter one." A more behavioral explanation was needed, and it was provided by Kenneth Spence (1937), using the framework provided by his colleague and teacher, Clark Hull (1943). Hull had proposed a mathematical explanation much like our original description of the discrimination process. This **algebraic summation theory** assumes that an excitatory potential builds up around the S+ training stimulus. That is, the learner acquires a tendency to respond to the S+, and this tendency generalizes around this stimulus. In addition, the theory assumes that the learner develops a negative or inhibitory tendency to the S–; he learns not to respond to it or anything like it. Spence and Hull suggested that the discrimination curve is the result of these two tendencies being combined. Because one is excitatory and the other is inhibitory, we can just subtract the amount of the inhibitory tendency that has generalized at any stimulus point from the excitatory tendency generalized to that point. Figure 7.7 illustrates this idea of combining tendencies. However, when Spence plugged in actual values from generalization data, he obtained curves of a different form. Nevertheless, the mathematical subtractions he performed accurately predicted the peak shift and the general shape of the discrimination curve.

Figure 7.7 The algebraic summation model of discrimination

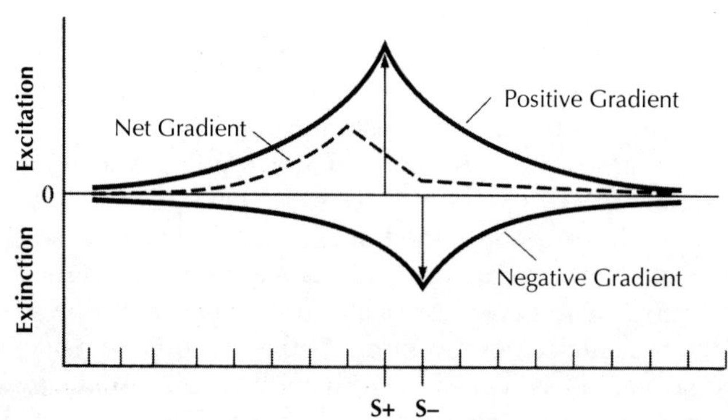

(Based on Hull, 1943)

The algebraic summation theory assumes much less than the relational theory; our learner doesn't have to understand relationships. Furthermore, we know that the nervous system operates by neurons stimulating each other with chemicals that can either increase (excite) or decrease (inhibit) the receiving neuron's tendency to respond. Finally, Spence provided an experimental test of the two theories. Although the two theories predict the same pattern of responding for most stimuli, his mathematical analysis suggested that at the far extreme away from the S– (on the other side of the S+ from the S–), the transposition reaction would disappear. That is, the transposition reaction is the result of adding together the two tendencies (positive and negative) at each point. However, near the opposite extreme from the S–, its negative influence has shrunk to zero. Because there is no longer anything to subtract, the only influence on responding is the excitatory tendency generated by the S+. Because this continues to decrease as we get further from the S+, Spence predicted that beyond the influence of the S– we would see a reversal of the response pattern.

This is the only difference in the predictions of the two theories. The relational theory predicts (for our example) always choosing the brighter light. On the other hand, the algebraic summation theory predicts that the learner will keep choosing the brighter light up to a point in testing and then switch to choosing the light most similar to the S+ training stimulus, which would be a dimmer light. So algebraic summation predicts that our learner will choose 130 watts over 120, and maybe 150 over 140, but perhaps choose 175 over 200. This occurs because the 175-watt bulb is closer to the 100-watt bulb, and there's no inhibitory tendency from the S– influencing either stimulus. In his experiments, that is what Spence (1937) found.

The pattern of results found in discrimination experiments has varied; sometimes the relational theory is supported (Gonzalez, Gentry, & Bitterman, 1954; Lawrence & DeRivera, 1954), sometimes the algebraic summation theory is supported (Hanson, 1959), and sometimes neither theory is supported (Riley, 1968). Schwartz (1978) has suggested that the results obtained depend on how you test for generalization. If you test by simultaneously presenting pairs of stimuli and allow the subject to choose between them, you tend to see results favoring the relational explanation. On the other hand, if you present one stimulus at a time (successive presentation), you are more likely to see results favoring the algebraic summation theory. It may be that both theories are partly correct and that creatures learn both some absolute characteristics of stimuli and some of the relationships between stimuli. Then, which piece of learning governs their behavior is determined by the situational requirements (how we test).

Both relational theory and algebraic summation theory have one serious drawback. Neither predicts the behavioral contrast effect; in fact, the algebraic summation theory predicts the opposite of behavioral contrast.

Algebraic summation depends on subtracting negative tendencies from positive. We should never get more responding as a result. But this is just what happens with behavioral contrast—we get more responding to the S+ when we also use an S– than if there is no S–. Currently there is no widely accepted explanation of the behavioral contrast effect. Probably the most plausible account involves noting the possible classical conditioning components of the operant conditioning situation. That is, the learner may come to find the stimulus that signals reinforcement (the S+) appealing and to react to the S– as if it were aversive. Its dislike of the S– may generate more motivation to bang away at the key when the S_D is present (Schwartz & Gamzu, 1977). Terrace (1972) has shown that the S– becomes somewhat aversive to the learner, presumably through classical conditioning. This emphasis on both classical and operant components of the operant situation is reasonable, but at this point we do not know enough about behavioral contrast to be sure of why it occurs.

We do know how to get and to eliminate peak shifts and behavioral contrasts. If we wish to eliminate the peak shift and have a nice symmetrical curve of generalization, we can do it by using several stimuli as S–. In our lightbulb experiment, we would have the 100-watt bulb as S+, one S– of 75 watts, and another S– of 125 watts. With an S– on either side of the S+, the peak would have to shift away from each, and it can't be shifted both directions at once. Such a procedure, using three training stimuli, produces a very steep but symmetrical curve such as the solid line in figure 7.8. The dotted line again shows the standard generalization curve for comparison. We can see the steep, narrow nature of generalization tendencies after this discrimination training. We would say that we have trained a very fine or precise discrimination.

Figure 7.8 The curve of generalization after discrimination training using one S+ and two S– stimuli

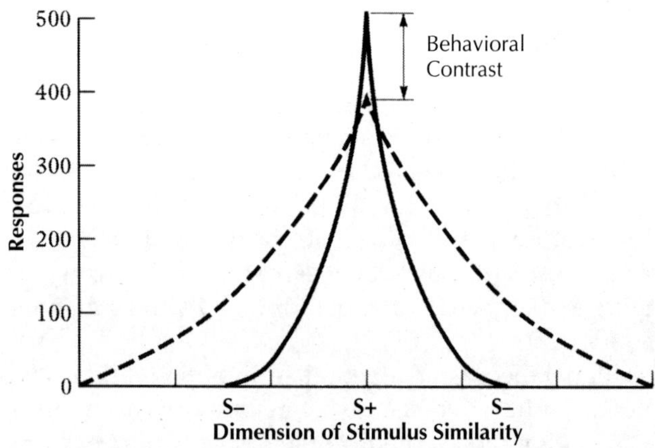

This is probably what happens to most of us in real life. We get a great deal of exposure to many varying stimuli. Many of them are not associated with any reinforcement (or with a US) and so cause fine discriminations to be learned for the fewer stimuli that are associated with reinforcement. This describes the role of experience just as Lashley did in his noncontinuity explanation for the shape of the generalization curve. The nonreinforced occurrences cause the tendency to generalize to anything to gradually become narrower until very fine discriminations are made. Another way of saying this is that we become more attentive to characteristics of stimuli as we learn more about them. Attention is a concept that is often used in discussing noncontinuity explanations of discrimination (Mackintosh, 1974; Sutherland & Mackintosh, 1971). We noted in our earlier brief discussion of noncontinuity theory that training may cause the learner to attend to one dimension and ignore others; this seems to be the basis of discrimination training. Discrimination training thus seems to have two effects: it teaches the learner to attend more to some dimensions of stimuli than others; and it also teaches the learner to respond more to one value or level of that dimension and not respond to other values.

Let us consider a real-life example of discrimination learning. Try to recall what your first experience with a jigsaw puzzle was like, or your first attempt at one after a long absence from them. This is an operant behavior in which the response of putting pieces together is reinforced by the feedback of seeing that they fit correctly. You poured the pieces out on a table, and looked at a bewildering array of pieces that all looked pretty much alike to you. As you began to sort them into groups, or tried to fit pieces together, you gradually came to notice small variations in shape, size, and coloring. Near the end of the task you have become an expert at seeing details of pieces. You have learned to make very fine discriminations between puzzle pieces. Another way of saying this is that you have learned to pay attention to details that you didn't notice or ignored before.

Although it may seem silly to think of a person as an expert at puzzles, the relationship between practice and the precision of one's discriminations is important. A doctor, who is an expert at medicine, is able to make much finer discriminations between physical symptoms than the average person. You or I might not notice the differences between small bumps on the skin, but the doctor can look at them and notice that they don't look like chicken pox but rather some other childhood virus. Part of becoming an expert is learning to make finer and more subtle discriminations as a result of differential experiences. The doctor has learned to attend to details differently than the rest of us do. But in fact, we all become expert at making some discriminations, such as noticing when it is safe to cross the street or drive through an intersection, or noticing that someone is singing off key or swinging at a baseball with poor form. In each case, we can notice differences in people's ability to attend to details of the stimulus that are the result of experience with that type of stimulation.

How to Analyze Generalization and Discrimination Problems

To analyze examples of generalization and discrimination, we must determine the amount of similarity between the learning experience and the generalization situation. In laboratory experiments, this similarity is almost always measurable using some numerical scale. So if we train a rat to respond to a particular sound, we choose one that is easy to describe. For example, suppose that we train a rat to press a bar for food when it hears a tone of 1000 Hz—a standard pitch heard on many stereo test discs. After training we test it for generalization using six tones of other pitches as follows:

1. 500 Hz
2. 1500 Hz
3. 750 Hz
4. 1100 Hz
5. 300 Hz
6. 2000 Hz

The tone that is most similar to the training tone and would lead to the greatest generalization is 4; 1100 Hz is only 100 Hz different from the training tone, which is the smallest difference. The tone most different from the training tone is 6; 2000 Hz is 1000 Hz different from the training tone, and this is the largest difference.

Now suppose we take another rat and try to study the effects of discrimination on it. We train it like the first rat except that we include some trials in which an S– tone of 1200 Hz is presented. When this rat hears the 1200 Hz tone, pressing the bar doesn't lead to any reward. If we test it using our same six test tones, we might find that the greatest response is to the 750 Hz tone (3). Even though it's further from the S+ than the 1100 Hz tone, it generates more responding because the 1100 Hz tone is also very similar to the 1200 Hz tone. We would expect very little responding to tones 2, 4, and 6, because these tones are all close to the S–, the 1200 Hz tone. The tones below 1000 Hz are much less affected by the S–, because they are on the other side of the S+ from it. However, the peak shift will occur for this rat, so that it may respond more to a tone of 900 Hz than to the S+ itself, and it may respond as much to the 750 Hz tone as it does to the S+.

Furthermore, the phenomenon of behavioral contrast means that our second rat will make more responses to the 900 Hz tone than the first rat did to 1000 Hz. Finally, this example of the transposition phenomenon might lead us to look for more examples of transposition. If we looked at tones not too far away from our S+, we should see a preference for the lower pitched tone when the second rat is given two choices; 500 Hz might generate more responses than 750 Hz, for example. But the algebraic summation prediction would be that this pattern would break down when we use sufficiently distant tones—in this case, very low tones. Therefore, our second rat might switch its pattern and respond more to 500 Hz than to 300 Hz, according to the Spence theory of algebraic summation. The relational theory would predict that the rat would continue to respond more to lower pitches.

This kind of detailed analysis is much more difficult when applied to real-life situations. Describing the characteristics of the real-life experience so precisely is not always easy, nor is focusing on just one dimension. For example, imagine that a person has been in a car accident and has developed a phobia as a result. This is a classical conditioning example in which the accident—the noise, commotion, and painful stimulation—is the US, and the car characteristics are possible conditioned stimuli. We could focus on characteristics of the car itself and note its color, make, and style; generalization on each of these dimensions might occur. Or we could focus on the driver or the neighborhood where the accident occurred. Generalization is possible along each of these dimensions; if we examined any one of them in a systematic way, we might see our generalization phenomena. For example, if the car were dark blue, we could show more fear of gray or green cars than of red or yellow cars. If the person had been a passenger in this blue car, but normally drove a green car, we could look for the discrimination phenomenon of peak shift, and we could expect to see the asymmetrical curve of responding. Thus, the peak shift might predict that the most feared color of car would be a shade of blue different from the original blue car, one with less greenish tinge in it, and the asymmetry would mean that we would see little fear of greenish-colored cars and more fear of bluish cars.

Summary

Generalization is the tendency to apply learning about one stimulus to new, similar stimuli. Without this tendency the usefulness of learning would be severely limited. The greater the physical similarity of a new stimulus to a training stimulus, the more likely a subject is to respond to it in the same way as he did to the training stimulus. Generalization occurs to a similar degree for all the learning procedures considered so far; habituation, sensitization, and classical and operant conditioning. A subject who has minimal experience with a physical dimension shows a symmetrical, tent-shaped generalization curve after training. Inhibitory generalization curves as a result of habituation, extinction, or punishment show the tent shape inverted. Lashley and Wade suggested that some minimal experience seemed to be necessary for this standard curve. They also suggested that a subject learns about the physical attributes of a stimulus in a noncontinuous fashion.

Discrimination is the opposite of generalization; the subject responds differently to a stimulus than she does to a training stimulus. Discrimination training consists of extinguishing the response to one stimulus while reinforcing the response to another stimulus. The two stimuli may be presented simultaneously or successively. This differential training causes the shape of the generalization curve to become asymmetrical and to exhibit a shift in the point of peak responding and an enhancement of that point; these changes in the point of greatest responding are called the peak shift and behavioral contrast.

Two major theories that attempt to explain changes in the shape of the curve after discrimination training are the relational theory and the algebraic summation theory. Kohler's relational theory suggests that subjects learn the relationship between stimuli (for example, "It's the larger one"), which determines their pattern of responding. Spence's algebraic summation theory suggests that differential training causes the development of excitatory response potentials to the S+ and inhibitory response tendencies to the S–. These tendencies generalize, and their combination produces the response pattern seen. Both theories have some experimental support; relational theory seems the best explanation when simultaneous presentation of stimuli is used, whereas algebraic summation seems to fit data from successive presentation studies.

Questions for Discussion, Thought, & Practice

1. Define and illustrate each key concept. Then group the concepts into two categories, one for generalization and one for discrimination. Which concepts are difficult to classify, and why?
2. Jimmy hit his finger with a hammer and now becomes upset when he sees one. Try to list at least three other objects that he might also fear because of generalization. Arrange them according to similarity to the hammer.
3. Imagine that we train a dog to come running for food when we whistle at 60 decibels. We test for generalization using whistles of (a) 25 dB, (b) 85 dB, (c) 50 dB, (d) 75 dB, (e) 40 dB, and (f) 90 dB. Which intensities will lead to the fastest running? Which will lead to the slowest?
4. Imagine that we train a second dog to discriminate, using the 60 db whistle as our S+ and another whistle of 70 dB as S–. Use the same six test whistles as in question 3, and determine which would lead to fastest and slowest running for this dog. Describe how this dog might illustrate the peak shift and behavioral contrast phenomena.
5. Using the dog example for discrimination in question 4, illustrate the predictions of the algebraic summation theory and the rela-

tional theory. Use two new test stimuli to show what each theory would predict.

6. In chapter 3 we described systematic desensitization, which was an extinction procedure based on generalization. This procedure depends on one of the assumptions of the algebraic summation theory. Which assumption, and how does it depend on that assumption?

A Comparison of Classical and Operant Conditioning

▲ KEY CONCEPTS ▲

autonomic nervous system
autoshaping
biofeedback
emit
evoke
external inhibition
interaction study
involuntary response
mediation
procedural
$r_g - s_g$
sign tracking
somatic nervous system
superstitious behavior
systemic
two-process theory
voluntary response

So far we have examined several forms of learning in some detail. The standard classification would be that we have considered four types of learning: habituation, sensitization, classical conditioning, and operant conditioning (Gould, 1986). This follows the tradition first proposed by Skinner (1938), which focuses on the differences between classical and operant conditioning, groups together all the variations of classical procedures, and distinguishes between them and all the variations in operant procedures. However, others have suggested that sensory preconditioning should be distinguished from other classical procedures, and that operant conditioning really groups together several separate forms of learning: positive reinforcement, punishment, escape, and avoidance conditioning (Razran, 1971). Furthermore, some researchers have distinguished between simple classical and operant learning versus discrimination learning (Gagne, 1965) or between these and higher, "symbolic" learning such as language learning and observational learning (Razran, 1971).

How many forms of learning are there? What is the basis for making these distinctions? Why do we group them all together and call them learning? In this chapter we will attempt to answer these questions by comparing the different types of learning. The general order of our discussion will follow a classic presentation by Kimble (1961) and consider many of the original distinctions made by Skinner (1938).

Similarities among the Forms of Learning

Similarities among the different forms of learning indicate that they are in fact related. The greater the similarities, the more likely it is that they are the result of the same process going on in an individual. If we look back at the phenomena we have described, we can note many important commonalities, both in the results of the processes and in the variables that influence the processes.

The curve of learning shows a similar shape for all the types of learning described (figure 8.1). For sensitization, excitatory classical conditioning, and positive and negative reinforcement, this curve shows great increases in performance on early trials and successively smaller increases as we give more trials, until we reach a leveling-off point or *asymptote*. This is the standard curve of learning, and although it may differ from one task to another or one subject to another, the differences are not caused by the type of learning studied. Rather, differences in the

Figure 8.1 The curve of learning. Response acquisition as a function of trials.

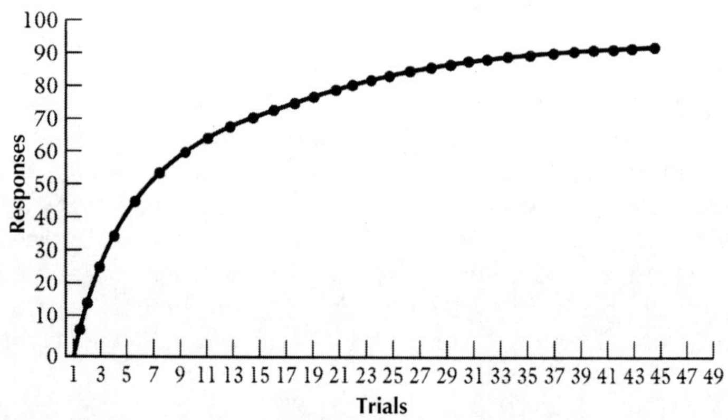

steepness of the curve may be due to having an especially good or poor learner or using an especially easy or difficult task. Differences in difficulty or subject ability occur without regard to whether we are studying classical or operant conditioning or sensitization. In other words very gradual learning can be found in operant conditioning tasks that are difficult, or very rapid learning in easier operant tasks; and the same holds true for the other forms of learning.

For habituation, inhibitory classical conditioning, extinction (of positively reinforced responses), and punishment, the curve has essentially the same shape, but it is upside down, as shown in figure 8.2. This is because for the other procedures we are causing the acquisition of a response, and with these procedures we are causing a response to be eliminated. However, we see the same pattern of big changes at first with successively smaller changes as we continue until no further change can be seen. The curve of learning reveals similar patterns for all forms of learning, which suggests that the underlying processes causing performance are the same for all forms of learning.

In addition, habituation and extinction of classically conditioned or positively reinforced responses all exhibit spontaneous recovery, and all for the same reason. In all cases, spontaneous recovery is easily obtained when there is a longer than usual delay between trials. Figure 8.2 also illustrates one occurrence of spontaneous recovery.

The phenomena of generalization and discrimination represent important similarities among all the forms of learning. The curve of generalization shows the same symmetrical tent shape for all excitatory forms of learning such as classical conditioning, positive reinforcement, and negative reinforcement. This suggests that the learning experiences have similar effects on our nervous systems and are represented by our

Figure 8.2 The curve of habituation or extinction showing spontaneous recovery on Trial 24.

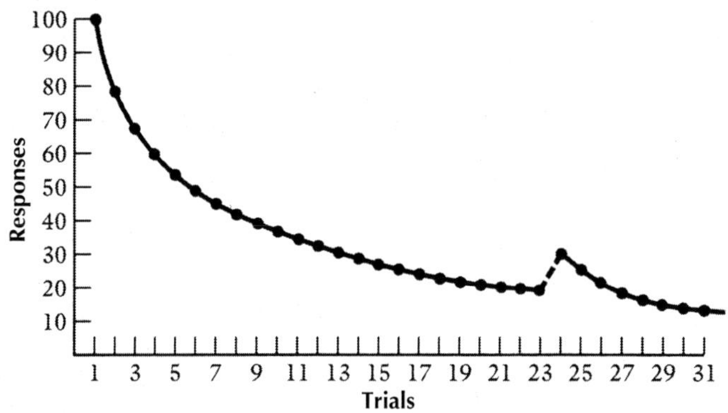

nervous systems in similar ways. Naturally, a curve of generalization for habituation, inhibitory classical conditioning, or punishment would again essentially be upside down, because these forms of learning eliminate responses rather than create them. However, the same principle applies in all cases: the degree of generalization is greatest for stimuli very similar to the training stimulus and successively decreases as we decrease this similarity by testing stimuli further from the training stimulus. There are exceptions to this principle, but they all involve aversive stimuli. In sensitization, classical conditioning using an aversive US, and punishment, the learning sometimes shows much broader generalization than in the other forms of learning. Apparently, aversive stimuli sometimes produce a general inhibition of all behavior.

Another response phenomenon common to several forms of learning is the partial reinforcement extinction effect (PREE). Remember that this refers to the fact that intermittently reinforced responses are more resistant to extinction than continuously reinforced responses. This effect is common to positive reinforcement (where it was first noted and most extensively studied), classical conditioning, punishment, and negative reinforcement. For classical conditioning, reinforcement would be interpreted as the action of the US; when it follows the CS on every trial, the response is easier to extinguish than when the US is occasionally omitted. This has been found in several classical conditioning procedures, but not all; eyeblink conditioning in animals seems much less likely to show the PREE (Gormezano, Kehoe, & Marshall, 1983). Thus, the forms of learning that involve several stimuli usually show the PREE. Of course, it cannot apply to the forms of learning that involve only one stimulus, such as habituation and sensitization.

The two most important variables in all the forms of learning are intensity of the stimulus (US or Sr) and timing. In all the forms of learning, the shorter the time interval, the more effective the learning procedure. For habituation and sensitization, shorter intertrial intervals result in the fastest learning. For classical conditioning, short CS–US intervals lead to learning in fewer trials. And for operant conditioning, the shorter the delay between the response and the reinforcement, the better the learning. The intensity variable works the same way for sensitization, classical conditioning, and all forms of operant conditioning; acquisition is faster with more intense unconditioned stimuli or reinforcers. In habituation, less intense stimuli lead to faster habituation because we are eliminating the response.

A final similarity among the several forms of learning is that they are all influenced by the presence of outside stimuli. In other words, if we are classically conditioning salivation to a bell and another noise accidentally occurs during a trial (such as someone dropping a box nearby), the course of learning will be somewhat disrupted—several more trials will be needed to return to the level before that trial (Pavlov, 1927). This is called

external inhibition. We noted the importance of this phenomenon in discussing habituation and sensitization, and it can also be demonstrated in operant conditioning (Kimble, 1961). Furthermore, the influence of external inhibitors decreases with more training trials, and repeated occurrences of external inhibitors leads to less inhibition—the subject "gets used to" the disruptive stimulus and learns to respond as it was trained in spite of the presence of extraneous stimuli. Both of these effects have been demonstrated in all four learning procedures.

Even though we have had to qualify most of these similarities, they represent a great deal of commonality and have suggested to some that all learning consists of one fundamental process. This argument usually focuses on classical and operant conditioning, although if pressed these theorists would probably place habituation and sensitization with classical conditioning and claim that they were some of the components of it. The emphasis would be that they must all be causing the same kinds of biochemical changes within the nervous system. Let us now consider some differences between classical and operant to determine whether they are significant differences or trivial ones. Although we will focus on classical and operant conditioning, many of our comments about classical could be applied to habituation and sensitization, and we will note some of these.

Differences between Classical and Operant Conditioning

We can generally note two kinds of differences between classical conditioning and operant conditioning: **procedural** differences and **systemic** differences. That is, we can notice differences in how the two types of conditioning are done, and we can note differences in what parts of the organism are affected and how they are affected. We will discuss several of each type of difference, weighing their significance as we go along. Generally, the systemic differences are regarded as more important because they would imply that creatures are functioning differently in the two learning situations.

Procedural Differences

The most obvious procedural difference is that the important stimuli in classical conditioning occur before the response, and the important stimulus (the reinforcer) in operant conditioning occurs after the response. This has two consequences. First, it means that in classical conditioning the learner must make an association between stimuli before the response, and in operant conditioning the learner makes an association between the response and a stimulus after it. In other words, in classical conditioning, the learner usually forms a connection between events (the CS and US), and this association allows each stimulus to evoke a reaction. Responses are evoked or elicited in habituation and sensitization in much the same way as in classical conditioning. In contrast, the important connection in operant conditioning is between the response and the reinforcer following it; here the response is not generated by the stimuli but rather by the learner. It may be that associations between stimuli are represented by different kinds of biochemical changes (or biochemical changes in different parts of the nervous system) than associations between a response and a stimulus following it; certainly these associations are representing different sequences of events. For example, in Pavlov's experiment, an association may be formed between signals in the dog's temporal lobe, where sounds are processed, and the portion of the brain where tastes are processed. On the other hand, in operant conditioning, associations may be formed between the motor cortex responsible for pressing the bar and the taste processing centers. The motor cortex may differ from the sensory cortex in the pattern of connections between neurons, in the length and number of axons the neurons have, or in the type of chemical transmitters used.

We say that what the learner does in operant conditioning is **emit** the response. The distinction between responses that are **evoked** and those that are emitted represents the second consequence of the order of events in the two forms of learning. In operant, the learner is free to respond when he wants, but in classical his pattern of responding is determined by our pattern of stimulus presentation. In classical conditioning the US is given at the experimenter's discretion, but in an operant conditioning situation the learner is free to obtain a reward whenever he chooses to perform. Thus, the occurrence of the unconditioned stimulus determines when the response will occur and also determines what kinds of responses we can study. If we use food as a US, we must look for digestive responses, and the use of a shock as the US causes us to look for fear responses. This cause-and-effect relationship also applies to habituation and sensitization but does not exist in such strict fashion for operant conditioning. We can use food as a reinforcer for a wide variety of responses, and we could use shock as a punisher to suppress those same responses.

Another way of describing these differences between classical and operant is to note that the learner has control over the environmental outcome in operant conditioning, and the experimenter (or the environment itself in nature) has control of the outcome in classical conditioning. In operant conditioning the learner determines when she receives the reinforcer by determining when to make a response; in classical conditioning the US is delivered totally independently of the learner's response. In classical conditioning the US is unaffected by the learner's response; however, several researchers have argued against this distinction between classical and operant. They note that the conditioned response may be either a preparatory response, such as salivation, or a compensatory response, such as heart rate decreases before shock. The nature of the CR is such that it allows the learner to cope with the US more effectively. Although it doesn't actually determine the occurrence of the US, the conditioned response does have an influence on the impact of the US. Making this distinction between classical and operant can be seen as a matter of degree rather than a truly qualitative difference. In other words, this distinction becomes one of degree of control, where control is a dimension rather than two opposite possibilities.

At one time, this "control over the outcome" issue was described in terms of the importance of a contingency in operant versus the emphasis on contiguity in classical. However, the research of Rescorla (1967) discussed in chapter 3 suggested that contingencies may be learned in classical conditioning as well. Today we can only state that the contingency in operant would be between a response and a reinforcer, but in classical it would be between two stimuli. Again, this distinction may not seem especially significant: the subject may be learning a contingency in both cases. It's just that the only contingency involving the response is in operant conditioning.

Another procedural distinction that can be noted is that timing seems to be much more crucial in classical than operant. Although both benefit from close contiguity between the important events, classical seems more dependent on this contiguity. With two exceptions, classical conditioning does not occur with delays beyond a few seconds. In operant conditioning, learning can often occur with much longer delays. Furthermore, the important time interval is between two stimuli in classical and between a response and a stimulus in operant. One counterargument to the timing distinction involves two cases in which classical conditioning can occur with longer interstimulus intervals. Taste aversion learning does occur with time intervals over an hour; in this procedure an individual comes to dislike or avoid a certain taste because it was paired with nausea or illness (Garcia & Koelling, 1966). The conditioning has been successful even though the occurrence of the taste and the illness are sometimes separated by more than an hour. Because the procedure must involve some classical conditioning elements, brief ISIs may not be absolutely necessary for classical conditioning. Taste aversion learning does not represent a very typical form of learning; in the next chapter we will discuss its relationship to other learning tasks. The questionable position of taste aversion learning makes it a poor criterion for evaluating the role of timing in classical conditioning.

The other case of longer time intervals in classical conditioning involves the use of shock and measurement of strength of conditioning by the CER procedure. When the conditioned suppression measure of conditioning has been used, significant amounts of suppression can be obtained with a memory trace interval as long as one minute (Kamin, 1965). This is a more serious problem for using timing as a distinction between classical and operant conditioning. For some aspects of classical conditioning, close temporal contiguity seems to be less essential than early researchers believed. Furthermore, the deemphasis on contiguity in operant conditioning is misleading. It might be that learning an operant contingency also requires close proximity of the response and the reinforcer, but that *after* this learning, performance can be maintained without contiguity. This idea suggests that in many everyday situations, behaviors are maintained by rewards given much later, when the behaviors have already been learned.

One illustration of the importance of contiguity in operant conditioning was the "superstition" experiment of Skinner (1948). He presented food to pigeons every 15 seconds in a Skinner box regardless of what the bird was doing. He found that after a while, most of his birds developed a specific pattern of behavior between food presentations. Each pigeon had a different behavior but stuck with it persistently. It was as if the birds "believed" that their responses were getting the food for them—thus, Skinner's label of **superstitious behavior**. The point is that the recurring responses were whatever responses the birds had been making just before the first few food presentations. The contiguity of their responses and the food actually served to make food reinforce the responses, even in the absence of a true contingency. At one time, contiguity was seen as the defining prerequisite of classical conditioning but unnecessary for operant conditioning. Learning theorists have generally moved away from this position to one in which timing represents a rather minor difference between the two. Thus, here again, this is a distinction of degree only, not a dichotomy (a two-choice, have-it-or-not distinction).

We have noted several times that the US in classical and the reinforcer in operant are the same kinds of things. However, our discussion here notes several differences in how they function. It could also be said that the conditioned stimulus and the discriminative stimulus are basically the same thing in different surroundings. However, here too there are several differences. The CS is usually presented rather briefly and in a discrete fashion—it's on for a few seconds, once for each trial. The discriminative stimulus, on the other hand, is often present while many responses are made and is thus on for a relatively long time, often 30 seconds or more. Also, by definition, the CR never occurs to the CS before conditioning. On the other hand, the operant response must occur in the presence of the discriminative stimulus at least once before we reinforce it. In other words, the classical baseline level of responding is zero, whereas the operant level must be greater than zero before conditioning.

An important part of most operant conditioning studies involves depriving the subject of the reinforcer for some time before studying learning. Thus, the rat is deprived of food for 8 hours or so before we train it in the operant chamber with a food reward. Along with this deprivation procedure, we often infer a drive state (in this case hunger), and we noted in chapter 6 that deprivation was an important factor determining the influence of a potential reinforcer. However, in classical conditioning, the procedure of deprivation is generally irrelevant. We don't have to deprive the rabbit of airpuffs to make it blink more effectively, or deprive the rat of shocks to classically condition a fear more effectively. The procedure of deprivation, and with it the concept of drives, are unimportant for classical conditioning procedures. Because deprivation is often essential for operant conditioning but irrelevant in classical conditioning, this represents an important procedural difference between the two.

A final procedural difference involves the measurement of the two forms of learning. The most widely used measure of classical conditioning is response strength or amplitude; this is basically irrelevant to the measurement of operant conditioning. On the other hand, the most widely used measure of operant conditioning is rate of response, which is impossible to measure in classical conditioning. This is a rather minor difference, because it is a consequence of the responses being conditioned and the way we condition them.

Systemic Differences

The nature of the responses and the response mechanisms involved represent the important systemic differences between classical and operant conditioning (Skinner, 1938; Solomon & Turner, 1962). Classical responses are either reflexive or emotional reactions. They generally involve glandular secretions or the action of the smooth muscles of the internal organs—the visceral organs. With the exception of some occurrences of reflexes, such as the eyeblink and the knee jerk, these responses are under the control of the **autonomic nervous system**. Most autonomic pathways involve the cranial nerves that bypass the spinal cord. This part of the nervous system usually operates automatically without conscious control, and these responses are often called **involuntary responses**. On the other hand, operant responses usually involve the striated skeletal muscles under the control of the **somatic nervous system**. The somatic nervous system operates through pathways in the spinal cord. We usually are conscious of these responses, and they are often called **voluntary responses**. These distinctions between autonomic and somatic systems represented such clear differences that even the exceptions could be explained without sacrificing the distinctions. For example, several investigators noted that the reflexive eyeblink was physically different in appearance from the voluntary eyeblink (Kimble, 1961; Spence & Ross, 1959).

Distinguishing between the autonomic and somatic systems in the brain is much more complicated. As we have seen in chapters 3 and 6, both classical conditioning and operant conditioning involve several central nervous system areas, with some different areas important for different classical procedures and a complex pattern for operant procedures as well. However, in general, autonomic functions are mostly controlled by subcortical areas of the brain (such as the hypothalamus and cerebellum), whereas voluntary responses involve more cortical activity (especially in the frontal lobes and motor cortex) in addition to subcortical activity.

The distinction between autonomic and somatic systems generated a great deal of crossover research in which investigators tried to operantly condition the autonomic nervous system or classically condition the somatic nervous system. Most of these studies had very poor results. For example, conditioning a dog to salivate as an operant response for food is trivial, because it would be very difficult to show that the results were not due to classical conditioning. On the other hand, conditioning the dog to not salivate to obtain food was very difficult and never led to results as satisfactory as a classical procedure (Sheffield, 1965). However, there are two notable types of experiments that we must consider further.

One case of a crossover procedure involves one of the most popular operant responses, the key pecking of the pigeon in a Skinner box. This response is easily shaped; in fact, often the experimenter doesn't really have to shape at all. Brown and Jenkins (1968) demonstrated that the pigeon would reflexively peck at anything paired with food in a classical procedure. In other words, they lit up the key for 8 seconds before delivering a piece of food to the pigeon. No response was required—the pigeon got the food regardless of whether it pecked or not. In fact, pecking of the key means that it takes longer to get to the food. Nevertheless, the pigeons all developed a pecking response directed at the key. Brown and Jenkins labeled this procedure **autoshaping**, suggesting that the pigeon would automatically shape itself to peck for food.

Later investigators have come to refer to the phenomenon as **sign tracking**. The relative roles of operant and classical conditioning in sign tracking are still being argued; however, classical conditioning clearly plays an important role. The response of pecking appears differently depending on whether the reinforcer is food or water; this is the way a conditioned response would occur (Moore, 1973), because in classical conditioning the US (food or water) determines the UR and CR. Trying to eliminate the response by withholding food when a peck is made is not very effective (Williams & Williams, 1969); thus, the procedure of operant extinction does not work very well for sign tracking.

If the only example of sign tracking were the pigeon pecking, the debate over its causes would be of limited significance. However, several examples of the sign tracking phenomenon have been observed in other species such as fish (Squier, 1969) and dogs. Some researchers have even suggested the possibility of sign tracking in humans (Wilcove & Miller, 1974). As a real-life human example, Domjan and Burkhard (1986) suggest that people riding in an elevator are engaged in sign tracking when they look at the numbers indicating which floors they are passing. Looking at the numbers doesn't make the elevator move any faster toward their destination. However, it does provide information about when they will arrive, just as a CS provides information about a US occurrence. On the other hand, "looking" is a voluntary behavior that appears to be an operant. Perhaps the informational interpretation provides an idea of why sign tracking occurs in other species as well. Thus, the existence of sign tracking represents a case of learning that is difficult to classify. Although the environmental circumstances are clearly classical in nature, the response is usually associated with operant. The ambiguity of sign tracking points out the problem with categorizing learning tasks—if tasks don't fit into the categories, perhaps the categories are wrong. Fortunately for the categorizers, relatively few of these problems have been discovered. The sign tracking phenomenon is relatively unique.

Operant Conditioning of the Autonomic Nervous System

Probably the most serious challenge to the idea of two separate forms of associative learning has come from the research of Neal Miller (1973, 1978; Miller & DiCara, 1968) and his associates. Miller analyzed the characteristics of classical conditioning and the autonomic nervous system by focusing on the lack of feedback in each. Feedback is information provided to the individual about the effectiveness of his own activity. When we pick up objects, messages from our fingertips tell us that we are holding it firmly enough to lift it. Picking up an object is an example of an operant activity. Miller noted that the autonomic nervous system does not usually need feedback for its normal operation; our autonomic system sends messages to our heart to beat at a certain pace without any feedback about what the heart rate actually is. Miller further noted that the reinforcement in operant conditioning provides feedback for the learner. He suggested that if a feedback mechanism could be developed for an autonomic response, it could be operantly conditioned.

Miller provided such a mechanism by monitoring heart rates with an EKG machine that was hooked up to a tone generator. The arrangement was such that a subject who was hooked up would hear a tone that changed pitch depending on heart rate. A lower-pitched tone meant a slower heart rate, and increases in the pitch meant increases in heart rate. The feedback was very accurate and immediate. Miller then introduced an operant contingency. For half of his subjects, a reward was given when the tone (and therefore the heart rate) increased; the other half received a reward for a lower tone and heart rate. Subjects were not given instructions in how to change their heart rate. Nevertheless, many subjects did show significant changes in their heart rates in the predicted directions, suggesting that the autonomic nervous system could be operantly conditioned. However, this is where things get complicated.

Miller's study and the many studies since have used two types of subjects: animals and people. The human studies are really inconclusive. Although humans can be quite successful at controlling their heart rates using this **biofeedback** technique, interpretation of these results is very difficult. Many investigators have shown that humans may be using mental or physical "tricks" in order to perform in the task. In other words, there are many ways to change your heart rate that might look like operant behaviors but are really the result of classically conditioned mechanisms or natural physiological mechanisms that are engaged through activity. This is called **mediation**, and it would be said that the individual is using a classical or physiological mediator to perform the task.

For example, if a person is told to increase her heart rate, she could do so by jumping up and down or by thinking about frightening things such as being in a car accident. Certainly, both jumping and thinking about things would be examples of operant activities; however, both of them have their effect on heart rate by means of mechanisms that are not operant—this is the mediation. Jumping up and down is an operant activity but automatically engages the autonomic nervous system, causing our hearts to beat faster without our having to voluntarily direct them to do so. Thinking about being in a car accident is similar; it could be interpreted as a self-generated CS that is associated with an unpleasant UR, pain, which reliably generates the classical UR of heart rate increases. Similarly, the person told to lower her heart rate could think peaceful thoughts, such as imagining lying on the beach on a warm summer day. These thoughts would generate lower heart rates through their classical associations with relaxation. Many studies have shown that these sorts of thoughts often occur in biofeedback experiments on humans (Katkin & Murray, 1968).

The strategy of selecting thoughts that generate particular emotions doesn't seem especially plausible as an explanation of biofeedback in rats, although they might be changing heart rates by changing activity levels. However, this possibility can be eliminated by paralyzing the animals with a drug such as curare. Thus, the animal data is crucial for interpretation of these experiments. Unfortunately, although the early experiments of Miller's on animals looked very promising, later experiments found smaller and smaller differences between experimental and control groups. In his later papers, Miller expressed doubt about the validity of his early animal research and uncertainty about the real cause of biofeedback performance (Dworkin & Miller, 1986; Miller, 1978). No satisfactory explanation of the variability in animal biofeedback studies exists. At this time, the biofeedback evidence that suggests that classical and operant conditioning are interchangeable is too controversial to warrant throwing out the distinction between them. The best interpretation of biofeedback studies is that it may be possible to operantly condition the autonomic nervous system, but it's much easier to classically condition the autonomic system. Similarly, it seems to be much easier to operantly condition the somatic nervous system.

Nevertheless, Miller's work on a theoretical question provided a powerful, practical tool for us. Many people who suffer from hypertension, high blood pressure, and the possibility of heart attacks can be helped by training them in biofeedback techniques. The equipment necessary for monitoring heart rate and providing a feedback signal is relatively cheap, and the technique has been shown to be effective in reducing the risk from these problems.

Interactions of Classical and Operant Conditioning

In our discussion of avoidance conditioning we saw that classical conditioning can interact with operant conditioning. That is, a creature may be learning to make an operant avoidance response because it is related to a classical fear response. The two forms of learning may be working together, and the response we see probably is a combination of the two processes. The presence of classically generated reflexes or tendencies may therefore exaggerate or inhibit operant behavior. This kind of interaction probably occurs in all examples of operant conditioning. In positive reinforcement, for example, rewarding the rat for pressing the bar also creates a positive classical reaction to the Skinner box environment. This can motivate the rat and make it more likely to be active and therefore more likely to press the bar. Likewise, rewarding a rat at the end of the maze causes the stimuli of the goal box and the alleyway areas near it to become conditioned stimuli associated with the food as a US. There are no *pure* examples of operant conditioning—all of them involve the possible occurrence of some classical conditioning as well. They would only be pure to the extent that the classical conditioning was irrelevant to the operant performance or neutral with regard to it, which is not especially likely given that any reinforcer also has a classical role in the learner's experience. Currently one of the hot research topics in learning is the analysis of the exact nature of these interactions in different operant procedures. From this perspective, sign tracking is just an extreme example of these more general interactions.

Generally, **interaction studies** focus on the fact that some responses that are easy to increase through positive reinforcement are very difficult to eliminate through punishment and vice versa. The reason for such patterns may be that the response bears some resemblance to the classical reaction to the reinforcer being used. Thus, the classical components enhance learning in one case and inhibit it in the other. The ideas originally proposed by Spence (1956) and Mowrer (1947, 1960)—that fractional anticipatory goal responses ($\mathbf{r_g} - \mathbf{s_g}$) or fractional anticipatory fear responses ($r_f - s_f$) are the learned components that mediate these interactions—have served as the basis for most of this research. However, Mowrer's original two-factor theory made a number of specific predictions that have been difficult to support fully. It emphasized a particular response component. Although this component was internal and just a part of a response tendency, it was still rather specific. The theory also required that this component occurred before the operant response, so that the operant response could be generated by the classical fractional response. Finding evidence for a specific response-generating tendency has been very difficult.

More importantly, when investigators have been able to observe classical responses in the operant situations, they have sometimes found these responses occurring at the same time or after the operant responses (Shapiro, 1960, 1961; Williams, 1965). For example, the dog pushing a pedal with its paw for food may salivate while pushing or after pushing; the theory requires salivation before the push. Modern **two-process theory** has altered the original description to focus on the creation of a central emotional state as a result of the classical aspects of the operant procedures (Rescorla & Solomon, 1967), which is rather more generalized and diffuse than that proposed in the original Mowrer theory. Four central emotional states were proposed: hope, fear, disappointment, and relief.

In the positive reinforcement situation, the animal is classically conditioned to feel hope when the discriminative stimulus occurs; our dog sees the light, which tells it that it should push, and "hopes" that it will soon have food. This hope motivates it to do anything associated with getting food, so it pushes the pedal. If we classically condition some other stimulus to shock, that CS should generate fear, which would counteract the hope and thus reduce responding. This is the conditioned emotional response that Rescorla and Wagner used to measure the amount of classical conditioning (see chapter 3). Remember that a CS for fear is presented while the rat is pressing a bar for food. The amount of suppression indicates that the fear is interfering with the hope in the operant chamber as predicted by the theory.

Most of the experiments examining combinations of the four emotional-motivational states have supported the theory. The most troublesome results have come from classically conditioning another stimulus that generates hope, for example, a bell. Then we add the bell to the dog's operant chamber when it is receiving positive reinforcement for pedal pushing when the light is on. If the dog pushes the pedal more often when the bell and light are both on than when only the light is on, the two stimuli both generate hope, and the two-process theory is correct. Unfortunately, this is not what usually happens. More often, the additional stimulus suppresses responding (Azrin & Hake, 1969; Miczek & Grossman, 1971). Currently there are no widely accepted explanations of why the two-process theory does not work in this case, although the two-process theory itself is generally regarded as the best analysis of interaction experiments.

Interaction studies represent the new perspective in learning that classical and operant are affected by the same principles and are often inseparable in actual behavioral situations. Rescorla and Holland (1982) were among the first to present this position. They argued from an associationist position that both forms of learning involve the formation of associations, and that association formation was influenced by the same basic variables in both cases. These basic variables were the contiguity between the events and the predictive nature (contingency) of the events being associated. They noted the similarities between classical and operant conditioning that we discussed at the beginning of this chapter and pointed out several others. For example, they noted similarities between the blocking of classical learning and the learned helplessness Seligman and Groves (1970) found in avoidance conditioning. Rescorla (1987) especially noted that analysis of the associations formed in operant conditioning (discussed in chapter 6) reveals that, of the three possible associations, two are classical-style relationships. The discriminative stimulus-response association is an S–R association like that which might occur if the subject associates a CS with a CR in classical conditioning. And the discriminative stimulus-reinforcer association suggested by some to occur in operant is similar to the classical CS–US association believed to occur. This emphasis on the associative nature of learning causes Rescorla to view all forms of learning as closely related.

This approach to the question of varieties of learning holds the most promise of eventually leading to a good understanding of the learning process. However, from the practical position of analyzing the way learning has occurred in an ordinary situation, the classical-operant distinction is probably more useful, and that is why it is the approach easiest to notice in a textbook. Now let us illustrate the practical value of the classical-operant distinction.

How to Recognize Classical or Operant Conditioning

Table 8.1 provides a summary of the main differences between classical and operant conditioning that we have considered. If we consider these differences from a practical point of view, they tell us how to go about recognizing examples of each form of learning in natural situations. Our best strategy is to look for the response first. Once we have identified a response that has changed in the situation, we can use this to answer two questions: (1) what kind of response is it?, and (2) when do the important stimuli occur? If we can identify the response as a reflex or emotional reaction, then we are looking at a classical response. Characterizing it as involuntary may be helpful in recognizing that it is an autonomic response, which is most easily classically conditioned. On the other hand, if we think it is a voluntary response involving the skeletal muscles and movement, action, or speech, then we are talking about the somatic nervous system and operant conditioning.

The second question involves the order of events in the situation: are all the important stimuli occurring before the response? If we can see more than one important stimulus before the response, they are probably

Table 8.1 Differences between Classical and Operant Conditioning

Paradigm	CS - - - → (CR) US ——— → UR Classical	S_D - - -R - → S_{r+} Operant
Procedural Differences		
Where is association?	Before response	After response
What causes response?	Evoked by CS or US	Learner emits response
Who controls outcome?	Experimenter or environment	Learner
Type of contingency	Between CS and US	Between response and reinforcer
Timing	Crucial, short intervals better (optimum = 1/2 to 2 sec)	Short delays better but not essential
Nature of signal	CS brief, sudden, one per CR	S_D longer, may be present for several responses
Correlation of signal and response before learning	CS – CR r = 0	S_D = R r > 0 (baseline)
Deprivation	Not necessary	Necessary; longer deprivation makes reinforcers more effective
Measurement	Strength or latency	Rate or latency
Systematic Differences		
Type of response	Reflexes or emotions	Actions or movements
Body parts	Glands, smooth muscles (viscera)	Skeletal (striped) muscles
Nervous system parts	Autonomic (cranial nerves), involuntary; hippocampus, cerebellum, etc.	Somatic (spinal nerves), voluntary; frontal lobes, motor cortex, amygdala, hypothalamus, etc.

the CS and US, and we are looking at an example of classical conditioning. However, if we can see an important stimulus occurring after the response, then we have found a reinforcer, and we are looking at operant conditioning. Let us apply this strategy to a few examples.

> At college, Alberto gets letters from his girl back home about once a week. As soon as he smells her perfume coming from his mailbox, his heart goes pitter patter and he starts breathing faster. Then he sees her handwriting on the envelope.

This seems to involve reflexive and emotional responses; Alberto's breathing and heart rate changes seem likely to be the result of feelings about his girlfriend. The perfume and the handwriting presumably were paired with the girl herself in the past. All of these stimuli (perfume, handwriting, the girl herself) occur before the response is generated. This is an example of classical conditioning. It's difficult to know which timing pattern best describes it: standard (delayed) conditioning if Alberto smells the perfume slightly before he sees her, but in real life it might be that simultaneous conditioning is more likely.

> Several times while they were painting their new apartment, Bonnie's roommate splashed her with paint. She always yelled, "Look out!" and so now, every time she hears, "Look out!" Bonnie flinches and blinks.

In this example, Bonnie is making a reflexive response of flinching and blinking. Reflexes suggest that this is classical conditioning. Because the exclamation and the paint splash both occur before her response, this also suggests classical conditioning. The paint splashing on her is probably the US and the words "Look out!" are the CS. It's hard to tell how the timing might be occurring here; it could be delayed conditioning, with the sound of the words overlapping in time with the feeling of getting splashed, or it could be trace conditioning, if the roommate gets the words out quickly (this is less likely).

> When Aphrodite's big brother loses a game, he comes stomping into her room and starts throwing her toys around, often at her. Luckily most of her toys are soft, but even a beany toy can hurt when thrown hard enough. Aphrodite now begins to cry whenever she hears him stomping her way.

In this example, Aphrodite's response of crying is clearly an emotional response. Also, all the important stimuli occur before she cries; both of these facts point to classical conditioning. The CS is the stomping sound, which occurs before the throwing and any painful consequences (the USs) and probably stops before the throwing, so this seems to be trace conditioning.

> Elbert is a devoted Republicrat. At a party, he enthusiastically talks to a group of eight people, which quickly dwindles to two, who take their leave by saying, "I'm gonna get a drink," and "Me too." Elbert walks up to another group and decides to just listen for a while.

Talking is a voluntary action; we choose to do it. Furthermore, something important happens after Elbert talks. People leave. Both of these facts suggest operant conditioning; this seems to be a case of something being removed (people's attention) as a result of Elbert talking. It can only be punishment type II (omission) or negative reinforcement. Since Elbert *stops* talking, this is punishment type II, much like a "time out" procedure being applied to Elbert. We might suspect that it may happen whenever Elbert gets carried away with talking, which would be continuous reinforcement, but that is not specified.

> Once when he was trying to buy candy from a machine, the machine jammed up on Muggsy. He banged it with his fist and a candy bar and some changed popped out. Now Muggsy bangs every machine whenever the machine operates slowly, and sometimes it seems to work.

Here the response that is changing is Muggsy's hitting of candy machines. This sounds like a voluntary action performed by the skeletal muscles and controlled by the somatic nervous system, which suggests operant conditioning. There is also an important event that happens after the response, the candy and change popping out. This also suggests operant conditioning. Because the response is occurring more frequently and something positive is being obtained, this must be positive reinforcement. The reinforcers are the candy and change, the response is hitting the machine, and a slow-operating machine seems to be the discriminative stimulus for hitting.

Actually, in most real-life situations, both classical and operant conditioning are occurring. Consider the following example:

> Little Gertrude burned her mouth on her first spoonful of hot tomato soup. Now just the sight of soup makes her start yelling and screaming until the soup is taken away.

This example has classical conditioning elements in which Gertrude learns to fear the sight of soup because the appearance of the soup or its aroma (CSs) were paired with burning her mouth (the US). However, it also has operant elements because Gertrude has learned that her reaction of yelling and screaming can lead to the removal of the soup. Removal of the soup represents a negative reinforcement procedure—something unpleasant is prevented by her responses of yelling and screaming. Here is a response that apparently can be either a classical reaction (the emotional feeling of fear, exhibited by the yelling and screaming) or an operant. In fact, children (and adults, for that matter) often learn that the display of their feelings can lead to reinforcing or punishing events. Emotional displays that may have originated as reflexive or classically controlled responses may come to function as operant responses; this is an example of the interaction between these two types of learning.

Summary

Similarities among the various forms of learning suggest that they involve the same internal processes in the learner. Phenomena common to all forms of learning include the shape of the learning curve, the occurrence of spontaneous recovery following rest in habituation and extinction, the shape of the generalization curve, the partial reinforcement extinction effect, the influences of intensity of stimuli and of timing on learning, and the influence of external inhibition on learning.

Differences between the forms of learning can be classified as procedural, involving the methods employed to get that form of learning, and systemic, involving the internal mechanisms and body systems used in the learning. Procedural differences are less convincing. They include the timing of events (in classical, the response is last, whereas in operant, the reinforcer is last), the fact that the subject determines when to respond and whether he receives reinforcement in operant (determined by the subject but determined externally in classical), and greater flexibility in the ways that responses and reinforcers may be combined in operant. Deprivation states are important in operant but irrelevant in classical conditioning. Another distinction often noted is that contiguity seems to be more important in classical than in operant. Each of these distinctions can be debated, and none is so absolute that it forces us to make a distinction between classical and operant.

The most striking systemic difference is that classical conditioning seems to involve involuntary reflexes and emotions, and operant involves voluntary actions. The internal organs and reflexes are involved in classical, and they are controlled by the autonomic nervous system. The skeletal muscles are involved in operant, and they are controlled by the somatic nervous system. However, there are some exceptions to these distinctions; one of the most notable is the phenomenon of autoshaping, which shows that the commonly used operant response of pigeons pecking a key can be obtained by a classical procedure.

An important attempt to refute the autonomic-somatic distinction between classical and operant was Miller's research on biofeedback. Miller monitored subjects' heart rates and provided feedback of tone changes. He was able to get subjects to deliberately raise or lower their heart rates for rewards, thus showing operant conditioning of the autonomic nervous system. However, the possibility of various mediational devices being used by humans makes their data inconclusive, and the animal data is inconclusive as well.

Most real-life situations involve both classical and operant elements. These components may work together, facilitating each other, or they may counteract each other. A generalized two-factor theory of learning seems to be the best analysis of these interactions at present.

Questions for Discussion, Thought, & Practice

1. Define and give an example of each key concept. Now group them into two categories, classical and operant terms.
2. Determine which type of conditioning is occurring for each example, and then analyze the example by labeling its components.
   a. Violet's parents always read her a story before they put her to bed. They would hold her in their laps and hug her while they read. As she got older, Violet found that having a book open in front of her made her feel contented—and sleepy.
   b. Victoria has a date with a new boy. He invites her to his room to see his "etchings." She readily agrees. He *really* shows her his etchings! Not wanting to seem rude, she smiles and nods her head whenever he looks up from another one, so her date keeps hauling out more and more etchings.
   c. Jesse held the 2, 3, and 4 of diamonds; the other poker players could see that. They didn't know that he didn't have the rest of the straight flush, but he bluffed very well and won a big pot. Now he's gotten very reckless when he plays poker, bluffing quite frequently. Sometimes it works, and sometimes it doesn't.
   d. Young Erlenmeyer (one of the Flask children) ran into the school bully near the swing one day, and the bully beat him up. Now Erlenmeyer gets very upset when he has to go out on the playground and usually asks to read in the library during recess.
3. When would classical conditioning interfere with operant conditioning, and under what circumstances would it enhance operant conditioning?
4. Young Leonardo steps on a jellyfish at the beach and gets stung. The next time the family goes to the beach, he starts to scream when he sees the surf. From then on, he starts to whine whenever the topic of the beach comes up. Is this an example of both classical and operant conditioning? Explain and describe the learning processes occurring.
5. Could the presence of operant contingencies interfere with the learning of classical conditioning? How would this work?
6. Which form of learning is the most common? Does this greater frequency of occurrence make it the most important form of learning? Which form of learning is the most important and why?

The Context of Learning

▲ Key Concepts ▲

attachment
bait shyness
contraprepared
fixed action pattern
imprinting
instinctive drift
interchangeable parts
modal action pattern
niche
novel CS
optimal foraging theory
phylogenetic scale
preparedness dimension
sauce béarnaise effect
taste aversion

The Traditional Model of Learning

When we discussed the nature of learning in chapter 1, we presented a simple distinction between learning and instincts. Instincts were entirely determined by genetic factors, and learning was entirely determined by experience. There was no indication of any overlap between the two; a behavior was entirely due either to the one or to the other. This led to attempts to identify examples of instincts in humans, which resulted in a proliferation of long lists of human instincts. When John B. Watson founded behaviorism, he rejected the concept of instinct almost entirely. He proposed that humans are equipped at birth with only some reflexes and basic emotional reactions and that all the rest of our behavior is learned. He doubted the value of the concept of instinct in general. This extended the earlier work of Thorndike (1898), which had essentially isolated researchers in learning from Darwinian ideas about evolution. For three decades this represented the dominant position in psychology, until Konrad Lorenz (1952) and other ethologists demonstrated convincingly that instincts (which they referred to as fixed action patterns) existed in at least some creatures.

Learning theorists then retreated to the position that although there were these two possible influences on behavior—learning and instinct—they were essentially independent of each other. This interpretation of learning and instinct as polar opposites carried along with it a number of implications. One implication was that "lower" animals' behavior was more likely to be governed by instincts, and "higher" animals, such as human beings, were more likely to be influenced by learning. This requires some independent way of determining which are the higher and lower creatures, and there has been quite a bit of disagreement about such classifications. Another implication was that, because the "higher" creatures generally evolved later, we would presume that instincts were already present in creatures when learning began to evolve in these more advanced creatures. Early learning theorists searched for the origins of learning in instincts and related behaviors. Because classical conditioning can modify reflexes, perhaps conditioning evolved from some combination of reflex-type activities. Such an interpretation would place habituation and sensitization as early steps on the way to classical conditioning, which might have later itself evolved into the potential for operant conditioning. Operant conditioning is often considered to be more advanced from this point of view, because it allows responses to be changed. Classical conditioning is seen as allowing for stimulus learning but little change in the nature of the response. More highly evolved creatures would be more capable of response modification.

This characterization of lower versus higher animals on an evolutionary ladder led some researchers, notably Bitterman (1965), to devise standard experimental procedures that they could use to compare animals of different species. Bitterman suggested an ordering of species' ability to learn, which progressed from earthworm through cockroach, fish, decorticated rat, turtle, pigeon, and rat, to monkey. Although such an ordering may seem plausible (and appealing to us monkey relatives), it ignores the branching nature of the evolutionary process. That is, it tends to treat the differences between species as if they can be placed on a single dimension, when in fact they should probably be arranged along several dimensions (Hodos & Campbell, 1969). As Hodos and Campbell point out, rats were not ancestors of monkeys, but rather the two species evolved from common ancestors. Therefore it's unclear whether each creature evolved behavioral abilities that diverged from this ancestor, whether one diverged and the other retained the ancestral behaviors, or what direction any divergence took. With physical changes, the fossil record often provides clues as to which characteristics appeared at what time; this kind of record doesn't exist for behavioral changes.

In addition, it's hard to remove our own perspective from such attempts, and the possible humanocentric chauvinism has prompted the comment that "Higher on the evolutionary ladder means closer to us." In fact, there is quite a bit of variation and overlap between species and phyla in complexity and sophistication of behavior. For example, most of us would describe the mollusks as relatively primitive creatures. The phylum Mollusca does include seemingly simple creatures such as slugs and snails. However, it also includes the octopus and squid, and octopi have been shown to be capable of fairly complex learning such as discrimination reversal learning (Mackintosh & Mackintosh, 1964) and problem solving. Even within our own order, the Primates, some species (such as lemurs and tarsiers) are considered to have rather primitive behavioral systems. A simple ranking of creatures soon becomes not only complex but also impractical. Creatures that seem primitive in one task seem more advanced in another.

Furthermore, such ideas have been heavily criticized by Bolles (1988) for ignoring the relationship of a learning task to the creature's environmental niche. Generally, what is meant by a **niche** is characteristics of the environment such as the availability and distribution of food and the nature and number of predators and other dangers the creature must live with. Bolles suggested that we see these discrepancies because we are comparing creatures on tasks that bear differing relationships to the behaviors they have developed to exist in their niches. We will discuss the role of niches more fully in the section on preparedness.

In spite of these pitfalls, the belief that innate behaviors are more primitive than learned behaviors was still implicit in most discussions of the importance of learning. Other implications of this position involve the nature of learning itself. If learned behaviors have evolved beyond innate tendencies, then learning represents a trend toward a "neutral" type of influence. Innate tendencies would predispose a creature to certain responses, but behaviors that could be learned would not reflect any built-in predisposition. That is, all stimuli would be equally good as potential conditioned stimuli and all responses would be equally conditionable. All organisms would be trainable in the same way, given that they are at comparable levels on the **phylogenetic scale** (Pavlov, 1927; Skinner, 1938; Spence, 1947). This is often referred to as the **interchangeable parts** assumption of learning theory, and it is basic to much of the research that we have discussed (Houston, 1981; Seligman & Hager, 1972).

For example, the principles of classical conditioning discovered by Pavlov using dogs and salivation to a sound should apply equally well to conditioning humans, rats, or cats to salivate or make any other unconditioned response, and it should apply equally whether we used a bell, a light, a touch, or a taste as the CS. The early research of Pavlov and others suggested that this was so. Similarly, the training of a rat to press a bar for food in an operant chamber represented a standard task that revealed general principles that were often also found to apply whether we were conditioning a child to raise her hand for praise or a dog to sit up for a pat on the head. Furthermore, we should be able to successfully punish any of these operants, which was also often found. The only limits on these learning principles occurred when we examined the "lower" organisms, which often seemed to be less capable of learning as many different things in as many different ways.

The Misbehavior of Organisms

During the 1960s evidence began to accumulate that this view of learning was too simple. Among the earliest indications was the report of Breland and Breland (1961) titled "The Misbehavior of Organisms." The Brelands were behavioral psychologists who used operant conditioning principles to train animals to perform tricks for circuses and amusement parks. In their article they gave numerous examples of cases where the animals did not learn very well or very easily.

One of the more dramatic examples involved their attempts to teach raccoons to deposit coins in a piggy bank. The idea was that customers would deposit quarters in a slot that would deliver the coins in front of the raccoon, who would then carry each coin to the piggy bank and drop it in. After initially shaping the animal to make the "depositing" response by using food reward, the Brelands reported that their raccoons' behavior degenerated when they were given more than one coin at a time to the point that they no longer deposited them. The animals appeared to make "washing" motions with the coins in their paws and then would put them halfway into the slot in the piggy bank, and then withdraw the coins. Often they would go through this washing sequence several times with the same coins.

The Brelands noted that raccoons in the wild routinely try to clean their food in this way. They suggested that this food-washing behavior was instinctive and might be triggered by the food reinforcement they were using. Because they thought that the form of the learned behavior was moving toward a relevant instinctive tendency, they called this phenomenon **instinctive drift**. Although their paper was widely read, it did not lead to any systematic reevaluation of the interchangeable-parts assumption. Instead, it was regarded as a collection of interesting behavioral oddities.

In addition to the Brelands' paper, there were several other examples of inequalities between learning tasks. For example, it was widely known among operant conditioners that the pecking response of the pigeon was easily reinforced with food but extremely difficult to use in a negative reinforcement procedure. In other words, pigeons could not often be trained to peck a key to escape or avoid shock (Rachlin, 1969). However, not much was made of this fact, and it rarely appeared in learning texts. This attitude began to change with the publication of Garcia and Koelling's (1966) research on learned taste aversions.

Taste Aversion Learning

Garcia and his colleagues set out to explicitly test the notion that all conditioned stimuli are equal and interchangeable. He originally became interested in the question because he had been studying the effects of radiation on feeding while working at a research unit at a Navy lab. Although the original experiments might be most appropriately described as avoidance conditioning procedures, it will be easier to follow their logic if we discuss them simply in terms of their classical components. Two types of CS and two types of US were used. The experiments involved teaching rats to fear or avoid the conditioned stimulus when it occurred while they were drinking water. One CS was a taste that was new to the rats; the other was a combination of a flashing light and a clicking noise that occurred while the rats drank. The distinctiveness of this CS has led to the study often being called the "bright noisy water" study. The unconditioned stimuli were (1) an electrical shock (which also occurred while the rats were drinking) or (2) lithium chloride in the water or exposure to X-rays, both of which generate nausea. The chemical itself or the X-rays are not very effective unconditioned stimuli; they were difficult for the animals to detect (impossible in the case of the X-rays) and caused little immediate physical reaction. The nausea they generated must be considered the functional stimulus, because it was the only sensation that the animals could detect. This nausea typically did not occur until half an hour to an hour after the rat drank the water. Each CS was paired with each US so that four different groups were trained as indicated in table 9.1.

The traditional learning theory prediction would be that Groups 1 and 3 should learn at a typical rate but that Groups 2 and 4 should not learn to fear and avoid, because they did not experience the US symptoms in close contiguity to the CS presentations. Contiguity or the lack of

Table 9.1

Group 1	Group 2	Group 3	Group 4
CS1 (flavored water)	CS1 (flavored water)	CS2 (bright, noisy water)	CS2 (bright, noisy water)
US1 (shock)	US2 (nausea)	US1 (shock)	US2 (nausea)

it would be the only factor influencing learning because the choice of CS or US was essentially irrelevant. However, this is not what occurred. Group 3 performed as expected, gradually learning to fear and avoid; and Group 4 performed as expected, because those animals didn't learn very well at all. However, Group 1 didn't learn very well, and Group 2 learned extremely well, usually in only one or two trials. Why didn't Group 1 learn, and why did Group 2 learn so well, violating the contiguity principle? Garcia argued that Group 2 was a case of an innate biological predisposition that allowed the creature to learn in spite of long delays between CS and US; at the same time he suggested that Group 1 didn't learn because the conditions were the opposite of the innate predispositions of the rats.

Seligman (1970) suggested that these and many other scavengers were biologically predisposed to make associations between internal signals (such as tastes) and internal distress (nausea) but were unable to associate an external cue (the bright, noisy CS) with these internal states, like Group 4, or internal cues with external pain, like Group 1. He suggested that these two groups failed to learn because they were biologically unprepared to learn such relationships, and that Group 2 learned extremely well because these animals were required to learn an association that they were biologically prepared to learn.

Carl Gustafson applied Garcia's findings to natural behavior to explain coyotes' scavenging behavior. Sheepherders had tried to poison coyotes with very little success. Gustafson decided to find out how the coyotes were able to avoid poisoning while still scavenging; his analysis suggested that most scavengers engage in a pattern of "nibbling," or just trying a few bites, anytime they encounter already dead animals (Gustafson, Garcia, Hankins, & Rusiniak, 1974). They then go away for some time; if they get sick, they don't return to that carcass. Ranchers call this behavior **bait shyness** because it leads the animals to avoid poisoned bait. If they don't get sick, they return later to consume the rest of the food. This pattern of behavior depends on the ability to associate stimuli at the time of eating with illness occurring up to several hours later.

Garcia called this ability to learn in spite of long delays **taste aversion** learning and pointed out several differences between it and standard classical conditioning. First, there is a lack of contiguity between CS and US. Second, in spite of the lack of contiguity the association is learned very quickly, usually in one or two trials. These two characteristics are relatively unique to taste aversion learning; the CER method of studying classically conditioned fear is the only other procedure that shows such rapid learning. The CER procedure also allows delays of up to a minute between CS and US but hardly seems likely to occur with delays of an hour or more. A third difference is that not all stimuli can serve as a CS for food aversions; usually only tastes (and to a lesser extent, odors) will work. Finally, new tastes (**novel CSs**) are more likely to be associated with illness than old familiar flavors. Although new or unfamiliar stimuli are more easily conditioned in standard classical conditioning experiments, this is not as powerful a factor as in the taste aversion procedure. In the taste aversion procedure, if familiar flavors occur between the novel taste and the illness, the creature nevertheless learns to avoid the novel flavor (Kalat & Rozin, 1970, 1971).

In contrast, as we saw in chapter 3, in standard classical conditioning procedures the stimulus closest to the US in time is the one associated with it. Furthermore, Lucas and Timberlake (1992) have shown that animals respond differently to a taste CS than to visual, auditory, or odor CSs when they are paired with a preferred food as US. It might appear that these differences make taste aversions very clearly a special form of behavior that involves both learning and innate mechanisms. However, each of these differences is one of degree or quantity rather than one of quality, and several researchers have emphasized that there are many similarities between taste aversion learning and standard classical conditioning (Domjan, 1980, 1983).

Many investigators since Garcia have shown taste aversion in various species, sometimes finding that for some species other types of stimuli are more effective than tastes. For example, quail are more easily conditioned to avoid foods on the basis of a visual CS (Wilcoxon, Dragoin, & Kral, 1971). Thus, the particular type of stimulus that is most effective as a CS depends on the species studied. The different ways in which creatures evolve require the use of different signals for indicating what is bad (or good) to eat. With regard to what's good to eat, in addition to the basic taste aversion phenomenon, Garcia has shown that a "medicine effect" also exists. Creatures that experience a flavor followed by relief from nausea develop a preference for that flavor (Green & Garcia, 1971). Subjectively, we learn to like the flavor of things that make us feel better.

Martin Seligman (1970) pointed out that taste aversions are learned by humans as well. He described an example in which he learned to avoid certain French foods and called it the **sauce béarnaise effect**. Since he proposed that taste aversions occurred in humans, many investigators have demonstrated this (Domjan, 1983). Perhaps the most interesting examples occur with cancer patients undergoing chemotherapy, who often come to dislike foods eaten just before a chemotherapy session (Bernstein & Webster, 1980). In most of these cases, the patient realizes that the chemotherapy is making him nauseous, and not the food. Yet these patients still lose their appetites, at least temporarily, for many foods this way. Seligman then proposed that taste aversions represented a "middle ground" between learning and instinct because of the differences between taste aversions and standard conditioning noted above. Furthermore, he suggested that the existence of such in-between cases required a reevaluation of the generality of the laws of learning and of the relationship between learning and innate influences on behavior.

The Preparedness Dimension

Seligman suggested that the causes of behavior were not totally separate categories but rather overlapping influences. He proposed a dimension or continuum, called the **preparedness dimension**, which went from one extreme of totally biologically determined behaviors (most prepared behaviors) to behaviors that the creature was incapable of doing (most **contraprepared**). Figure 9.1 illustrates the preparedness dimension with several types of behaviors positioned approximately. Standard learning tasks, such as rats pressing bars for food, were in the middle, or neutral. However, training raccoons to deposit coins for food reward was to the right of neutral, and the taste aversion task was halfway between neutral and the left end. Taste aversions, imprinting in some birds (Hess, 1973), and language learning in humans (Gleitman, 1984; Lenneberg, 1967) are examples of phenomena that truly seem to incorporate aspects of both innate mechanisms and learning in approximately equal measure. In all of these, the environment that the creature experiences determines what is learned: which tastes are avoided, which moving object is followed, which language is learned. However, in each case the genetic predispositions of the creatures place strong limits on the learning process: only tastes will serve as conditioned stimuli for most species, and birds can only be imprinted during a relatively short critical period and only to moving objects of moderate size.

Figure 9.1 The Preparedness Dimension

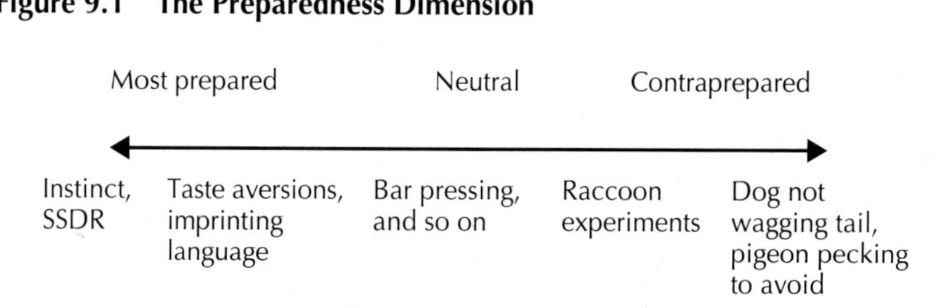

The evidence for an innate predisposition for language in humans is complex, but there are indications of a critical period (a part of the life span during which the individual is more likely to learn than at other times). For humans, the critical period is rather long—our entire childhood. In addition, language seems to be restricted to humans alone, early language development occurs in a fixed sequence despite differing language environments (Gleitman, 1984), and the human brain has some specialized language areas (Lenneberg, 1967). Although there are some arguments about the interpretation of each of these pieces of evidence, many psychologists now recognize that the important genetic basis of language means that there is an innate predisposition for language in humans, as Chomsky (1972) has suggested.

The most prepared extreme is characterized by behaviors totally independent of experience—true instincts (or **fixed action patterns**) such as the species-specific defensive reactions proposed by Bolles to account for avoidance responses in nature (described in chapter 5). Some species of birds (the song sparrow, for example) seem to be capable of developing their songs without any exposure to adult singing. This behavior would be at the most prepared end for these birds. On the other hand, other birds such as the white crowned sparrow require exposure to adult songs; for these birds we would place song development with taste aversions, between most prepared and neutral. Behavioral biologists are studying why some birds seem to have innate songs and others do not (Kroodsma, 1988); so far, variability of the species song over geographical region seems to be one of the best predictors. A species that shows little variation in its song from place to place does not seem to require experience to develop its song (Kroodsma & Miller, 1982).

Furthermore, some bird songs seem to be assembled from short bursts of song which are themselves unvarying, but which can be combined in differing arrangements. This kind of finding has led to modification of the original fixed action pattern definition of instinctive behavior. the more widely used term is now **modal action pattern** (MAP); this reflects the fact that these behaviors do show small amounts of variability in their performance and especially in the stimuli which trigger the response (Baerends, 1988). Baerends has shown that egg retrieval behaviors in birds can be produced to varying degrees by different coloration and size characteristics of the eggs. In fact, he has designed artificial eggs that are more powerful triggers for the birds than true eggs, even though the artificial eggs are abnormally large (too large to be mistaken for real eggs of that species) (Baerends & Drent, 1982). The MAP is produced by a small set of stimuli that have an ideal set of characteristics but can differ from these characteristics slightly and still be effective triggers. At the contraprepared end, we might appreciate how hard it would be to train a dog not to wag its tail when it sees its master or gets fed. This is comparable to the difficulty in teaching a pigeon to peck a key to avoid shock (Rachlin, 1969).

Bolles (1988) has suggested that whether a learning task is neutral on the preparedness dimension is a function of the relationship between that learning task and the animal's environmental niche. A *niche* is the position the creature occupies in its natural environment. The creature's size and other physical characteristics as well as its behavior make it best suited for a particular type of environment. This also means that the creature's behavior is tailored to best suit its environment and that some environmental conditions favor certain behaviors over others. Bolles suggests that the ability of a creature to learn is not a generalized given, but differs

niches & animals

depending on what is to be learned. If the learning task would be helpful and relevant to the creature's natural environment, then the creature probably does similar things already and learning should be easy. These tasks would appear toward the most prepared end of the dimension. Learning tasks that require behaviors that do not fit well into the creature's niche would be very difficult to learn. Because they might be behaviors that would make survival less likely, the creature would have evolved behaviors incompatible with them. This would make these tasks contraprepared for that creature. Finally, learning tasks that are irrelevant to the creature's behavioral niche would be near the neutral center of the preparedness dimension. Most of our examples seem well explained by Bolles's theory; pigeons don't learn to peck to avoid things because in nature, pecking hardly ever helps them escape danger. We have already seen how a taste aversion predisposition helps coyotes and other scavengers function in their environments.

Animal Cognition

During the 1980s researchers combined ideas from information-processing theories, ethology, and neuroscience to investigate animal behavior from a new perspective. These diverse experiments are generally classified as studies of animal cognition, and they are crucially concerned with the information-processing question of representation: do animals represent their world mentally, and if so, how (Gallistel, 1990b)? Do animals have "maps" of their environment stored in their heads, or concepts of what things are like? Are other creatures capable of manipulating their representations, as humans do (described in chapters 11–13)? That is, can animals compare two representations or modify one? Studies have employed many of the traditional learning procedures, but often with a new emphasis. We will consider several examples of this rapidly growing research area.

An illustration of how traditional techniques can be used with a new twist comes from a study by Matzel, Held, and Miller (1988) mentioned in chapter 3. Using a modification of the sensory preconditioning procedure, they presented rats with a tone followed five seconds later by a light. Then they shocked the rats and followed that five seconds later by the light, a backwards conditioning phase. They found no fear response to the light (as we should expect from backward conditioning) but a fear response to the tone did develop. The interesting aspect of this study is their conclusion: the animals must have been able to mentally connect their representations of the two separate pieces of conditioning to notice that the tone and the shock were occurring at the same interval ahead of the light. Thus, the animals were in some way mentally manipulating their representations of events ("five seconds ahead = five seconds ahead, so a shock should come five seconds after the tone").

Another example of animal cognition research involves the development of detailed models of what aspects of an environment would select for what kinds of behavior. One type of model, called **optimal foraging theory**, describes the influence of environmental factors such as the distribution of food (Kamil & Yoerg, 1982). If the preferred food of a creature is widely distributed in small patches that are slowly replenished, the environment favors a fast-moving, eat-and-run kind of behavior. Lots of food in a small area might encourage slower, "munch a bunch" behavior. Thus, the foraging behaviors that an individual learns may be specified by the natural environment; if many generations encounter the same environment, this selection may lead to innate tendencies to more easily learn one type of pattern.

Now recall the research described in chapter 4, in which animals placed on an interval schedule learn to respond at the proper time. As discussed there, they seem to have some kind of mental clock. Gibbon and Church (1990) suggest that animals may be able to use their timing abilities to forage for food more efficiently. These researchers describe natural scenarios that lead to hypotheses, which may generate laboratory experiments. For example, they suggest that birds could represent the travel time to a food source and compare that time (and effort) to the richness of the food supply of that food source to determine whether to go to that spot or to another. The bird gathering food for its newly hatched chicks must have not only a representation of the possible food destinations, their travel times, and the amount of food present at each, but also representations of the number of chicks and the time since they were last fed. The bird must also be able to compare these representations to choose an appropriate food location. Gibbon and Church examined performance on variable interval schedules to study aspects of bird timing suggested by the timing demands of this natural situation. Another, related scenario suggests that animals may also be able to use representations of the food source to determine whether it is depleted ("tapped out") too much to be worth the effort.

Similar functional analyses of defensive behavior have been suggested by Bolles and his colleagues (Bolles & Fanselow, 1980; Collier, 1981; Fanselow & Lester, 1988). These analyses suggest that the type of defensive behavior, and the degree that learning is involved in it, depends on the immediacy of the danger. They note that defensive behavior to a distant predator may be quite different from defensive behavior when the predator is very close or is actually attacking. Generally, they note a greater flexibility of response to the more distant threat. In addition, the relative density of predators in an environment and their type (big, fast cats or sneaky, deceptively colored snakes) may select for certain defensive strategies and behaviors over others. This view that learning allows selection of behaviors best suited to particular situations is consistent with the position taken by Timberlake and Allison (1974), who suggested that reinforcement operates to select an optimum pattern of responding. This optimum behavioral pattern means that reinforcement is actually another mechanism allowing creatures to adapt to their environment. Collier (1981) has explicitly noted the similarity between foraging theories and the behavioral regulation theories of reinforcement such as Timberlake and Allison's (1974).

Numerous studies have examined animals' abilities to remember food locations using a radial arm maze (see figure 9.2). The maze usually has no walls but is raised several feet off the floor; food is placed in a cup at the end of each runway. Thus, a rat placed in the center can see the laboratory walls and all the paths, but not whether a cup has food in it. The laboratory background provides visual cues to relate to locations just as an animal might encounter in foraging for food in the wild. Food is usually placed in all the goals for each trial; the questions are, can the rat remember which goals it has visited this time, and how does it do so? The paths that the animals follow indicate that they rarely enter the same goal twice in a trial; so they remember the goals at which they have eaten during that trial.

You may be thinking: If they just start with one path, then choose the next path on the right, and then the one after it on the right going in sequence, this isn't especially remarkable. But rats don't do that; their pattern of choices is random and haphazard (Olton, 1978). Yet Olton found that rats perform excellently; on a radial arm maze with 17 choices they averaged 15 correct (Olton, Collison, & Werz, 1977). As we will discover in chapter 11, this far exceeds the working memory capacity of people, which is usually around 7 items. So how do rats keep track of which paths they have visited on the current trial, while ignoring their choices from previous trials?

Figure 9.2 An eight-choice radial arm maze

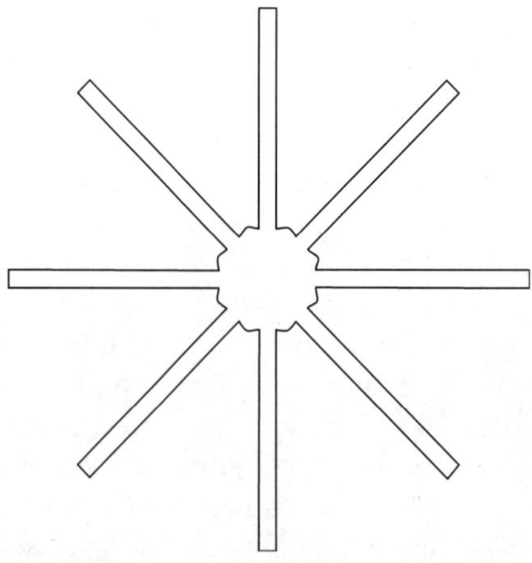

If we move the maze to a different spot in the room, we find that the rats make more errors. This indicates that the things in the room (windows, posters on the walls, benches with lab equipment, etc.) served as "landmarks" for the rats. Some research indicates that the rats form a mental map, with relationships between visual objects guiding their behavior (Gallistel, 1990a; Mazmanian & Roberts, 1983). O'Keefe and Dostrovsky (1971) found specific pyramidal cells in the hippocampus that responded selectively when an animal was in a particular location; these "place" cells retain their specificity for months (Thompson & Best, 1990) and develop this selective response pattern after only one exposure to an environmental location (Hill, 1978). These are the same cells that are said to form "neuronal models" of events during classical conditioning, so they apparently can serve at least two very different purposes (Macphail, 1993).

Several researchers have shown that rats use their working memory in a flexible way; analysis of the patterns of the few errors they make suggest that early in a trial, they are remembering which runways they have visited ("Let's see, I've been to A, B, and C"), but that they switch to keeping track of which runways they haven't visited yet ("Just X, Y, and Z to go") sometime after they have been to half the goals (Cook, Brown, & Riley, 1985). Cook et al. took the animals out of a 12-runway radial maze for 15 minutes after either 2, 4, 6, 8, or 10 visits during a trial and found the most errors when the rats were interrupted after the sixth runway visit. The fewest errors were for the interruptions after 2 and 10 visits; if the animals were only remembering which alleys they had visited, error rates should have increased all the way to the interruption after visit 10, because this would represent the greatest memory load. Cook and colleagues suggested that switching to remembering which runways remained to be visited after visiting their sixth runway minimized the amount to be remembered.

Researchers studying human memory in natural settings have suggested that people can use memory to remember details of past experience, which they called *retrospective memory*, and that people can also use their memories to perform some act in the future ("I've got to remember to get a birthday card for Mom"), which they referred to as *prospective memory*. By analogy, Cook et al. have described the rat as switching from retrospective memory to prospective memory as it progresses through a trial, indicating that animals can choose different ways of representing situations just as humans can. Kesner has shown that people may use the same strategy (Kesner & DeSpain, 1988). He duplicated the Cook et al. (1985) study with rats and also created a version of the task for people; the human subjects were shown grids of 16 squares with an X in one of the squares. They were tested after varying numbers of Xs had been shown. The test consisted of determining which of two Xs was in a new spot and which had been shown in its spot previously. Afterwards the human subjects were asked how they had tried to remember the locations of the Xs.

About half the people reported using only a retrospective technique—they tried to remember all the previous locations of Xs. They showed a continuous decline in performance with increasing numbers of locations to remember. The other half of the subjects described a pattern of switching from retrospective to prospective (as one person reported, "When there were more spaces I remembered Xs, when there were more Xs I remembered spaces"); these people showed an error pattern exactly like their rat counterparts. Since the animal studies do not show several patterns of errors but just the one switch from retrospective to prospective, we might conclude that both humans and animals may switch from one strategy to another, but that people have more control over whether they switch or not, and probably more options in what strategy they select.

A final example of animal cognition research involves conceptual ability: can birds learn concepts? A classic study by Herrnstein (Herrnstein & Loveland, 1964) indicated that they could. They showed pigeons 80 slides, 40 with all or part of a person and 40 without any people. Some pigeons were reinforced for pecking during the people slides and some for pecking during the no-people slides. All the pigeons were able to learn this discrimination. In other studies, the concepts of *water, tree, fish, artificial object*, and *Monet's paintings* vs. *Picasso's paintings*, among others, have been trained into pigeons. Furthermore, several studies have shown that the birds can apply their learning from pictures to the actual objects represented by the pictures (Honig & Stewart, 1988) or apply learning about real objects to responding appropriately to drawings or photographs of them (Delius, 1992).

Pigeons can learn concepts, just as people can. But do they learn and represent them the same way as humans? The "interchangeable parts" view of learning would assume that the two species are comparable and that we could learn much about human concept learning by studying pigeons this way. Unfortunately, according to a study by Edwards and Honig (1987), humans and pigeons differ in how they represent the environment. They compared pigeons' ability to learn using two kinds of training stimuli, a set similar to that used by Herrnstein and an additional set in which positive example pictures were identical to the negative examples except for the presence of the concept object (people). Herrnstein's picture sets were not matched in this way. Pigeons trained with the nonmatching backgrounds learned much faster than those trained with the matched sets, who learned very poorly.

In human studies, the opposite pattern occurs; we do much better with displays in which the only change is the crucial one. So humans learn concepts using different kinds of representations than those that pigeons use. Edwards and Honig suggest that the pigeons encoded the whole pattern as a single representation; two representations which differed by only one detail in the matched condition were hard to learn from. Humans are apparently much more likely to break up the experience and represent it as separate parts, so people learned better from the matched slides (see the discussion of criterial attributes in chapter 10).

Thus, both radial maze studies and studies of conceptual behavior in animals show some general similarities between people and other animals but also some differences of detail in how they function. Researchers in animal cognition have examined many additional fascinating topics, such as imitation, self recognition in mirrors, and tool use in animals (summarized by Boysen & Himes, 1999); these and the studies we have considered show us several things. First, complex creatures (everything from fish on up) are called complex for a good reason; they may have fixed characteristics in some of their behaviors, but they are also capable of very complicated learning. Second, creatures' learning abilities are often related to the tasks they encounter in nature. Third, when we discover a principle of learning, we have to study it across a wide variety of animals to look for variations in how it works and possible exceptions to it before generalizing the principle (especially to humans). If you review the previous chapters, you will find most of the described learning phenomena illustrated with research on several species, usually including people; those principles seem to be general characteristics of how most creatures learn.

Do Humans Have Instincts?

The neutral middle section of the preparedness dimension represents the kinds of tasks in which natural predispositions seem to play little role. Often this region is described as allowing for the greatest plasticity or flexibility of behavior. The important questions for most of us would be: How much of human behavior fits into this middle region, and what human behaviors fall closer to one extreme or the other? The traditional answer would be that most human behaviors are in the neutral zone, with the rather striking exceptions of language and taste aversions. To best answer these questions we must also determine what niche humans originally occupied. This is difficult because we probably are no longer restricted to that niche; in a sense we have become the creatures without a niche. Thus, there is still debate about whether humans evolved from a forest-type environment or a grassland plains environment. Our physical structure allows for either possibility and perhaps others as well. This way of viewing our origin favors the position that we have very few innate predispositions. A species-specific defensive reaction to run away isn't very useful if you live in a forest environment; it would be better to climb a tree. On the other hand, if you're on the plains with no trees in sight, being prepared to climb isn't much help when a sabertooth tiger is in the neighborhood. Furthermore, we aren't especially good runners or climbers compared to many other creatures. This kind of argument can be applied to much human behavior and suggests few prepared responses beyond our reflexes. However, our lack of outstanding physical skills might have forced us toward a pattern of social behavior such as cooperative hunting, which would have caused a pressure to develop better communication skills. Thus, language may have been a behavior that was selected by environmental pressure.

Various ethologists and psychologists have suggested that our facial expressions (Eibl-Eibesfeldt, 1972), certain phobias (fear of bugs and other creepy-crawly things for example [Seligman, 1971]), our affection for creatures with a babylike appearance, and our attachment to children (Bowlby, 1958), our territorial needs (Ardrey, 1966), and aggression (Lorenz, 1966) are at or near the prepared end rather than in the middle of the continuum. Most learning theorists have been reluctant to classify many of these anywhere but neutral. In most of them, there are many variations between individuals, and these variations are most easily explained by noting differences in experience and learning opportunities. The variability of a behavior within a species is one of the most important clues to the possible origin of the behavior.

Another clue is the occurrence of the behavior in other species. Generally, behaviors that always occur the same way, to the same stimuli, in all members of a species are more likely to have a genetic basis, and behaviors that only occur in a few species are more likely to be innate in those creatures. Phobias, aggression, affection for babies, and territoriality do not appear to hold up well to these criteria. The case for facial expressions is somewhat stronger. Smiling, laughing, and crying seem to be quite universal in humans, with little variation across cultures (Eibl-Eibesfeldt, 1972). These expressions occur in the congenitally blind and are associated with the appropriate emotions, even though these people could not have learned them through imitation.

The **attachment** phenomenon in humans is somewhat more difficult to evaluate than phobias or the other behaviors mentioned. In many ways, attachment resembles imprinting, a phenomenon that was originally presented as purely instinctive (Lorenz, 1935, 1952). This similarity was first suggested by John Bowlby (1958), and his analysis remains widely believed. **Imprinting** is a phenomenon that has been studied primarily in aquatic birds, although a few mammalian examples have been documented (primarily sheep: Collias, 1953; Smith, 1965). It is characterized by the tendency of the newly hatched chick to follow the first moving object it sees. During infancy, the chick seeks comfort, care, and protection from this imprinted object, and in adulthood it will attempt to mate with objects resembling it.

Imprinting has been distinguished from standard "neutral" learning in that (1) imprinting has a critical period; it is increasingly difficult to imprint the chick as more days pass since hatching; (2) only certain kinds of stimuli can serve as imprinting objects; they must move and be at least 4 inches in diameter (close to the size of an adult bird); (3) no practice is necessary; the first exposure is sufficient; and (4) extinction and punishment are relatively ineffective in eliminating the imprinted response. In our preparedness dimension, these characteristics place imprinting with taste aversions, or perhaps closer to the most prepared end of the continuum. However, each of these characteristics has been shown to require qualification. Generally, the criticisms note that each distinction is one of degree, rather than being absolute. So the critical period is not totally critical; imprinting is just much easier when done early. The idea that only certain stimuli can cause imprinting is important, but this limit is very broad. Finally, imprinting does require the minimum of one experience, making it different from a pure instinct.

In fact, the concept of instinct is not especially popular with comparative psychologists; at one time, the concept was more or less synonymous with the preferred term, fixed action pattern. However, more recent students of animal behavior have preferred the term modal action pattern to reflect the fact that even with many "instinctive" behaviors, there are slight variations in the behavior as a result of changing circumstances. Modal action patterns do occur in other creatures, but often these creatures exhibit many other learned complex behaviors, as illustrated by our discussion of animal cognition.

Is human attachment an example of imprinting and therefore largely innate? This is possible, although human attachment seems at best to be a very weak form of the phenomenon. The major similarity is that timing is important (just after birth is a crucial time, with the next six months also being very important [Klaus & Kennell, 1976, 1984]). On the other hand, during the first six months the baby becomes attached to the person who spends the most time with it (the primary caregiver). This suggests that much more experience is necessary for attachment than for imprinting.

Whether there is a limit to which kinds of stimuli may generate attachment in humans is a question that cannot ethically be studied, so we can only guess about this characteristic of imprinting. Many children remain attached to cruel or abusive parents, so it may well be more resistant to the effects of extinction and punishment than standard learned tendencies. Finally, the consequences of nonattachment, like the consequences of failure to be imprinted, are negative. However, here again it is unclear exactly what these consequences are for nonattachment. Many adverse personality and intellectual characteristics have been suggested, but because none of these studies are true experiments, conclusions must be made cautiously. Most importantly, the imprinting phenomenon specifies exactly what responses will be elicited from the bird. Attachment is much less specific; general tendencies such as greater shyness, or personality characteristics such as insecurity or low achievement, are the predicted types of behaviors in the poorly attached child. Our original statement seems the best interpretation: attachment may be a form of imprinting, but it's much weaker than the form seen in ducks and geese.

Are humans contraprepared for any behaviors? When I ask this in class students often shout, "Calculus!" (or any math). However, we must not try to make such a judgment on the basis of difficulty alone. Certainly, advanced math is difficult for many people. But it's much easier for us than for any other creatures; we even invented it. Clearly it's much easier to teach calculus to a college student than to a dog or a chimpanzee. We must evaluate the difficulty in learning a behavior for a species relative to that difficulty for other species. Furthermore, we must not choose responses that are impossible for the creature to make; it would be trivial to say that humans are contraprepared to fly or breathe underwater. Again, as we saw for attachment, the kinds of behaviors proposed as contraprepared in humans are very general categories, such as sharing or altruism. Children have a difficult time learning to share things (McCarthy & Houston, 1980). On the other hand, lions with a fresh kill don't share very well either. The dominant male (who often didn't participate in the kill) eats his choice; he shares whatever he is too full to finish.

Altruistic behavior, such as risking one's life to save a drowning child, is also something difficult. We hear about such cases in the news because they are unusual enough that each case is worthy of our attention and respect. But the very fact that these acts are rare implies that they don't come easy for us. Here, too, what is difficult for humans is rarer still in other creatures. No naturalist has ever reported zebras ganging up on the lions to protect an older, helpless zebra. To say that humans are contraprepared for sharing or altruism is to seriously weaken the concept of contrapreparedness. We clearly can learn such behaviors much better than any of the animal examples of contrapreparedness. At this point, there is no convincing evidence that any human behaviors belong near the contraprepared end of the preparedness dimension.

As we move from such "simple" creatures as the amoeba and earthworm to the more complex creatures such as mammals, there does seem to be a trend to rely less on prepared responses and to have a greater percentage of the species' behavior based on learning. However, we shouldn't fall into the trap of thinking that this is good, that learning is somehow "better" than prepared responding. The greater plasticity that learning allows us to have has made us able to adapt to most of the conditions on earth; however, the innate predispositions of ants and many other insects have also allowed them to populate a large portion of the planet. Judging the effectiveness of a survival strategy can be difficult. We must also recognize that all the creatures that exist today are currently at the top of their evolutionary "ladder." In this sense, perhaps they are all using equally effective behavioral strategies.

The greater flexibility conferred on us by learning carries a price. We spend a major portion of our lives learning things, and we are helpless for the first few years of life. On the other hand, the imprinted duckling is able to follow and survive within hours of hatching. This has caused one neurobiologist, Tierney (1986), to suggest that we've got it completely backwards in our traditional position. She suggests that learning didn't evolve from instincts and related innate tendencies, but the other way around. An instinct may be displayed the first time the triggering stimulus occurs. This allows the creature to be most effective in dealing with that stimulus from the outset, as we suggested in our discussion of SSDRs. Because the instinct is the most effective behavioral survival mechanism, Tierney suggests that eventually behaviors that may have to be initially learned may evolve into instinctive behaviors. She proposes that Darwinian survival principles would favor the creatures that could learn an effective defensive response in the fewest trials. Under this environmental pressure, eventually the only members of a species that exist are those with the defense prominent in their behavioral repertoire from the outset. This means that such instincts are highly tailored to particular niches. Tierney suggests that instincts evolve to allow creatures to better survive in their respective niches. It is only when we remove a creature from its normal environment that it looks like an ill-equipped animal. We then force it to learn, and having to learn a response would be its last resort. Tierney has called into question several of the implicit assumptions of learning theory. Specifically, she questioned the assumption that learning requires a larger, more flexible nervous system and the assumption that innate responses are programmed in by specific genes as well as the assumption that learning evolved more recently.

One possible difficulty with Tierney's position involves the time periods involved for evolutionary change and environmental change. Her suggestion seems plausible when we consider very short-lived creatures such as most insects. Insects that live less than a year would go through many thousands of generations before climatic or other environmental conditions could change. Thus, a stable environment would provide the pressure for evolutionary change in one direction. However, longer-lived creatures such as most mammals might face a different environment by the time they had gone through enough generations for evolution to select a specific behavior pattern to be built in. It may be that generational turnover, or reproductive speed, determines the extent to which behaviors can come to be programmed in. This is consistent with our contention that humans and other "higher" creatures display fewer instinctive behaviors. These "higher" creatures are generally longer lived.

Gould (1986) has suggested that the proper way to perceive the roles of learning and innate mechanisms is to see them as interacting with and enhancing each other. This can be seen in taste aversions, where an innate predisposition allows for quicker, more effective learning. The innate tendencies predispose the creature to more readily associate certain stimuli. Gould also notes that many documented cases show an interaction of the opposite form. That is, the creature has several innate subroutines, or small pieces of behavior, that are assembled into a useful sequence through trial-and-error learning. He mentions song learning in birds and food burying in squirrels as examples. Thus, there are cases of innate tendencies modifying the learning process, and learning influencing the use of innate action patterns. The attempt to integrate learning and instinct is possibly the most promising approach to this topic.

At the other extreme from our starting point (which was that there were general rules of learning that applied the same way when learning was possible) is the view that all learning is situation specific. This view suggests that every case of learning represents a situation in which the ability to learn has been "tuned" or refined to best fit some particular niche. Any cases where we fail to see this are the result of our not having identified the environmental constraints very well, or the result of the possibility that several different sets of environmental constraints might be dealt with using the same kinds of learning principles. These cases of common variables occurring in different situations (presumably by chance) would appear to us as suggesting general laws of learning even though there were none. When researchers discuss domain-specific learning, they may be illustrating this position (Cosmides & Tooby, 1987). However, the more traditional learning theorists would suggest that the domains of standard classical and operant procedures are so large that we might as well refer to them as general principles.

Learning theorists have been somewhat slow to accept these new ideas of interactions between learning and innate mechanisms. Most learning theorists remain closer to the traditional position than to Tierney's, Gould's, Cosmides and Tooby's, or even Seligman's. We began our discussion with the traditional position and ended with positions near the opposite extreme. This does not mean that the last positions described are correct—they're just the most recent. Each position has some merit, and at this point none has been fully accepted. In a sense this represents the limit of what we know about the nature of learning. We might tentatively conclude that many creatures have evolved innate patterns of responding that are tailored to the environmental conditions they usually encounter.

In addition, many creatures, including humans, have extensive learning capacities. It is difficult to determine which type of mechanism evolved first, or whether they evolved simultaneously. Some of these learning capacities may be modified to be especially effective for certain circumstances; taste aversions represent an example of this "fine tuning" of the general learning capacity to work especially quickly for a specific kind of situation. And sometimes learning may be operating on innate behavioral tendencies. The psychologist must determine the conditions under which the general principles of learning apply, the conditions under which these general principles are adjusted, and the conditions under which they do not apply. At this point, it seems that the general principles apply without modification to most human situations, with the exceptions of taste aversion learning, language learning, and facial expression learning.

Summary

The simple distinction between learning and instinct presented in chapter 1 assumed that the two were polar opposites totally separated from each other. Learning was assumed to represent a higher degree of evolution and was assumed to be equally effective for any arbitrarily chosen stimuli or responses that could be learned. Many problems exist for such assumptions; one is that they oversimplify phylogenetic relationships. Other problems come from research showing that some animals show an instinctive drift away from trained responses. The most serious challenge to these assumptions was the result of work on taste aversions, which showed that animals could learn to avoid flavors after very few presentations, even when the flavor occurred hours before the internal nausea.

The taste aversion research and Bolles's suggestion of innate species-specific defensive reactions caused Seligman to propose a preparedness dimension, which allowed for behaviors to vary gradually and continuously along a dimension from highly prepared or genetically determined behaviors (instincts or SSDRs), through neutral (most traditional learning tasks), to totally unprepared behaviors (which the creature would be incapable of learning). Taste aversions, imprinting in some species of birds, and human language seem to be behaviors falling midway between most prepared and neutral behaviors. The ease of learning something would depend on where that behavior lay along the dimension for the particular species of learner. The only strong case for a human prepared behavior seems to be language; infant attachment may be somewhat prepared, but it does not seem to be as powerfully determined by genetics as imprinting in ducks. No compelling examples of unprepared behaviors exist in humans.

The learner's innate predispositions are likely the result of the evolutionary and environmental demands placed on the creature by the ecological niche it occupies. Characteristics of the niche that might influence creatures to evolve particular innate behavior patterns include the distribution and quality of food and the distribution and nature of predators. Our initial presumption that learning is a more evolutionarily advanced mechanism than instinct can also be questioned. Although learning may be thought of as consisting of a set of general principles, there are clear cases where the principles are tailored to specific situations.

Questions for Discussion, Thought, & Practice

1. Define and give an example of each key concept. Also try to use each key concept in a sentence, and then arrange the sentences into an organized paragraph.
2. Are there any universal principles of learning? What are they?

3. Try to distinguish between general principles of learning and characteristics of learning that vary across situations. What kinds of phenomena are general and what kinds of phenomena have to be tailored to fit specific situations? Why might these differences occur?
4. Where does running in front of a truck to save a blind person from being hit belong on the preparedness dimension? Discuss the evolutionary value of such behaviors—what could have caused them to evolve?
5. Where does learning to play the guitar belong on the preparedness dimension? Is there any evolutionary value to this behavior?
6. Some researchers have suggested that our reactions to kinship relationships are based on an interaction of innate predispositions and learning. Discuss the human tendencies to protect one's sister, but not to marry her, from this perspective. What would be learned, and what might be innate? (Hint: start with face recognition.)

Verbal Learning
The Study of Transfer and Memory

▲ KEY CONCEPTS ▲

attributes
attribute theory
concept learning
consolidation
decay
differential encoding hypothesis
distributed practice
exemplar theory
frequency
imagery value
incidental learning
massed practice
meaningfulness
negative transfer
nonsense syllable
paired-associates learning
positive transfer
primacy effect
pronounceability
recency effect
release from proactive interference
response competition
retroactive interference
serial anticipation
serial position effect
unlearning

I heard an old favorite on the car radio recently, Donovan's "Sunshine Superman." It reminded me immediately of the times when it was popular; I was in college, and I remember hearing it a lot one summer as I cruised down Collins Avenue in Miami Beach in my Dad's white Ford Galaxie (with a red and white interior, the closest I could get to a girl magnet) looking for coeds. The bright blue sky, the storefronts, palm trees, beaches, hotels, and the people, all these stimulus elements, flash into my mind. This seems to be something that happens to lots of us; we are reminded of events when we hear a song from those times, or we remember events when we hear a line from a movie, or a slang expression from the past, or a smell, like the aroma of an elementary school cafeteria. It also represents a behaviorist view of memory: memories are sets of stimulus events connected together in the individual's mind because they occurred together; memories are sets of associations. When one of the stimuli occurs again, it evokes the other stimulus events, and we remember a pleasant experience.

Here are four questions about memory that illustrate the ideas we will be considering in this and the next several chapters:

1. What did you have for lunch the Tuesday before last?
2. What were you doing when you found out about the World Trade Center attack?
3. What was your favorite song in the third grade?
4. What is the name of the animal that lives in Australia, carries its young in a pouch, and hops around?

If you are like most people, you found questions 2 and 4 to be pretty easy, but questions 1 and 3 to be much harder. Why is this? The difficulty you had with the first and third questions, and the ease of number 2, can be at least partially explained by associative approaches to memory.

A fundamental question that often concerns students in discussions of learning is: Do these processes (classical and operant conditioning) really describe human behavior? As we covered these forms of learning, many of our examples were drawn from the realm of human behavior, yet often students remain unconvinced, and they are not alone. Critics of the behaviorist approach note that the principles of conditioning discovered in animal research apply to humans most clearly in cases where the human behaviors are "simpler" or closer to animal behavior—the behavior of the mentally handicapped, emotionally disturbed, or young children. These critics often feel that behaviorist descriptions omit that which is uniquely human—activities such as planning far into the future and the use of symbolic systems are often mentioned as complex behaviors not easily explained by learning theorists.

Learning theorists have also been concerned with these issues, and most of the findings from animal studies have been duplicated using human subjects. However, these replication studies do not always address the question of general applicability. To show that a study can be replicated in humans doesn't necessarily mean that it represents the typical way that humans function, or that it is a commonly found influence in everyday life. The attempt to answer these questions in domains of activity uniquely human has been the primary concern of a number of learning theorists who study verbal behavior. The study of verbal behavior does not necessarily mean the study of language; in fact, these psychologists have been most often concerned with memory. The term *verbal learning* comes from their choice of verbal stimuli and responses, which are very convenient materials to use when humans are being studied. Their approach to memory is perfectly illustrated by the power of old familiar songs to evoke memories in us.

Ebbinghaus and the Serial Anticipation Method

Hermann Ebbinghaus, a German psychologist, is generally acknowledged as the first person to conduct experiments on a "higher mental process" around 1885. Until his experiments, most of what we now call psychology was considered to be a branch of philosophy; like philosophy, psychology was thought to be an area that could not be studied experimentally. After all, how does one study the mind, thoughts, and emotions? Ebbinghaus had to start from scratch, devising techniques as well as materials and then devising ways to understand the results he obtained. He did all of this in his studies of how people learn and remember. For Ebbinghaus, and for many psychologists, the only difference between learning and memory is the timing involved—if one focuses on the immediate aspects of an experience, one is studying learning; and if one focuses on later consequences of the experience, one is studying memory. In fact, many of the same phenomena and independent variables occur in both learning and memory, as Ebbinghaus discovered, and in many cases the distinction between them is an arbitrary one made for convenience of discussion.

Ebbinghaus knew that to study learning he had to have materials to be learned that were totally new to his subject, materials uncontaminated by the subject's previous experience. For this purpose he developed a large pool of items that consisted of three letters: a consonant, a vowel, and another consonant. Most of these trigrams (three-letter strings) are pronounceable; therefore they are often referred to as **nonsense syllables** (any CVC combinations that were actual German words were thrown out of the pool). Because they were not words, the trigrams should have been unfamiliar to his subject and therefore equal in familiarity and meaningfulness at the beginning of his experiment. Research since Ebbinghaus's time has revealed that this is not always the case, but at the same time it has provided us not only with methods for determining the familiarity and meaningfulness of nonsense syllables and words but also with ways of controlling for such problems (these methods will be discussed later in the chapter). A short list of nonsense syllables might be the following:

XAB
PAQ
MIB
TOR
VOB
QUX
CUG
RIH
FUJ
CEW

Ebbinghaus also needed a method, or experimental task. The task he devised was gradually modified to eventually become the method of serial anticipation (Robinson & Brown, 1926). Serial anticipation could be easily studied with minimal equipment. The experimenter made up a list of 20 or so nonsense syllables, each on a 3 x 5-inch card. These were placed in a stack in front of the subject, with a blank card on top. The subject had to turn the cards over one at a time and look at the syllable printed on each card. When he was finished, he was to turn them back so that the blank was again on top. Then he was to try to remember what the first nonsense syllable was. After he made a guess, he turned over the blank, revealing the first card. This immediately gave him feedback, or knowledge of his results, and thus allowed for learning to continue while he was being tested. The first syllable was also a signal for the subject to try to guess what syllable was next, and so on through the list. Because the subject has to anticipate nonsense syllables in the order they occurred, this method is usually referred to as the **serial anticipation** technique.

When the subject was able to go through the whole list twice in a row correctly, the experimenter assumed that the list had been learned. Then the experimenter could wait for some specified amount of time (called the *retention interval*) and present the subject with the stack of cards again. The number of presentations required to reach the all-correct level this time around could be compared to the original number of training trials, and the difference would reveal how much had been forgotten during the retention interval. This is the most sensitive measure of memory, called *savings*, and is reported as percentages of the original total. After a number of experiments using different retention intervals, Ebbinghaus was able to construct his famous curve of forgetting, which has been verified in its general form many times since. Figure 10.1 shows the results he obtained described under the heading of *percent retained*, which is a little easier to follow than Ebbinghaus's original savings measures. It suggests that people forget over half of what they learn in the first 20 minutes after learning. This is the period of greatest forgetting. Another 10% to 15% is lost in the next half hour or so, and then only about 10% more is lost after longer intervals of hours, days, or even weeks.

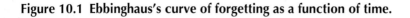

Figure 10.1 Ebbinghaus's curve of forgetting as a function of time.

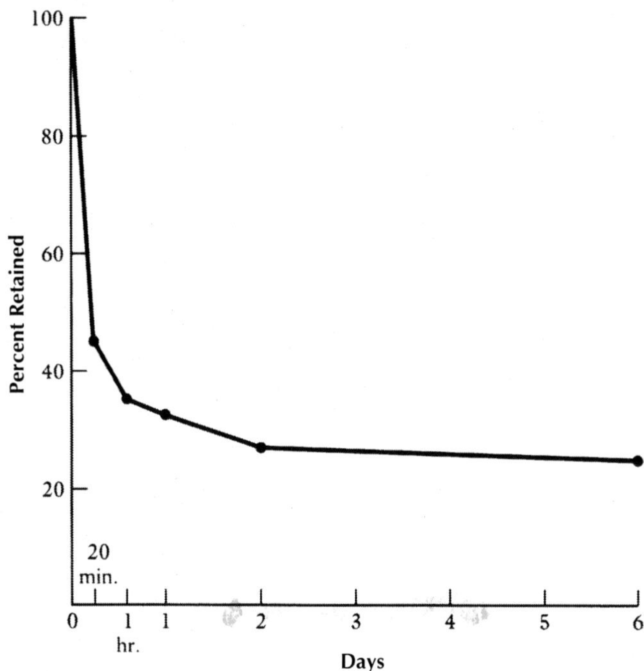

Adapted from *Memory: A Contribution to Experimental Psychology*, by H. Ebbinghaus, 1885, H. A. Ruger & C. E. Bussenins (Trans.). New York: Dover.

Interference versus Decay

Because the amount remembered shows a steady decline with increasing time intervals (up to a point), it is tempting to conclude that the passage of time causes memories to fade away. This is referred to as **decay**, an explanation often given by the average person on the street to explain forgetting. However, one would need to explain why the effect is so much more powerful immediately after learning, and why it does not continue until the material is completely forgotten. Any such explanation would require mechanisms in the nervous system that operate differently at different time intervals after learning. As you might imagine, such explanations are not popular with behaviorists, who wish to explain behavior as a consequence of external factors rather than internal factors. Verbal learning theorists also have consistently tried to reject the notion of decay and have had a reasonable amount of success in doing so. The alternative explanation emphasizes interference, the idea that the things one has learned can get in the way of each other when one tries to recall them. This is also often suggested by the person in the street, and in fact Ebbinghaus himself proposed it to explain many of his results. However, although the average person might feel that both decay and interference explain forgetting, the verbal learning theorists have focused exclusively on interference.

As stated earlier, Ebbinghaus's curve of forgetting has been confirmed many times by later investigators. However, these later studies have generally found a smaller amount of forgetting at each point than Ebbinghaus found, and the reason seems to be in their choices of subjects. Most studies have used college freshmen; Ebbinghaus used himself. Why would the memory ability of a brilliant scientist such as Ebbinghaus be consistently worse than that of the average college freshman? The answer is that Ebbinghaus used himself as a subject in study after study—hundreds of lists of nonsense syllables were learned and recalled. The average college freshman learns one or two lists in somebody's experiment and is not used again. Verbal learning theorists suggested that the memory traces of the previously learned lists interfered with Ebbinghaus's ability to accurately recall the list he had most recently learned. Older memories interfering with the ability to remember more recently learned things is referred to as **proactive interference**. Many experiments have demonstrated the very powerful effects of proactive interference; they generally are conducted in three stages in the following way:

Group	Stage 1	Stage 2	Stage 3
Experimental	Learn List A	Learn List B	Recall List B
Control	Neutral	Learn List B	Recall List B

The control or comparison group is first required to do some neutral activity (circling every *e* on a page of a newspaper has been a popular task) so that they are engaging in some activity likely to generate similar amounts of mental effort and fatigue while in the laboratory. They do this for the same amount of time it takes the experimental group to learn the first list. Then both groups learn list B. After some time interval, both groups are tested for their recall of list B. Invariably the control group recalls list B better than does the experimental group. The difference in their performance is due to the proactive interference effects of the experimental group having learned list A earlier. In addition, these differences usually account for most of the differences between the level of original performance and recall performance by the control group. In other words, these interference effects consistently appear more powerful than effects that might be due to decay. We will shortly suggest that even these differences within the control groups' performance are due in large part to interference.

Examples of proactive interference occur regularly in everyday life. Whenever some activity is regularly repeated, our recall of the details of the most recent occurrence is disrupted by the many previous occurrences. A common example involves college students who drive to campus and park in a neighborhood near the campus. If they must hunt for a spot and don't get the exact same one day after day, they will occasionally have trouble remembering where they parked on the current day. The previous memories "confuse" them due to proactive interference.

Another form of interference is possible; newer memories might interfere with the recall of previously learned material. This is referred to as **retroactive interference** and would be studied in the following way:

Group	Stage 1	Stage 2	Stage 3
Experimental	Learn A	Learn B	Recall List A
Control	Learn A	Neutral	Recall List A

Again, the control group outperforms the experimental group during recall, and the difference represents the amount of retroactive interference affecting the experimental group. Pure examples of retroactive interference in everyday life involve the problems we have recalling the details of "firsts"—for example, can you recall the first time you went to see a movie at a theater? What was the movie? Who were you with? When was it? Often these details are hard to recall because of the interference of the details of all the later experiences. The more such experiences one has, the more retroactive interference there is. Therefore, retroactive interference may account for the everyday suspicion that we "forget" long ago events; actually, the further back in our past they are, the more retroactive interference there is for them.

Question 1 at the beginning of the chapter, which asked about what you had for lunch last Tuesday, can be seen as both retroactive and proactive interference at work. Many lunch experiences on previous days cause proactive interference, and the lunches you ate on days since last Tuesday caused retroactive interference. Because these experiences had so many similarities, the result was lots of interference and therefore poor recall for last Tuesday. On the other hand, you have experienced only once the news of the World Trade Center attack (question 2); there's very little to interfere with it.

Both forms of interference are influenced by the same major variables (with one exception, discussed shortly). The three most important variables influencing interference are (1) the meaningfulness of the material to be remembered, (2) the similarity of the materials involved, and (3) the time intervals between learning and recall and between the original learning experiences. These variables work in a very straightforward way. As you might suspect from our discussion of Ebbinghaus's original experiment, more meaningful material is more easily remembered and therefore in a sense more resistant to interference. Materials that are more similar are more likely to interfere with each other, either proactively or retroactively, than less similar materials. Finally, the longer the retention interval, generally the poorer the recall.

In our descriptions of experiments, we had our experimental groups learn two lists of nonsense syllables, which are more likely to interfere with each other than a list of nonsense syllables and an activity such as circling *e's* as the control group did. The greater the physical similarity of the materials, the greater the interference they generate for each other. This is a wonderful variable for the empirically oriented behaviorist; a behavioral result is predicted by an external variable that is physically measurable. In addition, these effects can be explained as being the result of generalization, tying the learning of verbal materials in humans to the learning of classical and operant behaviors in animals. The idea is that the associations formed to one stimulus would generalize most to another stimulus very similar to it; if the two stimuli must be distinguished, generalization would lead to confusion. When dealing with nonsense syllables, physical similarity—the appearance or sound of the syllables when pronounced—is the only way in which they can be similar. However, when meaningful words are used in interference studies, their similarity of meaning becomes the more important factor. Words that are similar in meaning will interfere with each other more than words with little similarity in meaning.

Although similar materials interfere with each other to the greatest extent, any two experiences may interfere with each other a little, as Jenkins and Dallenbach (1924) demonstrated in an important experiment. They studied retroactive interference in a curious, "naturalistic" way; the interfering material was normal daily activity. Their experimental subjects learned a list of nonsense items in the morning and then went through their normal daily activities until tested for recall. The control subjects learned the list at night and then slept in the lab until tested for recall. Again, the control group recalled better, demonstrating that even very dissimilar activities generated a little interference, which could add up to a lot when there were many such activities. This experiment further weakens the value of decay as an explanation of forgetting; as more time goes by, more little bits of experience can occur, which lead to greater amounts of retroactive interference. Although the curve of forgetting may look like the result of decay, it may merely be the result of the buildup of lots of small amounts of interference. Because in everyday life the two factors will be highly correlated (more time would naturally be associated with more experiences), we find it easy to assume that the mere passage of time causes memories to be lost when in fact they are suffering from more interference.

What causes interference? The problem of too much generalization might have an effect during the original learning, in which case we should see that learning the second list takes longer than learning the first list. In addition, this suggests that learning the second list might cause the first list to be **unlearned** or extinguished. On the other hand, the effect may only occur during recall, in which case both sets of responses are available to the subject, but she is confused about which responses to give. This **response competition** idea (McGeoch, 1932) should be easy to test—we notice how many responses the subject gives from the wrong list. Unfortunately, although there are some of these errors, they are relatively few and therefore seem to account for only a little bit of the total amount of interference (Melton & Irwin, 1940).

The other possibility, unlearning, is unfortunately also not well supported. Initially, researchers proposed that because unlearning was the same as extinction, we should be able to detect spontaneous recovery in retroactive interference. That is, if we test for recall of the first list immediately after learning the second list, we should see the maximum amount of extinction of the first list and therefore lots of retroactive interference. But if we waited a while, spontaneous recovery of the first list should occur and we should see less retroactive interference. Initially, this led to promising results; Underwood (1945) found just this predicted pattern. However, later research made it seem much less plausible. In particular, Postman and Stark (1967) found that if, instead of requiring recall of items, they gave subjects a recognition test immediately after the second list, the subjects showed little evidence of retroactive interference. Unlearning does not seem to be a major cause of interference.

The most widely accepted explanations of interference effects allow for the possibility of some response competition both from within a list and from outside of it, but emphasize an inhibitory process that causes a response set predisposition (Postman, Stark, & Fraser, 1968). This explanation is referred to as list differentiation and suggests that when a subject receives a lot of practice on one list, her tendency to recall other material is inhibited. In a sense she "prefers" to give responses from the highly practiced list or from the most recently practiced list. For the retroactive interference situation, her inability to differentiate newer material from the older test list should lessen as time passes since the last practice on the new list, thus causing the improvement that looked like spontaneous recovery. This idea also suggests that things that make the two lists easier to distinguish would lessen the amount of interference obtained.

Houston and Reynolds (1965) were able to do just this, merely by altering the pacing of study on the two lists. For one list study was massed—that is, there was no intertrial interval; the other list was studied with rest intervals between each trial through the list. This made the two lists more distinctive from each other without altering the similarity of the stimuli themselves. This did reduce the retroactive interference obtained. The list differentiation idea is best understood as a refinement of the competition notion; something like competition is occurring to cause interference, but it's not the item-versus-item competition that the original simple competition idea proposed.

Ebbinghaus discovered another unique finding. No matter which items he used in his lists, the first few and the last several were easier to learn and remember than the items in the middle of the list. Again, this finding has been confirmed many times since and is referred to as the **serial position effect**. It can be found in memory for lists even when serial anticipation is not required. For example, we could give a list of words or nonsense syllables to our subject and later just ask her to write down as many as she can remember in any order. Such a free recall task will also show the serial position effect; the items with the greatest probability of recall will be those at the beginning and end of the list. Figure 10.2 shows an idealized graph of the percentage of correct responses for each position in a list of about 20 items; this is a typical serial position curve. It can be readily observed in any list of items that are about equal in meaningfulness and familiarity.

For example, figure 10.3 shows actual data obtained in a classic study by Murdock (1962). In such experiments, ease of learning depends on whether an item is among the first two or three on the list (referred to as the **primacy effect**) or among the last five to seven (the **recency effect**). Ebbinghaus and later verbal learning theorists attempted to explain the serial position effect by noting that items at the beginning of a list can

Figure 10.2 The serial position curve. Recall as a function of position on the list.

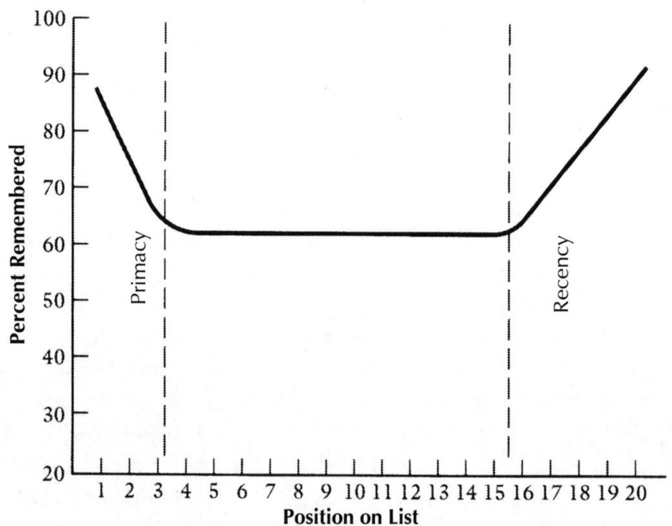

only suffer from the interference of later items (retroactive interference), and items at the end of the list can only suffer from the interference of earlier items (proactive interference), but items in the middle could be interfered with by items both before and after them. Thus, there are more sources of interference in the middle of the list. Unfortunately, although there is evidence for rather generalized effects of this type (Deese & Kresse, 1952), experiments have generally failed to provide detailed support for interference effects operating in this manner.

As an example, this theory would predict substitutions or confusions between TOR, VOB, and QUX (items 4, 5, and 6 in our sample list) with VOB sometimes given as a response instead of TOR or QUX and TOR given for VOB and QUX, but only PAQ and XAB substituted for each other at the beginning of the list or CEW and FUJ substituted for each other at the end of the list. Although fewer numbers of substitution errors at the beginning and end of the list do occur, even errors in the middle of the list are only occasionally the result of "neighbors" being shifted around in this manner. Usually, poor performance is most often seen as a total failure to respond rather than making wrong responses.

Figure 10.3 The serial position curve for a 20-word list presented at a rate of 2.5 seconds per word.

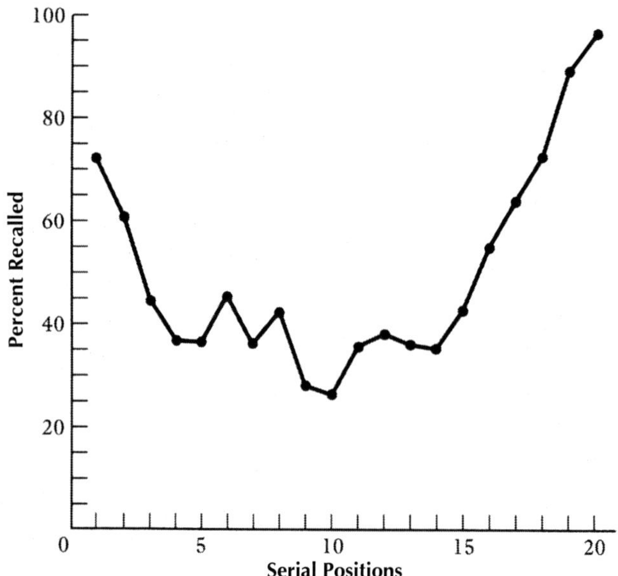

From "The Serial Position Effect of Free Recall, by B. B. Murdock, Jr., 1962, *Journal of Experimental Psychology, 64,* 482–488. Reprinted by permission of the author.

A more satisfactory explanation of part of the serial position curve comes from an experiment by Rundus (Rundus & Atkinson, 1970), who gave subjects lists and asked them to rehearse out loud. He then counted the number of times that each item was rehearsed as a function of its position on the list. He found that the first item was rehearsed the most, second item next most frequently, third next, and then number of rehearsals leveled off; a curve of rehearsals for each position exactly parallels the primacy effect and the middle portion of the serial position curve. The recency portion of the curve was not explained very well by amount of practice. In fact, the recency effect has been very troublesome for behaviorally oriented theorists. The most widely accepted behavioral explanation involves the notion of "landmarks"; the first and last items on a list are distinctive simply because they are the first and last. This distinctiveness makes them better remembered. However, the landmark idea has trouble accounting for the recall advantage seen for the second and third items and for the next-to-last items. (The best current explanation requires an assumption that involves the two different memory mechanisms described in the information-processing theory in the next chapter.)

A good real-life example of the serial position effect in action comes from the performance of most people when asked to recall the presidents of the United States. Typically, people easily recall the first few, Washington, Adams, and Jefferson, and the most recent few, Bush, Clinton, Bush, Reagan, and Carter, but have much more difficulty with many in the middle, such as James K. Polk (11) or Rutherford B. Hayes (19). In fact, two psychologists (Roediger & Crowder, 1976) conducted an experiment that demonstrated this, with one glaring exception; the sixteenth president was much better remembered than the others in the middle of the list (right, it was Lincoln). This also very nicely illustrates the influence of meaningfulness and distinctiveness; most of us know much more about "Honest Abe" than we do about many of the others in the middle, and our added knowledge makes Lincoln more unique to us. The fact that distinctive stimuli are more easily learned and better remembered than others is called the *von Restorff effect* (von Restorff, 1933) and occurs in a wide range of memory tasks. Together, the effects of meaningfulness and distinctiveness make the terrible events of 9/11 in our second example very well remembered; it was very meaningful, and there are few events like it in our experience.

In addition to these findings, Ebbinghaus demonstrated many principles that are exactly the same as, or totally consistent with, the principles of learning revealed in animal experiments on classical or operant conditioning. Several should be obvious from the gist of our discussion so far. For example, he found that the size of the list determined the ease of learning and remembering it. Although short lists (four or five items long) could often be learned in one trial, longer lists took more trials; the longer the list, the more trials required. Also, he found a straightforward practice-effect for longer lists; the more times he went through a list, the better it was learned and recalled. His practice effect curves duplicate the standard learning curves found in earlier chapters, with the greatest improvements found on the earliest trials and smaller and smaller amounts of improvement on later trials.

Yet, even here Ebbinghaus was able to contribute something unique; he found that it was better to spread out the practice (referred to as **distributed practice**) than to lump it all together at one time (**massed practice**). This is essentially the same effect as the intertrial interval variable discussed in chapters 2 and 3. One possible reason for this effect may be understood by referring to nonverbal, skill-learning tasks such as shooting foul shots in basketball or learning to play the guitar. Massed practice on such tasks will lead to fatigue effects, which will lower performance after a while; distributed practice does not lead to quite so much fatigue and therefore is more effective (Irion, 1966). However, although fatigue in such situations would clearly be affecting performance, it might not have an effect on the underlying learning (remember that we excluded fatigue from our definition of learning in chapter 1).

The fact that distributed practice has an advantage over massed practice in verbal tasks, where fatigue is less important, as well as in physical tasks, indicates that the underlying learning is influenced by the spacing of practice. Several reasons have been suggested for this. Some emphasize that the learner has an easier time "consolidating" the memory trace—that is, the memory trace requires some time to become engraved in the nervous system well enough to resist disruptive influences (Hebb, 1949). Such **consolidation** theories suggest that the nervous system may be likened to potter's clay—when it is formed into a vase, the shape may be distorted and deformed until it has been baked into a hardened form. Forming the clay into a shape is like having an experience that causes some chemical or physical change in nerve cells; baking is the consolidation process whereby the change in nerve cells is made permanent. When new learning is still being consolidated, extra practice has less value; if you take your sculpture out of the oven "half baked" and work on it some more, the material may crumble instead of becoming properly hardened. Generally, the consolidation process is believed to require about 20 minutes. The time requirement for consolidation thus suggests that material should be rehearsed within 15 or 20 minutes to ensure the strongest memory trace.

Other explanations emphasize cognitive rather than physiological factors and suggest that distributed practice provides for greater variations in the context surrounding each presentation of the material. It is assumed that the context is associated with the material to be learned to some extent. More different contexts mean more pathways to the same memory—more roads leading to Rome, as it were. This is often referred to as the **differential encoding hypothesis** (Melton, 1967). Using the technique of differential encoding to improve memory is a bit complicated because one could create pathways that interfere with each other rather than enhance each other. Generally, a new pathway should be an elaboration on the older pathway for the differential encoding to be helpful rather than troublesome. We will discuss these ideas in more detail in chapter 12. Let us now turn to some other important findings in verbal learning.

Paired-Associates Learning

Earlier in the chapter the nature of the materials to be learned was mentioned as an important influence on ease of learning. Two variables were listed, similarity of the materials and their meaningfulness. The effects of these variables on learning and memory have been more carefully examined using a technique somewhat different from the serial anticipation method; this slightly newer technique invented by Mary Calkins (1894) is called the paired-associates technique. In **paired-associates learning** the subject must learn to give a particular response to a particular stimulus; a typical list is shown below.

S	R
WIF	– Tranquil
DEX	– Barren
GOZ	– Spoken
LOH	– Worthy
PEC	– Fearful
JAL	– Insane

In this list, after the learner has seen it once, he is shown the stimulus item WIF and must give "Tranquil" as the response. Often the learner is tested in a random order; he may have to respond correctly to PEC, then GOZ, then JAL, and so on, so that he is indeed forced to learn that "Spoken" is the response to GOZ rather than the third response to be given. Usually after the learner responds, he is shown the correct response for feedback. Note that in this list, the learner must come to recognize that the nonsense syllable LOH is the signal to give the response of the meaningful word "Worthy." We could have given such a list to one group and reversed the items for a comparison group, asking them to learn to respond to "Insane" with JAL. We could then compare the two groups. If the first group learned and remembered better, we could conclude that it is harder to learn new responses (because that is what is required when the responses are nonsense syllables) than it is to learn new signals for making old (already learned) responses such as familiar words. In this fashion the influence and nature of meaningfulness can be studied in some detail.

This might give the impression that verbal learning theorists have defined meaningfulness as simply *familiarity.* Clearly, familiarity is an important factor determining meaningfulness; correlations between the two range from r = .33 (Paivio, Yuille, & Madigan, 1968) to r = .83 (Noble, 1963).

In these studies, **meaningfulness** is usually defined as the average number of responses given to an item in 60 seconds in a word-association task (Noble, 1952). The most objective definition of familiarity is in terms of frequency of occurrence in large samples of writing or speech (Thorndike & Lorge, 1944). We can see from the range of correlations that familiarity influences meaningfulness, but there must be other factors involved as well. One is pronounceability; words that are harder to say often have lower meaningfulness scores than words that are easy to pronounce. **Pronounceability** and **frequency** are themselves interrelated (Ley & Locascio, 1970).

These variables, frequency and pronounceability, have been extensively studied and are clearly very influential in determining the meaningfulness and therefore the ease of learning materials. However, it is also clear that they omit some components of meaningfulness, components that are very difficult to study. The most obvious of these involves the specific nature of the **contexts** in which items occur. Two items may be equally easy to pronounce and occur equally often, but one may occur in richer, more detailed contexts than the other. The one in the richer contexts will become more meaningful. Or one item may occur in more pleasant contexts than the other, and this may make it more meaningful. These variables are so difficult to define and measure accurately that we are just beginning to explore them. The research on complex meaning interrelationships between items and their contexts is best understood in the information-processing context discussed in chapters 11 and 12.

Finally, in addition to familiarity, pronounceability, and contextual factors, the imagery value of an item may be related to its meaningfulness. **Imagery value** is a rating of how strong or vivid a visual or sensory image is generated by a word. Usually words referring to concrete objects (such as "butterfly") receive higher imagery ratings than abstract words (such as "virtue"). Paivio, Yuille, and Madigan (1968) obtained ratings from a large number of subjects of the imagery value of 925 nouns varying in frequency of occurrence. The average imagery ratings correlated very highly with concreteness ratings ($r = .83$), moderately highly with meaningfulness ratings for the words ($r = .72$), but not very much at all with familiarity ($r = .23$). That is, generally words with the ability to generate vivid images are concrete rather than abstract words; they are also rated as more meaningful, but there is more variability in this relationship. Thus, the ability of a word to generate a strong visual image in your mind is somewhat related to the meaningfulness of that word, but is not especially influenced by the word's familiarity. Paivio concluded that images represent a separate component of meaning, at least somewhat independent of the verbal associations given to a word (Paivio, 1971). Paivio and his colleagues also showed that high-imagery words are more rapidly learned and better recalled than low-imagery words, even when the two sets of words are equated for meaningfulness and familiarity (Paivio, Yuille, & Rogers, 1969). The value of mental images as a powerful memory aid has long been known; discussion of this topic and some tips for imagery use are presented in chapter 13.

Positive and Negative Transfer

The most common uses of the paired-associates method have been in the study of interference and a closely related phenomenon, transfer. Usually when these phenomena are studied, two paired-associates lists are used, just as in an interference study using the serial learning method. If we examine how one piece of learning influences the *ability to remember* another piece of learning, we are studying interference. If we examine how one piece of learning influences the *ability to learn* another thing, we are studying transfer. Thus the most important difference between transfer and interference is procedural in that we look for the effects either during learning (transfer) or after learning (interference).

Another difference is that transfer effects can be either positive or negative, but interference effects are thought of as exclusively negative. That is, it might be that having learned one thing makes it easier to learn another; this would be **positive transfer**. If learning one thing gets in the way of learning something else, that would be **negative transfer**. An example of positive transfer from everyday life might be the assertion often made by Latin teachers that learning Latin will aid in the learning and understanding of English grammar and vocabulary. However, evidence for this effect is very weak; in general, positive transfer is fairly hard to demonstrate both in the laboratory and in real life. Negative transfer is unfortunately much more common, as we shall see.

The amount and type of transfer has been found to depend very heavily on the similarity of the materials in rather complex ways. We must describe degree of similarity rather precisely, from exactly the same (HOUSE on both lists, for example), through slightly different (HOUSE on one list and HOME on the other), to totally dissimilar. In addition, we must do this separately for the stimulus-learning aspects and the response-learning aspects of our tasks. Paired-associates learning tasks have proven ideal for this. Let us look at a few examples of different types of transfer tasks.

A – B, C – D

List 1	List 2
Beach – Clock	Broom – Pelican
String – Pony	Mask – Table
Fire – Letter	Shoe – Waffle

This is referred to as an A – B, C – D design because the stimuli in list 1, the A items, are unrelated to the stimuli in list 2, the C items, and the responses in the two lists, represented by B and D, are also unrelated. If the responses were the same, the design would be classified as A – B, C – B and might look like this:

A – B, C – B

List 1	List 2
Beach – Clock	Broom – Clock
String – Pony	Mask – Pony
Fire – Letter	Shoe – Letter

The A – B, C – D design generally leads to so little *specific* transfer that it is often used as a standard comparison or control group. Thus, by definition any positive transfer generated in the A – B, C – D design is classed as *nonspecific* or *general* transfer effects; all transfer designs show these sometimes substantial benefits, described as learning-to-learn (Postman & Schwartz, 1964) and warm-up effects (Thune, 1951). They refer to the likelihood that the learner has to learn what to pay attention to, how to study it, and so on, for a task; and once she has done this, it will benefit her in any following tasks of that type. If the nature of the tasks is similar (in this case, learning lists), the learner benefits somewhat from having seen a list-learning task before. This effect has resulted in many high school students retaking the SAT tests several times to benefit from their previous practice at taking such tests. Clearly they don't expect to see the same questions, but they do expect to have some improvement. On the other hand, specific transfer would refer to the consequences of seeing the same questions again. In transfer tasks, we can study this more precisely and examine the effect of having learned BEACH – CLOCK on the learning of BROOM – CLOCK, for example. One might expect that there would be some benefit in this case (the A – B, C – B design); however, a variety of results have actually been found from moderately positive to slightly negative transfer (Twedt & Underwood, 1959).

Positive transfer is actually rather hard to find; it does occur fairly reliably for the A – B, A' – B design (below), and weak positive transfer occurs in the A – B, A – B' design. Using the same letter and adding an apostrophe indicates that we are using similar, but not the same, materials (as in the HOUSE versus HOME situation described earlier). The A – B, A' – B design would consist of pairs like these:

A – B, A' – B

List 1	List 2
Clock – Beach	Watch – Beach
Pony – Letter	Horse – Letter
String – Fire	Thread – Fire

You can see how similar the two lists are; the only difference is that the stimulus words from list 2 are synonyms of the stimulus words for list 1. Given this high similarity, if we didn't obtain positive transfer here, we would probably doubt that it could be obtained. But this high degree of similarity is what we need in order to see positive transfer (Dallett, 1962;

Wimer, 1964). If we make the stimuli a little less similar (for example, by changing WATCH to HOUR, HORSE to SADDLE, and THREAD to NEEDLE in list 2), we see a reduced amount of positive transfer (Brown, Jenkins, & Lavik, 1966; Dallett, 1962).

Thus, we can expect positive transfer only in circumstances where the stimuli change just a little and the responses don't change at all, such as learning to use a metal tennis racket after having used a wood one, or changing from playing on cement courts to clay courts. However, we probably would find negative transfer from hitting a tennis ball to hitting a golf ball or baseball (of course, the changes in response requirements would also generate negative transfer in these cases, making these examples of the A – B, A' – B' design). If we reverse the stimulus items and response items for each list above, we would have an A – B, A – B' transfer design. Here the stimuli are identical and the responses are very similar, and we might expect positive transfer. Weak positive transfer is obtained (Bastian, 1961), but sometimes zero transfer is obtained (Wimer, 1964), and the degree of similarity again seems to determine whether any positive transfer is obtained. Table 10.1 summarizes the transfer designs discussed in this chapter.

In general, attempts to find a systematic pattern to transfer effects have not been very successful. Osgood (1949) provided an early summary of these effects with his transfer surface model, but his presentation focuses on results from transfer studies using meaningful items (words). Studies using nonsense syllables show different results for some designs. Furthermore, Osgood's surface fails to include several important transfer

Table 10.1 Typical Transfer Designs

Type	List 1	List 2	Result
A – B, C – D	Beach - Clock XAB - PAQ	Broom - Pelican VOM - CEW	0 (by definition)
A – B, C – B	Beach - Clock XAB - PAQ	Broom - Clock VOM - PAQ	Mixed
A – B, A – D	Beach - Clock XAB - PAQ	Beach - Pelican XAB - CEW	Negative
A – B, A – B'	Bach - Clock XAB - PAQ	Beach - Watch XAB - VAQ	Weak Positive
A – B, A' – B	Clock - Beach XAB - PAQ	Watch - Beach XAV - PAQ	Positive
A – B, A – Br	Beach - Clock XAB - PAQ	Beach - PAQ Xab - Clock	Strong Negative

designs. An analysis by Martin (1965) provides a somewhat better and more inclusive description. Generally, both approaches note that responses are harder to learn than stimulus signals, as we have shown, and therefore changing the responses from one list to the next (A – B, A – D) usually generates negative transfer. When the responses remain unchanged, making the stimuli more similar (A – B, A' – B) leads to greater positive transfer. In addition, Martin pointed out that the connection or association itself is an element that must be learned. This gives his analysis much broader explanatory power. Consider the following transfer experiment, called A – B, A – Br.

List 1	List 2
Beach – Clock	Beach – Letter
String – Pony	String – Clock
Fire – Letter	Fire – Pony

In this design, the stimuli and the responses are the same for list 1 and list 2; the only difference is that they are matched up differently. The little r after the second A – B indicates that the associations are rearranged. Instead of responding to BEACH with CLOCK the subject must give LETTER, and respond with CLOCK to STRING. This procedure often leads to the greatest degree of negative transfer, even though the subject already knows the responses and the stimuli when she gets to list 2. Because the only change we have made is in the pattern of associations, these results demonstrate that the associations must be learned as well as the responses to make and the signals for making responses. Osgood's transfer surface has no provision for these association effects, because it only deals with stimulus similarities and response similarities.

Generally, at least five different pieces of learning have been identified in transfer tasks: (1) learning forward associations, such as CLOCK is the response that goes with BEACH; (2) learning to make the responses or integrate response elements into a unitary response; (3) learning to differentiate responses from each other; (4) learning to differentiate stimuli from each other; and (5) learning backward associations such as BEACH was the signal for CLOCK. Usually, distinguishing stimuli turns out to be the easiest thing for subjects to learn, and learning new responses is the most difficult thing to do. Backward associations are not especially well learned because they are generally of little use to the subject in these tasks. Nevertheless, they seem to come along for the ride when the forward associations are learned.

Transfer occurs regularly in everyday life. Learning to drive a manual transmission with reverse at the lower right, as on some foreign cars, after having driven an American car with reverse at the upper left should result in specific negative transfer because we are changing the response requirement. We would probably classify this as an A – B, A' – D transfer task because the stimulus situations are similar but not exactly the same, but the responses are different. There would also be some general positive transfer (learning to learn) for that individual compared to someone who hasn't driven a manual transmission car before, so that the individual with the previous stick shift experience should shift gears better than the inexperienced person, except for difficulty with reverse. Thus, predicting who would more easily shift into reverse might be difficult.

This is exactly the kind of problem the transfer researchers encountered—transfer effects are difficult to predict. Another, personal example involves the characteristic of some CD changers that require that the compact discs be placed label-side down in the player. Once I got used to this, I was continually placing CDs label-side down in the single-play CD player I have—and wondering why I wasn't hearing anything. Again, this is negative transfer because I have to change my response. Also, the stimuli that signal what response to make are quite similar—CD players don't look too different, so this is an A – B, A' – D example, and negative transfer usually occurs here.

Learning the vocabulary of a foreign language can also be viewed as a paired-associates task. Translating from Spanish, for example, to English is similar to a transfer design with nonsense items as stimuli and meaningful words as responses; and translating from English to Spanish would have meaningful words as the stimuli and items that function like nonsense syllables as the responses, and probably will be the more difficult task. A common finding from laboratory studies is that nonsense syllables are not all equally nonsensical. Many of them remind subjects of real words to some degree. Remember that we can measure this by asking subjects to write down all the associations they can think of to a given item in one minute. The average number of associations given is an indication of the meaningfulness of the item. These associations to meaningful words make the nonsense items easier to learn.

This process, called *natural language mediation,* suggests a good strategy for learning foreign language vocabulary. Use the associations to the foreign word as go-betweens or mediators to help in bridging the gap between the foreign word and its English meaning. A good way to do this is to use the pronunciation of the foreign word as your starting point. Find an English word (or words) that rhymes with the foreign word. Then associate this rhyming word with the English word. For example, for the Spanish word *casa,* which means house, note that casa sounds like castle (I give it the British pronunciation to emphasize the similarity and to make it distinctive) and create the phrase, "A man's house is his castle." Remember the phrase; along with it will go the memory that you distorted the Spanish word somewhat. When you need either the Spanish or the English translation, recall the phrase and use it to produce the needed response. This technique is quite effective if you can produce good rhyming words.

Atkinson and Raugh (1975), who call this the "keyword" technique, suggest three criteria for selecting keywords: (1) the rhyming word or words must sound as much like the foreign word as possible (this is the most important principle); (2) it must be distinctive—different from other keywords; and (3) it must easily form an interactive image with the English word. This technique could also be used with definitions of terms from the sciences, which often use Latin words for concepts. Treat the science term or Latin word as the nonsense item and find some rhyming English word—this ought to be easy because so many English words were derived from Latin. For example, many students of physiological psychology must learn about the part of the brain called the pons. Often they are told that the term comes from the Latin word for bridge and that the pons is a set of connections or bridges between other sections of the brain. Remembering that pons sounds like pontoon, which is a term associated with crossing bodies of water, may help in remembering some of the facts about it.

Incidental Learning

Transfer and interference effects were studied extensively during the 1950s and 1960s. As we have seen, the type of task and the results often fit well with data and theories from animal studies of classical and operant conditioning. Because these behavioristic principles were being tailored to complex human activities, the researchers who studied them were often called *neobehaviorists*. However, when cognitive psychologists began proposing information-processing theories of memory and cognition during the late 1960s, many researchers drifted away from the neobehaviorist position and embraced these new theories and paradigms. One traditional type of verbal learning study that has remained a popular research procedure throughout this transition is the **incidental learning** procedure. In this procedure, subjects are exposed to material that they must respond to in some way, but that they don't actually have to learn. For example, suppose we show subjects pairs of words and tell them that one of each pair is "correct." The *intentional* task they must master is the identification of which are the "correct" items. That is, this is what they intend to do, and of course the subjects can do it.

But they also learn the "wrong" items, and which wrong items are associated with each "right" item, even though they were not asked to do so (McLaughlin, 1965); furthermore, they often learn this incidental information about as well as subjects who are intentionally asked to learn the same material as a paired-associates task (Postman, 1964). Generally, researchers found that if the orienting tasks were comparable (in other words, if the subject had to spend about the same amount of time and effort studying the items), the instruction to deliberately memorize items showed little or no advantage over incidental learning instructions.

A variety of incidental learning tasks have been used in the study of a wide range of theoretical questions. Many incidental learning studies involve perceptual or categorization tasks. That is, the subject is asked to identify briefly presented items or to group words into categories. Then the subject is given a memory task even though she was not expecting that she would have to remember the items. The original tasks were proposed to investigate the nature of the associative process involved in verbal learning, such as the development of backward associations in paired-associates tasks. More recent research uses incidental learning procedures to study the effect of cognitive strategies on memory and is usually discussed within the information-processing framework, especially the levels of processing model. These positions, discussed in the next three chapters, allow for a more complete understanding of memory.

Concept Learning

Another area studied by the neobehaviorists and verbal learning researchers was the area of concept formation—how do people learn and remember concepts? And what are concepts, anyway? Students don't usually have a good definition of what a concept is, but they can come up with examples when pressed. However, they almost always come up with abstract academic concepts like *liberty,* or the *atom,* or *electricity.* Most psychologists and philosophers have a somewhat different interpretation of concepts. Any word that groups several objects or events together is an example of a concept; the words concept and category mean about the same thing to them. The words book, car, red, and square are examples of *concrete* concepts whereas liberty, the atom and electricity are examples of *abstract* concepts.

Both abstract and concrete concepts seem to be learned by a process of being given examples and having to figure out why they are grouped together and separated or distinguished from other things. Consider the child learning the concept of *sock* as a result of her mother saying, "Pick up your sock," while pointing it out on the floor one day and saying, "Now let's put on your socks" another day. The child must notice the similarities between the referents (the socks—white one day and perhaps blue the next) and ignore the differences (the fact that some socks are white and some blue, etc.). The child must also notice the differences between things labeled socks and other things—for example, Mom tossing her a blue shirt and saying, "Now put on your shirt" (implying that it's not a sock). This learning process can be studied from beginning to end by using artificial concepts and examples so that the learner's previous experiences do not influence the results.

Such studies use stimuli like those in figure 10.4, from classic experiments by Jerome Bruner. They were designs drawn on 3 × 5 cards. The stimuli could be displayed all at once (simultaneous presentation) or displayed one at a time (successive presentation). They differed on the basis

Figure 10.4 Designs used by Bruner to study concepts

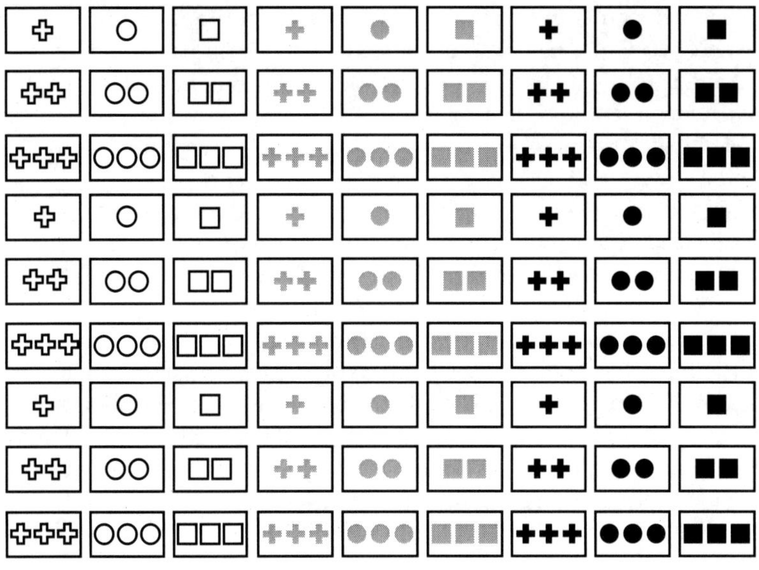

Adapted from Bruner, Goodnow and Austin, *A Study of Thinking*, 1956.

of shape (cross, circle, square), color (black, white, and gray), number of shapes (one, two, or three), and number of borders (none, one, or two). These properties are called **attributes**, and their combinations give us a total of 81 patterns. A concept could be simple (all the crosses or all those with two borders, for example), involving just one attribute, or complex (all the black ones which are circles, using two attributes, or all the ones with two things which are gray and which are square, using three attributes). The attributes which served to define the concept are referred to as *relevant attributes*, *critical attributes*, or *criterial attributes*, while the other attributes are *irrelevant or noncriterial*.

In studies before Bruner's, a learner would be shown one example and would be told that it was an example of the concept to be learned. Then the learner would be shown another stimulus and asked to guess whether it was an example or not, and then given feedback about whether she was correct or not. The learner was considered to have learned the concept when she "guessed" correctly five or so times in a row. For example, the experimenter might point to the third card from the left on the top row, a white square with no border, and say that it was an example of the concept, and then point to the sixth card in the second row, two gray squares with no border, and ask the subject whether she thought it was also an example. Suppose our learner says, "Yes." The experimenter says "That's right." The learner has been shown that color and number don't matter, but that shape (square) and number of borders might be relevant attributes and therefore might define the concept. The experimenter could then choose to point to a nonexample, such as the card with two white circles and no border, the second card in the second row. If the learner says, "No, it's not," our experimenter will suspect that the learner thinks the concept is square, not border. By analyzing the pattern of subject responses in this way, we know what the subject has learned and we can measure how long it took to learn.

Using this procedure, early studies revealed that simple concepts (using just one critical or criterial attribute) were generally learned more quickly than complex concepts that used several relevant attributes (Walker & Bourne, 1961, Bulgarella & Archer, 1962). So, our child should learn simple concepts like *red* or *spoon* fairly easily and, indeed, most of us learn them at an early age. *Sock* is probably learned as if it were a simple concept based only on the criterial attribute of shape; as adults most of us would probably say that socks need to be made of cloth as well. Thus the definition of a particular concept is just the complete list of its critical or relevant attributes—the attribute theory of concepts.

Studies also showed that people were consistently better at learning from examples than at learning from nonexamples. That is, if we are trying to teach our child the concept of *sock*, it wouldn't be too helpful to show our child a spoon, a book, or a bicycle and tell her "Now these aren't socks") (Hovland, 1952). There seem to be two important reasons for this: positive examples usually provide more information to the learner than negative ones (positive examples narrow the field of possibilities much more), and people are also usually better at analyzing the information in the positive examples. If we carefully choose a small set of stimuli, it is possible to generate artificial concepts for experiments in which the positive and negative examples convey equal amounts of information. Hovland and Weiss (1953) did this and discovered that adults *still* learned more quickly from the positive examples. Bruner, Goodnow and Austin (1956) suggested that our greater ability to use positive examples was the result of encountering many more situations involving positive examples than situations involving negative examples in everyday life.

Freibergs and Tulving (1961) showed that people improved in their ability to use information from negative examples with practice. Their subjects had to learn 20 concepts, with half of them being given only positive examples and the other half being given negative examples. The subjects in the negative example group started out far worse than their positive counterparts; both groups improved with practice, but the group given negative examples improved more rapidly (they had much more to learn) and were performing about as well as the positive example group by the eleventh example.

Therefore, it seems that we learn to use positive examples better because we have so much more practice with them. It also implies that if we wanted to teach someone a new concept, we ought to do so by using positive examples (which generally occurs in most children's home experiences but may not be the way it happens in school, where many concepts are taught primarily through giving a definition). However, studies have also shown that the learner needs to encounter some negative examples as well, after having seen several positive examples, in order to keep from overgeneralizing the concept.

This approach to studying concepts is based on the assumption that the concept is stored in our memories as a list of criterial attributes. That is, along with the verbal label, the learner stores a set of attributes that define the concept and may not remember much about the details of specific examples. While the research described supports that theory (for example, the more criterial attributes involved, the more difficult the concept is to learn), not all research supports it. Word association data does not especially show patterns of attributes being given in response to natural concepts ("round" is only occasionally given in response to the concepts of balloon or barrel, for example; Kausler, 1974), and definitions of concepts vary greatly between individuals in the occurrence of criterial attributes mentioned (Komatsu, 1992).

In addition, some examples are often well remembered by people (usually the first and most recent examples). Thus one alternative to a critical attribute theory of concepts is that people actually remember particular examples of concepts and compare what they are currently encountering to these examples; this is called the **exemplar theory.** An exemplar theory implies that there is much less analysis and abstraction involved in the conceptual process than is required by the attribute theory; people simply memorize examples, grouping examples together when they have a common label.

Yet a third theory of concepts (the prototype theory) is discussed, along with supporting research that is difficult for an attribute theory to explain, in the information-processing chapters to follow. Each of these three theories has research supporting it, although theories relying purely on criterial attributes have declined in popularity among researchers in favor of the exemplar and prototype theories. That is, each theory may be partly correct; no single one seems to give the whole story.

Summary

Verbal learning researchers attempt to extend the principles of learning described in animal research on classical and operant conditioning to uniquely human behaviors. They use verbal materials to study complex, multiple discrimination tasks such as memorizing and recalling lists of nonsense syllables in order (as Ebbinghaus did in his early version of the serial anticipation task) and learning lists of paired-associates items. Ebbinghaus described the curve of forgetting, which shows that most loss from memory occurs within the first 20 minutes after learning. The most important factor that influences remembering seems to be interference, which is determined by the similarity of the materials to be remembered, their meaningfulness, and the time intervals between the three events (learning a first list, learning a second list, and recalling one of them). Interference can be either retroactive, in which newer material makes it harder to remember previously learned material, or proactive, in which older material makes it more difficult to recall more recently learned material. It seems likely that interference effects account for the great majority of forgetting, with very little forgetting likely to be due to decay (the loss of memories just because of the passage of time).

In addition to describing interference effects, Ebbinghaus also described the serial position effect, in which the first few items (the primacy effect) and the last several items (the recency effect) on a list are learned more quickly and remembered better than items in the middle of the list. Ebbinghaus also showed that distributed practice was more effective than massed practice.

Meaningfulness has been related to frequency of occurrence of items in speech and writing, pronounceability of the items, and the imagery value of the items. The use of the paired-associates task allows the study of transfer, in which the influence of previous learning on learning a new set of materials is examined. Transfer effects can be positive or negative, but negative transfer is much more common. The direction and amount of transfer obtained is a consequence of the similarity of the materials. A wide variety of transfer designs have been studied; these designs are classed in terms of the similarities between the stimulus elements and the response elements of the two tasks (as in an A – B, C – D design). The learning of new responses and competition between responses are the most important sources of negative transfer effects, although the subject must also learn the stimulus signals and the pattern of connections between stimuli and responses.

Conceptual behavior has also been studied by the neobehaviorists, who used geometric patterns and artificial laboratory concepts to determine that positive examples were easier to learn from than negative examples. They also indicated that more complex concepts (those with more criterial attributes) were more difficult to learn.

Questions for Discussion, Thought, & Practice

1. Define and give an example of each key concept. Then try to group the key concepts into four categories: procedures, variables, results, and explanations.

2. Imagine trying to learn to play tennis after having played baseball for a while. Try to classify this in terms of changing stimuli or response, and determine whether it would lead to positive or negative transfer.
3. Imagine that you have learned French in high school. Now, in college you want to learn either Spanish or German. Which language would suffer the greatest interference effects from French? Why?
4. Discuss the roles of retroactive and proactive interference in each of the following situations (some situations may involve both):
   a. Forgetting where you left your keys last night
   b. Trying to remember details of your first date
   c. Forgetting what items you needed to get at the grocery store
   d. Forgetting the name of an old high school pal
5. Describe how you could use the serial position effect to make a list of concepts easier to learn for a class. In what cases would the serial position effect cause the most problems for learning?

Information-Processing Models of Memory

▲ KEY CONCEPTS ▲

acoustic coding
bottom-up processing
chunk
displacement
distinctive features
distractor task
echoic memory
edge detectors
encoding
executive
free recall
iconic memory
long-term memory
masking
overwriting
pattern recognition
probe task
rehearsal
release from proactive interference
retrieval
sensory memory
sensory register
short-term memory
storage
top-down processing
verbal rehearsal loop
visuospatial sketch pad

As described in the previous chapter, we often remember things because of hearing an old song, or because of something that someone says or does, or because of some other triggering event. Our subjective experience is that "all of a sudden" we remember something. But where was the memory before the trigger? Clearly it was somewhere in our brains, but we weren't aware of it. If the memory brought back an image, where did that come from? Do we have "pictures" stored away in our heads? Our everyday experience suggests that we have memories of many things but that we are not always aware of these memories. Research beginning in the 1960s lends credibility to this idea; much of it assumes that we develop permanent memories that are stored in what has come to be called long-term memory and that we can call these up to our awareness, at which time they are in our short-term memories. There is also a large body of research investigating the nature of visual images and how they are represented in long-term and short-term memory.

The previous chapters have been based on behavioral theories that emphasized research on animals. In this and the next chapter we will present information-processing models, which are based on quite different research. The information-processing position was originally derived from attempts to design and describe computers and the recognition that many computer mechanisms must serve the same function as human systems. Many analogies can be made between computer functions and human brain functioning. For example, computers consist of several parts, each of which performs a different function. Do humans work the same way? Certainly there are some general similarities. The computer has an input device for receiving information, usually a keyboard; so do people (our eyes, ears, and other senses). Both computers and humans also have output devices: the monitor or the printer for the computer and hands, legs, mouths, and so on for humans. The computer has parts that store information (floppy disks or hard drives) that are separate from the "working" part (the "chip" or CPU)—do people also have separate storage and working components? The first information-processing models of memory proposed that we do.

In this chapter we approach our topic somewhat differently than in earlier chapters. The studies of learning described in the previous chapters were often guided by the behaviorists' emphasis on observable relationships between variables, with a deemphasis on theory. Theories were the result of the research. Information-processing approaches have emphasized the development of the theories first, with research generated to test the theory. To best represent the area, we will follow a similar pattern. Rather than presenting a basic experimental procedure and describing independent and dependent variables, we present a model of memory and the evidence for that model. We then present the evidence critical of the model, followed by alternatives that attempt to accommodate these criticisms. Finally, in the last chapter we present a very different attempt to describe memory.

All of the theories discussed in these next chapters can be characterized as S–O–R theories. That is, these theories quite willingly accommodate events and mechanisms intervening between the observable stimuli and responses as explanatory devices. In contrast, most of the research and theory in the previous chapters can be characterized as S–R theory, with a deemphasis on any internal (and therefore difficult to detect) events. Watson and Skinner especially represent the S–R position in our earlier discussions, whereas two-factor theory and some of the neobehavioristic research in chapter 10 are examples of S–O–R approaches.

The Stage Model of Memory

Stage models suggest that information coming into the human nervous system gets analyzed by some initial processing mechanisms. Then the results of these analyses are sent on to the next processing mechanisms, where further analyzing is done and the results then sent on to a possible next stage, and so on, until the last bit of processing results in a response. The most detailed of these models was described by Atkinson and Shiffrin (1968). Although these models have had a controversial history with memory researchers (Crowder, 1982; Greene, 1992; Watkins, 1990), they still have much to tell us about human functioning and provide a useful starting point. Figure 11.1 shows a diagram of the model.

Figure 11.1 The Atkinson and Shiffrin stage model of memory

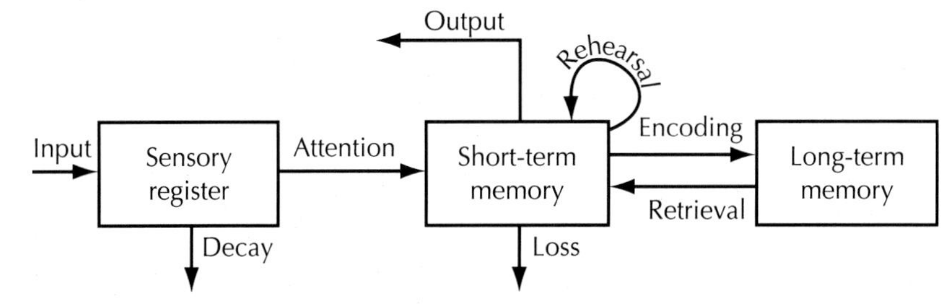

Input enters the system by way of the senses. These **sensory registers** (sometimes referred to as **sensory memory**) change the external physical energy (light waves or sound vibrations) into nervous system energy (neurochemical reactions or nerve impulses) and thus make a "copy" of the input that the rest of the system can use. This copy is usually thought to be an exact replica of the stimulation but is very brief, lasting only 1/4 second for visual traces (Sperling, 1960) (referred to as the "icon" by Neisser, 1967), or 2 to 4 seconds for hearing (the "echo") (Darwin, Turvey, & Crowder, 1972). Therefore, the visual sensory register is often referred to as **iconic memory** and the auditory sensory register as **echoic memory**. If the rest of the system doesn't notice the contents of the registers within these intervals, it could be lost. Normally most stimulus events last much longer than 1/4 second, so it's not so much a case of not having enough time but rather of having so many other things competing for our attention. However, the stimulation coming in usually changes rapidly, and details of a stimulus pattern could be lost when not attended to. The new information continuously bombarding our senses will always obscure and replace the current contents of our sensory registers. This is called **masking**.

Short-term memory (STM) refers to the component that does the attending. It can be thought of as representing the things a person can be aware or "conscious" of because it selects which stimulation gets further processing and may also select the type of processing. There is a heavy price for this active processing: a small capacity of about seven items and a time limit of about 20 seconds. However, STM can rehearse material to prevent it from being lost after the 20 seconds. With continued **rehearsal** material may be encoded or entered into permanent **long-term memory** (LTM). Long-term memories can be stored or retained, presumably for life, apparently without any need for additional conscious effort to be made in maintaining them. Material in **storage** may be retrieved from LTM later by STM for use in processing the current input. As we all know, this **retrieval** can and often does require effort.

The term **encoding** is used essentially to refer to the original learning of some material. This word was chosen to emphasize that learning is an active process that usually involves some interpretation of the experience, whereas our previous discussions of conditioning allowed for learning to be understood as a passive, somewhat mechanical reaction to experience. Therefore, information-processing models emphasize that the learner may choose to attend to some aspects of the situation, ignore other aspects, and may perceive those aspects somewhat differently than the way they actually occurred. This is an important difference between most information-processing models and the behavioral models we considered previously. Let us now look at each of the processing stages in some detail.

The Sensory Register

The sensory register is most easily understood as the sense organs, particularly the eyes and ears. The retina of the eye contains about 5 million cone cells and 15 million rod cells. These rods and cones contain chemicals that decompose when exposed to light. The breakdown of the light-sensitive chemicals causes the rods and cones to send nerve impulses to the optic nerve. When the occipital lobe at the back of our brain receives this pattern of nerve impulses, we experience the sensation of seeing something. In a very clever experiment, Sperling (1960) demonstrated that these internal events in the visual system last about 1/4 second. He presented three rows of random letters for a very brief time (50 milliseconds—about 1/20 of a second). Then he would give the subject an auditory signal that told the subject to report one of the rows of letters.

Note that the signal telling which row to report came after the stimuli were gone. In fact, Sperling could delay the signal for up to 250 milliseconds

(1/4 second) and still have his subjects report the letters accurately. Longer delays led to the performance equivalent of no signal at all—the subjects would be able to give some letters but were generally best at the letters starting in the upper-left-hand corner of the display. This suggests that the subjects had the whole stimulus array present somewhere in their nervous or sensory systems and had 1/4 of a second for the rest of the nervous system to "read" as much of it as possible. If instructed to attend to one line during that 1/4 second, they could do so accurately. With no instructions, people in our society began reading at the upper-left-hand corner and continued until the visual trace or icon faded too much to make out. Sperling's interpretation was that the sensory system could retain the icon for this 1/4 of a second, but that it was rapidly decaying and was undecipherable by the end of that time. Whatever was attended to during that time was available for further processing by the short-term memory system; whatever was not attended to during that time was lost through decay.

In a variation of Sperling's experiment, Averbach and Coriell (1961) showed that iconic storage suffered from what they called "masking" as well as decay. They used a visual signal presented after the array of letters. When they followed the letters with a circle around the spot where the subject was to identify the letter, their subjects were unable to accurately report any letters at any time interval. They concluded that the circle pattern was stimulating an overlapping set of visual detectors and essentially obscuring, or *masking*, the visual icon. These experiments suggested to many that visual iconic storage was performed by the rods and cones themselves—it was the result of the process of chemical deterioration and regeneration going on in the retina. Although several experimenters have suggested that the sensory registers are actually in the sensory cortex of the brain (see Haber, 1983; and Kolers, 1984, for detailed discussions of the issues involved), it may give you a feel for the nature of the system to think of the sensory registers as consequences of the sense organs. The implications of such a view are that (1) although this form of storage is very brief, it is a fairly accurate copy of the input, (2) all of the stimulation occurring is stored, indicating a very large capacity, (3) this represents an unanalyzed copy, and (4) the learner has little control over the nature of the copy. In other words, sensory registers are automatic mechanisms that cannot be improved through practice or training.

Sperling was able to use position cues such as signaling to report the middle row successfully, but was unable to use such cues as "report all the vowels" successfully. This and several other similar studies (Crowder & Morton, 1969) suggest that the sensory registers retain the physical features of visual stimuli without any further analysis (such as interpreting the meaning of the stimulus). These findings also imply that the sensory registers operate automatically without our conscious control.

Experiments similar to Sperling's but using auditory stimuli to be recalled have suggested a slightly longer duration for the echoic sensory register of about 2 to 4 seconds (Darwin, Turvey, & Crowder, 1972). Because of this longer duration, the existence of the echo is much more noticeable to us than the existence of the icon. If you have ever had the experience of concentrating on one thing (for example, reading a thriller) while someone asked you a question, you may have experienced the echoic sensory register in action. If you don't respond, the person prompts you with a "well?" Occasionally when this happens, we say "what?" and immediately realize what was actually asked without having to have it restated. In these cases we have "read" what was in the echoic sensory register after the sounds themselves were gone and were therefore able to respond to the question. This only works with impatient friends who deliver the prompt fairly quickly; after a few seconds, your friend will have to repeat the question. This precategorical acoustic storage (PAS) (Crowder & Morton, 1969) system can hold the acoustic features of spoken stimuli (an echo) for a few seconds at the same time our iconic memory system is holding its representation of the visual stimulation around us; our attentional mechanisms must choose what of this and the material in the other possible sensory registers (smell, body position feedback, etc.) to process further.

The data generated by Sperling and others since his original experiments have caused researchers to describe the icon as considerably more complex than Sperling's original description, allowing for the likelihood of some categorical analysis. Probably the most widely accepted model is the dual-buffer model of Mewhort, Marchetti, Gurnsey, and Campbell (1984), which proposes that physical features such as curves, straight lines, and angles are stored in a feature buffer, which is then analyzed by a recognition mechanism. This mechanism sorts features into coherent units and then generates a list of the possible identities of these groups of features. These possible identities are then stored in a character buffer, which is thus a system that involves some categorization. This might still be called an iconic store because no semantic categorization (meaning analysis) has occurred, but it's much more complex than Sperling's original icon, and nothing like the picture in the head that his original conception implied.

Pattern Recognition

The nature of the "copy" held in the visual sensory register has been carefully studied. Early research by Neisser (1967) indicated that the human nervous system worked quite differently than the early computer systems designed to recognize patterns. The first computer recognition systems utilized descriptions of whole patterns as unitary objects called templates. However, a system based on sets of stimulus *parts*, or **distinctive features**, describes human recognition of patterns much more accurately. A good illustration of this is the early work of Eleanore Gibson

(1969), who designed a set of about a dozen different features that could be used to describe all the letters of the alphabet. These features included straight line segments or edges, curved line segments, and angles or intersections of two lines, as shown in table 11.1. Actually, such a set of features could be used to describe printed digits as well as letters, or indeed, could be used to produce most objects. We could, for example, use them to draw a picture of a house. Therefore, one of the advantages of describing whole objects with a set of features is that we can use that same set of a dozen features to describe thousands of objects—there's a kind of economy to this approach.

Distinctive features explain patterns of recognition errors much better than the whole-pattern templates. People often confuse the letters E and F, but rarely confuse the letters S and P. A glance at table 11.1 shows that E and F share almost the same set of features (as is obvious from looking at the letters) but S and P don't share any features; this fits with the error patterns. Template models, on the other hand, don't explain such patterns of confusions at all: since each template is stored as a whole unit, each template is equally different from all the others. Furthermore, we would need a lot of templates (for three dimensional objects, rather than things printed on a page, we would need a different template for each possible viewing angle), rather than a small set of features. So, what works for computers in the limited setting of reading bar codes (which are printed, flat, and a standard size) on products doesn't fit human needs very well.

Table 11.1 Gibson's distinctive features

Features	A	E	F	H	I	L	T	K	M	N	V	W	X	Y	Z	B	C	D	G	J	O	P	R	Q	S	U
Straight																										
Horizontal	+	+	+	+		+	+								+				+							
Vertical		+	+	+	+	+	+	+	+	+				+		+		+				+	+			
Diagonal /	+							+	+		+	+	+	+	+											
Diagonal /	+							+	+	+	+	+	+	+									+	+		
Curve																										
Closed																+		+			+	+	+	+		
Open *V*																				+						+
Open *H*																	+		+	+					+	
Intersection	+	+	+	+			+	+					+			+						+	+	+		
Redundancy																										
Cyclic change		+							+			+				+									+	
Symmetry	+	+		+	+		+	+	+		+	+	+	+		+	+	+			+					+
Discontinuity																										
Vertical	+		+	+	+		+	+	+	+				+								+	+			
Horizontal		+	+			+	+								+											

Physiological psychologists have shown that vertebrate visual systems have specialized neural cells that are sensitive to the presence of edges, that is, borders between lighter and darker areas. These are apparently the feature detectors (Lettvin, Maturana, McCulloch, & Pitts, 1959; Hubel & Wiesel, 1965), and in us they are the result of the neural connections between our occipital lobes and the rods and cones in the eye. That is, their activity is relatively automatic; if it gets to the retina, our occipital lobe receives it as edges and angles. These pieces of the pattern are combined on the basis of position and motion information to form representations of objects that we can match with representations from memory so that we recognize words or objects.

The distinctive features model proposed by Gibson has required modification; it was designed to describe reading, a two-dimensional stimulus/analysis task, but the world is a three-dimensional place. Biederman (1987) has proposed that the features are actually three-dimensional shapes called *geons* that are constructed from the two dimensions present on the retina. He has shown how a set of about 24 simple geometric features can be used to reconstruct objects for recognition.

Unfortunately, even Biederman's geons don't answer all the perceptual questions. A phenomenon called the **word superiority effect** (Reicher, 1969) requires that perception involve top-down as well as bottom-up processing (Lindsay & Norman, 1977). The word superiority effect shows up in a letter identification task. Suppose you are asked to identify the fourth letter from the left in strings of letters we show you. If we show you a string like QAZK and time your response latency, you will be slightly slower than if we show you the string BOOK; people are consistently faster to identify letters when they form part of a word than when they are part of a random string of letters. This is the word superiority effect. Since it is the same K in both our examples, the letter itself can't be the cause of the advantage. Analyzing its features should be the same in both contexts. It is the context that is providing the advantage.

Processing that proceeds in steps from analyzing one piece of input, combining this analysis with analyses of other pieces of the input, analyzing the result, and so on, is called **bottom-up** (or data-driven) **processing**. Recognition that comes from the context causing you to "expect" to see a K, for example, is **top-down** (or conceptually driven) **processing**; instead of proceeding through the stages from start to finish, top down processing requires using information already present in long-term memory or short-term memory to evaluate incoming information. Expectations based on previous experience and context often influence our recognition of objects, and therefore seem to be a part of the perceptual process.

A nice illustration of this "top-down" effect is a study by Brewer and Treyens (1981) in which college students who were brought into a professor's office to "wait their turn for the experiment" frequently reported seeing books in the office when asked to remember what they had seen there. In fact, there were no books, but one expects to see books in a professor's office, so many students just seemed to assume that they had seen some. How top-down and bottom-up processing are used in combination is not really known at this time, but it is certain that both types of processing are being used, automatically and usually without any awareness on our part that we are doing it.

Short-Term Memory (STM, or Working Memory)

The division of memory into two components was originally suggested by William James before the turn of the century (James, 1890). However, the idea was neglected until information-processing models were developed. An experiment conducted independently by two Americans and an English psychologist did the most to popularize the concept. In this experiment, Peterson and Peterson (1959) and Brown (1958) found essentially chance-level memory performance for material after just 20 seconds! Why did these subjects perform so poorly? The Petersons and Brown both suggested that the reason for their subjects' poor performance was that they had prevented their subjects from rehearsing the material, and that unrehearsed material just decayed away within 20 seconds. In their experiments, the Petersons and Brown prevented rehearsal by making subjects count backwards by threes immediately after they had seen the material to be remembered. The longer they were made to count backwards, the poorer their recall was until they reached a minimal level after 18 seconds. The Petersons and Brown suggested that the distractor task of counting backwards by threes prevented the rehearsal of material. They suggested that rehearsal had two functions: the maintenance of material for immediate use, and eventually, with more rehearsal, the permanent storage of material for later use. The immediate use of material was done by the short-term memory system, and the permanent storage was done by long-term memory. Short-term memory was subject to decay, but long-term memory was not. Thus, they proposed a two-part memory system with each part having different properties.

Researchers immediately began looking for other explanations; interference was the most obvious alternative. But in the distractor experiments, why would counting backwards interfere with remembering letters or words? The lack of stimulus similarity would not lead to predictions of the high degree of interference seen. Nevertheless, one investigator, Reitman (1974), compared the interfering effects of counting backwards with another distracting task, detecting tones. At first, she seemed to have clear evidence that counting backwards was interfering; because each task should have served equally well as a distractor, subjects should have done equally poorly in each condition. However, the subjects who had to detect tones remembered significantly better; the only apparent reason would be that detecting tones interferes less with remembering than counting backwards.

However, when Reitman looked at her tone-detecting subjects more closely, she found that they differed in their approach to the task. Some of them concentrated on remembering, and remembered well but had poor tone-detection scores. Others had good tone-detection scores but poor memory scores. She concluded that her tone-detection subjects were either rehearsing surreptitiously or not rehearsing and concentrating on the tones (i.e., attending to one aspect of the task or another). Lumping all her subjects, and thus, these two approaches, together led to an average that was better than that of the counting-backwards subjects. However, this conclusion also still allowed for the possibility of decay in a short-term memory system.

A more recent set of studies by Cowan (Cowan, Saults, & Nugent, 1997, 2001) led to a similar pattern of results: they presented two tones and subjects had to decide if the second tone was higher or lower in pitch than the first. There was a delay of up to 12 seconds between tones, during which subjects had to track the movement of a visual icon on a computer screen (two tasks, visual and auditory, which should interfere with each other very little). In their 1997 study Cowan et al. found that length of delay determined performance, but a reanalysis of their data in 2001 revealed that the difference between the tones predicted the performance of subjects as well or better than the passage of time.

Another attempt to show interference effects in the distractor task was more successful. Keppel and Underwood (1962) pointed out that the Petersons and Brown had failed to note an important source of interference. In their original experiment they had presented a list of items to be remembered, then had their subjects count backwards, then tested them for recall. This first sequence was for practice to ensure that the subjects understood the task. Therefore it was not scored. Subjects then would be given a second list of items, asked to count backwards, and then asked to recall this second list. Data from this second trial and several other later trials were recorded. Keppel and Underwood suggested that proactive interference could have been generated by the first, "practice" trial. When they measured recall for a first list, they found it to be far better than the following trials—in fact, first-trial memory was usually perfect well beyond the 18-second limit.

Wickens, Born, and Allen (1963) provided an even better demonstration of the proactive interference from earlier lists in an experiment that generated a **release from proactive interference**. They did this by using words from the same category (for example, all animal names) for four lists. The recall scores for their groups got successively lower from list 1 to list 4. Then on a fifth list half of their subjects received words from a different category (for example, a set of words naming foods), and the other half received more animal names. The category shift allowed that group to perform almost as well as on the first list; they experienced a release from the proactive interference that had built up. The other subjects continued to recall poorly. Here was an interference effect in the task based on stimulus similarity. Furthermore, it is semantic similarity. Several advocates of the short-term model had pointed to evidence that short-term memory was influenced primarily by acoustic or phonemic sources of interference and differed from long-term memory on this characteristic.

Currently, most memory researchers have concluded that decay may occur during the first two seconds or so after material has entered short-term memory (Baddeley, 1990), but that any loss during the next 15 seconds or so is the result of acoustic and semantic interference and not decay (Nairne, 2002).

Coding in STM

Conrad (1964) first suggested that items stored briefly were represented by an acoustic trace (acoustic coding). He presented groups of randomly chosen letters to his subjects. Half of the subjects listened to strings of letters, and the other half saw slides with letters on them. This is not an especially difficult task, so subjects make few errors. Nevertheless, there are some, and Conrad presented enough letters to obtain a trustworthy sample of errors. For both presentation conditions, Conrad found that errors were primarily the result of similarities of sound. That is, even when the subject initially saw the letters, her mistakes would be based on their sound; she might be confused and give B when V had been presented, or S when she had seen F. Although these letters don't look very much alike, they do have similar sounds. Because the letters were subject to acoustic interference even when presented visually, Conrad concluded that they were converted to an acoustic representation when they left the sensory register and entered short-term memory.

Because long-term interference effects are predominantly based on semantic similarity, it would seem that the short-term and long-term memory systems rely on two different coding mechanisms. However, as we noted above in the Wickens, Born, and Allen (1963) study, semantic interference does occur in short-term memory as well as in long-term memory. Shulman (1971, 1972) has also presented clear evidence for semantic representation in short-term memory; however, his conclusions favor the notion that the effects of acoustic interference are much greater than the effects of semantic interference in short-term memory. In a similar fashion, there is evidence for acoustic interference in long term memory, but these effects are not as powerful as semantic interference effects (Bruce & Crowley, 1970; Nelson & Rothbart, 1972).

Capacity of STM

So far we have found that working memory, or short-term memory, and long-term memory may differ in duration and may encode material in different formats. A third major difference that has been suggested is that short-term memory has a very limited capacity, and long-term memory has an apparently unlimited capacity. This limit on our working memory was first noted by George Miller in a classic paper titled "The Magical Number Seven Plus or Minus Two" (1956). Miller surveyed many different studies and concluded that people have a limit of about seven things (or different pieces of information), or chunks, as he called them (see chapter 13 for a more detailed discussion), that they can attend to at one time. For example, he noted the routine procedure of measuring the Digit Span on IQ tests, which generally shows people being able to repeat about seven or eight digits correctly and faltering with longer strings. The Atkinson and Shiffrin model takes Miller's idea as representing our short-term memory capacity. It may be helpful to think of this limit as representing our attentional capacity—generally, we are attending to the contents of our short-term memory. The material in long-term memory is not being attended to, and long-term memory apparently has no limit on its capacity.

The difficulty with Miller's idea was in his definition of the unit used for measuring capacity. His definition of a chunk allowed for chunks of different sizes. For example, our capacity for numbers (the digit span) is about seven, and our capacity for randomly chosen letters is close to six, but our capacity for random words is about four or five. Although four words would usually have a dozen or more letters in them, Miller suggested that the letters in a word don't actually have to be remembered all by themselves. They are parts of the word; the word is the unit or chunk. In this way, Miller suggested that short-term memory has a very powerful mechanism at its disposal: the ability to combine small, related units into larger chunks and to treat these chunks as if they were the units. Thus, the size of the chunk varies depending on the type of material and the relations between items. It is even possible to combine chunks into still larger chunks and use these larger chunks as units to remember more than four words at a time. For example, a subject may be given several very familiar sayings such as "a penny saved is a penny earned" and "a stitch in time saves nine" and remember them in an attention span task. In this case, instead of remembering 7 + 6 = 13 chunks when treating the words as independent units, our subject could remember the two sayings as one chunk each. The phenomenon of chunking represents one of the most interesting and important capabilities of our memory system; we shall consider some of the useful applications of this kind of ability more thoroughly in chapter 13 when we discuss memory strategies.

The size of Miller's chunks changes depending on the nature of the material being represented. This is both an advantage for the memory system and a problem for the psychologist studying memory. The problem is that the variable size of the chunk makes it difficult to predict ahead of time how much capacity short-term memory will display; if we assume chunks of one size and predict a capacity of seven chunks, what does it mean when we actually obtain a capacity of four chunks? Did we fail to analyze the size of the chunk, or overestimate the capacity of short-term memory? So far, no one has been able to specify clearly and in advance how chunks will be formed or used.

An alternative that has become the experimental standard is the number of syllables a person can articulate in two seconds (Baddeley, 1990). Baddeley discovered this while examining the digit span of English and Welsh school children. When he examined the Welsh students, who mostly spoke both Welsh and English, he found that each child's span would be smaller when trying to remember Welsh digits than when trying to remember English digits. The pronunciation of the Welsh digits takes a bit longer and is phonetically more complicated than their English equivalents. Since then, researchers have noted that an individual's memory span can be predicted by measuring the person's articulation rate – how fast he or she speaks (Baddeley, Thompson, & Buchanan, 1975, Tehan & Lalor, 2000). The people who can pronounce the most syllables in two seconds seem to have larger short-term capacities. Another consequence of this is that a person's short-term capacity will appear smaller when tested using a set of long words than when using a set of short words (Baddeley, Thomson, & Buchanan, 1975).

The capacity limit has been suggested as the explanation for one of the other characteristics of working memory, its brief duration. The argument is that, if we have just seven "slots" or spaces in short-term memory, when all seven slots are filled and new material comes along, something old has to go. Thus, the **displacement** hypothesis suggests that old material may be displaced in this way fairly rapidly in normal experience. That is, maybe normal experience consists of so much continual stimulation that we encounter seven or more new pieces of information within 20 seconds. We would therefore have a complete turnover of the contents of working memory every 20 seconds whether working memory had a time limit or not.

This idea was suggested and supported in an experiment by Waugh and Norman (1965), which they called a **probe task.** They presented a random string of digits to subjects. Some of the repeated digits would be followed by an auditory signal. The subject was required to repeat the digit that followed the previous occurrence of the signaled or "probe" digit. For example, in the string "6, 8, 3, 4, 5, 2, 8*" if the asterisk indicates the signal sound, the subject would have to remember back to the previous occurrence of 8 and recall that it was followed by 3, which occurred four items previously. Because this is within our span of seven items, it is still in STM and the subject is fairly accurate. However, in the string "9, 5, 2, 1, 3, 8, 0, 4, 6, 3, 7, 6, 0, 2*" there are 10 digits between occurrences of the probed digit, and few subjects are able to correctly recall that the following digit was 1.

The clever thing that Waugh and Norman did was to present these digits at different speeds in addition to varying the number of intervening items. They found that time intervals had no effect; performance was much better predicted by number of intervening digits. Thus, they suggested that in normal experience stimulation occurred rapidly enough that the contents of our seven "slots" in STM were constantly being replaced at a rate that caused a complete turnover in 18 seconds for unrehearsed material.

Although some displacement may occur, this is unlikely to be the full explanation of loss from STM. Such an explanation would require a capacity that is more rigidly fixed than the chunk concept and would suggest that the 18-second limit should apply no matter how we test for memory. However, estimates of STM duration of 90 seconds can be obtained in the Peterson distractor procedure if recognition instead of recall is used to measure memory (Lutz & Wuensch, 1989).

The evidence for the existence of two separate parts to our memory system therefore consists of the following: (1) time differences; (2) capacity differences; and (3) coding differences. However, the time differences appear to vary depending on the way we test. Also, the coding differences are not absolute, but relative. In other words, acoustic interference is more powerful in STM, but semantic interference also occurs. Likewise, semantic interference is more significant in LTM, but acoustic interference also occurs in long-term memory.

Two other pieces of evidence have been suggested in support of the distinction, but these also have been contested. One is that the recency effect in the serial anticipation task (see chapter 10) may be due to the presence of the last few items in STM. The idea is that those last four or five items on the list are still present in STM but the earlier items are not—they must be retrieved from LTM. Because it's more difficult to retrieve items from LTM than to simply repeat them out of STM, the last several items show higher memory rates than the rest of the curve. Extensive analysis of the serial position effect has in fact shown that one set of variables affects the recency part of the curve, and a totally different set influences the rest of the curve (Glanzer, 1972). This supports the distinction between STM and LTM. However, you may also recall from chapter 10 that the whole serial position effect can be shown in a totally long-term situation, such as recalling the presidents. This means that the recency effect cannot be totally explained by reference to the STM–LTM distinction.

The final piece of evidence comes from the study of individuals who suffer head injuries. Several of these cases reveal that damage in the area of the temporal lobe (specifically the hippocampus) of the brain—the areas on the side of the head around our ears—can cause a disruption to the link between STM and LTM. In the most famous case, an individual with such an injury was able to remember new material as long as he attended to it, but lost it after a short delay (Milner, 1966). This person was apparently unable to transfer new material from STM to LTM—he was unable to encode anything new. However, over the years, study of the individual has shown that in fact sometimes he can encode some aspects of new material into LTM (Milner, 1970).

The net result of all the evidence cited above is that it can be considered inconclusive. It seems generally supportive of a distinction between STM and LTM, but each point in favor of the distinction can be argued. It's a matter of which experiments a memory researcher finds most convincing. For example, Glenberg (1987) has proposed a model of temporal discriminability that explains much of the data described in this chapter without resorting to stages of memory at all. Essentially, in his model recently presented items are easier to distinguish from one another, like telephone poles passed on the highway. When we take into account the actual similarity of the items involved, such a model can predict recency effects quite well. That is, the last two items presented would be easiest to tell apart, like the telephone poles we are currently passing; therefore accuracy in recalling or analyzing them would be very good. The second and third from last items would be a little more difficult to distinguish, and items farther back would begin to blur together just as telephone poles half a mile away would. In this book, we will generally lean toward the distinction between STM and LTM, because it still seems to accommodate more of the data than any of the alternatives (e.g., Baddeley, 1990). This is a reasonable position, but not one that is proven beyond doubt.

How Many Parts Does STM Have?

One of the problems raised by critics of the STM–LTM distinction is the issue of coding in STM. One researcher, rather than abandoning the distinction, has attempted to modify the STM concept to accommodate these coding differences. Baddeley (1982, 1990) has proposed dividing STM into three components, each of which has some independence from the others. He proposed an **executive** or decision-making part, a **verbal rehearsal loop** component, and a **visuospatial sketchpad** component. The verbal rehearsal component and the sketch pad are slave systems that are called into action by the executive when we need to rehearse something or if we need to visualize something. Baddeley has presented evidence that visual or motor stimulation will interfere with image generation by the sketch pad but cause much less interference for the verbal rehearsal loop. On the other hand, he also has shown that verbal sources of interference interrupt the rehearsal loop but have small effects on the sketch pad.

Although this approach seems to have some potential, it's too early to tell if it represents the best description of the STM system. If it is correct, we will almost certainly find that three divisions of STM are not enough. In this case, we may end up with a description of several somewhat interrelated systems that will appear to have been thrown together because they all show some time-dependent characteristics, such as deterioration after about 20 seconds. One illustration of this is provided by Watkins and Peynircioglu (1983), who were able to produce three recency effects at the same time by using a list made up of three very different kinds of items: riddles, sound effects obtained from sound-effects recordings, and objects shown to their subjects. While overall recall was lower than for a simpler list, each type of item showed a recency effect comparable to that obtained when each item type was presented alone.

Additional support for a working memory system that consists of several components comes from research indicating that they are supported by different parts of the nervous system. The verbal rehearsal loop is clearly associated with the left temporal lobe, and the occipital lobes at the back of the brain are active when the visuospatial sketchpad is being used (Farah, 1995) to form images. Furthermore, research on primates strongly indicates that the frontal lobes of the brain are active in many working memory tasks (Goldman-Rakic, 1993). This activity probably represents Baddeley's executive component at work, directing the activity of the other working memory components and combining their results. Thus much of the brain is engaged in working memory activity. The idea of an executive system and a set of processing systems that may be engaged independently of each other has some intuitive appeal and is probably on the right track. In addition, it provides a useful context for presenting various memory strategies. This will be the focus of our discussion in the last chapter.

Table 11.2 presents a summary of the major differences suggested to exist between the three stages proposed by Atkinson and Shiffrin (1968). We have discussed most of these characteristics for STM; it might be useful for the student to go back and match the discussion of the evidence with the descriptions in table 11.2. For example, the mode of representation in STM is described as "primarily acoustic" because of Conrad's (1964) work on acoustic confusions and Wickens, Born, and Allen's (1963) release from proactive interference experiment.

STM seems to operate by using serial processing. This represents our subjective experience of a "stream of consciousness" in which we think about one thing at a time in sequence. Sternberg (1966) attempted to show that this was the case and also showed that it took about 38 milliseconds to examine the contents of each "slot." He gave subjects sets of digits to remember and then asked whether a particular digit was among the set. In other words, the subject might study a set of four digits, "6, 2, 4, 1," and be asked, "Was one of the digits 4"? She would report that, yes, 4 was in the set. Sternberg varied the size of the set from one to six digits and found that responding when the set had one item took about 438 milliseconds. Each additional digit added 38 milliseconds to this. Four hundred milliseconds seems to be required to say the response, but clearly, the number of items to be searched determined the *rest* of the reaction times so that the inspection time was quite constant for each item. Furthermore, each item appeared to be examined in turn, in a serial fashion.

However, since Sternberg's original experiments, many researchers have shown that parallel processing models can explain Sternberg's data adequately (Ratcliff, 1978; Townsend, 1971, 1990). Ratcliff's model, which is the most mathematically precise, assumes that the subject responds in Sternberg's task by comparing the features of the probe to all the features of all the stimuli in the memory set simultaneously. In a situation involving many comparisons, even a parallel search can lead to longer times for larger memory sets, as Ratcliff showed.

Table 11.2 Characteristics of the Memory Stages

Characteristic	Sensory Register	Short-Term Memory	Long-Term Memory
Duration	1/4 sec. (V) 2–4 sec. (H)	18 sec (recall)	Lifetime
Capacity	Approx. 1000 + bits	7 +/– 2 chunks	Unlimited?
Causes of Loss	Decay, masking	Decay, acoustic interference, displacement	Semantic interference, retrieval failure
Mode of Representation	Sensory features (analog replica)	Primarily acoustic (verbal description)	Primarily semantic (meaning or proposition)
Operation	Automatic (reactive)	Optional (conscious) (active)	Automatic (unconscious) (passive)
	Parallel processing	Serial processing?	Spread of activation
Recall		Complete, accurate, takes 38 msec per item	Incomplete, inaccurate, no time limit

Ratcliff's model implies that STM does not maintain a representation of the stimulus itself, but rather a record of the set of features representing the stimulus. Such lists would involve many more than seven items, but the feature lists would presumably be easily chunked. Nevertheless, most memory researchers favor the idea that STM uses serial rather than parallel processing because STM seems to impose a limit on how much we can deal with at one time. This position is more consistent with our understanding of consciousness and attention.

STM, Consciousness, and Attention

Several times during our discussion of working (or short-term) memory, we have described it as reflecting our consciousness or what we are attending to. While this seems like a reasonable enough description, it is not entirely accurate. The relationship between working memory and consciousness is very poorly understood, primarily because we have a very poor idea of what consciousness is to begin with. The most convincing analysis of this issue I have encountered is Bernard Baars' description. Baars (1988) suggests that the contents of working memory are the things that are available to our conscious selves, but that we can only be fully conscious of one of these items at a time, and that it will occupy our consciousness for less than about half a second. He suggests this to reflect our subjective experiences of a "stream of consciousness," which can sometimes wander from topic to topic (as when we daydream). He also suggests that we are only conscious of the *results* of the analyses performed by working memory, not the *nature* of the analyses themselves or the incoming raw information.

Finally, Baars argues that consciousness does have a purpose: it allows us to deal with new situations by presenting unfamiliar stimulation to a wide range of automatic processing modules. He therefore follows the thinking of neuroscientists who have found that the brain has many sections designed to automatically perform some analysis on stimuli possessing certain properties (as we have seen with pattern recognition, etc.). These "dedicated modules" are automatically activated when that kind of stimulus occurs, and therefore we are not conscious of having engaged them; they do their jobs automatically. According to Baars, when a stimulus occurs that does not automatically activate some module, consciousness allows us to seek a set of modules that might come closest to allowing us to respond appropriately. Thus, he believes that consciousness is a constantly shifting awareness of parts of our working memory that is designed to allow us to properly understand new, complex situations. This description seems similar to Baddeley's executive component of working memory and would suggest that consciousness resides in the frontal lobe (remember that this is all very speculative at this point).

Attention is also a poorly understood topic, although it has been much more carefully studied. Donald Broadbent (1958) devised a task that is still widely used to study attention, called the **dichotic listening** task. People wearing headphones received a different message in each ear and were told to repeat aloud what they heard in one ear. A person might get a male voice reading Shakespeare in the left ear and a female voice reading a physics text in the right ear, and be asked to tell what he was hearing in the left ear. The requirement to repeat what they heard in one ear allowed Broadbent to be sure that they were actually paying attention to it. He found that people's ability to tell afterward what they had received in the other ear was severely limited, and he initially concluded that accessing the meaning of what one heard required attention; meaning processing was prevented by an attentional filter.

Later research has in fact found that even the unattended material is processed to the point that meanings are accessed, but that the results of these semantic analyses are mostly lost before they have much of an impact on us (Duncan, 1999). For example, receiving the word *money* in the unattended ear causes a person to interpret the attended sentence "They threw stones at the bank" as involving vandalism at the savings and loan rather than kids tossing rocks across the river (MacKay, 1973). This means that the unattended word *money* was processed enough to obtain its meaning, which then biased the interpretation of the ambiguous sentence.

If unattended material is analyzed, what good is attending to things? Ann Treisman proposed that attention allows us to put together the results of our perceptual analyses more accurately (Treisman & Gelade, 1980). She studied visual attention using letters randomly spaced in a display and printed in two colors. For example, a person might have to find a blue T among a display of red Ts and red Ss. In this case, the target very quickly "pops out" at the person; reaction time is not only fast, it is equally fast for a display with many distractor letters or a display with only a few distractors. The same is true if the subject must find a red T among a field of red and blue Ss. Treisman concluded that a search requiring use of only one property (either color or shape but not both) is automatic, parallel, and does not require attention. Because it is a parallel (simultaneous) search, the number of distractors makes no difference.

However, if Treisman's learner must find a red T among blue Ts and red Ss, then the person's reaction time is dramatically affected by the number of distractors. More distractors result in slower reaction times. She concluded that attention was required to correctly combine two or more details of a complex stimulus, and that this forced the person to examine each item one at a time, leading to longer times for more items. She called this combination process **feature integration**, and it seems the most likely description of what working memory might be like. The material we are attending to gets entered in working memory so that many pieces of information (several details of an event, or the meanings of words in a paragraph) can be accurately combined to give us an understanding of the whole experience, rather than isolated fragments of events.

A nice illustration of the way automatic processing allows stimulus patterns to "pop out" at us is provided by Hoffman (1986). Look at figure 11.2. Pattern A is obviously separated into a left and a right half; so is pattern B. Pattern C is also separated into a left and right half, but it is not obvious until you look closely. The A and B patterns can be automatically separated on the basis of one characteristic each: color for A and shape for B. Pattern C uses these same colors and shapes, but the left half combines them into black squares and white diamonds whereas the right half combines them as black diamonds and white squares. The recognition of the different combinations requires attention and the use of working memory to integrate the features.

Figure 11.2 Patterns A and B can be automatically divided preattentively, while pattern C requires attention.

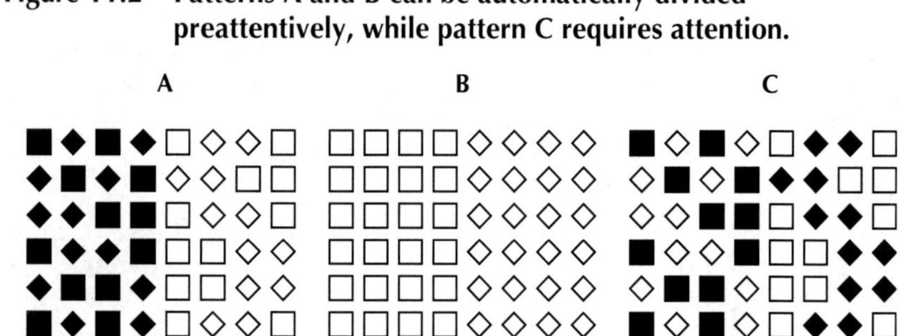

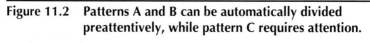

Adapted from Hoffman, 1986.

Long-Term Memory (LTM)

Duration of LTM

Long-term memory is supposed to be permanent. This is implied not only by the information-processing model of Atkinson and Shiffrin but also by the interference data generated by the verbal learning researchers. However, there is no conclusive evidence for this, only implications. Interference data suggest a very small role for decay through disuse but do not eliminate decay due to the passage of time completely (see chapter 10). Nevertheless, most memory workers assume that long-term memories are permanent, based on the available evidence.

There are two other pieces of suggestive data in addition to the interference data presented in chapter 10. One is a series of studies done by Wilder Penfield (1954). Penfield was a brain surgeon who investigated the functioning of the parts of each patient's brain before operating. He did so by stimulating the area with a very mild electrical current. Because most brain surgery is done using only a local scalp anesthetic with the patient remaining conscious, he was able to ask the patient to report the results of his stimulation. Sometimes patients would report sensations, sometimes they would make various movements, and sometimes they would report memories. The memories were usually reported as being very vivid and detailed, and the patients would often feel as if they had relived the events. This was in spite of the fact that some of the memories were of things and events that the patient claimed to have forgotten or not thought about in many years. Penfield concluded that, even though some memories are not normally recalled, they are nevertheless there, stored away for life, just needing the correct stimulus to retrieve them.

You might think that Penfield's research answered the question of permanence. This was in fact the belief of memory researchers for several years thereafter. However, the brain stimulation studies suffer from a lack of supporting evidence. In most cases, Penfeld had only the patients' word that they had not recalled events before the stimulation, or even that the events actually happened. In addition, Penfield actually obtained such memory reports from only about 8% of his patients.

The best evidence suggesting that long-term memories are very durable comes from a much different kind of study. This study used high school yearbooks (Bahrick, Bahrick, & Wittlinger, 1975). The experimenters took names and pictures from the yearbooks of people who had graduated from high school from 3 months to 47 years earlier. They used a variety of procedures to test memory, first asking subjects to recall as many classmates' names as they could. Recall performance was not especially good, but when asked to recognize classmates' names from a list of names including their own and other subjects' classmates, memory performance was much better. Even for the people who had graduated more than 40 years earlier, name recognition was 69% accurate. Recognition of faces was even better, revealing no decline at all from the three-month group to the next-to-oldest group, which averaged 34 years since graduation. The eight groups examined averaged 90% face recognition accuracy! The last group, the oldest subjects who were tested 47 years after graduating, averaged 71%. This high level of accuracy suggests that if there is any decay of memories, it's a very small amount. But again, that is only suggestion. Bahrick (1984) has also shown that subjects such as Spanish learned in high school can last a lifetime if they were well learned initially. Initial learning was estimated by asking about grades in the original courses; he also asked his subjects how much they had practiced the language and found little relation between that later practice and retention.

The reason that memory researchers have become so cautious of such data, calling them suggestive rather than compelling evidence, is primarily because of the research of Elizabeth Loftus. Loftus examined the accuracy of the kind of *eyewitness testimony* given in court. She showed her subjects a set of pictures portraying events such as cars involved in a fender bender. Later she would ask her subjects simple questions about the pictures. Several types of questions were asked, differing only in their wording. Some questions were asked so that they implied things about details of the pictures that were misleading. In one experiment (Loftus & Palmer, 1974), subjects were asked, "How fast were the cars going when they ______ each other?" Each group of subjects was asked this question with a different word inserted in the blank space. When subjects saw the word *smashed* in that sentence, their average estimate of the speed of the cars was 40.8 mph. The subjects who saw the word *contacted* in the sentence averaged 31.8 mph in estimating the speed of the cars. Loftus suggested that the actual memory was distorted by the way in which she had asked for recall. In another experiment using a four-second film of a fender bender, subjects were more likely to report having seen broken glass on the street when asked after they had responded to the version of the speed question using *smashed*, even though there was no broken glass shown.

Loftus called the memory distortions *overwriting*. In another experiment she showed that even very subtle wording changes could have overwriting effects (Loftus & Zanni, 1975). Some subjects were asked, "Did you see *the* broken headlight?"; others were asked, "Did you see *a* broken headlight?" (without, of course, any emphasis on the words "the" or "a" to cue subjects). This seemingly trivial change actually conveys an important implication that in the first case there actually was a broken headlight to see. Subjects were significantly more likely to respond "yes" to the version of the question using *the*.

Loftus suggested that the original memories had actually been changed by the misleading questions into new versions of the events, and these new memories were the only ones retained. Several investigators have challenged this idea and suggested that both memories might be present, but that the demand characteristics of the situation (Orne, 1962) led subjects to choose to report things consistent with what they thought the experimenters expected. Current research suggests that both of these possibilities actually occur, although coexistence is more probable (Zaragoza, McCloskey, & Jamis, 1987). Sometimes old memories are modified by new information, and sometimes both the old memories and the new ones coexist and the individual has at least some access to both.

The trouble with this possibility is that it still presents a major problem for evaluating eyewitness testimony, Loftus's original interest. Consider a witness to a crime who is first asked to go through a series of "mug shots" to identify a potential criminal. If the witness later sees one of the mug-shot people in a police lineup, will the witness be able to tell whether he had seen that face during the crime or just during the viewing of the mug shots? Brown, Deffenbacher, and Sturgill (1977) found that seeing people's faces in mug-shot arrays made subjects significantly more likely to identify them as criminals and also more likely to implicate them in the crime in question. Thus, their subjects became confused about the source of their memories.

Research on which factors lead to overwriting a memory and which ones lead to two memory traces indicates that practice or repetition is a very powerful factor, and even a little contradictory evidence is enough to weaken the effect. Kroll and Timourian (1986), in a replication of Loftus's original study, showed that allowing their subjects to see the slides again after they answered the misleading recognition questions substantially reduced the effect of a second set of misleading recognition questions. In addition, Bekerian and Bowers (1983) found that asking the questions in the same order as the events occurred also made subjects less susceptible to an overwriting effect. Misinformation effects seem to be stronger for peripheral details than for centrally important details, for longer retention intervals, and when the misleading information is presented as part of a question or as something that can be assumed to have occurred (see Loftus' wording) (Koriat, Goldsmith, & Pansky, 2000).

Awareness of how the effect works has led to the development of standard procedures for obtaining accurate eyewitness accounts of crimes, such as beginning with open-ended questioning ("Just tell the whole story from the start in your own words") rather than directed questions. A case study of 13 witnesses to an actual murder committed in broad daylight indicated that the witnesses were very accurate, with little change in their accounts over a five-month period; the most errors occurred in estimates of height, weight and hair color of the people involved (Yuille & Cutshall, 1986). These researchers suggested that memory for actual events is less likely to suffer from distortion than memory for things in laboratory experiments.

Loftus has also done research related to the *recovered memory – false memory* controversy. During the 1990s several psychological therapists apparently encountered cases of individuals, usually women, suddenly remembering being abused as children after many years of seeming unawareness of it. These recovered memories seem to contradict all the principles of memory we have encountered: powerful emotional events are usually remembered better; repeated experiences are generally better remembered, and we don't usually see memories improve with longer retention intervals. Loftus' research indicates that at least some of the legal cases of childhood abuse were created in adult clients by the therapists (sometimes unwittingly) and are false memories rather than recovered ones. Loftus conducted several studies in which entirely new memories were implanted in people. She and her colleagues were able to convince people that they had been lost in a mall when they were five

(Loftus & Pickrell, 1995), or spilled punch on the parents of the bride at a wedding (Hyman, Husband, & Billings, 1995), or that they had been born left-handed (Kelley, Amodio, & Lindsay, 1996); in all cases these were not actual events that happened to the people, yet the people came to believe that they had. As a result of this research, some convictions of abuse on the basis of recovered memories have been overturned. Most memory researchers consider the circumstances of recovered memories to be unlikely (remember that a good scientist never says "never").

Research on false recall now includes studies of distortions that may occur during the original encoding as well as distortions occurring during or near retrieval. A clever study by Roediger and McDermott (1995) used *free recall* (see chapter 12) of specially constructed word lists to induce people to recall having seen a word on the list (the target word) that wasn't there. For example, if you are given a list of 20 words that include *loan, money, vault,* and *teller,* you might mistakenly later think that the word *bank* was also on the list. Roediger and McDermott (1995) found the likelihood of such mistakes being made equal to the recall of actual items from the middle of the list (remember the serial position effect) in immediate recall, and McDermott (1996) found higher recall for such nonpresented items than for actual presented items in a delayed recall task. Other studies have indicated that these false memories can be relatively long lasting. Robinson and Roediger (1997) found that more false recognitions and false recalls occurred when the study list included more words associated with the targets.

Clearly, long-term memories are not permanent in the same way as a videotape recording. The Penfield and Bahrick research suggests that memories may persist for a very long time, but the Loftus research suggests that memories may be distorted or become inaccessible because of intervening events. However, remember that our definition of learning was a "relatively permanent" change in behavior. We took that to mean that the memory of an experience would remain with the individual for his lifetime unless something happened, like a brain injury or a new experience, to change it. The experiments of Loftus are extremely important in that they emphasize the caution we must have in trusting memories. However, they do not say that memories are temporary, merely that they can be changed by new, related experiences. It still seems quite likely that both the original memories and the new, revised memories could be retained for a lifetime. At this time our best answer to the question, "Are memories permanent?" is a qualified "yes."

Organization and Long-Term Memory

Many analogies have been suggested to help explain the Atkinson and Shiffrin model. We might think of STM as a secretary in an office and long-term memory as the filing cabinet. This analogy implies that STM is the active decision maker, deciding what input (correspondence) to give to the boss, file away, or ignore by trashing it. LTM just passively stores the material placed in its files by the STM secretary, who also searches among the files to retrieve needed information. We might be tempted to think that the success of STM searches depends on how much material is stored. However, if the secretary had to search all of the files for each piece of correspondence, she wouldn't be too efficient, and our retrieval times from LTM would usually be very long. Retrieval times also would invariably get much longer as we acquired more memories, which means as we got older we would always be slower to recall things. This might seem like a plausible description of people's recall behavior if we focus on the elderly, but it certainly doesn't apply to the differences between children and teenagers or teenagers and adults.

There is no systematic increase in retrieval times from LTM with increases in age. This is because we never search all of our permanent memories at any one time, only some of them. The contents of a secretary's filing cabinets are organized, usually alphabetically, and the secretary only searches the part that probably contains what is needed. Apparently, much of the contents of long-term memory is also organized to aid in retrieval, but not alphabetically. Instead, our memories tend to be organized topically, according to the meaningful relationships between items, a little like the organization found in a library. This makes the search process much easier for the organized material. The organized material is said to be in *semantic memory*, and the experiences that do not fit well into this organization are remembered in *episodic memory*. The differences between these two types of long-term memory, and the organization of semantic memory, are the topics of the next chapter.

Summary

The information-processing approach attempts to analyze the psychological events that occur when we encounter stimulation, often by making an analogy between human functioning and computer functioning. One of the first such models was Atkinson and Shiffrin's stage model of memory. It proposed that information was processed in three stages, a sensory register, short-term memory, and long-term memory. The sensory registers consisted of brief "icons" for visual stimuli or "echoes" for auditory stimuli that maintained a fairly exact copy of the stimulus for about 1/4 second for vision or 2 to 4 seconds for hearing. The short-term memory system could "read" the contents of these sensory registers and select some of this material for further analysis. Thus the things we "attend to" are the things that pass from the sensory registers to STM. Short-term memory has a time limit of about 20 seconds; unrehearsed or unattended material disappears from STM in this time. STM also has a severe capacity limit of 7 +/– 2 "chunks" of information. However, the chunk itself differs in size depending on the complexity of the material. STM seems to be more susceptible to interference on the basis of acoustic similarity, and therefore is believed to usually operate as a verbal or phonemic representation of the input. STM may be characterized as the active, "conscious" part of the information-processing system, but some researchers feel that STM is not a single entity, but rather a set of several somewhat related processing mechanisms.

Long-term memory is supposed to be unlimited in capacity and last for a lifetime. However, the memories stored in LTM may be altered by later experiences, as Loftus revealed in her eyewitness testimony studies. LTM is characterized as a passive storage mechanism that receives material encoded into it by STM, and from which STM can retrieve stored material. Much of the material in LTM seems to be stored in a highly organized semantic memory; however, some idiosyncratic experiences are not easily integrated into this semantic network. These other episodic memories are more difficult to retrieve because there is no efficient search strategy for retrieving them.

Questions for Discussion, Thought, & Practice

1. Define and give an example of each key concept. Then try to arrange the terms into three categories: sensory register, STM, and LTM.
2. Describe how short-term and long-term memory would function in each of the following examples:
   a. Figuring out in your head approximately what your change will be at the grocery store.
   b. Recognizing that Ms. Flootsnoot is wearing her hair differently.
   c. Figuring out your path to your car from your current location.
3. Identify each example as involving top-own or bottom-up processing, feature detection, visuospatial sketch pad, or verbal rehearsal loop.
   a. When Donatello hears his girlfriend's voice down the hall, he picks her face out of the crowd very quickly and smiles.
   b. It's easy to pick out Dontello's girlfriend because of her purple spiked hair and the dimple on her cheek.
   c. Phil is on the phone trying to describe to his roommate where he left his history homework in their room.
4. Give examples of interfering words in short-term and in long-term memory for the stimulus words *house, tire, person*. Why do different words cause interference for short- and long-term memory systems?

Knowledge Representation in Permanent Memory

Key Concepts

basic-level category	prototype
clustering	schema
cognitive economy	script
episodic memory	semantic memory
fan effect	semantic network
feature comparison	semantic priming
free recall	spreading activation
fuzzy boundary	subordinate category
hierarchical organization	superordinate category
natural concepts	

The last chapter ended by describing the difference between episodic long-term memories and semantic long-term memories. I suggested that semantic memories were highly organized and that this made them more easily retrieved than episodic memories. One of the earliest pieces of evidence for organization in our permanent memories comes from the verbal learning studies discussed in chapter 10. Besides the serial anticipation task of Ebbinghaus and the paired-associates task, that chapter mentioned a third task that was widely used by verbal learning researchers from the 1940s through the 1960s (McGeoch, 1942). This was the **free recall** task, which consisted of a list of items, usually words, in a random order. The learner had to recall what items were on the list after some delay but was free to recall the items in any order.

In addition to the phenomena of primacy and recency effects, the free recall task revealed something else. Typically, learners would recall items in a much different order than that originally given. They would rearrange the items, recalling them in groups of words with related meanings, which is called **clustering**. The pattern of clusters generally could be predicted by noting which words had related meanings or belonged to the same category (Bousfield, 1953). In addition, errors made in the free recall task were almost always substitutions of words semantically related to the actual words on the list.

For example, if the words *potato, cupboard, plateau, liver, bathtub, collards, fireplace,* and *canyon* were presented in that order to a person, she might recall them this way: "potato, collards, liver, onions, bathtub, cupboard, fireplace, plateau, canyon" The grouping of the foods together represents one cluster and the household characteristics represent another. In addition, the person would have made one error; *onions*, a word clearly related to the other foods. The given list is especially sensitive to these semantic interrelationships. However, we can easily design free recall lists that avoid this kind of categorical relationship. They generally lead to poorer recall, although the learner does impose his own subjective organization on them (Tulving, 1972).

Episodic vs. Semantic Memory

Tulving proposed that information to be stored in permanent memory could be classified into two types: material that could be easily organized, and material that had little or no objective organization. He suggested that the unorganized material was stored in an **episodic memory**, and the organized material was stored in a **semantic memory**. He pointed out several differences between the two types of material and the two types of storage. Episodic material refers to specific details of events, such as when they happened, who you were with, or where you were. The question at the beginning of chapter 10 about your favorite song in third grade asks about a typical episodic piece of information. There is no logical reason for one particular song to have been popular at that time; it just happened that way. On the other hand, semantic material is factual and independent of context, and the relations between facts do have a logical reason underlying them. Question 4, about kangaroos, represents a question about your factual knowledge; you were not asked about when or where you learned it, just what the information was. Most importantly, Tulving suggested that the categorically organized semantic material would be much easier to retrieve from LTM than the episodic material, which could only be organized temporally. If you think back to your reactions to the two questions, you can easily appreciate that episodic memories, even when they represent things that were important to you, can be difficult to retrieve. In comparison, semantic memories sometimes are ridiculously easy to retrieve, such as the meaning of the word *kangaroo*.

As a brief digression, we should note that material the learner *perceives* as possessing a systematic organization is much better retrieved than material for which the learner fails to see an organization. Therefore, if a student memorizes material for a test and perceives it as a collection of unrelated things to be remembered as episodic events, he is less likely to recall it on a test than someone who has attempted to perceive the relationships between the pieces of material and has tried to integrate them with her existing semantic network. We pursue this idea in more detail in the next chapter.

Tulving (1972) suggested that episodic memories were actually stored by different LTM systems than semantic memories. It seems more likely that semantic memories can be more richly encoded—that is, more connections can be made between the semantic item and other semantic material than between episodes. The idea of richness of encoding has become a popular research area. If additional facts make already known relationships clearer or more easily perceived, then they can enhance recall. However, if they are just additional facts which do not clarify existing relationships, then they can reduce recall (Lesgold, Roth, & Curtis, 1979). Semantic memories seem to be those in which richer encoding usually enhances existing relationships, making material much more accessible.

Hierarchical Organization

The nature of semantic memory may be best understood by consideration of a model proposed by Collins and Quillian (1969), which they originally devised as a learning system for computers. They called their model TLC, for Teachable Language Comprehender, and the goal was to create a program that could be "taught"—that is, that could receive information in the form of sentences and that could integrate that information with its existing knowledge base. To test the program's ability to do this, they wanted to be able to ask it questions about the new information. To provide a useful framework for storing information that could be expanded to include new facts, they developed a hierarchical network.

A portion of a network with a **hierarchical organization** is illustrated in figure 12.1 for some of our knowledge about birds. Basically, this portion represents the relationship between the relatively comparable categories of *birds* and *fish,* above them their superordinate category of *animals*, and some examples below them. Properties of each category are stored with the category at each level in the hierarchy. The two most important properties of the model are that each connecting arrow represent an association that has to be traveled to remember the relationship and that properties are represented in the most economical way. The associational "roads" all had about the same travel time. The **cognitive economy** principle meant that a

Figure 12.1 An illustration of a portion of the model of a semantic network for the "Animal" superordinate category

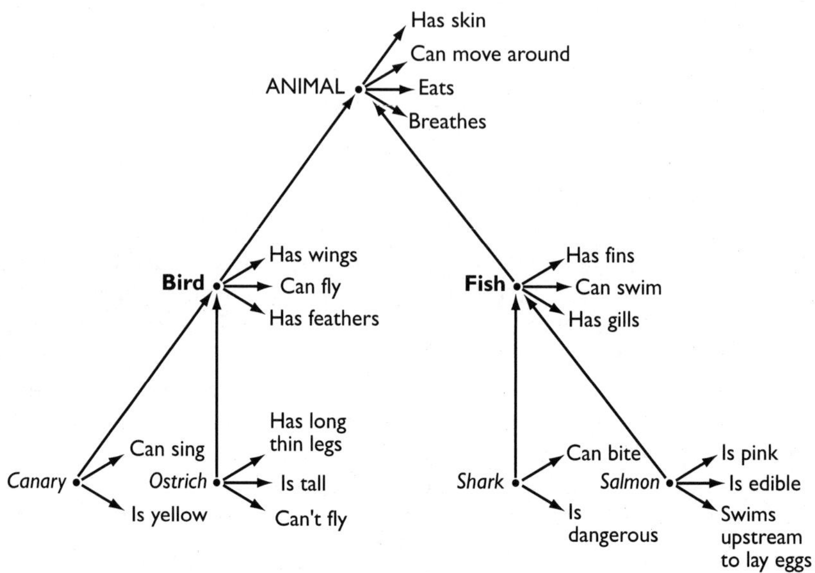

Reprinted from A. M. Collins & M. R. Quillian, "Retrieval Time from Semantic Memory," *Journal of Verbal Learning and Verbal Behavior, 8,* 240–247.

property such as "Has feathers" was not stored with *canary, ostrich,* and so on, but only at the higher level of *bird,* and similarly the property of "breathes" is only directly connected to *animal.* Thus to answer a question such as, "Is a canary yellow?", the user of a **semantic network** need only travel the direct pathway between them. However, to answer a question such as, "Does a canary breathe?", the computer program must travel three pathways. This second question should take somewhat longer because of the additional travel. In a computer program the difference would be difficult to notice, but if humans used a similar arrangement, their reaction times to such questions should be measureable. Collins and Quillian (1969) were able to show the predicted pattern of reaction times to many questions about birds and animals; people took longer to answer questions that involved more pathways to travel.

Unfortunately, several researchers have shown that TLC has some severe limitations and failings as a model of human semantic memory. Many exceptions to its predictions have been found. Some, such as the "mammal problem," may not be too serious. The "mammal problem" is that questions such as "Is a lion a mammal?" should be answered faster than "Is a lion an animal?" according to the model. People actually take longer to answer the mammal question (Rips, Shoben, & Smith, 1973).

However, this may be because the concept of *mammal* is learned much later than the concepts of *animal, bird,* and so on. Most of the others are learned by most children before school, but *mammal* is learned by most children after several years of education. That is, *mammal* might have been shoved into the network rather late; perhaps it's just not as well integrated into the network as the concepts learned earlier. In other words, it may be an enrichment that does not clarify the already existing relations unless you're very knowledgeable about biology. A similar problem exists for the term *primate* and may be explained the same way. This notion means that some connections would be better learned than others, and we have to add a concept of repetition to the network model. Then not all pathways would be equal. Paths that received more practice would be traveled faster or more easily; they would be better learned. The addition of a practice principle would probably improve the TLC model, but it would be an important change that might have major effects on the overall nature of the model.

Concept Structure

One of the more severe problems of the original TLC model involved the comparison of the questions "Is a canary a bird?" and "Is an ostrich a bird?" The TLC model predicts that these two questions would take about equally long to answer; unfortunately, the ostrich question takes consistently longer (Smith, Shoben, & Rips, 1974). This finding is general to most of our semantic categories. It means that the examples of categories are not all equally "good" examples. In the TLC model the assumption was that all examples are equally representative of their category and thus are equally easily associated with it. However, there is much data to contradict this idea. Think of any category you like, and you will find that some examples come more easily to mind than others. For example, when people are asked to give examples of the category *dog*, they respond with some typical dogs such as Labradors, collies, German shepherds, and cocker spaniels. They rarely respond with dachshunds or Chihuahuas (except for people who own one of these dogs). Or think of some examples of *furniture*; you might have thought of a chair or sofa, but you probably didn't think of a vase or a clock. Eleanor Rosch and her colleagues (Rosch, 1973, 1975, 1977; Rosch & Mervis, 1975) have provided a great deal of evidence that shows that category relationships are much more complex than the TLC model assumes.

Recall our discussion of concepts at the end of chapter 10. It was noted that encoding concepts as consisting of a list of criterial attributes allowed prediction of many of the findings of early concept learning studies. However, Rosch and her colleagues suggested that these experiments were not studying real-life concepts but rather artificial laboratory concepts. She suggested that, whereas the concepts devised by psychologists for experiments had very clear boundaries and consisted of a set of examples that were all equally good (and nonexamples that were equally poor), real life or **natural concepts** had a much more complex structure. She suggested that natural concepts had one best example, called a **prototype**, and that other examples would be associated with that concept to the degree that they were similar to the prototype. Furthermore, she suggested that there would be examples that would be *very* different from the prototype and might be difficult to classify because of their dissimilarity to the prototype. These confusing examples were called "**fuzzy boundary**" examples.

For our concept of *dog*, Labrador might be close to a prototype example, and dingoes, wild dogs, or foxes might be near the fuzzy boundary. Are dingoes dogs? Perhaps, sort of, and this is the case for wild dogs and foxes as well. Rosch would give a category name to subjects and ask them to give examples. The first several examples would invariably be given by almost all her subjects; these would be the prototype or other examples close to it. The last few responses given by individuals would be much more idiosyncratic; only one or a few people would give each of them. So, for our concept of *furniture*, almost everyone responds quickly with table and chair, but only a few people respond with vase, clock, or mirror, and they do so late in their recall session (Rosch, 1973, 1975, 1977; Rosch & Mervis, 1975). Table and chair are approximately prototypical; and vase, clock and mirror are probably near the fuzzy boundary of the concept *furniture*. These characteristic patterns occur for most of our concepts; even those which we think of as artificial (such as the concept of an *odd number*) show such patterns. Before you read on, think of an example of an odd number.

People almost always respond to the odd-number question with a single digit number, 1, 3, 5, 7, 9 and not a two- or three-digit number like 23 or 461, even though they all should be equally good examples of odd numbers. So this very abstract mathematical concept is treated by people the same way as concrete concepts like *dog* or *furniture* (although the concept of *odd number* doesn't have fuzzy boundaries). Remember that Smith, Shoben, and Rips (1974) showed that people verified questions faster for prototypical examples (Is a canary a bird?) than for non-prototype examples like *ostrich*. Rosch was able to predict these reaction times on the basis of the word association data; words given as associations early and given by most subjects functioned like prototypical examples in sentence verification tasks.

Rosch's research suggests an alternative to the description of concepts as lists of *criterial attributes*. It is possible that people see examples of a concept and construct an imaginary example in their heads (more or less finding an average of the examples) which best represents the attributes of the concept—the prototype. They remember the prototype and compare new examples to it to determine how the new examples should be labeled. Although people would still be analyzing examples in terms of attributes, the terms criterial or critical attribute used in chapter 10 no longer fit very well; we could have no fuzzy boundary if there are attributes that the example must possess. Instead, Rosch proposed that concepts have *characteristic attributes*; the more characteristic attributes an example has, the closer to prototypical it is. For the concept *bird*, characteristic attributes would be *flies* and *small*; most birds fly and are small, but ostriches, penguins and a few others do not fly and are larger than other birds. We all still agree that ostriches and penguins are birds, so they possess enough characteristic attributes to be properly classified. Bats have the attributes of flying and are the right size, but do not have other characteristic attributes of birds, and so most of us realize that they are not birds.

Concepts as Categories

Rosch also proposed an organizational pattern relating concepts to each other, and it resembles the Collins and Quillian hierarchical structure. She suggested that concepts at the middle level would be special; she referred to them as **basic-level categories** (*dog* or *chair* are examples). Categories which were more general (like *animal* or *furniture*) she called **superordinate categories**, and subdivisions of basic-level categories (like *Labrador* or *rocking chair*) she called **subordinate categories**. The basic-level categories were special for several reasons: they were learned first by children; they generally had shorter names; they shared more characteristic attributes than higher level concepts; there would be more concepts at that level than any other; and they would be the label supplied when people were shown pictures (e.g., the average person would look at a picture of a cocker spaniel and name it as a dog first). People are also quicker to identify a picture as an example of a dog or a chair than to identify it as an animal or a piece of furniture. A cross-cultural study by Berlin, Breedlove, and Raven (1973) that examined 66 different cultures and languages (mostly those of isolated groups which would be uninfluenced by our Western ways of thinking) found that these characteristics showed up in them all. Basic, superordinate, and subordinate categories could be identified in all these cultures (as well as up to two other intermediate levels in many cultures). The basic categories were learned first by children, and the people tended to use the basic level as the names of the objects. They also found that the basic level had the most categories, usually around 500. Note that although the basic level is special, the hierarchical arrangement of categories matches well with the TLC idea of Collins and Quillian.

There is some evidence that different categories of word meanings and knowledge are stored in different locations in the brain. Most words and their definitions seem to be represented in the left temporal lobe (interior to the left ear) of the brain. Damasio and colleagues (Damasio, Grabowski, Tranel, Hichwa, & Damasio, 1996) studied 127 adults with small areas of damage to parts of their temporal lobes. They were able to group these people into three different types of damage. Damage to one region only caused loss of the ability to name animals, although the person would be able to describe the animal's characteristics (e.g., when shown a skunk, the person would say, "That animal makes a terrible smell and is black and white"); damage to another area caused loss only of ability to name tools, and damage to a third area caused loss of recognition of familiar faces. The three areas were next to each other in the left temporal lobe but were nevertheless quite distinct. When they studied normal, uninjured individuals using PET scans, the appropriate areas were activated by the pictures. Note that the meaning attributes of the items were available in the brain damaged patients although the names were not; Caramazza (1996) pointed out that the Damasio study's results imply that words are stored in several separate brain systems: one for phonological representation (how the word sounds), and one for meaning representation.

All our examples have involved objects or "things"; in case you are wondering if psychologists recognize concepts which are not nouns (objects), some psycholinguists have identified the important distinctions between object concepts and action or relation concepts (verbs). Generally, it has been easier to devise methods of studying object concepts. Gentner (1981) suggests that verb concepts are more complex (and therefore more difficult to learn; see Gentner & Boroditsky, 1999) and their meanings more variable across cultures. However, they also seem to exhibit the properties of prototypical examples and fuzzy boundaries; when a child hits another child after seeing a Volkswagen ("Punch buggy no punch back"), is this as good an example of hitting as a boxer's punch in the ring? Is the child's punch truly hitting? Much of our analysis of object concepts seems to apply to other types of concepts as well.

Spreading Activation and Semantic Priming

The last major problem for a network model is that TLC (and indeed most networks) predicts very long response times for questions such as "Is a canary a plant?" When a question involves two very unrelated items, network models predict that the paths from each item would have to be traced to determine that they never meet. This should take a relatively long time. However, such questions are usually answered very quickly; in this case, the absurdity of the question leads to a very quick "no."

Collins and Loftus (1975) proposed a modification to the TLC model that they called **spreading activation**, which was an attempt to handle this problem and the problem of unequal examples. This model allows for some associations to be stronger than others and also allows for some negative relationships to be built in. The activation idea suggests that stimulation of any one point in the network flows out from that point (or spreads) equally along all the paths connecting it to other points. The more paths connecting a point, the more diluted the activation will be for any particular path. Therefore, the more examples there are in a category (such as *mammal*), the less activation each example receives, and this will make it less well recalled later. Each example in a small category (such as *type of family relationship* or *seasons*) receives more activation and is more easily recalled later. This is called the **fan effect** and has been verified in several experiments involving priming (Anderson, 1976).

Priming occurs when earlier activation of a memory trace makes current retrieval of it more likely. There are several forms of priming. The form in which we are interested involves activation of one trace that spreads from that point to other points nearby, making them also more easily accessed. This is called **semantic priming**. For example, all our talk of dogs and birds has caused some activation of the facts related to those animals for you. If we then ask you to name the bird that lives in the South Pole and doesn't fly, you might be able to answer "penguin" faster and more easily than someone who has not been primed with discussion of birds. The amount of priming a stimulus receives can be accurately predicted by examining the semantic relationship between it and the priming item. Although the TLC model predicts many patterns of priming effects, it is not very accurate in predicting the findings of fan effect studies. The activation model handles these findings better (Foss, 1982; Meyer & Schvaneveldt, 1971).

Figure 12.2 is Collins and Loftus's (1975) attempt to illustrate an activation model of a semantic network. Although it is considerably less orderly looking than the TLC model, it also represents a greater variety of interrelationships. If a model were created that retained the orderly semantic relationships of the TLC model while incorporating the richer variety of interrelationships suggested by the activation model, we might well have a reasonable description of long-term memory. Such a model might also be able to interconnect semantic and episodic information, allowing for integration of these two aspects of experiences.

The many studies of priming have supported the idea that there is indeed a complex network of interconnections among the facts that we have stored in our long-term memories (Chang, 1986). Activation of one spot causes some spread of partial activation to its neighbors, which are related semantically to it. The spread of activation illustrated by the priming effect is actually a very familiar phenomenon for most students. The time-honored advice given on how to take multiple-choice tests is based on priming. That is, when you are advised to skip questions that you don't know and come back to them later, it's in the hope that other questions will prime the necessary memories and aid in retrieval that second time around.

The existence of priming effects illustrates how partial activation may occur (Anderson & Bower, 1973; Graf & Mandler, 1984). It is partial because the memory is not fully activated until the next bit of stimulation occurs. Because of priming, that next stimulus does not need to be as powerful to fully activate the memory. In such cases, we might say that the priming stimulus has generated subthreshold activation; it makes it easier to retrieve the memory, but the memory is not actually retrieved because of the priming stimulus.

Many times, however, priming stimuli themselves actually cause a memory to be recalled. This could be called above-threshold priming, but is more often referred to simply as cued recall. In actuality, when we consider this point, the activation model provides an additional model of the whole memory system. In such a model, long-term memory is simply the stored representations of experiences that are currently not stimulated (or activated). When these stored representations are fully activated, they could be said to exist in short-term memory. Therefore, in such a model, the only difference between short-term and long-term memory is the level of activation; when a certain threshold is reached, that material would be said to be present in short-term memory.

Furthermore, the model implies a dimension of activation in which some representations could be just below threshold. These would be the primed representations, and they might be responsible for subjective experiences such as dreaming—primed subthreshold material might be more likely to show up in our dreams. The representations far below threshold would be fully "unconscious." If our nervous systems operate by a gradually changing pattern of infinitely variable levels of activation, the distinctions between short-term and long-term memory and between conscious and unconscious become blurred and somewhat less significant.

Figure 12.2 A representation of a semantic network for an activation model

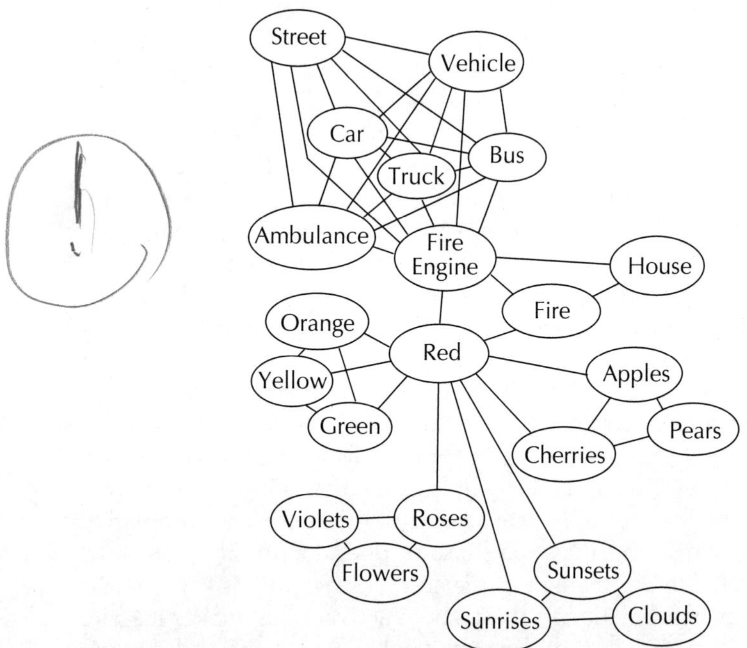

From "A Spreading-Activation Theory of Semantic Processing," by A. M. Collins, and E. F. Loftus, 1973, *Psychological Review, 82,* 407–428. Copyright © 1973 by the American Psychological Association. Reprinted by permission.

spreading activation

As an alternative to the stage model, an activation model like that described above has some appealing points. For example, the problem for the stage model of how to represent recognition in the diagram (figure 11.1) doesn't exist for activation models. The stimulation of a representation is recognition, and such stimulation causes those representations to exist in our short-term memories or our consciousness without any need for shuttling back and forth between STM and LTM, as the stage model implies. Our lack of any subjective awareness of trying to recognize familiar stimuli is thus easily accommodated by activation models. Also, the 20-second duration of short-term memory could just be the result of activated material that is unrehearsed losing its activation energy to the point where it falls below the threshold. Perhaps it takes 20 seconds for this to happen; after that time, the material might be just below the threshold, which would make it look like primed material. The fact that a Peterson-Brown type distractor task using recognition rather than recall leads to longer estimates of STM duration (Lutz & Wuensch, 1989) supports such an interpretation. Here recognition does not require as high a level of activation as is required by recall.

Unfortunately, an activation model must also explain all the other memory phenomena: Why are there different patterns of interference effects for brief time intervals and long time intervals, and why does there seem to be a capacity limit for our attention span? There are no obvious answers to these questions at this time. Pure activation models have an especially difficult time with the first of these questions, and the second is somewhat troubling for any model.

Is Memory Reconstructive? Script and Schema Theories

All memory theorists agree about one thing: your memory is not like a videotape recording. This analogy has become very distasteful to memory researchers. The research that Loftus related to eyewitness testimony (Loftus & Palmer, 1974), discussed in chapter 11, illustrates the frail nature of our memories compared to many artificial systems. Yet we do retain much of what we experience. What is kept and what is lost? Some theories, which emphasize the reconstructive nature of memory, assume that we develop frameworks or standard scenarios for many sequences of events we regularly experience. One of the first such theories called these mental structures or sets of procedures scripts (Schank & Abelson, 1977). Basically, the script tells us what should happen in a given situation, when it should happen, and what causes it to happen. For example, most of us have a script for what happens at a restaurant, which includes a host seating us and giving us a menu, a server taking our order and delivering the food, and so forth. Each restaurant experience follows this script to some extent. Details of a particular experience that are consistent with and easily generated from our knowledge of the script need not be remembered separately for each experience. Thus, scripts employ a cognitive economy principle. Only details of the experience that are unique to that particular time have to be specifically encoded in memory. Furthermore, the unique aspects of the experience that are relevant to the goal of the script should be remembered very well. Thus, if you order a ribeye steak and five minutes later the server returns to tell you that they are out of ribeyes and asks about an alternative choice, you should remember that particular restaurant trip and that detail well. On the other hand, details of the experience that are irrelevant to the script, such as the fact that the server knew someone in your party, are likely to be poorly remembered.

Bower, Black, and Turner (1979) constructed six script-based stories that included not only the script actions, but also relevant and irrelevant actions that deviated from the basic script. Shortly after their subjects had read all six stories, they were asked to write down all they could recall about them. Subjects recalled 53% of the relevant distinctive actions, 38% of the script actions, and 32% of the irrelevant actions. Thus, we remember specific details best when they have an important relationship to the purpose we have for being there and when they diverge somewhat from our typical expectations. On the other hand, details of an experience that are similar to the underlying script are not remembered much better than totally irrelevant details.

Researchers have also shown that memories may be altered to make them more consistent with scripts. In an interesting study of visual memory, Thorndyke and Stasz (1980) showed that their subjects' recall of map details became distorted toward more geometrically "regular" patterns. Details that are very different from the way the "script" reads may be remembered very well because of their distinctiveness. Alternatively, such memories may be difficult to retrieve because the script context does not provide useful retrieval cues for them. Thus, slightly different experiences may become distorted, and very different experiences may become either very well remembered or more difficult to remember. Scripts are similar to semantic memory networks in that they provide a complex, usually hierarchical framework for incorporating new information. However, the focus of scripts is to describe sequences of events or procedures, and semantic networks provide frameworks for relating objects and word meanings. No one has proposed an overall structure that relates different scripts to each other in the way that our semantic network interrelates all its contents.

A concept very similar to that of the script is the concept of the **schema**. A schema is a standardized description of a commonly encountered environment, like what we might think of as a typical grocery store design, a doctor's waiting room, or a professor's office. The Brewer and Treyens (1981) study, mentioned briefly when we discussed top-down processing in the previous chapter, was a study of the influence of schemas on memory. Just as with scripts, our memories for details of settings can be distorted by our expectations of what ought and ought not to be there. In that study, subjects who waited in a professor's office remembered that there were books in it, even though there weren't any. Their schema of what a professor's office should have in it led them astray. Many of them also failed to remember that there was a human skull in plain view on one shelf of the office, because their schema for a professor's office was not compatible with such an object being there.

Schemas and scripts seem to be the same idea applied to two different aspects of events that frequently occur the same way; how they proceed for scripts, and what was there for schemas. We can also note that they bear a strong resemblance to semantic networks, the major difference being that schemas and scripts don't have a systematic relation to each other. The restaurant script has not been related to a "going to a rock concert" script or to a "what my history class looks like" schema or to any other schema or script. Semantic networks propose that a very large body of different kinds of information might be organized and all the pieces of information eventually connected. Nevertheless, schema theory and script theory emphasize that we don't store a perfect copy of events in our memories; schemas and scripts cause us to select some pieces of experiences to store and some to leave out, and they can cause us to interpret the stored pieces in ways consistent with the schema or script (Alba & Hasher, 1983).

While there is still much about the nature of our long-term memory structure that is not well understood, we can make several statements about the nature of long-term memory organization:

1. Many long-term memories are highly organized according to semantic relationships.
2. There is a hierarchical nature to LTM semantic networks.
3. There probably is some use of a cognitive economy principle so that information is not redundant, but there are clearly exceptions to this principle.
4. Common or frequently encountered relationships create stronger, more easily accessed associations (practice).
5. Recently accessed memories are more easily retrieved (priming).

These principles provide a more accurate account of our semantic knowledge, but the TLC model still gives us a good general idea of the nature of our memories. Each of us probably has some very complex pattern like it in our heads, not just for birds and other animals, but for a multitude of objects and activities—indeed, for everything we've learned about the basic nature of our environment! In addition, it's likely that some combination of activation principles and a stage model would provide a good overall model of memory. At this point, however, no combination has been presented that is satisfactory to the majority of memory workers.

Feature Comparison Models

An alternative to organizational models was proposed by Smith (Smith, Shoben, & Rips, 1974), who chose to emphasize the search process used during retrieval rather than the encoding process (we would organize material in a semantic network during the original learning). Smith and his colleagues assumed that word meanings are stored as sets of attributes which they labeled features. (This was in keeping with previous research on semantic features in psycholinguistics; we shall use the term *attributes* to avoid confusion with distinctive features, which are not related to this usage). They assumed that a question like, "Is a canary a bird?" could be answered by a simple one-step count of attributes; if two terms shared a lot of attributes, then one could quickly answer "Yes." Similarly, a question like "Is a canary a fish?" would result in a quick answer, "No," because they share few attributes. This handles the problem that semantic networks have with "no" responses. However, if a pair of terms shared an intermediate number of attributes, a second, slower step was required. This second step examined *which* attributes were shared. If these were criterial or critical attributes, then we might answer yes; but if they were simply characteristic attributes or irrelevant attributes (like size or ability to fly in our "Is a bat a bird?" example), then we would answer no.

The appeal of the feature comparison model is that it does not assume that people systematically organize information during learning; it's more like an Internet search engine such as Google than a model of storage or encoding. The task of working memory becomes one of *retrieval* rather than one of encoding; this aspect of memory, although important, was somewhat neglected by researchers initially. Unfortunately, we have encountered sufficient evidence to suggest that some organization does exist in long-term memory; therefore, the feature comparison model is incomplete by itself; it is a model of retrieval only. Probably some combination of search strategies with a semantic network would provide the best description of long-term memory performance. Some consideration of retrieval is presented in the next chapter.

Summary

Much of the material in long-term memory seems to be stored in a highly organized semantic memory; however, some idiosyncratic experiences are not easily integrated into this semantic network. These other episodic memories are more difficult to retrieve because there is no efficient search strategy for retrieving them. The semantic memories are hierarchically arranged as sets of superordinate and subordinate categories, with properties of categories stored along with the categories usually using a cognitive economy principle (Collins and Quillian's TLC).

However, categories have a more complex structure than the TLC model assumed, as revealed by experiments in which some examples are more typical of their categories than others. A model called spreading activation attempted to incorporate the findings of typicality effects and the fan effect. The fan effect is the result of a category having many members; the activation from the category is diffused among many pathways. Therefore any one pathway receives less activation than a pathway for a category with fewer members. This is revealed by the strength of priming effects for different-sized categories.

Several memory researchers have shown that we may learn structures or frameworks for common events or circumstances, such as going to a restaurant. These scripts or schemas allow us to remember just the distinctive characteristics of individual occurrences of these events and to "fill in" the rest of the details based on our knowledge of the script. However, this can also lead to errors of recall when specific details conflict with the script or are unrelated to it. An alternative to organizing at input is the feature comparison model, which describes retrieval as either a one-step or a slower two-step process depending on the amount of attribute overlap.

Questions for Discussion, Thought, & Practice

1. Define and give an example of each key concept.
2. Construct a section of your semantic network for the superordinate category of *tools*. Include scissors, pliers, and electric drill at the bottom level. Include some attributes at each level in the network.
3. You are primed with the superordinate category *games*, and your friend is primed with the superordinate *seasons*. Discuss the amount of activation that the item *monopoly* would have for you versus the amount of activation *spring* would have for your friend.
4. Construct your semantic network for the superordinate category *learning*. The more attributes you can list, the better your prospects for an "A" in the course!
5. A current and controversial social issue can be described as a "fuzzy boundary" problem: What are the limits (boundaries) of marriage? What is the prototypical marriage? Are marriages in religious groups that practice polygamy (usually several wives) or gay marriages at a fuzzy boundary?

Processing and Remembering

KEY CONCEPTS

acoustic analysis
automaticity
chunking
completion task
deep processing
elaboration
elaborative rehearsal
encoding specificity
imagery
implicit memory
levels of processing
maintenance rehearsal
method of loci
organization
parallel distributed processing
peg-word technique
perceptual identification task
phonemic processing
precise elaboration
prospective memory
recall
recognition
retrospective memory
rote rehearsal
self-reference effect
semantic analysis
sensory analysis
shallow processing
state-dependent learning
transfer-appropriate processing

Psychologists generally agree about the importance of interference effects as discussed in chapter 10. They are also in agreement about the existence of an organized set of permanent memories as illustrated by semantic networks as presented in chapter 12. However, they are more divided over the issue of stages of memory; probably at least half of the researchers in memory currently feel that the concept of short-term memory is unnecessary and should be discarded (Crowder, 1982; Greene, 1992; Watkins, 1990). Craik and Lockhart (1972) were among the first to reject stages; they described an alternative based on differences in encoding processes. They demonstrated very clearly that people can analyze material in many different ways and that some analyses lead to better recall than others.

One of the assumptions of the Atkinson-Shiffrin stage model was that rehearsal in STM eventually led to permanent encoding in LTM. They didn't make any distinctions between ways of rehearsing for maintenance of material in short-term memory and rehearsal mechanisms for permanent encoding in long-term memory. An experiment by Craik and Watkins (1973) demonstrated that such differences existed and were under the control of their subjects. They presented "random" lists of words to their subjects and, for each list, instructed them to remember the last word beginning with a particular letter.

For example, let's say you are the subject, and you are asked to remember the last word beginning with G. You hear the words, *daughter, oil, rifle, garden, grain, table, football, anchor, giraffe, hammer.* You respond with "giraffe," and it seems to be a very easy task. You think you're through with that list, but you're not. After 27 such lists, you get a surprise final recall task: "Write down as many of the G words from *all* the lists as you can." Imagine the irritation you feel as you say, "But I wasn't trying to remember them—I was only trying to remember until you stopped." Then you try to write down as many of the words as you can. Now notice that the list is arranged so that you had only a second to rehearse the word *garden* before the very next word, which was *grain*. But you have several intervening words—much more rehearsal time—for *grain* before the next G word. If all types of rehearsal are the same, *grain* should be much better recalled than *garden* on the final recall task because it received more rehearsal.

However, Craik and Watkins found that there was no difference in final recall for the two items. They point to just the kinds of differences that I attributed to you as the hypothetical subject. They suggested that their subjects were engaged in **maintenance rehearsal**, so named because its only purpose was to maintain material until it was used. Once the material had served its purpose, it was abandoned. This is the sort of thing we do when we get the phone number of a mechanic on our cell phone when we require roadside assistance on the highway. We maintain it until we have dialed it and then we "forget" it.

Craik and Watkins (1973) also suggested that we deal with material differently when we want to remember it permanently. They called this other processing **elaborative rehearsal**. If you imagine yourself getting the phone number of a very attractive member of the opposite sex you meet at a party, you can appreciate the difference between this type of rehearsal and the type you would use for the mechanic's number. You can also appreciate that it might take more effort. Now we have established that people can choose to rehearse for a temporary purpose or for permanent storage. As a personal confession, I must admit that in college I occasionally fell prey to using the easier maintenance rehearsal while hunched over a textbook. I would be reading the words, but actually thinking about watching television or going out after I finished studying. To soothe my conscience, I maintained each sentence long enough to verify that I had indeed read it. However, at the end of the page I couldn't recall what was said on that page. If this experience sounds familiar, then you too suffer from the affliction. You must avoid maintenance rehearsal and take steps to use elaborative rehearsal while studying. Otherwise you're wasting your time.

The Craik and Lockhart model was explicitly designed to describe differences in the processing of written text. Thus, understanding means the comprehension of sentences; however, with a little thought, the ideas can easily be seen to apply to understanding social situations, such as the mechanic versus party examples just mentioned. As we discuss the Craik and Lockhart model, ways of generating elaborative rehearsal strategies will become apparent.

Levels of Processing

Craik and Lockhart suggested that rehearsal was just one processing strategy at our disposal. They suggested that some processes were automatic and rather easily done; these they described as **shallow processing**, because they thought that easy, automatic processing didn't lead to very durable memories. Generally, processing strategies that are highly practiced become more automatic and seem to take less "mental effort" or attention. Because shallow processing was fairly easy, it could often result in the same analyses being repeated, which was also of limited value for memory. They suggested that deeper processing resulted in longer-lasting memories, although the greater duration was really just a by-product. **Deep processing** for them really meant the processing needed to understand something—understanding was the goal, and remembering came along as a bonus. Although it is difficult to pin down a concept such as "understanding," we might think of understanding as the examination of the nearby associations in the individual's semantic network or the addition of new relevant associations to the network. This suggests that deeper processing is more effortful and is not automatic. Instead, deeper processing is initiated at the learner's option once the initial shallow processing is complete. Because deep processing requires more effort and is explicitly chosen, the same analyses were unlikely to be repeated; instead it was more likely that different deep analyses would be performed with each opportunity.

In their 1972 paper, Craik and Lockhart directed subjects to use strategies at three different levels. They did this by presenting a question before each stimulus word was viewed on a computer screen. The question would bias the subject to use one strategy in analyzing the stimulus word. If the subject is asked, "Is the word in capital letters?" she will be encouraged to process the visual sensory characteristics of the word and little more. This was assumed to represent a superficial **sensory analysis**. Her response to this pattern recognition question should be based on fairly shallow processing. To generate an intermediate level of processing, Craik and Lockhart used questions such as, "Does the word rhyme with weight?" This is somewhat deeper than the capital letters question because the visual pattern must be converted to an acoustic representation to answer the question; this represents an **acoustic analysis**. At the deepest level, Craik and Lockhart asked such questions as "Does the word fit in the sentence, 'I met a ____ in the street'?" This requires that the pattern be analyzed, then used to access the meaning of the stimulus word. Then this meaning must be integrated with the meaning of the sentence to see if they fit together. After their subjects had answered a lot of these easy questions about many stimulus words, they were given a surprise final recall test; Craik and Lockhart thus employed a variation on the incidental learning procedure discussed at the end of chapter 10. As predicted, the deepest-level semantic questions led to the highest likelihood of recall, and the shallowest sensory questions led to the poorest recall. The rhyming or phonemic questions were in between in recall, just where they were supposed to be. A flood of research followed that demonstrated the tremendous value of the ideas underlying the model while also revealing drastic limitations to the model itself.

One of the appealing qualities of the model was the elegant way in which Craik and Lockhart and their colleagues were able to use it to explain standard memory phenomena. For example, one of the problems in memory data concerned the reason for the recency effect in serial anticipation and free recall tasks. Remember that the stage model explained the recency effect by suggesting that the last few items were still in short-term memory and were thus more easily recalled than later items. Thus the existence of a recency effect was evidence in support of the stage model. However, the **levels of processing** theory suggests that the recency effect is the consequence of a shift in processing strategy from elaborative to maintenance rehearsal. This explanation suggests that the learners in memory tasks are engaging in elaborative rehearsal for most of the list because they know that they will have to recall the items later. However, when they know that they are near the end of the list, they shift to the easier maintenance rehearsal, counting on being able to write those last few items down right away. Presumably the maintenance rehearsal would be very effective for a brief time but very ineffective over longer intervals.

Watkins and Watkins (1974) tested this possibility by giving their subjects lists of varying length. Because the subjects never knew when the list was going to end, they couldn't shift to the maintenance rehearsal strategy. These subjects showed a reduced (although not totally eliminated) recency effect. Another group of subjects was given the same lists, but was told before each list how long it would be. They showed the standard recency effect. In addition, after a number of lists, both groups were given a surprise final recall task. For this task, the two groups' performance on the last few items was reversed. Subjects who knew the length of the list and showed a sizable recency effect in immediate recall showed poor recall for the last few items in the later final recall task. On the other hand, the subjects who didn't know the list lengths did as well on the last items from the lists as on earlier items during final recall. As the theory predicted, the switch to maintenance rehearsal had immediate benefits but long-term drawbacks.

Be careful in interpreting these results, though. We might be tempted to think that it is the intention to remember permanently that is the key to remembering. However, a better interpretation is that this intention causes us to use the deeper and more effective semantic processing strategies. These more effective strategies do not necessarily depend on trying to remember; they are also engaged by trying to understand. Wanting to understand the material is a more important goal than wanting to remember it, because the goal of understanding will bring memory along with it. In this context, wanting to understand means that you try to integrate the new material into your existing semantic network. According to our discussion of semantic and episodic memory in chapter 11, this would make the material more easily remembered. The goal of memorizing does not necessarily bring understanding along with it, because you could be storing the experience as an episodic memory, not integrated into semantic memory and less easily retrieved than semantic information.

The levels model makes several very specific assumptions: (1) shallow processing is automatic, and deep processing is optional; (2) deep processing makes use of the results of the shallow processing and so is dependent on the shallower levels; (3) shallow processing leads to temporary memory traces, and deep processing leads to longer-lasting traces. Assumption 1 is fairly reasonable and generally seems correct; however, there is one qualification that must be added to it. Deep processing can become more automatic with lots of practice. This is what Fiske and Schneider (1984) showed; they gave their subjects extensive training in semantic categorization so that such tasks became easier and more automatic for them. They found that material processed semantically was poorly recognized when the semantic processing had become automatic. This actually calls into question one of the model's basic ideas; it might be that **automaticity** rather than depth is the factor determining memory. Perhaps the more automatically we process, the poorer the memory trace we form.

In the original Craik and Lockhart study, these two factors of depth and automaticity were not distinguished, but in fact they can be separated. Normally, the shallow processes are the most practiced and therefore the most automatic; we begin analyzing the auditory and visual patterns around us on the day we are born and continue doing it all our waking hours. The deeper semantic processing of verbal and especially written stimuli develops later and probably receives less practice. Although normally shallow processes are more automatic, this is a consequence of our more extensive experience with them, rather than a consequence of the processing systems themselves. Therefore, there may be exceptions to this rule. Certainly there are variations in the level of automaticity for many semantic tasks; an example can be found by observing an expert in any area. The expert's extra practice in his area makes him more capable of automatic "deep" semantic processing of input relevant to his specialty; however, his semantic processing of material out of his specialty is much less automatic.

Assumption 2 was that the shallow processing must be done first so that the deeper processing mechanisms could use the products of the shallow analyses. In the original Craik and Lockhart description, the results of the shallow pattern-recognition processing are used by the intermediate **phonemic processing** systems to generate a phonemic representation, which can then be processed for semantic content. Although it seems obvious that a pattern must be recognized (at level 1) before it can be interpreted (at levels 2 or 3), this doesn't mean that the second level (phonemic processing) must occur before the third (semantic processing). Several experimenters have shown that in some circumstances semantic processing may occur independently of, or without, phonemic processing (Baddeley, 1978; Craik, 1979).

This also is a specific illustration of a more general underlying problem. That is, although the description of three levels presented by Craik and Lockhart seemed plausible, there was no real evidence in support of that particular order of the three levels, nor even any evidence that there were three levels rather than six or sixty. In fact, Craik and Lockhart admitted that there *were* likely to be more than three levels in their basic description. They describe the levels as a continuous dimension of depth rather than as a series of steps; their experiment merely illustrated depth by selecting those three levels for study. The only evidence for differences between levels is their different effect on memory. However, this is the result of the levels and is not an independent measure of the differences between them. So far, no one has come up with an independent objective measure of depth that is satisfactory, and this remains the major stumbling block for the levels theory (Nelson, 1979; Postman, Thompkins, & Gray, 1978). The ordering of levels proposed by Craik and Lockhart seems plausible but has not been proved correct.

The most important consequence of this problem of defining levels is that several studies indicate that the semantic processing level can actually be subdivided into several levels that differ in their effect on memory. In particular, several investigators have shown the **self-reference effect**, wherein questions involving self-reference are more effective in enhancing memory than the more typical semantic questions used by Craik and Lockhart. In the standard Craik and Lockhart procedure, a self-reference question would be "Does it apply to me?" This requires a semantic analysis of the stimulus word, as does the sentence-frame question illustrated above, but is for some reason much more effective as a retrieval aid (Klein & Kihlstrom, 1986; Rogers, Kuiper, & Kirker, 1977). It's difficult to suppose that personal reference is a deeper level than semantic processing and fully separate from it; the only reason for supposing so is the better recall. At this time, we have very little idea of how many semantic levels might exist, or even how we might begin to separate them from one another.

The final assumption of the levels model is that shallow processing only leads to temporary memories. However, several different kinds of studies demonstrate that shallow processing can lead to permanent memories. Generally, these studies suggest that memories generated by shallow processing are there but are harder to retrieve. Two reasons have been suggested for this. One is that probably most people have become used to trying to remember things by conducting a semantic search. Shallow processing would provide a poor basis for a later semantic search, especially in comparison to deeper semantic processing.

Morris, Bransford, and Franks (1977) demonstrated this idea by asking for the later recall with the original questions used during encoding. They used the same procedure as in the original Craik and Lockhart (1972) study until the final recall test, which they changed from a free recall situation to a cued recall task. When the recall questions matched the encoding (or "study") questions, recall was equally good regardless of level. This is what happened when the subjects were asked, "Was there a word that rhymed with weight?" or "Was there a word that was in capital letters?" and these questions matched the original encoding tasks. However, when the recall questions differed from the questions used during original encoding, recall was poor and semantic encoding questions showed their usual advantage. This would occur in our examples if our subject was asked, "Was there a word in red ink?" or "Was there a word that rhymed with vase?" when they had not originally analyzed any words for these requirements.

Basically, the Morris et al. study suggests that the way we try to recall should be similar to the way we originally encode the material. This is an old principle that has been demonstrated in many ways and goes by several names. In the present context, it may be seen as an example of the **encoding specificity** principle, which is basically the same idea as the **state-dependent learning** principle. Both versions of this idea suggest that conditions during original learning and during recall should be as similar as possible for maximum recall. Encoding specificity focuses on the psychological context similarities, and state dependency focuses on the physical condition of the learner's nervous system. The tendency to use one search strategy (a semantic one) when trying to remember means that encoding specificity will lead to better recall for semantically encoded material than for material encoded using other processing strategies.

An extension of this idea is **transfer-appropriate processing** (TAP) (Morris, Bransford, & Franks, 1977), a model which simply assumes that memory performance can be predicted on the basis of the similarity between the operations performed during encoding and the operations performed during retrieval. The greater the similarity the better the memory performance. The extension consists of the emphasis on active processing by the learner rather than any external circumstances. According to transfer-appropriate processing models the learner should choose encoding strategies which he is likely to also choose during retrieval. Possibly a useful interpretation of this would be to try to ask yourself questions about the material being learned. The closer you can mimic the questions of the teacher, the better your performance on the test. Generally, transfer-appropriate processing would suggest that for most verbal materials some kind of semantic encoding would be best because we will usually choose to retrieve these items using semantic searches.

We might conclude that shallow processing may lead to permanent memories, which are harder to retrieve than memory traces based on deeper processing. Thus, if we can reduce the retrieval or searching portion of the memory task, we might find more effective memory traces based on shallow processing. This is exactly how a recognition task works, and several experimenters have shown that allowing the subject more time for shallow processing results in better recognition, even though it doesn't help recall. A clever revision of the Peterson-Brown distractor task has been used by several investigators to demonstrate this (Glenberg, Smith, & Green, 1977; Rundus, 1977). They told their subjects that they had to remember short lists of digits. After the digits were presented, the subjects had to repeat a word (or a few words) during a retention interval. The subjects were told that these words were merely distractors and that the recall of the digits was the important task. Thus, the words were more likely to be processed by a maintenance rehearsal mechanism at a shallow level. Then, at the end of the experiment, the subjects were given an unexpected recognition test on the "distractor" words. The amount of rehearsal time significantly affected recognition accuracy, but was much less influential on recall accuracy (Rundus, 1980).

This process may be similar to the way students prepare for tests. Many students believe that they need to study differently for essay tests (involving **recall**) than for multiple-choice tests (involving **recognition**). If shallow, maintenance rehearsal helps recognition accuracy, then it might be acceptable to study this way for a multiple-choice test, but it would be a poor way to study for an essay test. Unfortunately, the use of maintenance rehearsal for multiple-choice tests is still risky unless the test items use wrong distractors that didn't appear in the studied material. Multiple-choice tests can use sets of distractors that all appeared in the studied material, which would minimize the value of responding on the basis of a simple decision about familiarity (such as "Have I seen this choice before?").

The second reason for the advantage of semantic processing over sensory processing has to do with the degree of interference to which each is subject. A great deal of evidence suggests that basic sensory information is represented by a limited set of features. Remember from chapter 11 that Gibson (1969) suggested that about a dozen features could be combined in various ways to represent all the visual patterns we see. A dozen elements combined and recombined in different ways allows for tremendous interference effects. It would be hard to make a particular stimulus distinctive or memorable with just those physical features. Although there is much less agreement about the nature and number of semantic attributes, there is agreement that many more than a dozen are necessary (probably they number at least in the hundreds). The much greater variety of semantic characteristics allows for a greater degree of distinctiveness for semantic encodings, thus reducing the problems caused by interference (Eysenck, 1979; Moscovitch & Craik, 1976).

In 1990 Lockhart and Craik reviewed the status of the levels of processing model. They recognized the problem of a lack of independent ways of identifying levels that we have discussed and specifically admitted difficulties properly explaining the self-reference effect. They also admitted that sensory (shallow) processing could lead to retrievable memories, but in spite of these issues they still claimed that the general idea that deeper levels of processing lead to better memory was correct. Although they remained critical of the term *short-term memory*, they were willing to accept the term *working memory* as indicating that some set of processing mechanisms were operating on some current material.

Implicit Memory

A large body of current research on **implicit memory** fails to support the levels model of memory. The distinction between implicit and explicit memory tasks was proposed by Graf and Schacter in 1985. Explicit memory tasks are those in which the subject is directly required to remember a past experience. Virtually all the memory tasks discussed in these chapters falls into this category; recall and recognition tests are the most common examples. On the other hand, implicit memory tasks do not require the subject to specifically remember a past experience. However, they reveal that the earlier experience has some effect on current performance. There are several variants of these implicit tasks. We will describe two, perceptual identification tasks and completion tasks.

In an implicit memory **perceptual identification task**, we show the subject a list of words one at a time. Then we present individual words to her in a perceptual task. In this second stage the words are presented very briefly (a small fraction of a second) and the subject must identify what word she is seeing. Some of the words in the perception task were on the first list. These words are perceived much more easily than words not on the first list; in a typical study, Jacoby (1983) found 61% recognition for the primed words (those that were also on the first list) compared with 34% for the unprimed words. This is an implicit task because we didn't ask our subject to use her memory, but she was clearly influenced by the previous experience.

Jacoby and Dallas (1981) used an implicit memory task such as this to study the effects of levels of processing by asking different types of questions before each item on the first list. In other words, the subjects were asked shallow, sensory-level questions about some words and deeper, semantic-level questions about others. Then they were asked to identify words in the perception phase. New words were identified correctly 65% of the time, and previously seen words from the first list were identified about 81% of the time—this is the implicit priming effect. However, processing at a deep or shallow level made no difference in the implicit memory test of the primed words; sensory questions led to 80% perceptual identification, and semantic questions led to 82% identification accuracy. In comparison, a control group explicitly asked to recognize items from the first list showed the standard levels effect, with 50% recognition of the words processed with shallow questions and 86% recognition of the words that had received semantic processing.

In a **completion task** the first stage would occur in the same fashion as the perception tasks just described, but the second task would differ. The second task would involve the presentation of fragments of words, and the subject would have to fill in the missing letters to identify the word. If this target word was seen in the first list, completion times are significantly faster. Furthermore, if a fragment can be completed with several possible words, priming with one of them appearing on the first list makes it much more likely to be the one given. However, manipulating the level of processing during the first stage again has no effect on the strength of the priming obtained.

Graf and Mandler (1984) demonstrated this and were able to design the experiment so that the instructions for stage 2 served to make subjects treat it as either an implicit or explicit test. In stage 2 the subjects saw three-letter word stems, some of which could be completed by words seen in stage 1. Subjects in the implicit condition were told to complete the stems with the first word that popped into their mind; in contrast, subjects in the explicit condition were told that it was a cued-recall task and they should complete the stems only with words from the first list. The level of processing required on the first list had a significant effect on the subjects' cued recall but no effect on the implicit completion task.

Studies of implicit memory are consistent with the Morris et al. (1977), Glenberg et al. (1977), and other studies suggesting that shallow and deep processing do not differ in the durability of the memory traces they create. Instead, these processing strategies differ in how accessible the resulting memory traces will be. Apparently, deliberate search strategies used during retrieval benefit from deeper processing during encoding, but tasks requiring implicit use of memories do not.

One of the most interesting findings from studies of implicit memory involves special populations such as amnesic subjects. As you know, amnesia is a memory deficit as a result of brain damage, and amnesics typically show poor performance on standard memory tasks such as paired-associate learning, free recall, and recognition. However, they appear to do about as well as normal people on implicit memory tasks (Shimamura, 1986). In addition, age differences in memory ability appear to be much smaller when implicit tasks are used. That is, very old and very young subjects show very small deficits in implicit memory tasks compared with young adults (Light & Singh, 1987; Parkin & Streete, 1988) but show much larger deficits on explicit memory tasks compared with young adults. It is easy to conclude from this pattern of findings that implicit and explicit tasks differ in their demands on retrieval strategies, because we would assume that young children and the elderly would be less capable of efficient use of deliberate controlled search strategies than young adults. However, this is actually implied by the names of the tasks themselves and does not necessarily provide understanding of the different mechanisms underlying these tasks.

For example, Roediger (1990) has presented a strong argument in favor of a processing strategy explanation of implicit memory findings. He suggests that transfer-appropriate processing can explain these results simply by assuming that the very different ways used to test in implicit tasks and explicit tasks require different retrieval strategies. The implicit strategies do not match up well with deliberate encoding strategies. Unfortunately, his analysis is inconsistent with some findings with amnesic subjects (Shimamura, 1986). Perhaps implicit memory merely reflects different ways of using the memory trace, as we (and Roediger) suggested. On the other hand, implicit memory may reflect different ways in which aspects of experiences are stored—that is, different kinds of memory traces. The topic of implicit memory is currently one of the most popular areas for memory research, but as yet we have a very poor understanding of the nature of implicit memory itself.

Another distinction based on how we use our memory systems is that between **retrospective memory** and **prospective memory**, mentioned briefly in chapter 9 (see the radial arm maze section). All the studies we have considered in chapters 10–13 have examined retrospective memory, the ability to retrieve learned information. Prospective memory, the ability to perform some action in the future (send that card to Mom, go get groceries this afternoon), requires some use of retrospective memory but also involves other processes, such as planning and initiating actions at the appropriate time or place. Many of the variables we have discussed in regard to retrospective memory work similarly in prospective memory tasks; both benefit from additional rehearsal and distinctiveness of encoding, and both show decreased levels of performance with increased delays. Both show primacy effects and both benefit from additional retrieval cues (in prospective tasks, retrieval cues occur for event-based prospective memory, which is usually better than time-based prospective memory). An important difference, though, is that people's ability to do prospective tasks seems to decline much less in the elderly than is seen in retrospective tasks (Einstein & McDaniel, 1990; d'Ydewalle, 1996)—a pattern similar to that seen in implicit memory tasks. As yet, the relationship between prospective memory and retrospective memory is not well established.

Encoding and Control Processes

The processes the individual uses for analyzing stimulation actually control what happens to this input. The processes described by Craik and Lockhart represent attempts to describe what happens to input. It is clear from this, and from the transfer-appropriate processing research, that we humans have at least two general ways of representing stimulation (visual and verbal) and have great flexibility in how we mentally manipulate these representations. Subjectively, these processes are experienced as ways of trying to understand the stimulation in order to respond to it appropriately. Although the researchers who emphasize a processing approach focus on these analyses to explain mental functioning, we can also discuss their results as strategies for trying to learn. If we were to try to describe the processes subjectively, we might come up with about five general types of strategies. These control processes would be (1) rote rehearsal, (2) organization, (3) chunking, (4) imagery, and (5) elaboration or coding. Generally, rote rehearsal involves relatively little effort directed at understanding, whereas the other four techniques involve considerably more effort directed toward understanding the material. These processes and their combinations are present in the majority of mnemonic devices for remembering. Consideration of each of them will give some idea of the richness of possibilities that Craik and Lockhart envision for actively analyzing our world. It will also provide many suggestions for how to better use them to remember academic material.

Rote Rehearsal

The continued repetition of an experience, called **rote rehearsal**, usually does lead to a permanent memory; this principle is nicely illustrated by classical and operant conditioning studies, where the environment causes the event to be repeated. It is also illustrated by the kind of rehearsal many of us used as children for learning the alphabet or the multiplication tables. In this case the learner has to generate the repetition himself. As we have seen, rote or maintenance rehearsal does work, but it is the least effective method for remembering. An excellent demonstration of the limits of rote rehearsal was provided by Nickerson and Adams (1979). They showed people drawings of 15 variations of a very frequently experienced object (a penny) and asked them to recognize the correct drawing. Their subjects' ability to accurately recognize the exact arrangement of a penny's details was shockingly poor. You can appreciate the subjects' performance if you try to recall which side has the phrase "E pluribus unum" and which side has "In God we trust" on it. The levels explanation of our poor performance is that these details are not often necessary for recognizing whether you have a penny or not; usually you need only note the size, shape, and especially the color of the coin. Therefore, the other details merely receive maintenance rehearsal and are thus poorly learned.

When we think about how many times we see pennies, we can appreciate that rote rehearsal is not necessarily the best way to learn something. Although no one study has compared all the encoding strategies, several have compared rote rehearsal to others, and it has generally led to the poorest performance. On the other hand, it seems to be the easiest to master. Young children show signs of limited use of rehearsal by the age of 4 (Brown, Campione, & Barclay, 1979), and mildly mentally handicapped individuals can be taught to rehearse (Brown & Campione, 1977).

Rote rehearsal involves a rather minimal manipulation of material. The individual doesn't change the material in any way, she just re-presents it to herself over and over. The following strategies emphasize changing the material, either by rearrangement, restatement, expansion, or condensation. The goal is to make the material more meaningful, more distinctive, or more vivid; that is, the goal is to try to understand the material. These kinds of changes and analyses may be beyond many creatures, even beyond some humans. For example, young children show signs of organization, although their ability to group is limited (Ornstein, Naus, & Liberty, 1975). Piagetian studies have shown that children's classifications tend to stray off target as they are asked to group more examples (Piaget called this syncretic reasoning). This is characteristic of children up to about age 6 or 7. They are also unable to properly use hierarchical relationships (Piaget's class inclusion studies) until about 8 or 9 years of age. Children also seem to use chunking much less than adults

(Belmont & Butterfield, 1971) and are less capable of generating and using images. These limits suggest that these more complex processing strategies are probably not very useful as memory strategies for children until they are about 8 or 9 years old. It also suggests that a certain level of intellectual ability is necessary to use these strategies; probably, some mentally handicapped individuals are not capable of using them.

Organization

We have already established that much of our permanent memory has some kind of organization. The clustering phenomenon in free recall and the studies of Collins and Quillian (1969) demonstrate that. In addition, Gordon Bower and his colleagues (Bower, Clark, Lesgold, & Winzenz, 1969) demonstrated that material presented in an organized fashion is better remembered than unorganized material. They presented the same 26 words describing minerals to two groups. One group received the words in the logical format shown in the top half of figure 13.1, and the other half received them in the scrambled format shown in the bottom half of figure 13.1. Note that the logical format resembles the hierarchy described by the Collins and Quillian TLC model. This arrangement led to significantly better recognition than the other (84% versus 60%). The only difference between the two conditions was the use of the pattern: the words themselves, and the structural format, were the same. However, if the arrangement of the words in the structural format makes sense to us, it helps us remember better.

Many experimenters have shown this to be true. In free recall tasks, for example, we can present the words randomly or group them by categories. Grouping consistently leads to better recall (Cofer, Bruce, & Reicher, 1966). Further, the prompting of subjects to organize is also effective. In other words, if we give subjects a randomly arranged list of words and provide them with category labels for the words ("The list will have animals, tools, and so on in it"), or give them the categories as cues during recall ("What were the animals?"), they recall more than if we don't provide the category names (Tulving & Pearlstone, 1966). It seems that it is the perception of an organization or structure that is important.

If you perceive that material to be learned and remembered is organized, then you will be able to remember it better. For example, let's imagine we give a stack of 40 note cards to two people. Each card has a word on it, and the 40 words fall into four categories: jobs, names, animals, and foods. One person is told to sort the cards into groups, and she does this in 2 or 3 minutes. Then we ask her to write down as many as she can. After she curses us for this trick (because she wasn't expecting to have to remember them!), she writes down about a dozen words from the list. Our second subject is handed the stack of cards and told to study them for recall. We give him the same amount of time as our other subject (only a few minutes). He also remembers about a dozen words. He doesn't

Figure 13.1 The two training arrangements used in the memory experiment of Bower et al.

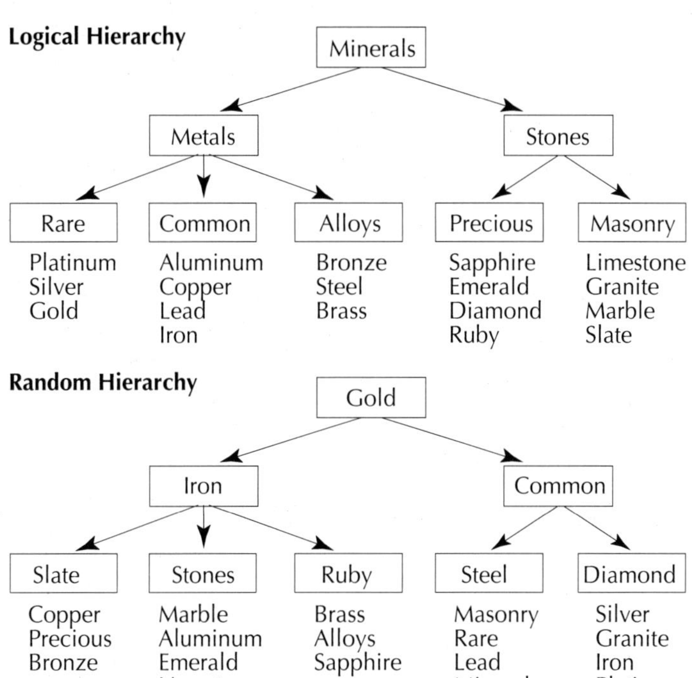

From *Journal of Memory and Language*, vol. 8. G. H. Bower, M. C. Clark, A. M. Lesgold, & D. Winzenz, "Hierarchical Retrieval Schemes in Recall of Categorized Word Lists," pp. 323–343.

remember any more words than our organizing subject, even though he was studying with the intent to remember. Our organizing requirement generated just as effective a memory trace as the desire to remember.

You can easily generate a method to help yourself notice the organization of academic material. One way is to use lists of key concepts at the beginning or end of chapters. Many times these concepts are presented alphabetically in the list. Write each term on a card and then sort them into groups based on their meanings. Start at the top with the most general division and work down, trying to make finer distinctions as you proceed. Even if you have a text that does not provide concept lists for each chapter, you can use this technique. Go to the index of the text and use it as your concept list. Although this may seem to be tedious, if you just start with the most familiar terms, you will find this a very effective study technique—in fact, many graduate students have been advised to take an introductory textbook and "know every term in the index" to prepare for comprehensive exams. The number of categories that you use in your grouping is important, and so is the number of terms per category. In both cases, the magic number is about six.

G. Mandler (1967, 1968) and J. M. Mandler and Z. Pearlstone (1966) asked subjects to group unrelated words into from two to seven categories in any way they chose. The subjects who had used the most categories recalled the most words. Best performance seemed to be the result of having about five words per category. However, six categories seems to be the limit; using more than six categories decreases recall (Dallett, 1964). It seems that when subjects use more than six categories, they are likely to forget some of the categories, which means all of the words in them (Tulving & Pearlstone, 1966). Six categories with six terms in each category gives us a maximum of about 36 terms, plus the category names, which brings us up to about 42 items. In these experiments, words are used that belong to different categories, but the categories themselves are unrelated.

In using this technique for studying course material, presumably the categories you create will be related. That means that you might be able to generate a structure that allows you to go beyond the six-category limit, especially if you follow the technique of generating categories from the top down as recommended. During recall (on the test), you should try to generate your organizational structure, again starting from the top down.

Another mechanism for noticing the organization of material is to outline it. This is probably more useful when the material emphasizes relationships between concepts rather than lots of new concepts. The important thing to do when using outlining is to be able to compare your outline with a standard. Often the table of contents of a text can be used to at least verify the accuracy of the major headings. After you have created an outline, going back and adding details (attributes) will lead to an outline with the properties of a semantic network, although it might not look much like one.

Finally, one can use organization to learn a list of terms by linking the terms together in a brief story. This is called the narrative technique, and in one study it resulted in six times as many items being recalled as were recalled by a group told simply to study the list (Bower & Clark, 1969). If the story can be easily recalled and its parts "hold together" for you, this can be very effective.

Chunking

We have already introduced the idea of chunking as a characteristic way STM organizes input, You perceive the letters C-A-T not as separate stimuli but as one chunked stimulus, the word *cat*, just as you perceive a pair of eyebrows, a nose, chin, cheeks, and wrinkles as a face rather than as a collection of face parts. Chunking is not only a mechanism for STM to get around its capacity limit, it's also a very effective technique for long-term remembering.

In his classic paper, Miller (1956) illustrated the value of chunking for memory. Suppose you try to remember the following letters: TVFBIJFK-CIAIBM. If you just rehearse them as they are, you far exceed your STM capacity limit and it will take a lot of rote rehearsal. You will also need lots of practice if you group them as TVF-BIJ-FKC-IAI-BM. But if you group them this way: TV-FBI-JFK-CIA-IBM, you have only five sets of meaningful items to remember, and it's relatively easy.

In several experiments, Bower (1970, 1972) showed that memory for letter strings was highly influenced by presentation formats that emphasized meaningful chunks. In one experiment, subjects heard the strings read at a one-per-second pace, or read with pauses at the meaningful spots (where the dashes are). The "phrased" presentation led to superior recall. In another study, the letters were presented visually, but in two different colors, which either corresponded to the meaningful groupings or did not. Again, when the meaningful groupings are made obvious to the learner, his recall is better.

Chunking therefore involves condensing a large amount of material into a smaller package and storing the small package. This condensation should emphasize any meaningful relationships that exist among the items. When the material is needed, the small package is retrieved and used to generate the material. That is, during retrieval you go through the condensing process in reverse, expanding the chunk back into the material you needed to recall. Many popular mnemonic devices use chunking; the classic example is the familiar Roy G. Biv for remembering the colors of the spectrum. Although it certainly is an example of chunking, your experience with this mnemonic probably does not do justice to the value of the chunking technique. The reason is that this mnemonic was taught to you, and you may well have learned it just by using rote rehearsal. Chunking works much better when the individual makes up her own chunks. If you make up your own chunks, it will be easier for you to remember how the chunks were formed, and thus easier to reverse the process after retrieving the chunk. This "do-it-yourself" principle will apply to most of these processing strategies.

Recent research has shown that the generation effect, as it is now called, does lead to better retrieval most of the time (Gardiner, 1988). Generally, it is consistent with the orientation of the levels theorists, who emphasize the active nature of the optional processing strategies. Generation effects were nicely demonstrated in an experiment by Slamecka and Graf (1978). Their subjects learned 100 paired associates items. Half of the items were studied in the standard way, but for the other half subjects were required to complete one item for each pair. Thus, a subject might be given the rule "opposite" and shown "long–s." The subject would have to complete the item to form "short." This generation of the rest of the item led to both better recall and better recognition while employing several generation rules, even some very elementary ones such as switching the first two letters in ehAVEN to form HEAVEN.

The size of the chunk should be around six items or less, although this is less important than the nature of the chunk. Notice that our chunking examples use chunks that are themselves meaningful units. The whole idea of chunking is to turn a batch of material that has limited meaning and impact for you into a unit that is highly meaningful to you. This more meaningful material will be easier to retrieve.

Imagery

Imagery is perhaps the most widely used memory strategy, and it is remarkably effective. For some reason not yet understood, visual images are much more effectively remembered than words. This has been demonstrated in numerous and varied ways. The long-term memory study using yearbooks by Bahrick et al. (1975) cited in chapter 11 is one example, but the most impressive illustrations of the power of imagery come from the work of Roger Shepard (1967; Shepard & Cermak, 1973). In his classic 1967 study, Shepard showed subjects 612 pictures. They were tested using pairs of pictures in a recognition task. For each pair the subjects had to recognize which one was one of the original 612. Although this is a rather lenient test, the subjects' performance was still remarkable: virtually perfect after two hours (97%) and 87% accuracy after a week. This was considerably better than subjects shown words instead of pictures; the word group recognized only 88% immediately after studying them. Standing (1973; Standing, Conezio, & Haber, 1970) used a more stringent recognition procedure and picture sets numbering in the thousands and obtained the same very impressive recognition scores.

Imagery can be used for a large number of academic subjects. For history, cast your favorite movie stars as historical characters and turn the history lesson into a soap opera (e.g., Russell Crowe as Napoleon and Angelina Jolie as Josephine). The action has to include important things such as dates and locations, so your characters need to look at a calendar on the wall and look out the window at the skyline of Paris (put in the Eiffel tower and digital watches if you want; it's your image, so make it useful to you). Imagery can also be used for such subjects as biology, geology, and astronomy. Imagine yourself shrunk to the size of a virus, traveling through a cell or the human body. Each part along the way has a road sign in front of it ("nucleus," "liver," etc.), and you have to use the signs to find your way to the mouth to exit. This is a method very popular with the folks at Disney World, as it makes for very entertaining rides, but it's also effective for learning.

One of the important characteristics of the use of imagery is that it can make abstract material more concrete and tangible to the learner (recall from chapter 10 that concrete words generate more vivid images than abstract words). Your images seem vivid and distinctive to you; perhaps this is why images are more easily retrieved. Once the image has been retrieved, you simply inspect it, almost as if you were looking at a picture and examining it for details. Many experimenters have shown that people using images seem to be examining them as if they were looking at pictures (Finke & Pinker, 1982; Kosslyn, Ball, & Reiser, 1978; Shepard, 1978).

Imagery techniques have been known since the time of the ancient Greeks. Traditionally, imagery instructions recommend that the images should be unusual or even bizarre. Modern research on this has been inconclusive, with some experiments showing an advantage for bizarreness whereas others do not (McDaniel & Einstein, 1986). On the other hand, research has been in high agreement about the need for interaction of the parts of the image (Wollen, Weber, & Lowry, 1972). In other words, in your history image if you imagine Josephine turning the pages of the calendar or looking out the window, you will remember the time and place better than if you form an image where the calendar and view out the window are merely elements present during her scene with Napoleon. Similarly, using the "road signs" on your tour of the body to determine your next steps leads to better recall than just noticing them.

There are two classic mnemonic techniques that rely on imagery, the method of loci and the peg-word method. The method of loci is attributed to the ancient Greek storyteller Simonides. Simonides had been reciting a story for a banquet, but reportedly the story did not amuse his host. After Simonides was dismissed, the roof of the building collapsed and all inside were killed. Simonides was called in to help identify the victims. He walked through the rubble, pointing out where each nobleman sat, and thus identified all the bodies. The idea behind the **method of loci** is to associate or link each thing to be remembered with a very familiar place among a set of very familiar places. So you could remember a grocery list (eggs, ham, green beans) by visualizing each item on the list on the front door of each house in your family's neighborhood. Or, you could take a mental tour of the kitchen, placing each item in a familiar spot—eggs in the sink, green beans on top of the stove, and ham in the oven. When you need to recall the groceries, you mentally walk through the kitchen or around your block, examining the locations for the grocery items. A recent study of experts at the World Memory Championships in London indicated that nine out of ten of the best memorizers used the method of loci for remembering numbers, faces, and even snowflake patterns (Maguire, Valentine, Wilding, & Kapur, 2003). Brain imaging of these individuals indicated no differences between them and average people; their use of the technique provided their advantage.

The peg-word method uses this same idea of associating images along with a strong organizational aid. This combination of organization and imagery make it a very effective memory technique. The **peg-word technique** involves a rhyming scheme for the numbers from one to ten. The rhyming words are the "pegs" on which you hang the items to be remembered (TBR items). The way you hang them is to form an image of the rhyming word interacting with the TBR items. The traditional instructions emphasize that the interaction should be bizarre or unusual. This is the rhyming scheme:

One is a bun
Two is a shoe
Three is a tree
Four is a door
Five is a hive
Six are sticks
Seven is heaven
Eight is a gate
Nine is a line
Ten is a hen

Although the rhyme seems childish, it is remarkably effective. I demonstrate it regularly in class, and all my students act embarrassed when I ask them to repeat it aloud after me. Then I give them ten words, allowing about 10 seconds for them to form images. Then I amaze them when I ask them, "What was number five?" After one repetition of the words, my students are able to answer correctly when I skip around in the list, or even if I give them an item and ask which number it was. I've had students recall most of the list as long as a year later!

Research on the peg-word method, initiated by Bower (1970), has revealed that it is powerful and surprisingly resistant to interference. In other words, it can be used over and over with little fear of previous uses getting in the way of your current need. As noted earlier, the value of bizarreness has not received strong support, but the peg and the TBR item must be interacting. Virtually all studies of these mnemonics show powerful effects caused by instructing the subjects to visualize the two things doing something together or doing something to each other. Note that all of these imagery examples illustrate the generation effect as well; it has been shown to improve memory in imagery tasks as well as in verbal tasks (Ironsmith & Lutz, 1994).

Elaboration

Our last encoding strategy is kind of a catch-all for many ways of adding to, or elaborating on, the TBR material. Craik and Lockhart (1972) originally described elaboration as **semantic analysis**. This included not only their experimental task, but also the activation of semantic associations as described by many previous researchers. For our purposes, the idea of elaboration includes these and many other related processes. In a sense, **elaboration** is the opposite of chunking—instead of condensing down into a smaller package, here you are asked to create a larger package and remember it. However, the larger package is supposed to be more meaningful to you than the original material. This is nicely illustrated by the familiar mnemonic for the notes of the musical scale, "Every Good Boy Does Fine." Here we have five letters to remember (EGBDF), and we do it by adding lots of other letters to them to turn them into words. The reason this works is that the five letters themselves are a meaningless random bunch of letters, but the five words have meanings and in fact form a meaningful phrase. This kind of mnemonic technique is useful for relatively short lists of things that are initially not very meaningful. You can use it for algebraic or chemical formulas or for other abstract materials. But it represents a wide range of other, more flexible strategies.

Semantic elaboration has been studied in a wide variety of ways, from tasks like those of Craik and Lockhart to classification tasks. Subjects can determine whether stimuli belong to a certain category, how strong or potent they are, their pleasingness, or their relevance to the individual himself. All these decisions about stimuli lead to better recall than rote rehearsal, with personal relevance superior to the others.

We may profitably apply each of these tasks to the learning of academic material. Most generally, a paraphrase is a semantic elaboration; when you paraphrase, you convert some sentences into "your own words." To do this, you must access the semantic associations of the words in the original sentences and choose among them so that you construct sentences that retain the essential "gist" of the original. Paraphrasing or summarizing chapters of a text is an excellent way to try to learn and remember a text if you do it properly. To do it correctly, you must have a source of feedback about the accuracy of your paraphrase. The best source is the text itself, if it has a good summary at the end of the chapter. You compare your paraphrasing to the chapter summary; things you left out are important points you missed. Things that you remember but the chapter summary omits may not be as important as you thought. For books without summaries, having the teacher check your work is the best procedure, with using a peer a distant second (unless the peer is an "A" student).

In addition to paraphrases, you can elaborate on text material by evaluating the importance of each sentence. After you read a paragraph, decide which was the most important sentence in it. This decision will make all the sentences in the paragraph a little better remembered, because you will have to rate each of them for importance. This is the essence of the "highlighting" many students do using bright yellow or pink marking pens. Highlighting is therefore a good study technique (as most students believe), but is not necessarily used properly. From our discussion, you should recognize that the value of highlighting comes during the initial decision making. That is, if you select only a few things to highlight in each passage, you arc doing the processing necessary to remember the material well. This is when the true encoding of the information occurs. However, the use of these highlights later, the night before the test, is of little value. In fact, it probably causes more harm than good. If you just attempt to read your highlights, you often get a disconnected set of sentences that can easily generate a rote rehearsal review or lead to confusing, disorganized attempts at encoding. On the other hand, if you try to recall why you highlighted one sentence and not another, you are engaging in a distracting task that will probably take longer than studying a nonhighlighted text. The task is distracting because it's not directly related to the sentences' content, and you can get caught up in re-creating your state of mind rather than concentrating directly on the meanings of the sentences. It would be best to use disappearing ink when highlighting!

In addition to ranking text sentences for importance, you could evaluate the relations between sentences. In other words, you could construct new paragraphs with the sentences in a different order that makes sense to you, or with only the three most important sentences in the paragraph rearranged. However, this is rather difficult to do and probably is not as effective as other evaluative techniques. In creating a durable, easily accessed memory trace, evaluations of the pleasingness of the content of text material or its personal relevance are the most effective questions that you can ask. For our history example, this consists of imagining how you would have behaved in Napoleon's or Josephine's position, or whether you would have enjoyed those circumstances—a future of being beheaded or stuck on a remote island.

Personal relevance or pleasingness can be used for a variety of subjects, but perhaps most obviously for our subject, psychology. If you try to think of personal experiences you had in which you might have been classically conditioned, the material in chapter 3 will be much more memorable to you. The key here would be to analyze your personal example in the same ways that Pavlov would, trying to assess the strength of the US, and so on. One limitation of these elaborative strategies needs to be noted, however. If your decision about a piece of material is "Yes, it fits me" or "Yes, I like it," your memory for it will be better than if you feel it doesn't apply to you or is unpleasant. A technique similar to the personal relevance decision task is to relate the text material to someone you know or some event you personally experienced; this can also be effective for many subjects.

One final elaborative strategy is to simply add some adjectives to the sentences studied. Thus if you read "Pavlov rang a bell while he fed the dog," you might add the adjective *hungry* to get "Pavlov rang a bell while he fed the hungry dog." The need to choose the right adjective and put it in the right place is crucial; the adjective must be relevant to the important idea in the sentence. Adding *brown* instead of *hungry* is of little help; brown goes along with dog well enough, but it isn't as relevant to Pavlov's use of food as is hungry. The use of hungry here represents what Stein and Bransford (1979) call **precise elaboration,** which they found far superior to the imprecise elaboration illustrated by the use of brown.

Most of the memory techniques presented in books of memory aids involve some combination of two or more of the processes we have discussed; for example, the peg-word system involves imagery and organization. Combining elaboration with chunking is also useful sometimes, particularly with long numbers. For example, in order to remember a string of numbers like an ATM number, break the number down into small segments which you can then associate with familiar things. If the number was 21963531, breaking it into 21 (legal age to vote), 96 (year you graduated), 35 (your rank in your very large senior class), and 31 (maximum days in a month) creates chunks which have some meaning for you, and would make the numbers easier to remember.

Which Memory Model Is Correct?

As we stated at the end of the last chapter, memory researchers agree that there is a semantic organization to much of our permanent memory and that interference causes difficulty in remembering. Although many memory researchers dislike the terms *long-term memory* and *short-term memory,* the idea they represent of a two-part memory system is probably here to stay. On the other hand, the levels of processing approach, although it has generated a great deal of research and a rich body of ideas about memory, is not itself a complete theory. At the present time, the most satisfactory model of memory would have to combine the ideas of the stage model with those from activation models, levels of processing, and theories about retrieval processes. Such a combination would suggest that we have a short-term memory and a long-term memory; however, these are not separate "boxes" but rather are differing states of activation. Short-term memory would be the currently activated material, and the rest of LTM would be inactive. There would be some voluntary control over which parts of LTM became activated and some control of the type of processing that activated material received. The pattern or spread of activation could be hampered by interference. The duration of STM would be partly due to activation effects weakening after a short time unless renewed stimulation of those memories occurred. The capacity of STM would suggest that there is a limit to how much activation could occur in the brain at any one time. Short-term memory would consist of a set of somewhat independent processing strategies and the materials that they were actively analyzing. At present, no researcher has developed a model such as this in any reasonably complete form.

Some researchers prefer an alternative that does not emphasize one active system and one passive system. Rumelhart and McClelland (1988; McClelland & Rumelhart, 1988) have proposed what they call a **parallel distributed processing** (PDP) model. This model essentially assumes that each of the processing strategies we have discussed is independent of the others and may be carried out at the same time as the others. That is, several analyses of a stimulus may be carried out simultaneously or in parallel. We can see this as an extreme extension of the levels idea. In addition, the parallel distributed processing model assumes that memories are not stored as points in a network, but as patterns distributed over the whole network. That is, for PDP models, a "fact" causes a complex pattern of activation over a large portion of the brain. When we learn this fact, all the neurons stimulated are changed a little bit, so that they become slightly more (or less) likely to fire. Distributed models describe these changes in the neurons as changes in "weights" assigned to each neuron; these weights may be represented by numbers. This leads to a mathematical description in which the overall pattern of all the changes in weights represents the long-term storage of the experience.

When we recognize that fact later, a match is made between the current pattern of stimulation and the permanent changes made earlier. Thus, a neuron may record many "facts" that have overlapping territories or patterns of activation. The fact is stored as the pattern, rather than as a change in a particular neuron. If two facts use many of the same neurons, they would be likely to interfere with each other when they must be distinguished. On the other hand, two overlapping patterns would easily explain spreading activation or priming data. The neurons shared would be partly activated or primed by the first item, making retrieval of the second item more likely. Patterns are generally thought to exist at two or three separate but interacting levels: an input or sensory level, an output (response) level, and an intermediate level of "hidden units" (Hintzman, 1990). The PDP model employs all three levels, but some distributed models do not.

The preceding discussion assumes that the two overlapping patterns use the neurons they share in the same way—the two patterns don't disrupt each other. One of the major problems encountered by any "whole brain" or distributed model such as the PDP model is called *catastrophic interference* (McClosky & Cohen, 1989). This refers to the fact that any new pattern representing a new piece of information, which is superimposed on an already existing pattern, can completely disrupt the old pattern, and the old information will be lost. That is, the new pattern may require changes in the neurons that had been encoding the old information; all the weights might be changed to new weights. These changes would eliminate the way in which the old information had been encoded. McClosky and Cohen (1989) found this to be the case for PDP and many other distributed models. The problem is implicit in a distributed model; if most of a system (a large portion of the brain) is necessary to store a representation of an experience, then experiences will be superimposed on one another. How many superimposed patterns can coexist before chaos results?

Rumelhart and McClelland present extensive research, and many other distributed models have been proposed since the late 1980s (Hintzman, 1990; Raaijmakers & Shiffrin, 1992). Thus, there has been a great deal of research and attention devoted to distributed processing models in recent years. They appeal to memory researchers for several reasons. First, a pattern of neuron weights seems to appear closer to actual physiological mechanisms than many other descriptions of memory. Second, these models are almost universally mathematical, allowing for very precise predictions. Third, the system used with these models allows for categories to have "better" and "poorer" examples (e.g., the frequently given examples of birds mentioned in chapter 12). The models also eliminate the short-term versus long-term memory distinction.

Finally, distributed processing models also eliminate the need for an executive or decision-making component. Any executive component (such as STM or "working" memory) must have its own characteristics and be distinct from other components of the system. This is reminiscent of the "homunculus" criticism leveled at many early cognitive theories by Watson and the early behaviorists. The homunculus was caricatured as a little man inside your head, pulling levers to control your actions. But who controls the controller? An STM executive must also have its mechanisms well specified to avoid this problem. Distributed models such as the PDP model bypass this problem completely. However, the problem represented by catastrophic interference is a serious weakness in most distributed models, and at this time it is too early for us to determine whether they represent a better description of human memory than some combination of stage models, processing strategies, and activation principles. One possibility is that PDP models describe the characteristics of learning and memory at a relatively microscopic level and that the working memory models are more useful descriptions at the larger scales that are easily noticed in everyday experience. Perhaps both are correct at their own level.

Summary

Craik and Lockhart proposed an alternative to the stage model of memory, which they called levels of processing. They suggested that memory was a by-product of the depth of processing that material received. They described shallow processing as just the analysis of the sensory or physical characteristics of stimuli, but deep processing involved converting the stimuli to a phonemic representation. The deepest processing involved an analysis of the meaning of the stimuli. Shallow processing was fairly automatic and often required little effort, and deep processing was optional and required more concentration. Craik and Lockhart tried to show that when subjects were directed to do shallow processing, a poor memory trace resulted, but that deep processing led to superior memory. Maintenance rehearsal was a form of shallow processing that led to a poorer memory trace than the deeper elaborative rehearsal. Although there are several important problems for a strict levels of processing model, the emphasis on active analysis and manipulation of material as a determiner of memory has been a very useful idea.

We can distinguish several types of control processes that people can use to encode material. Rote rehearsal is the simplest procedure, but it requires the most repetitions of the material for learning. In addition, because it does not emphasize the meaning of the material, memories encoded this way are the least useful. Encoding strategies such as organization, chunking, imagery, and elaboration are much more effective than rote rehearsal. Organizational techniques involve grouping terms into categories or outlining. Chunking involves combining items into units that have more meaning—smaller packages such as the Roy G. Biv mnemonic for the colors of the spectrum. Imagery involves the creation of mental pictures of the material to be remembered. Elaboration represents a category of diverse procedures that all involve adding to the material to be remembered. This makes it essentially the opposite of chunking. Elaborative techniques involve paraphrasing, rating sentences for their importance or personal relevance, or adding adjectives or other modifiers to sentences. Finally, recent models of memory suggest that memories are created by parallel processing of stimuli and are represented as a pattern distributed over the whole brain rather than being encoded in one spot in the brain.

Questions for Discussion, Thought, & Practice

1. Define and give an example of each key concept. Then try to group as many of the terms as you can into two categories: shallow processing and deep processing. There are about 10 terms that don't fit easily into one of these two categories.
2. Analyze the control processes involved in the following examples:
   a. Going over your Spanish vocabulary 10 times.
   b. Sorting your Spanish vocabulary items into groups of words that refer to eating, recreation, studying, and so on.
   c. Using the phrase, "Spring forward, fall back" to help remember how to adjust your clock.
3. You remember what page of the text some information was on, but you can't remember the facts themselves. Discuss your encoding in terms of episodic and semantic storage.
4. Discuss your encoding problem in question 3 in terms of levels of processing. (Hint: Does this imply that shallow processing can be permanent?)
5. Suppose your friend has to memorize the Greek gods and their Roman counterparts to make the school's "College Bowl" team. Design a mnemonic strategy for this problem and explain it in terms of the levels of processing model.

epilogue

We have covered a great deal of territory. What we have seen is that much of our behavior is understandable through the use of principles discovered by learning researchers and memory researchers. Learning principles show us that we come to ignore common weak stimuli through the habituation process; we "tune out" the sound of the traffic outside. We attend more carefully to stronger stimuli because of sensitization, and these strong stimuli often become associated with other signaling stimuli through classical conditioning. This allows us to anticipate when something painful might hit us, or when someone else's anger might be followed by pain.

Classical conditioning influences our feelings and motivations. Our likes and dislikes, our desires and hatreds, are extended to a wider range of events through classical conditioning. We come to like baseball, clothing styles, types of cars, and many other things, and we come to dislike Arab terrorists, visits to the doctor, and so forth, through classical conditioning. Operant conditioning allows us to learn new behaviors for obtaining our likes and avoiding our dislikes. We learn how to behave so that our parents give us what we want, and eventually we learn how to earn money to get what we want ourselves. Combined, these principles provide a basis for understanding the general characteristics of simple everyday activity.

However, the principles of conditioning don't seem to do justice to the complex activities especially characteristic of people, such as planning a whole day's activity. Operant conditioning by itself doesn't go far enough in explaining how sequences of behavior emerge. Planning, and the integration of sequences of responses into complex activities, require more complex explanations such as those suggested in our discussion of memory models. The stage model suggests, for example, that our classically conditioned preferences for certain foods and associations of those foods with certain stimuli cause working memory to retrieve the factual information we need from semantic long-term memory, and script information from long-term memory that allows us to plan a trip to the grocery store. Our ability to consider several things at once in STM allows us to anticipate that if we get in the car, drive in such and such a direction, go in this particular store, collect certain items, take them home, and prepare them, then we will be rewarded with a tasty meal. Each step requires explanation at both the simple classical and operant level and the more complex level represented by memory models. By using all of these principles, we can at least begin to explain why and how we do things.

acoustic analysis the first stage of processing speech, performed by the sensory register. Meanings are associated with the speech sounds.

acoustic coding a mental representation of a stimulus (usually a word) as a set of phonemes or sound features, usually occurring in short-term memory.

acquisition training a new association or response tendency; the development of a CR in classical conditioning or the development of an operant response.

algebraic summation theory the Hull-Spence theory of discrimination, which assumes the mathematical combination of excitatory and inhibitory response tendencies.

alternative responses when a response is punished, the likelihood that the learner will stop making it depends partly on whether other responses are available.

anticipatory response in classical conditioning, a CR that is similar to a UR and therefore seems to be a reaction in anticipation of the US.

asymmetrical a generalization pattern that shows different amounts of responding to stimuli for the two halves of a generalization curve.

attachment the emotional relationship that develops between parent and child and child and parent.

attribute some aspect or property of an object, such as its size, shape, or color.

attribute theory the neobehaviorist theory that concepts are learned by noticing the attributes which are common to all examples and which are not found in nonexamples. These attributes are called relevant, critical, or criteria attributes whereas others are irrelevant or noncritical.

automaticity the degree to which a task can be performed without conscious attention or effort.

autonomic nervous system the portion of the nervous system responsible for regulating basic bodily functions such as heart rate and digestion; especially important in classical conditioning.

autoshaping the process whereby a pigeon learns to peck at a stimulus associated with food reward; a classical conditioning reaction that functions as an operant response.

avoidance in operant conditioning, making a response to prevent an unpleasant stimulus from occurring before that stimulus occurs.

backward conditioning in classical conditioning, the presentation of the US before the CS; leads to extremely poor learning.

bait shyness the tendency of wild animals to avoid poisoned food successfully by using taste aversion learning.

basic-level category categories or concepts at a middle level of generality, learned first, before either more general or more specific concepts are learned.

behavioral contrast the increased responding to a training stimulus as a result of discrimination training.

behaviorism (the school of psychology) founded by John B. Watson, which attempts to explain psychological phenomena by exclusive focus on observable stimuli and responses without reference to internal events.

behavior modification the application of operant conditioning principles to the control of human behavior, usually in schools or institutions.

biofeedback providing accurate and immediate information to an individual about his or her internal autonomic activity so that the individual is better able to regulate that activity.

blocking effect in classical conditioning, making a potential CS ineffective by presenting it in a situation in which it is redundant with another previously learned CS.

bottom-up processing also called data-driven processing, this refers to the perception of basic sensory properties first, which serves as the basis for further analysis.

central theory theories that attempt to explain motivation by describing central nervous-system events.

chunk a combination of several stimuli into one meaningful unit by a learner.

chunking in human memory experiments, the process of forming meaningful combinations of stimuli in order to learn and remember them more easily.

classical conditioning the process of pairing a neutral conditioned stimulus with an unconditioned stimulus.

clustering in a free recall memory task, the rearranging of words into meaningful groups when trying to recall them.

cognitive economy the idea that long-term memory for knowledge or semantic information is coded so that redundant information is not repeatedly represented.

cognitive neuroscience a new theoretical background based on information-processing theories and physiological research.

completion task an implicit memory task in which a subject is able to finish a word fragment more quickly because of previous exposure to the target word.

concept learning also called concept formation, this refers to any task in which objects must be grouped on the basis of similarities in their properties (attributes).

conditioned emotional response (CER) the decrease in an ongoing operant response because of the presence of a CS associated with an unpleasant US; an indication of classical conditioning.

conditioned response (CR) the response newly acquired by the conditioned stimulus as a result of classical conditioning.

conditioned stimulus (CS) a previously neutral stimulus that comes to elicit a new response through pairing it with an unconditioned stimulus during classical conditioning.

conditioning the process of the modification of mental associations, primarily through classical or operant conditioning.

configural learning in classical conditioning, the idea that an individual may learn to treat two CSs as a combined, single complex stimulus pattern.

consolidation the physiological process of permanently storing an experience in memory; it seems to take about 20 minutes, and the memory is susceptible to damage during this interval.

contiguity how close together two or more stimuli occur in time and space; especially important in classical conditioning.

contingency a dependency or "if-then" relationship; the US is contingent on the CS in classical conditioning and the reinforcer is contingent on the response in operant conditioning, meaning that the occurrence of the contingent stimulus depends on the occurrence of the previous event.

contingency management the application of operant reinforcement principles to the control of human behavior, especially in schools or institutions.

contingency theory Rescorla and Wagner's theory that emphasizes the value of a CS as a source of information about the occurrence of a US.

continuity theory the Hull-Spence idea that all aspects of discriminative stimuli are learned bit by bit simultaneously.

continuous reinforcement in operant conditioning, the delivery of a reinforcer for every single response.

contrapreparedness Seligman's idea that some creatures are innately incapable of learning certain tasks.

control group a group that serves as a comparison group or standard for evaluating the performance of the experimental group.

counterconditioning classically conditioning a subject by pairing a previously conditioned CS with a US that generates a response the opposite of that generated by the original US.

cumulative recorder a device for automatically recording the rate of a frequent operant response.

decay the idea that a memory may weaken or disappear just as a result of the passage of time; not widely believed.

deep processing Craik and Lockhart's idea that stimuli may be more thoroughly analyzed, leading to more durable memories.

delayed conditioning in classical conditioning, the timing procedure in which the CS occurs before, but overlaps in time with, the US.

dependent variables the things being influenced in an experiment; in psychology, some measure of responding.

depression effect the early name given to an individual's dramatic decrease in operant responding when the reward is decreased (now called negative contrast effect).

deprivation restricting an individual's access to something to be used as a reinforcer.

determinism the idea that all behavior is caused and does not occur at random.

differential encoding hypothesis the idea that experiences repeated in different situations may be stored in slightly different ways, allowing for more different ways to remember them.

discrimination the process of making one response to one circumstance and a different response to another circumstance.

discriminative stimulus a signal that a particular reinforcement contingency is in effect.

displacement the loss of an item from short-term memory due to the capacity limit of STM; when items over the STM capacity of about seven must be processed, some items must be dropped or displaced.

distinctive features the small pieces of a visual stimulus, such as the edges and intersections (angles) that make up letters.

distractor task a procedure such as counting backward used in some memory tasks to prevent rehearsal of other material.

distributed practice experiences that are repeated with relatively long time intervals between repetitions; this almost always leads to better learning.

drive-reduction theory theory that assumes motivation to be the result of reducing a psychological state by reducing a physical need.

echoic memory a brief (2 to 4 seconds), relatively unanalyzed sensory representation of a sound in the nervous system.

edge detectors neurons which respond only to contrasts between neighboring regions of the visual field, thus detecting the boundaries between objects and the background.

elaboration a human information-processing strategy that involves adding context to the material.

elaborative rehearsal when a person uses deep processing, performing multiple analyses, to remember something permanently.

elation effect an increase in an individual's responding as a result of increasing the reinforcement; also called positive contrast effect.

emit a response that is performed by the subject without the requirement of a preceding stimulus said to be emitted; an operant that is said to be "voluntarily" produced.

encoding placing material in permanent memory; a term approximately equivalent to "learning."

encoding specificity the fact that material is easier to retrieve when the retrieval situation is similar to the way it was originally learned.

episodic memory memories for events that have no inherent organization to them.

escape a negative reinforcement situation in which the learner experiences something unpleasant and its response stops the unpleasantness.

evoke a response that is brought forth or elicited from the subject by a preceding stimulus said to be evoked; classical responses said to be evoked.

excitatory conditioning in classical conditioning, pairing a CS with a US.

executive a hypothetical decision-making component of short-term memory.

exemplar theory a theory of concept learning which states that the learner memorizes specific examples of the concept and compares new stimuli to those examples.

external inhibition the fact that adding a new stimulus to a learning situation may interfere with the learning.

extinction the elimination of a classical or operant contingency.

fan effect the fact that when terms have many associations, the associations may be harder to access.

fatigue the result of rapidly repeated practice, such as the buildup of waste products in the muscles; a change in behavior that is not learning.

feature comparison the hypothesis that people compare two things by first noticing how many features or attributes they share and then, if necessary, noticing *which* features are shared.

fixed action pattern early scientific term for instinct, defined as a species specific, species characteristic, rigidly fixed complex behavior.

fixed interval an operant conditioning procedure that involves reinforcing the first response after a specific time interval.

fixed ratio an operant conditioning procedure that involves reinforcing the last of a specific number of responses.

free recall a memory procedure in which the learner is allowed to respond in any order she chooses.

frequency how often a word occurs in a large sample (1,000,000 words is typical) of speech or writing (radio broadcasts, newspaper articles, for example).

generalization the process of applying learning from one situation to new, similar situations.

gradient the graph of levels of responding to stimuli other than the training stimulus in testing generalization.

habituation a decrease in responding to the same stimulus repeatedly presented; the simplest form of learning.

hierarchical organization an arrangement of material (usually words) in a system involving categories and subcategories.

higher-order conditioning using a previously trained CS as if it were a US in another classical conditioning procedure.

homeostasis the idea that the body may maintain an ideal state either by increasing or decreasing some physiological process.

hypothalamus a part of the nervous system that influences many bodily conditions such as hunger.

hypothesis a scientific idea that is a testable explanation of some phenomenon.

iconic memory the visual representation of a stimulus, lasting about 1/4 second.

imagery a mental activity in which a stimulus is recalled as a direct analogue of the sensory experience.

imagery value the average rating given by subjects who are asked to rate the vividness or intensity of an image.

implicit memory tasks that indicate through an indirect measure that an event has been learned.

imprinting an innate tendency of many aquatic birds in which the young follow the first moving object they see.

incidental learning an individual unintentionally learning additional aspects of a situation beyond those requested.

independent variables the elements that may be changed in an experiment that influence or cause changes in other (dependent variable) elements.

information processing a theoretical position which analyzes behavior by using computer mechanisms as models of behavior.

inhibitory conditioning in classical conditioning, deliberately pairing a CS with the absence of a US.

innate (native response tendency) the idea that a response is genetically determined (instinctive or reflexive) with little or no environmental influence.

instinct a specific innate response, genetically predetermined to occur to specific stimuli.

instinctive drift the tendency of a learned response to be distorted by its relationship to innate tendencies.

instrumental conditioning a form of operant conditioning in which only one response at a time is possible.

interaction study an experiment that attempts to examine the relationship between classical and operant conditioning by combining the procedures in some way.

interstimulus interval the time interval between start of the CS and start of the US in classical conditioning.

intertrial interval the time interval between trials or occurrences of individual CS–US pairings or response-reinforcer pairings.

involuntary response automatic, unconscious activity performed by the autonomic nervous system; often influenced by classical conditioning.

Lashley-Wade hypothesis the idea that at least two experiences are necessary for normal generalization to occur.

latency the time interval between a stimulus and a response.

latent inhibition see preexposure effect.

law of effect Thorndike's idea that behaviors are influenced by their consequences; associations are strengthened by rewards and may be weakened by punishers.

learned helplessness the inability of a subject to learn to escape an unpleasant stimulus because it had previously been classically conditioned with that stimulus.

learning a relatively permanent change in behavior or behavioral potential as a result of (reinforced) practice.

levels of processing Craik and Lockhart's idea that better memory traces are the result of processing the material using deep semantic rather than shallow sensory strategies.

local theory the idea that drives such as hunger are caused by sensations in one peripheral organ such as the stomach.

long-term memory the stage of memory that stores representations of events potentially for a lifetime.

long-term potentiation a relatively permanent change in neurons (especially hippocampal pyramidal neurons) which makes their synapses more likely to stimulate receiving neurons. It may be the basis of learning.

maintenance in operant conditioning, using a partial reinforcement schedule after acquisition to keep responding at a stable level.

maintenance rehearsal the idea that material may be rehearsed in a shallow way that does not result in a permanent memory trace.

masking in the visual sensory register, the obscuring of a pattern of features by a new pattern.

massed practice repetition of an experience with no time interval between repetitions; zero ITI.

matching law formula relating the relative rates of two operant responses to the proportionate rates of reinforcement for them.

maturation a physical or psychological age-related change in an individual due to a genetically determined sequence.

meaningfulness the significance of a verbal item, often measured by the average number of words given in response to the item in a fixed amount of time.

mediation the process of bringing together two separate processes; the process of acting as a go-between.

memory the representation of an experience in the nervous system after the experience is over.

method of loci a traditional memory strategy relating to-be-remembered material to familiar locations.

modal action pattern the current term for an instinct, indicating that genetically determined behaviors show small degrees of variation in some aspects of how they occur as a result of environmental influences.

natural concepts "real life" categories, as opposed to artificial concepts devised for psychological experiments.

negative reinforcement an operant conditioning procedure in which a response causes an undesired reinforcer to be removed or prevented.

negative transfer when one piece of learning makes it more difficult to learn a second item.

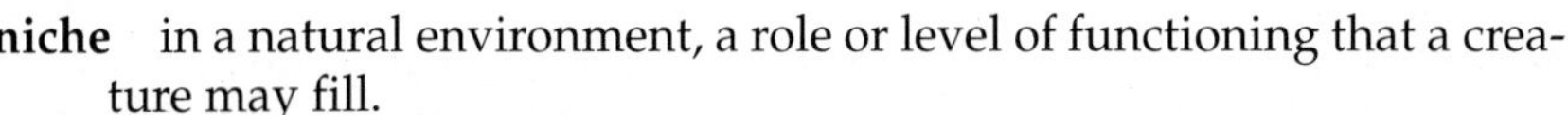

niche in a natural environment, a role or level of functioning that a creature may fill.

noncontinuity theory theories such as Lashley and Wade's that assume learning occurs in sequences in which later events are dependent on earlier ones.

nonsense syllable a pronounceable string of three letters that have no meaning; invented by Ebbinghaus for the study of memory.

omission training a form of punishment in which a desired reinforcer is removed because of a response; also called punishment type II.

operant conditioning a learning procedure in which a voluntary response is followed by a consequence.

operational definition an attempt to define a term by reference to the actions needed to observe the phenomenon.

opponent process theory a theory that any repeated stimulation causes both habituation and sensitization, and the change in behavior is the result of the relative amounts of each when they are combined.

optimal foraging theory a theory that describes food-gathering behavior in terms of its relevance to environmental niches.

organization a memory technique emphasizing the relationships between items to be remembered.

overshadowing in classical conditioning, a creature's natural tendencies to be more likely to learn to respond to one CS over another when both are paired with a US.

overwriting Loftus's idea that memories can be changed by later events.

paired-associates learning a memory task in which the subject must learn a different specific response to be given to each stimulus.

parallel distributed processing memory models that emphasize that stimulation could be analyzed in several ways simultaneously, and memories are represented by large portions of the brain.

partial reinforcement extinction effect the fact that operant responses rewarded intermittently are more resistant to extinction than responses rewarded continuously.

pattern recognition processing the details of a visual or auditory stimulus in order to match it with a learned pattern.

peak shift the fact that discrimination training causes the greatest degree of responding to occur to a different stimulus from the positively trained stimulus.

peg-word technique a memory technique in which the to-be-remembered items are combined in images with rhymes for the first 10 digits.

perceptual identification task a person is asked to identify a stimulus (usually words or nonsense syllables) when the stimuli are presented very briefly and/or under poor illumination.

phonemic processing analysis of the sound properties of stimuli (usually printed words) as proposed by many information-processing models.

phylogenetic scale a description of the biological relationships between species, usually involving some arrangement of species in order of complexity.

positive reinforcement the operant conditioning procedure of following a response with delivery of a desired reinforcer.

positive reinforcer any stimulus or event that increases the likelihood or probability of a response when it is delivered as a consequence of that response.

positive transfer the possibility that a piece of learning may make it easier to learn another task later.

postreinforcement pause a creature's tendency to stop responding briefly after reinforcement on fixed ratio or fixed interval schedules in operant conditioning.

precise elaboration a memory enhancement technique in which relevant details are added to the material.

preexposure effect in classical conditioning, the fact that a familiar stimulus is often less effective as a CS than a new stimulus.

Premack principle the idea that frequently made responses can be used as reinforcers for less frequently made responses.

preparatory response a conditioned response that makes the individual better able to tolerate a US.

preparedness dimension Seligman's idea that the ability to learn is influenced by a creature's biological predispositions.

primacy effect the fact that the first three or so items on a list are learned more easily than items in the middle of the list.

primary reinforcer a reward such as food or drink that satisfies bodily needs and is innately effective.

proactive interference the fact that previously learned material makes it more difficult to remember more recently learned material.

probe task after a subject has been exposed to a list of items, a signal is given to report about the presence of a particular item with a cue called a probe.

procedural a distinction between the forms of learning (usually classical vs. operant) on the basis of the operations or procedures involved in each.

pronounceability the ease or difficulty involved in saying a word. Generally, one-syllable words are relatively easy to pronounce, for example. More easily pronounced items are usually more easily learned.

prospective memory remembering to do something at a specified time or place in the future.

pseudoconditioning a sensitization procedure in which a CS occasionally occurs randomly among occurrences of a US, without pairing the two.

punisher a stimulus that causes a behavior to decrease when it is presented contingently upon that behavior.

punishment the process of eliminating operant responses by following them with presenting undesired stimuli or removing desired stimuli.

punishment type I the presentation of an undesired stimulus (punisher) contingent on an operant response.

punishment type II see omission training.

rate of response the most common way of measuring the degree of operant conditioning, consisting of counting the number of responses and dividing by the time involved in making them.

recall the most stringent measure of memory, asking the subject to reproduce the stimulus with minimal cues.

recency effect the fact that the last several items on a list are learned and remembered better than items in the middle of a list.

recognition a memory test in which the learner is given the material and asked to identify if it was in fact what he or she experienced.

reductionism the attempt to make theories that explain phenomena by using lower or more basic levels of explanation; for example, explaining psychology using biological principles.

reflex an innate, fairly simple response to a stimulus, which may be modified.

reflex arc the portions of the nervous system that are responsible for a creature's ability to make a reflexive response to a stimulus; it consists of three parts for the simplest reflexes: sensory neurons, association or interneurons, and motor neurons.

rehearsal the repetition of a stimulus (or, more often, repetition of a mental representation of that stimulus) initiated by the learner.

reinforcement the instrumental or operant procedure of making the occurrence of a stimulus contingent on a preceding response.

reinforcer a powerful stimulus or condition that may be used to modify the occurrence of operant behaviors through reinforcement.

relational theory the idea that subjects in discrimination procedures are learning relationships between stimuli rather than absolute properties of the stimuli.

response any glandular secretion, muscular action, or other objectively identifiable aspect of the behavior of a creature.

response competition in verbal learning studies, the idea that several potential responses are available to the subject, who has difficulty choosing the correct one.

response hierarchy Thorndike's idea that in an operant situation, the subject can make many responses that can be arranged in order of relative frequency.

response selection the idea that reinforcement has its effect through informing the learner which responses should be made most often.

response strengthening the idea that reinforcement has its effect through making the connection between a stimulus and an operant response stronger.

retrieval the last part of the memory process, wherein a stored experience is activated, or wherein a memory may influence current behavior.

retroactive interference the fact that more recently learned material may make it harder to remember older material.

retrospective memory remembering past events and previously learned information.

r_g–s_g the mediational mechanism proposed by Spence to explain movement toward a previously reinforced goal.

rote rehearsal repetition of items by a person without any attempt at elaboration or deeper processing.

S+ the stimulus consistently rewarded in a discrimination study. Also called the discriminative stimulus in operant conditioning.

S– the stimulus consistently extinguished in a discrimination study; called the S delta (SΔ) in operant studies.

salience the fact that some stimuli seem to be more easily noticed than others.

satiation the fact that unlimited access to a reward eventually makes that reward ineffective as an operant reinforcer, at least temporarily.

sauce béarnaise effect Seligman's description of learned taste aversions in humans.

schedule Skinner's term for the patterning of the delivery of reinforcements in operant conditioning.

schema a set of learned ideas about how a large part of the environment should be arranged (for example, our expectations about what pieces of furniture should be in a bedroom).

script a memory for a sequence of events or a procedure.

secondary reinforcer a stimulus that has come to acquire reinforcing properties through its association with primary reinforcers.

self-reference effect the fact that relating material to one's personal characteristics makes it more easily remembered.

semantic analysis the deepest level of analysis proposed by information-processing models (especially Craik and Lockhart's), emphasizing the analysis of the meaning of stimuli.

semantic generalization generalizing from a training word to other words on the basis of their similarity of meaning.

semantic memory human long-term memories for word meanings and interrelationships, or knowledge.

semantic network the idea that semantic memories are arranged in a complex hierarchical pattern of superordinate and subordinate categories.

semantic priming the fact that recently activated words can increase the activation level of other, meaningfully related words.

sensitization an increase in an innate response tendency as a result of repeated stimulation.

sensory adaptation a decrease in the sensitivity of sensory receptors due to repeated stimulation; sensory fatigue.

sensory analysis the initial processing of a stimulus performed by the sensory register.

sensory memory see sensory register.

sensory preconditioning the process of pairing two conditioned stimuli, then pairing one with a US, and finding that the other has also acquired CR generating capacities.

sensory register the first stage of processing in the Atkinson and Shiffrin memory model, where the physical features of stimuli are briefly stored; also called the sensory memory.

serial anticipation the memory procedure of learning a list in order, in which the learner must show her learning by responding with each item in advance of its presentation.

serial position effect the fact that items at the beginning and end of a list are more easily learned and remembered than items in the middle of the list.

shallow processing Craik and Lockhart's theory that repeated automatic sensory analysis of a stimulus will lead to a poor memory trace.

shaping Skinner's procedure of rewarding successive approximations to a final desired response to gradually change the form of the operant response into a desired response pattern.

short-term memory the second stage of memory proposed in Atkinson and Shiffrin's model, assumed to be active but retaining material for only about 20 seconds without rehearsal.

shuttle box a device for studying negative reinforcement in which the animal must move from one compartment to another to avoid or escape shock.

sign tracking see autoshaping.

simultaneous conditioning in classical conditioning, presenting the CS and the US beginning at exactly the same time.

simultaneous discrimination presenting the S+ and the S– at the same time during discrimination training.

somatic nervous system the parts of the nervous system responsible for our voluntary actions and whose nerve paths go through the spinal cord.

species-specific defensive reaction the idea that some creatures may have innate preprogrammed responses to danger.

spinal animal a creature whose spinal cord has been surgically cut just below the neck.

spontaneous recovery an increase in responding after a longer delay than usual in extinction trials.

spreading activation the fact that stimulation of one part of the nervous system will cause other, related parts to be more easily stimulated.

state-dependent learning the fact that memory performance is better when the individual is in the same state (sober or drugged, for example) during the testing situation as when he originally studied the material.

stimulus any adequate change in energy falling on an appropriate sensory receptor; any event that can be shown to cause a measurable change in the individual.

stimulus substitution a name for the S–S associative interpretation of classical conditioning.

storage the maintaining of a memory trace until needed, presumably in long-term memory.

successive discrimination training a subject using trials with the S+ and S– alternating randomly.

superstitious behavior Skinner's description of the fact that pigeons repeat whatever they were doing just before reinforcement occurred, even when their behavior had no influence on the occurrence of reinforcement.

symmetrical in testing for generalization, the finding that response to changes in the stimuli occurs equally on either side of the training stimulus.

systematic desensitization Wolpe's procedure for eliminating phobias through a combination of extinction, relaxation, and generalization procedures.

systemic having to do with the body or nervous system; systemic distinctions between classical and operant conditioning focus on the different parts of the nervous system involved in each.

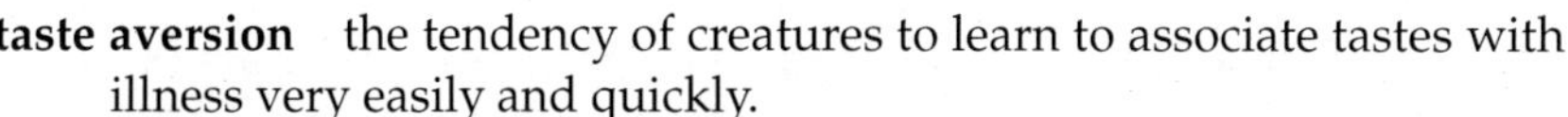

taste aversion the tendency of creatures to learn to associate tastes with illness very easily and quickly.

temporal coding hypothesis the hypothesis that creatures learn the duration of the CS–US intervals involved when they are classically conditioned, as well as the nature of the stimuli.

three-term contingency the name Skinner used to refer to the fact that operant conditioning involves a relationship between three elements: a discriminative stimulus, a response, and a reinforcer.

time out a form of omission training in which the individual is isolated from potential positive reinforcers because of her response.

token economy an application of operant conditioning procedures to schools and institutions in which secondary reinforcers are used.

top-down processing the idea that we use our expectations and the contexts surrounding a stimulus in order to recognize and process it accurately.

trace conditioning in classical conditioning, the procedure of starting and stopping the CS before the US starts, so that the learner must have a memory trace of the CS to associate with the US.

transfer-appropriate processing using the same analyzing strategies during learning (encoding) as will be used during retrieval.

transposition Kohler's finding that subjects in simultaneous discrimination tasks respond according to a relational principle.

transsituationality the idea that a stimulus determined to be a reinforcer in one situation should function that way in all situations.

trial-and-error learning Thorndike's description of the gradual change in responding in instrumental situations; responses were attempted, and those that were not rewarded were gradually omitted from the learner's repertoire.

two-factor theory Mowrer's attempt to explain avoidance conditioning by using classically conditioned fear as a mediating device for maintaining the operant response.

two-process theory a modification and extension of two-factor theory that does not specify specific emotional components but rather generalized emotional states, which enhance or inhibit operant responding.

unconditioned response the innate or naturally occurring response to a strong stimulus (the US) in classical conditioning.

unconditioned stimulus a stimulus that reliably (always) causes a particular response.

unlearning in verbal learning studies, a term equivalent to extinction, in which old associations are destroyed because of the learning of new associations incompatible with the original associations.

variable interval an operant schedule in which reinforcers are available for the first response after a variable amount of time, which averages out over many intervals to some predetermined interval value.

variable ratio an operant schedule in which the individual receives one reinforcement for several responses; the number of responses required varies but averages out to the ratio value.

verbal rehearsal loop a short-term memory component proposed by Baddeley in which verbal material may be maintained through rehearsal.

visuospatial sketch pad a short-term memory component capable of generating and manipulating mental visual images.

voluntary response an operant response that is emitted, mediated by the somatic nervous system.

Abramson, L. Y., Seligman, M. E. P., & Teasdale, J. D. (1978). Learned helplessness in humans: Critique and reformulation. *Journal of Abnormal Psychology, 87,* 49–74.

Alba, J. W., and Hasher, L. (1983). Is memory schematic? *Psychological Bulletin, 93,* 203–231.

Albert, M., & Ayres, J. J. B. (1989). With number of preexposures constant latent inhibition increases with preexposure CS duration or total CS exposure. *Learning and Motivation, 20,* 278–294.

Alberto, P. A., & Troutman, A. C. (1982). *Applied behavior analysis for teachers: Influencing student performance.* Columbus, OH: C. E. Merrill.

Allison, J. (1989). The nature of reinforcement. In S. B. Klein & R. R. Mowrer (Eds.), *Contemporary learning theories: Instrumental conditioning theory and the impact of biological constraints on learning* (pp. 13–40). Hillsdale, NJ: Lawrence Erlbaum.

Allison, J., & Timberlake, W. (1973). Instrumental and contingent saccharin-licking in rats: Response deprivation and reinforcement. *Bulletin of the Psychonomic Society, 2,* 141–143.

Allison, J., & Timberlake, W. (1974). Instrumental and contingent saccharin-licking in rats: Response deprivation and reinforcement. *Learning and Motivation, 5,* 231–247.

Anderson, J. R. (1976). *Language, memory, and thought.* Hillsdale, NJ: Lawrence Erlbaum.

Anderson, J. R., & Bower, C. H. (1973). *Human associative memory.* Friday Harbor, WA: Winston-Books.

Ardrey, R. (1966). *The territorial imperative.* New York: Dell.

Ashton, A. B., Bitcood, S. C., & Moore, J. W. (1969). Auditory differential conditioning of the rabbit nictitating membrane response: III. Effects of US shock intensity and duration. *Psychonomic Science, 15,* 127–128.

Atkinson, R. C., & Raugh, M. R. (1975). An application of the mnemonic keyword method to the acquisition of a Russian vocabulary. *Journal of Experimental Psychology: Human Learning and Memory, 104,* 126–133.

Atkinson, R. C., & Shiffrin, R. M. (1968). Human memory: A proposed system and its control processes. In K. W. Spence (Ed.), *The psychology of learning and motivation: Advances in research and theory* (Vol. 1, pp. 89–195). New York: Academic Press.

Averbach, E., & Coriell, A. S. (1961). Short term memory in vision. *Bell System Technical Journal, 40,* 309–328.

Ayllon, T., & Azrin, N. H. (1968). *The token economy: A motivation system for therapy and rehabilitation.* New York: Appleton-Century-Crofts.

Azrin, N. H. (1956). Some effects of intermittent schedules of immediate and non-immediate punishment. *Journal of Psychology, 42,* 3–21.

Azrin, N. H., & Hake, D. F. (1969). Positive conditioned suppression: Conditioned suppression using positive reinforcers as the unconditioned stimuli. *Journal of Experimental Analyses Behavior, 12,* 117–173.

Azrin, N. H., & Holz, W. C. (1966). Punishment. In W. K. Honig (Ed.), *Operant behavior: Areas of research and application* (pp. 380–447). New York: Appleton-Century-Crofts.

Azrin, N. H., Holz, W. C., & Hake, D. F. (1963). Fixed ratio punishment. *Journal of Experimental Analysis of Behavior, 6,* 141–148.

Baars, B. (1988). *A Cognitive Theory of Consciousness.* Cambridge: Cambridge University Press.

Baddeley, A. D. (1978). The trouble with "levels": A reexamination of Craik and Lockhart's framework for memory research. *Psychological Review, 85,* 139–152.

Baddeley, A. D. (1982). Domains of recollection. *Psychological Review, 89,* 708–729.

Baddeley, A. D. (1990). *Human memory: Theory and practice.* Boston: Allyn & Bacon.

Baddeley, A. D., Thomson, H., & Buchanan, J. (975). Word length and the structure of short-term memory. *Journal of Verbal Learning and Verbal Behavior, 14,* 575–589.

Baerends, G. P. (1988). Ethology. In R. C. Atkinson, R. J. Herrnstein, G. Lindzey, & R. Luce (Eds.), *Stevens' Handbook of Experimental Psychology,* Vol. 1, 765–830. New York: Wiley.

Baerends, G. P., & Drent, R. H. (1982). The herring gull and its egg, part II. The responsiveness to egg features. *Behavior, 82,* 1–417.

Bahrick, H. P. (1984). Semantic memory content in permastore: Fifty years of memory for Spanish learned in school. *Journal of Experimental Psychology: General, 113,* 1–29.

Bahrick, H. P., Bahrick, P. O., & Wittlinger, R. P. (1975). Fifty years of memory for names and faces: A cross-sectional approach. *Journal of Experimental Psychology: General, 104,* 54–75.

Barnet, R. C., Arnold, H. M., and Miller, R. R. (1991). Simultaneous conditioning demonstrated in second-order conditioning: Evidence for similar associative structure in forward and simultaneous conditioning. *Learning and Motivation, 22,* 253–268.

Barnet, R. C., and Miller, R. R. (1996). Second-order excitation mediated by a backward conditioned inhibitor. *Journal of Experimental Psychology: Learning and Behavior Processes, 22,* 279–296.

Bastian, J. (1961). Associative factors in verbal transfer. *Journal of Experimental Psychology, 62,* 70–79.

Baum, W. M. (1974). On two types of deviation from the matching law: Bias and undermatching. *Journal of the Experimental Analysis of Behavior, 22,* 231–242.

Baum, W. M. (1979). Matching, undermatching, and overmatching in studies of choice. *Journal of the Experimental Analysis of Behavior, 32,* 269–281.

Beery, R. G. (1968). A negative contrast effect of reward delay in differential conditioning. *Journal of Experimental Psychology, 77,* 429–434.

Bekerian, D. A., & Bowers, J. M. (1983). Eyewitness testimony: Were we misled? *Journal of Experimental Psychology: Learning, Memory, and Cognition, 9,* 139–145.

Belmont, J. M., & Butterfield, E. C. (1971). Relations of storage and retrieval strategies as short term memory processes. *Journal of Experimental Psychology, 89,* 319–328.

Berger, T. W., & Thompson, R. F. (1978). Neuronal plasticity in the limbic system during classical conditioning of the rabbit nictitating membrane response. I. The hippocampus. *Brain Research, 145,* 323–346.

Berlin, B., Breedlove, D. E., & Raven, P. H. (1973). General principles of classification and nomenclature in folk biology. *American Anthropologist, 75,* 214–242.

Bernstein, I. L., & Webster, M. M. (1980). Learned taste aversions in humans. *Physiology and Behavior, 25,* 363–366.

Bersh, P. J. (1951). The influence of two variables upon the establishment of a secondary reinforcer for operant responses. *Journal of Experimental Psychology, 41,* 62–73.

Biederman, I. 1987. Recognition-by-component: A theory of human image understanding. *Psychological Review, 94,* 115–147.

Bindra, D. (1974). A motivational view of learning, performance and behaviour modification. *Psychological Review, 81,* 199–213.

Bitterman, M. E. (1965). Phyletic differences in learning. *American Psychologist, 20,* 396–410.

Black, A. H., Nadel, L., & O'Keefe, J. (1977). Hippocampal function in avoidance learning and punishment. *Psychological Bulletin, 84,* 1107–1129.

Blakemore, C., & Cooper, C. F. (1970). Development of the brain depends on the visual environment. *Nature, 228,* 477–478.

Bliss, T. V. P., & Gardner-Medwin, A. R. (1973). Long-lasting potentiation of synaptic transmission in the dentate area of the anaesthetized rabbit following stimulation of the perforant path. *Journal of Physiology, 232,* 357–374.

Blough, D., & Blough, P. (1977). Animal psychophysics. In W. K. Harris & J. E. R. Staddon (Eds.), *Handbook of operant behavior* (pp. 514–539). Englewood Cliffs, NJ: Prentice-Hall.

Boe, E. E., & Church, R. M. (1967). Permanent effects of punishment during extinction. *Journal of Comparative and Physiological Psychology, 63,* 486–492.

Bolles, R. C. (1970). Species-specific defense reactions and avoidance learning. *Psychological Review, 77,* 32–48.

Bolles, R. C. (1988). Nativism, naturalism, and niches. In R. C. Bones & M. D. Beecher (Eds.), *Evolution and Learning.* Hillsdale, NJ: Lawrence Erlbaum.

Bolles, R. C., & Fanselow, M. S. (1980). A perceptual-defensive-recuperative model of fear and pain. *Behavioral and Brain Science, 3,* 291–323.

Boring, E. G. (1950). *A History of Experimental Psychology* (2nd Ed.). New York: Appleton-Century-Crofts.

Bousfield, W. A. (1953). The occurrence of clustering in the recall of randomly arranged associates. *Journal of General Psychology, 49,* 229–240.

Bouton, M. E., & Nelson, J. B. (1998). The role of context in classical conditioning: Some implications for cognitive behavior therapy. In W. T. O'Donohue (Ed.), *Learning and Behavior Therapy,* 59–84. Boston: Allyn & Bacon.

Bower, G. H. (1961). A contrast effect in differential conditioning. *Journal of Experimental Psychology, 62,* 196–199.

Bower, G. H. (1970). Organizational factors in memory. *Cognitive Psychology, 1,* 18–46.

Bower, G. H. (1972). Mental imagery in associative learning. In L. W. Gregg (Ed.), *Cognition in learning and memory.* New York: Wiley.

Bower, G. H. (1981). Mood and memory. *American Psychologist, 36,* 129–148.

Bower, G. H., Black, J. B., & Turner, T. J. (1979). Scripts in memory for text. *Cognitive Psychology, 11,* 177–220.

Bower, G. H., & Clark, M. C. (1969). Narrative stories as mediators for serial learning. *Psychonomic Science, 14,* 181–182.

Bower, G. H., Clark, M. C., Lesgold, A. M., & Winzenz, D. (1969). Hierarchical retrieval schemes in recall of categorized word lists. *Journal of Verbal Learning and Verbal Behavior, 8,* 323–343.

Bowlby, J. A. (1958). The nature of the child's tie to his mother. *International Journal of Psychoanalyses, 39,* 350–373.

Boysen, S. T., & Himes, G. T. (1999). Current issues and emerging theories in animal cognition. *Annual Review of Psychology, 50,* 683–703.

Breland, K., & Breland, M. (1961). The misbehavior of organisms. *American Psychologist, 61,* 681–684.

Brewer, W. F. (1974). There is no convincing evidence for operant or classical conditioning in adult humans. In W. B. Weimer & D. S. Palermo (Eds.), *Cognition and the symbolic processes* (pp. 1–42). Hillsdale, NJ: Lawrence Erlbaum.

Brewer, W. F., & Treyens, J. C. (1981). Role of schemata in memory for places. *Cognitive Psychology, 13,* 207–230.

Broadbent, D. E. (1958). *Perception and communication.* London: Pergamon Press.

Brogden, W. J. (1939). Sensory pre-conditioning. *Journal of Experimental Psychology, 25,* 323–332.

Brooks, D. C., & Bouton, M. E. (1994). A retrieval cue for extinction attenuates response recovery (renewal) caused by a return to the conditioning context. *Journal of Experimental Psychology: Animal Behavior Processes, 20,* 366–379.

Brown, J. (1958). Some tests of the decay theory of immediate memory. *Quarterly Journal of Experimental Psychology, 10,* 12–21.

Brown, A. L., & Campione, J. C. (1977). Training strategic study time apportionment in educable retarded children. *Intelligence, 1,* 94–107.

Brown, A. L., Campione, J. C., & Barclay, C. R. (1979). Training self-checking routines for estimating test readiness: Generalization from list learning to prose recall. *Child Development, 50,* 501–512.

Brown, E., Deffenbacher, K., & Sturgill, W. (1977). Memory for faces and the circumstances of encounter. *Journal of Applied Psychology, 62,* 311–318.

Brown, L. K., Jenkins, J. J., & Lavik, J. (1966). Response transfer as a function of verbal association strength. *Journal of Experimental Psychology, 71,* 138–142.

Brown, P. L., & Jenkins, H. M. (1968). Autoshaping of pigeon's key peck. *Journal of Experimental Analysis of Behavior, 11,* 1–8.

Bruce, D., & Crowley, J. J. (1970). Acoustic similarity effects on retrieval from secondary memory. *Journal of Verbal Learning and Verbal Behavior, 9,* 190–196.

Bruner, J. S., Goodnow, J. J., and Austin, G. A. (1956). *A Study of Thinking.* New York: John Wiley.

Bucher, B., & Lovaas, O. I. (1968). The use of aversive stimulation in behavior modification. In M. R. Jones (Ed.), *Miami symposium on the prediction of behavior: Aversive stimulation* (pp. 77–145). Coral Gables: University of Miami Press.

Bulgarella, R., & Archer, E. J. (1962). Concept identification of auditory stimuli as a function of relevant and irrelevant information. *Journal of Experimental Psychology, 663,* 254–257.

Burr, D. E. S., & Thomas, D. R. (1972). Effect of proactive inhibition upon the post-discrimination generalization gradient. *Journal of Comparative and Physiological Psychology, 81,* 441–448.

Calkins, M. W. (1894). Association. *Psychological Review, 1,* 476–483.

Camp, D. S., Raymond, G. A., & Church, R. M. (1967). Temporal relationship between response and punishment. *Journal of Experimental Psychology, 74,* 114–123.

Campbell, B. A., & Kraeling, D. (1953). Response strength as a function of drive level and amount of drive reduction. *Journal of Experimental Psychology, 45,* 97–101.

Campbell, D. J. (1984). The effects of goal-contingent payment on the performance of a complex task. *Journal of Personnel Psychology, 37,* 23–40.

Canli, T., & Donegan, N. H. (1995). Conditioned diminution of the unconditioned response in rabbit eyeblink conditioning: Identifying neural substrates in the cerebellum and brainstem. *Behavioral Neuroscience, 109,* 874–892.

Cannon, W. B., & Washburn, A. L. (1912). An explanation for hunger. *American Journal of Physiology, 29,* 441–454.

Capaldi, E. J. (1966). Partial reinforcement: A hypothesis of sequential effects. *Psychological Review, 73,* 459–479.

Capaldi, E. J. (1971). Memory and learning: A sequential viewpoint. In W. K. Honig & P. H. R. James (Eds.), *Animal memory* (pp. 115–154). New York: Academic Press.

Caramazza, A. 1996. The brain's dictionary. *Nature, 380,* 485–486.

Carpenter, R. G., & Grossman, S. P. (1983). Reversible obesity and plasma fat metabolites. *Physiology and Behavior, 30,* 51–55.

Carr, E. G., & Lovaas, O. I. (1983). Contingent electric shock as a treatment for severe behavior problems. In S. Axelrod & J. Apsche (Eds.), *The effects of punishment on human behavior.* New York: Academic Press.

Castelluci, V. F., & Kandel, E. R. (1974). A quantal analysis of the synaptic depression underlying habituation of the gill-withdrawal reflex in *Aplysia. Proceedings of the National Academy of Sciences, 71,* 5004–5008.

Catania, A. C. (1984). *Learning* (2nd ed.). Englewood Cliffs, NJ: Prentice-Hall.

Chang, T. M. 1986. Semantic memory: Facts and models. *Psychological Bulletin, 99,* 199–220.

Chomsky, N. (1972). *Language and the mind.* New York: Harcourt, Brace, Jovanovich.

Church, R. M. (1969). Response suppression. In B. A. Campbell & R. M. Church (Eds.), *Punishment and aversive behavior* (pp. 111–156). New York: Appleton-Century-Crofts.

Church, R. M., & Raymond, G. A. (1967). Influence of the schedule of positive reinforcement on punished behavior. *Journal of Comparative and Physiological Psychology, 63,* 329–332.

Church, R. M., Raymond, G. A., & Beauchamp, R. D. (1967). Response suppression as a function of intensity and duration of a punishment. *Journal of Comparative and Physiological Psychology, 63,* 30–44.

Cofer, C. N., Bruce, D. R., & Reicher, G. M. (1966). Clustering in free recall as a function of certain methodological variations. *Journal of Experimental Psychology, 71,* 858–866.

Collias, N. E. (1953). Some factors in maternal rejection by sheep and goats. *Bulletin of the Ecological Society of America, 34,* 78.

Collier, G. H. (1981). Determinants of choice. *Nebraska Symposium on Motivation, 29,* 69–127.

Collins, A. M., & Loftus, E. F. (1975). A spreading activation theory of semantic processing. *Psychological Review, 82,* 407–428.

Collins, A. M., & Quillian, M. R. (1969). Retrieval time from semantic memory. *Journal of Verbal Learning and Verbal Behavior, 8,* 240–247.

Colwill, R. M., & Rescorla, R. A. (1986). Associative structures in instrumental learning. In G. H. Bower (Ed.), *The psychology of learning and motivation* (Vol. 20, pp. 55–104). New York: Academic Press.

Conrad, R. (1964). Acoustic confusions in immediate memory. *British Journal of Psychology, 55,* 75–84.

Conrad, R. (1966). Short-term memory factors in the design of data-entry keyboards: An interface between short-term memory and S–R compatibility. *Journal of Applied Psychology, 50,* 353–356.

Cook, R. G., Brown, M. F., & Riley, D. A. (1985). Flexible memory processing by rats: Use of prospective and retrospective information in the radial maze. *Journal of Experimental Psychology: Animal Behavior Processes, 11,* 453–469.

Corning, W. C., Dyal, J. A., & Willows, A. O. D. (1973). *Invertebrate learning: Protozoans through annelids.* New York: Plenum Press.

Corning, W. C., & Lahue, R. (1971). Reflex training in frogs. *Psychonomic Science, 23,* 119–120.

Corte, H. E., Wolf, M. M., & Locke, B. J. (1971). A comparison of procedures for eliminating self-injurious behavior of retarded adolescents. *Journal of Applied Behavior Analysis, 4,* 201–213.

Corteen, R. J., & Wood, B. (1972). Automatic responses to shock-associated words in an unattended channel. *Journal of Experimental Psychology, 94,* 308–313.

Cosmides, L., & Tooby, J. (1987). From evolution to behavior: Evolutionary psychology as the missing link. In J. Dupre (Ed.), *The latest on the best. Essays on evolution and optimality* (pp. 277–306). Cambridge: MIT Press.

Cowan, N., Saults, J. S., & Nugent, L. D. (1997). The role of absolute and relative amounts of time in forgetting within immediate memory: The case of tone pitch comparisons. *Psychological Bulletin Review, 4,* 393–397.

Cowan, N., Saults, J. S., & Nugent, L. D. (2001). The ravages of absolute and relative amounts of time on memory. In Roediger, H. L., Nairne, J. S., Neath, I., and Suprenant, A. M. (Eds.), *The nature of remembering: Essays in honor of Robert G. Crowder* (pp. 315–330). Washington, DC: American Psychological Association Press.

Craik, F. I. M. (1979). Human memory. *Annual Review of Psychology, 30,* 63–102.

Craik, F. I. M., & Lockhart, R. S. (1972). Levels of processing: A framework for memory research. *Journal of Verbal Learning and Verbal Behavior, 11,* 671–684.

Craik, F. I. M., & Watkins, M. J. (1973). The role of rehearsal in short-term memory. *Journal of Verbal Learning and Verbal Behavior, 12,* 599–607.

Crespi, L. P. (1942). Quantitative variation of incentive and performance in the white rat. *American Journal of Psychology, 55,* 467–517.

Crowder, R. G. (1982). The demise of short-term memory. *Acta Psychologia, 50,* 291–323.

Crowder, R. J., & Morton, J. (1969). Precategorical acoustic storage (PAS). *Perception and Psychophysics, 5,* 365–373.

Dallett, K. M. (1962). The transfer surface re-examined. *Journal of Verbal Learning and Verbal Behavior, 1,* 91–94.

Dallett, K. M. (1964). Number of categories and category information in free recall. *Journal of Experimental Psychology, 68,* 1–12.

Damasio, H., Grabowski, T. J., Tranel, D., Hichwa, D., & Damasio, A. R. (1996). A neural basis for lexical retrieval. *Nature, 380,* 499–505.

D'Amato, M. R. (1955). Secondary reinforcement and magnitude of primary reinforcement. *Journal of Comparative and Physiological Psychology, 48,* 378–380.

D'Amato, M. R., Fazzaro, J., & Etkin, M. (1968). Anticipatory responding and avoidance discrimination as factors in avoidance conditioning. *Journal of Experimental Psychology, 77,* 41–47.

Darwin, C. J., Turvey, M. T., & Crowder, R. G. (1972). An auditory analogue of the Sperling partial report procedure: Evidence for brief auditory storage. *Cognitive Psychology, 3,* 255–267.

Davey, G. (1981). *Animal learning and conditioning.* Baltimore, MD: University Park Press.

Davis, M. (1974). Sensitization of the rat startle response by noise. *Journal of Comparative and Physiological Psychology, 87*(3), 571–581.

Dawson, M. E., & Schell, A. M. (1987). Human autonomic and skeletal classical conditioning: The role of conscious cognitive factors. In Graham Davey (Ed.), *Cognitive processes and Pavlovian conditioning in humans* (pp. 27–55). New York: Wiley.

Deese, J., & Kresse, F. H. (1952). An experimental analysis of the errors in rote serial learning. *Journal of Experimental Psychology, 44,* 199–202.

Delius, J. D. (1992). Categorical discrimination of objects and pictures by pigeons. *Animal Learning and Behavior, 20,* 301–311.

Dennis, W. (1940). The effect of cradling practices upon the onset of walking in Hopi children. *Journal of Genetic Psychology, 56,* 77–86.

Dinsmoor, J. A. (1954). Punishment: I. The avoidance hypothesis. *Psychological Review, 61,* 34–46.

Dinsmoor, J. A. (1962). Variable-interval escape from stimuli accompanied by shocks. *Journal of the Experimental Analysis of Behavior, 5,* 41–48.

Dinsmoor, J. A. (1977). Escape, avoidance, punishment: Where do we stand? *Journal of the Experimental Analysis of Behavior, 28,* 83–95.

Domjan, M. (1980). Ingestional aversion learning: Unique and general processes. In J. S. Rosenblatt, R. A. Hinde, C. Beer, & M. Busnel (Eds.), *Advances in the study of behavior* (Vol. 11, pp. 276–306). New York: Academic Press.

Domjan, M. (1983). Biological constraints on instrumental and classical conditioning: Implications for general process theory. In G. H. Bower (Ed.), *The psychology of learning and motivation* (Vol. 17, pp. 216–277). New York: Academic Press.

Domjan, M., & Burkhard, B. (1993). *The principles of learning & behavior* (3rd ed.). Pacific Grove, CA: Brooks/Cole.

Donahoe, J. W., & Palmer, D. C. (1994). *Learning and complex behavior.* Boston: Allyn & Bacon.

Duncan, J. 1999. Attention. In R. C. Wilson and F. C. Kell (Eds.), *The MIT encyclopedia of the cognitive sciences.* Cambridge: MIT Press.

Dworkin, B. R., & Miller, N. E. (1986). Failure to replicate visceral learning in the acute curarized rat preparation. *Behavioral Neuroscience, 100,* 299–314.

Dyal, J. A., & Corning, W. C. (1973). Invertebrate learning and behavior taxonomies. In J. A. Dyal, W. C. Corning, & A. D. Willows (Eds.), *Invertebrate learning* (pp. 1–48). New York: Plenum Press.

d'Ydewalle, G. (1996). Are older subjects necessarily worse in prospective memory tasks? In J. Georgas, M. Manthoouli, E. Besevegis, and A. Kokkevi (Eds.), *Contemporary psychology in Europe.* Seattle: Hogrefe & Huber.

Ebbinghaus, H. (1885). *Memory: A contribution to experimental psychology* (H. A. Ruger & C. E. Bussenius, Trans.). New York: Dover.

Edwards, C. A., & Honig, W. K. (1987). Memorization and "feature selection" in the acquisition of natural concepts in pigeons. *Learning and Motivation, 18,* 235–260.

Eggar, M. D., & Miller, N. E. (1963). When is a reward reinforcing?: An experimental analysis of the information hypothesis. *Journal of Comparative and Physiological Psychology, 56,* 131–137.

Eibl-Eibesfeldt, I. (1972). Similarities and differences between cultures in expressive movements. In R. A. Hinde (Ed.), *Nonverbal communication. Love and hate: Natural history of behavior patterns* (pp. 297–314). New York: Holt, Rinehart, & Winston.

Einstein, G. O., & McDaniel, M. A. (1990). Normal aging and prospective memory. *Journal of Experimental Psychology: Learning, Memory, and Cognition, 16,* 717–726.

Eisner, T., & Meinwald, J. (1966). Defensive secretions of arthropods. *Science, 153,* 1341–1350.

Estes, W. K. (1944). An experimental study of punishment. *Psychological Monographs, 57* (Whole No. 263).

Eysenck, H. J. (1979). The conditioning model of neurosis. *Behavior and Brain Science, 2,* 155–199.

Fanselow, M. S., & Lester, L. S. (1988). A functional behavioristic approach to aversively motivated behavior: Predatory imminence as a determinant of the topography of defensive behavior. In R. C. Bolles & M. D. Beecher (Eds.), *Evolution and learning* (pp. 185–212). Hillsdale, NJ: Lawrence Erlbaum.

Farah, M. J. (1995). The neural basis of visual imagery. In M. J. Gazzaniga (Ed.), *The Cognitive Neurosciences* (pp. 963–975). Cambridge: MIT Press.

Felton, J., & Lyon, D. O. (1966). The post-reinforcement pause. *Journal of the Experimental Analysis of Behavior, 9,* 131–134.

Ferster, C. B., & Skinner, B. F. (1957). *Schedules of reinforcement.* New York: Appleton-Century-Crofts.

Finke, R. A., & Pinker, S. (1982). Spontaneous imagery scanning in mental extrapolation. *Journal of Experimental Psychology. Learning, Memory, and Cognition, 8,* 142–147.

Fiske, A. D., & Schneider, W. (1984). Memory as a function of attention, level of processing and automatization. *Journal of Experimental Psychology: Learning, Memory, and Cognition, 10,* 181–197.

Flaherty, C. F. (1982). Incentive contrast: A review of behavioral changes following shifts in reward. *Animal Learning and Behavior, 10*(4), 409–440.

Foss, N. J. (1982). A discourse on semantic priming. *Cognitive Psychology, 14,* 590–607.

Fowler, H., & Miller, N. E. (1963). Facilitation and inhibition of runway performance by hind and forepaw shock of various intensities. *Journal of Comparative and Physiological Psychology, 56,* 801–805.

Fowler, H., & Trapold, M. A. (1962). Escape performance as a function of delay of reinforcement. *Journal of Experimental Psychology, 63,* 464–467.

Franzisket, I. (1963). Characteristics of instinctive behavior and learning in reflex activity of the frog. *Animal Behavior, 11,* 318–324.

Freibergs, V., & Tulving, E. (1961). The effect of practice of utilization of information from positive and negative instances in concept identification. *Canadian Journal of Psychology, 15,* 101–106.

Friedman, M. L., & Stricker, E. M. (1976). The physiological psychology of hunger: A physiological perspective. *Psychological Review, 83,* 409–432.

Furedy, J. J., & Riley, D. M. (1987). Human Pavlovian autonomic conditioning and the cognitive paradigm. In Graham Davey (Ed.), *Cognitive processes and Pavlovian conditioning in humans* (pp. 1–25). New York: Wiley.

Gagne, R. M. (1965). *The conditions of learning.* New York: Holt, Rinehart & Winston.

Gallistel, C. R. (1990a). Representations in animal cognition. *Cognition, 37,* 1–22.

Gallistel, C. R. (1990b). *The organization of learning.* Cambridge: MIT Press.

Garcia, J., & Koelling, R. A. (1966). Relation of cue to consequence in avoidance learning. *Psychonomic Science, 4,* 123–124.

Gardiner, J. M. (1988). Generation and priming effects in word-fragment completion. *Journal of Experimental Psychology: Learning, Memory, and Cognition, 14,* 495–501.

Gentner, D. (1981). Some interesting differences between nouns and verbs. *Cognition and Brain Theory, 4,* 161–178.

Gentner, D., & Boroditsky, L. (1999). Individuation, relativity and early word learning. In M. Bowerman & S. Levinson (Eds.), *Language acquisition and conceptual development.* Cambridge: Cambridge University Press.

Gibbon, J., & Church, R. M. (1990). Representation of time. *Cognition, 37,* 23–54.

Gibbon, J., & Church, R. M. (1984). Sources of variance in an information processing theory of timing. In H. L. Roitblat, T. G. Bever, & H. S. Terrace (Eds.), *Animal cognition.* Hillsdale, NJ: Erlbaum Press.

Gibson, E. J. (1969). *Perceptual learning and development.* New York: Appleton.

Gibson, J. J. (1950). The implications of learning theory for social psychology. In J. G. Miller (Ed.), *Experiments in social process* (pp. 147–167). Ithaca, NY: Cornell University Press.

Gibson, J. J. (1966). The problem of temporal order in stimulation and perception. *Journal of Psychology, 62,* 141–149.

Glanzer, M. (1972). Storage mechanisms in recall. In G. H. Bower (Ed.), *The psychology of learning and motivation: Advances in research and theory* (Vol. 5, pp. 129–193). New York: Academic Press.

Glanzman, D. L. (1995). The cellular basis of classical conditioning in *Aplysia californica*—It's less simple than you think. *Trends in Neuroscience, 18,* 30–36.

Gleitman, L. R. (1984). Biological predispositions to learn language. In P. Mader & H. S. Terrace (Eds.), *The biology of learning* (pp. 553–584). Berlin: Springer-Verlag.

Glenberg, A. M. (1979). Component levels theory of the effects of spacing on recall and recognition. *Memory and Cognition, 2,* 95–112.

Glenberg, A. M. (1987). Temporal context and recency. In D. S. Gorfein & R. R. Hoffman (Eds.), *Memory and learning: The Ebbinghaus Centennial Conference* (pp. 173–190). Hillsdale, NJ: Lawrence Erlbaum.

Glenberg, A. M., Smith, S. M., & Green, C. (1977). Type I rehearsal: Maintenance and more. *Journal of Verbal Learning and Verbal Behavior, 16,* 339–352.

Glickman, S. E. (1973). Responses and reinforcement. In R. A. Hinde & J. Stevenson-Hinde (Eds.), *Constraints on learning: Limitations and predispositions* (pp. 207–241). New York: Academic Press.

Glickman, S. E., & Schiff, B. B. (1967). A biological theory of reinforcement. *Psychological Review, 74,* 81–109.

Goldman-Rakic, P. S. (1993). Working memory and the mind. *Mind and Brain: Readings from Scientific American Magazine* (pp. 67–77). New York: W. H. Freeman.

Gonzalez, R. C., Gentry, G. V., & Bitterman, M. E. (1954). Relational discrimination of intermediate size in the chimpanzee. *Journal of Comparative and Physiological Psychology, 47,* 385–388.

Good, M., & Macphail, E. M. 1994. Hippocampal lesions in pigeons (*Columbia livia*) disrupt reinforced preexposure but not overshadowing or blocking. *Quarterly Journal of Experimental Psychology, 47B*, 263–291.

Goodall, G. (1984). Learning due to the response-shock contingency in signaled punishment. *Quarterly Journal of Experimental Psychology, 36B*, 259–279.

Gordon, B. (1983). Lexical access and lexical decision: Mechanisms of frequency sensitivity. *Journal of Verbal Learning and Verbal Behavior, 22*, 24–44.

Gordon, W. C. (1989). *Learning and memory*. Pacific Grove, CA: Brooks/Cole.

Gormezano, L., & Kehoe, E. J. (1981). Classical conditioning and the law of contiguity. In P. Harzem & M. D. Zeiler (Eds.), *Advances in analysis of behavior: Vol. 2. Predictability, correlation, and contiguity* (pp. 1–45). New York: Wiley.

Gormezano, L., Kehoe, E. J., & Marshall, B. S. (1983). Twenty years of classical conditioning research with the rabbit. In J. M. Prague & A. N. Epstein (Eds.), *Progress in psychobiology and physiological psychology* (Vol. 10, pp. 197–275). New York: Academic Press.

Gould, J. L. (1986). The biology of learning. *Annual Review of Psychology, 37*, 163–192.

Graf, P., & Mandler, G. (1984). Activation makes words more accessible, but not necessarily more retrievable. *Journal of Verbal Learning and Verbal Behavior, 23*, 553–568.

Graf, P., & Schacter, D. A. (1985). Implicit and explicit memory for new associations in normal and amnesic subjects. *Journal of Experimental Psychology: Learning, Memory, and Cognition, 11*, 501–518.

Green, K. F., & Garcia, J. (1971). Recuperation from illness: Flavor enhancement for rats. *Science, 173*, 749–751.

Green, L., Fischer, E. B., Perlow, S., & Sherman, L. (1981). Preference reversal and self-control: Choice as a function of reward amount and delay. *Behavior Analysis Letters, 1*, 43–51.

Greene, R. L. (1992). *Human memory: Paradigms and paradoxes*. Hillsdale, NJ: Lawrence Erlbaum.

Groves, P. M., & Thompson, R. F. (1970). Habituation: A dual process theory. *Psychological Review, 77*, 419–450.

Gustafson, C. R., Garcia, J., Hankins, W. G., & Rusiniak, K. W. A. (1974). Coyote predation control by aversion conditioning. *Science, 184*, 581–583.

Guthrie, E. R. (1934). Reward and punishment. *Psychological Review, 41*, 450–460.

Guthrie, E. R. (1935). *The psychology of learning*. New York: Harper & Row.

Guttman, N. (1953). Operant conditioning, extinction, and periodic reinforcement in relation to concentration of sucrose used as reinforcing agent. *Journal of Experimental Psychology, 46*, 213–224.

Guttman, N., & Kalish, H. I. (1956). Discriminability and stimulus generalization. *Journal of Experimental Psychology, 51*, 79–88.

Haber A., & Kalish, H. I. (1963). Prediction of discrimination from generalization after variations in schedule of reinforcement. *Science, 142*, 412–413.

Haber, R. N. (1983). The impending demise of the icon: A critique of the concept of iconic storage in visual information processing. *The Behavioral and Brain Sciences, 6*, 1–54.

Hall, J. F. (1976). *Classical conditioning and instrumental learning: A contemporary approach*. Philadelphia: Lippincott.

Hanson, H. M. (1959). Effects of discrimination training on stimulus generalization. *Journal of Experimental Psychology, 58*, 321–334.

Harris, J. D. (1943). Studies of nonassociative factors inherent in conditioning. *Comprehensive Psychological Monograph, 18,* (1, Serial No. 93).

Hearst, E. (1988). Fundamentals of learning and conditioning. In R. C. Atkinson, R. J. Herrnstein, G. Lindzey, and R. D. Luce (Eds.), *Stevens' handbook of experimental psychology, Vol. 2: Learning and cognition.* New York: Wiley.

Hearst, E., & Koresko, M. B. (1968). Stimulus generalization and amount of prior training on variable interval reinforcement. *Journal of Comparative and Physiological Psychology, 66,* 133–138.

Hebb, D. O. (1949). *The organization of behavior.* New York: Colley.

Herman, R. L., & Azrin, N. H. (1964). Punishment by noise in an alternative response situation. *Journal of Experimental Analytical Behavior, 7,* 185–188.

Herrnstein, R. J. (1961). Relative and absolute strength of response as a function of frequency of reinforcement. *Journal of the Experimental Analysis of Behavior, 4,* 267–272.

Herrnstein, R. J., and Loveland, D. H. (1964). Complex visual concept in the pigeon. *Science, 146,* 549–551.

Hess, E. H. (1973). *Imprinting.* New York: Van Nostrand Reinhold.

Heth, C. D., & Rescorla, R. A. (1973). Simultaneous and backward fear conditioning in the rat. *Journal of Comparative and Physiological Psychology, 82,* 434–443.

Hetherington, A. W., & Ranson, S. W. (1940). Hypothalamic lesions and adiposity in the rat. *Anatomical Record, 78,* 149–172.

Hilgard, E. R., & Bower, G. H. (1966). *Theories of learning.* New York: Appleton-Century-Crofts.

Hill, A. J. (1978). First occurrence of hippocampal spatial firing in a new environment. *Experimental Neurology, 62,* 282–297.

Hillman, B., Hunter, W. S., & Kimble, G. A. (1953). The effect of drive level on the maze performance of the white rat. *Journal of Comparative and Physiological Psychology, 46,* 87–89.

Hindley, C. B., Filliozat, A. M., Klackenberg, G., Nicolet-Meister, P., & Sand, E. A. (1966). Differences in age of walking in five European longitudinal samples. *Human Biology, 38,* 364–379.

Hineline, P. N., & Rachlin, H. (1969). Escape and avoidance of shock by pigeons pecking a key. *Journal of Experimental & Analytical Behavior, 12,* 533–538.

Hintzman, D. L. (1990). Human learning and memory: Connections and dissociations. *Annual Review of Psychology, 41,* 109–139.

Hiroto, D. S. (1974). Locus of control and learned helplessness. *Journal of Experimental Psychology, 102,* 187–193.

Hiroto, D. S., & Seligman, M. E. P. (1975). Generality of learned helplessness in man. *Journal of Personality and Social Psychology, 31,* 311–327.

Hodos, W., & Campbell, C. B. G. (1969). *Scala naturae*: Why there is no theory in comparative psychology. *Psychological Review, 76*(4), 337–350.

Hoffman, J. E. (1986). The psychology of perception. In J. E. Le Doux, and W. Hirst (Eds.), *Mind and brain: Dialogues in cognitive neuroscience.* Cambridge: Cambridge University Press.

Honey, R. C., & Good, M. (2000). Associative components of recognition memory. *Current Opinion in Neurobiology,* Vol. 10(2), 200–204.

Honig, W. K., & Stewart, K. E. 1988. Pigeons can discriminate locations presented in pictures. *Journal of the Experimental Analysis of Behavior, 50,* 541–551.

Houston, J. P. (1981). *Fundamentals of learning and memory* (2nd ed.). Orlando, FL: Harcourt, Brace, Jovanovich.

Houston, J. P., & Reynolds, J. H. (1965). First-list retention as a function of list differentiation and second-list massed and distributed practice. *Journal of Experimental Psychology, 69,* 387–392.

Hovland, C. I. (1952). A communication analysis of concept learning. *Psychological Review, 59,* 461–472.

Hovland, C. I., & Weiss, W. (1953). Transmission of information concerning concepts through positive and negative instances. *Journal of Experimental Psychology, 45,* 165–182.

Hubel, D. H., & Wiesel, T. N. (1965). Receptive fields of single neurons in two nonstriate visual areas (18 and 19) of the cat. *Journal of Neurophysiology, 28,* 229–289.

Hull, C. L. (1943). *Principles of behavior.* New York: Appleton.

Hull, C. L., Livingston, J. R., Rouse, R. O., & Barker, A. N. (1951). True, sham, and esophageal feeding as reinforcements. *Journal of Comparative and Physiological Psychology, 44,* 236–245.

Hyman, I. E., Husband, T. H., & Billings, J. F. (1995). False memories of childhood experiences. *Applied Cognitive Psychology, 90,* 181–197.

Irion, A. L. (1966). A brief history of research on the acquisition of skill. In E. A. Bilodeau (Ed.), *Acquisition of skill* (pp. 1–46). New York: Academic Press.

Ironsmith, M., & Lutz, J. (1994). The effects of bizarreness and self generation on mnemonic imagery. *Journal of Mental Imagery, 20,* 113–126.

Jacoby, L. L. (1983). Remembering the data: Analyzing interactive processes in reading. *Journal of Verbal Learning and Verbal Behavior, 17,* 649–667.

Jacoby, L. L., & Dallas, M. (1981). On the relationship between autobiographical memory and perceptual learning. *Journal of Experimental Psychology: General, 22,* 485–508.

James, W. A. (1890). *The principles of psychology* (Vols. 1 and 2). New York: Holt.

Jenkins, J. G., & Dallenbach, K. M. (1924). Obliviscence during sleep and waking. *American Journal of Psychology, 35,* 605–612.

Jenkins, H. M., & Harrison, R. H. (1960). Effect of discrimination training on auditory generalization. *Journal of Experimental Psychology, 59,* 246–253.

Jenkins, J. G., & Harrison, R. H. (1962). Generalization gradients of inhibition following auditory discrimination learning. *Journal of the Experimental Analysis of Behavior, 5,* 435–441.

Jones, M. C. (1924). The elimination of children's fears. *Journal of Experimental Psychology, 7,* 383–390.

Kagan, J., & Klein, R. E. (1973). Cross-cultural perspectives on early development. *American Psychologist, 28,* 947–961.

Kaiser, D. H., Zentall, T. R., & Neiman, E. (2002). Timing in pigeons: Effects of the similarity between intertribal interval and gap in a timing signal. *Journal of Experimental Psychology: Animal Behavior Processes, 28,* 416–422.

Kalat, J. W., & Rozin, P. (1970). "Salience": A factor which can override temporal contiguity in taste-aversion learning. *Journal of Comparative and Physiological Psychology, 71,* 192–197.

Kalat, J. W., & Rozin, P. (1971). Role of interference in taste-aversion learning. *Journal of Comparative and Physiological Psychology, 77,* 53–58.

Kamil, A. C., & Yoerg, S. I. (1982). Learning and foraging behavior. In P. P. G. Bateson & P. H. Klopfer (Eds.), *Perspectives on ethology* (Vol. 5). New York: Plenum.

Kamin, L. J. (1963). Backward conditioning and the conditioned emotional response. *Journal of Comparative and Physiological Psychology, 56,* 517–519.

Kamin, L. J. (1965). Temporal and intensity characteristics of the conditioned stimulus. In W F. Prokasy (Ed.), *Classical conditioning* (pp. 118–147). New York: Appleton-Century-Crofts.

Kamin, L. J. (1968). "Attention-like" processes in classical conditioning. In M. R. Jones (Ed.), *Miami Symposium on the Prediction of Behavior. Aversive stimulation* (pp. 9–33). Miami: University of Miami Press.

Kamin, L. J. (1969). Predictability, surprise, attention, and conditioning. In B. A. Campbell & R. M. Church (Eds.), *Punishment and aversive behavior* (pp. 279–296). New York: Appleton-Century-Crofts.

Kamin, L. J., & Brimer, C. J. (1963). The effects of intensity of conditioned and unconditioned stimuli on a conditioned emotional response. *Canadian Journal of Psychology, 17,* 194–198.

Kamin, L. J., Brimer, C. J., & Black, A. H. (1963). Conditioned suppression as a monitor of fear of the CS in the course of avoidance-training. *Journal of Comparative and Physiological Psychology, 56,* 497–501.

Kandel, E. R. (1979). Small systems of neurons. *Scientific American, 241,* 66–76.

Kandel, E. R., & Tauc, L. (1964). Mechanisms of prolonged heterosynaptic facilitation. *Nature, 202,* 145–147.

Kandel, E. R., & Tauc, L. (1965). Heterosynaptic facilitation in neurons of the abdominal ganglion of *Aplysia depilans. Journal of Physiology, 181,* 1–27.

Katkin, E. S., & Murray, E. N. (1968). Instrumental conditioning of autonomically mediated behavior: Theoretical and methodological issues. *Psychological Bulletin, 70,* 52–68.

Kaufman, A., Baron, A., & Kopp, R. M. (1966). Some effects of instructions on human operant behavior. *Psychonomic Monograph Supplements, 1*(11), 243–250.

Kausler, D. H. (1974). *Psychology of verbal learning and memory.* New York: Academic Press.

Kazdin, A. E. (1994). *Behavior modification in applied settings* (2nd ed.). Pacific Grove, CA: Brooks/Cole.

Kelley, C., Amodio, D., & Lindsay, D. S. (1996). The effects of diagnosis and memory work on memories of handedness shaping. Paper presented at the International Conference on Memory, Padua, Italy, cited in E. R. Loftus, The dangers of memory. In R. J. Sternberg, (Ed.), *Psychologists defying the crowd.* Washington, DC: APA Press.

Kennedy, G. C. (1953). The role of depot fat in the hypothalamic control of food intake in the rat. *Proceedings of the Royal Society of London,* B 140, 578–592.

Keppel, G., & Underwood, B. J. (1962). Proactive inhibition in short-term retention of single items. *Journal of Verbal Learning and Verbal Behavior, 1,* 153–161.

Kesner, R. P., & DeSpain, M. J. (1988). Correspondence between rats and humans in the utilization of retrospective and prospective codes. *Animal Learning and Behavior, 16,* 299–302.

Kimble, D. P., & Ray, R. S. (1965). Reflex habituation and potentiation in *Rana pipiens. Animal Behaviour, 13,* 530–533.

Kimble, G. A. (1961). *Hilgard and Marguis' conditioning and learning* (2nd ed.). New York: Appleton-Century.

Klaus, M. H., & Kennell, J. H. (1976). *Maternal-infant bonding.* St. Louis: Mosby.

Klaus, M. H., & Kennell, J. H. (1984). Mother-infant bonding: Weighing the evidence. *Developmental Review, 4,* 275–282.

Klein, M., Shapiro, E., & Kandel, E. R. (1980). Synaptic plasticity and the modulation of the calcium current. *Journal of Experimental Biology, 89,* 117–157.

Klein, S. B., & Kihlstrom, J. F. (1986). Elaboration, organization, and the self-reference effect in memory. *Journal of Experimental Psychology: General, 115,* 26–38.

Kohler, W. (1939). Simple structural functions in the chimpanzee and the chicken. In W. D. Ellis (Ed.), *A source book of gestalt psychology* (pp. 217–227). New York: Harcourt Brace.

Kolers, P. A. (1984). Perception and representation. *Annual Review of Psychology, 34,* 129–166.

Komatsu, L. K. 1992. Recent views of conceptual structure. *Psychological Bulletin, 112,* 300–328.

Konorski, J. (1948). *Conditioned reflexes and neuron organization.* New York: Cambridge University Press.

Koriat, A., Goldsmith, M., & Pansky, A. (2000). Toward a psychology of memory accuracy. *Annual Review of Psychology, 51,* 481–537.

Kosslyn, S. M., Ball, T. M., & Reiser, B. J. (1978). Visual images preserve metric spatial information: Evidence from studies of image scanning. *Journal of Experimental Psychology: Human Perception and Performance, 4,* 1–20.

Kraemer, P. J., Randall, C. K., Dose, J. M., & Brown, R. W. (1997). Impact of d-amphetamine on temporal estimation in pigeons tested with a production procedure. *Pharmacology Biochemistry & Behavior, 58*(2): 323–327.

Krechevsky, I. (1932). "Hypotheses" in rats. *Psychological Review, 39,* 516–532.

Kroll, N. E., & Timourian, D. A. (1986). Misleading questions and the retrieval of the irretrievable. *Bulletin of the Psychonomic Society, 24,* 165–168.

Kroodsma, D. E. (1988). Contrasting styles of song development and their consequences among passerine birds. In R. C. Bolles & M. D. Beecher (Eds.), *Evolution and learning* (pp. 157–184). Hillsdale, NJ: Lawrence Erlbaum.

Kroodsma, D. E., & Miller, E. H. (1982). *Acoustic communication in birds.* Orlando, FL: Academic Press.

Larson, J., and Lynch, G. (1986).Induction of synaptic potentiation in hippocampus by patterned stimulation involves two events. *Science, 232,* 985–988.

Lashley, K. S. (1929). *Brain mechanisms and intelligence.* Chicago: University of Chicago Press.

Lashley, K. S. (1942). An examination of the "continuity theory" as applied to discriminative learning. *Journal of General Psychology, 26,* 241–265.

Lashley, K. S., & Wade, M. (1946). The Pavlovian theory of generalization. *Psychological Review, 53,* 72–87.

Lawrence, D. H., & DeRivera, J. (1954). Evidence for relational transposition. *Journal of Comparative and Physiological Psychology, 47,* 465–471.

Leaton, R. N. (1976). Long-term retention of the habituation of lick suppression and startle response produced by a single auditory stimulus. *Journal of Experimental Psychology: Animal Behavior Processes, 2,* 248–259.

Lenneberg, E. H. (1967). *Biological foundations of language.* New York: Wiley.

Lesgold, A. M., Roth, S. F., & Curtis, M. E. (1979). Foregrounding effects in discourse comprehension. *Journal of Verbal Learning and Verbal Behavior, 18,* 291–308.

Lett, B. T. (1975). Long delay learning in the t-maze. *Learning and Motivation, 6,* 80–90.

Lettvin, J. Y. Maturana, H. R., McCulloch, W. S., & Pitts, W. H. (1959). What the frog's eye tells the frog's brain. *Proceedings of the IRE, 47,* 1940–1951.

Ley, R., & Locascio, D. (1970). Associative reaction time and meaningfulness of CVC response terms in paired-associate learning. *Journal of Experimental Psychology, 96,* 255–262.

Light, L. L., & Singh, A. (1987). Implicit and explicit memory in young and old adults. *Journal of Experimental Psychology: Learning, Memory, and Cognition, 13,* 531–541.

Lindsay, P. H., & Norman, D. A. (1977). *Human information processing* (2nd ed.). New York: Academic Press.

Lockhart, R. S., & Craik, F. I. M. (1990). Levels of processing: A retrospective commentary on a framework for memory research. *Canadian Journal of Psychology, 44*(1), 87–112.

Loftus, E. F. (1979). *Eyewitness testimony.* Cambridge Harvard University Press.

Loftus, E. F., & Palmer, J. C. (1974). Reconstruction of automobile destruction: An example of the interaction between language and memory. *Journal of Verbal Learning and Verbal Behavior, 13,* 585–589.

Loftus, E. F., & Pickrell, J. (1995). The formation of false memories. *Psychiatric Annals, 25,* 720–725.

Loftus, E. F., & Zanni, G. (1975). Eyewitness testimony: The influence of the wording of a question. *Bulletin of the Psychonomic Society, 5,* 86–88.

Logan, F. A. (1956). A micromolar approach to behavior. *Psychological Review, 63,* 63–73.

Logan, F. A. (1970). *Fundamentals of learning and motivation.* Dubuque, IA: Wm. C. Brown.

Logue, A. W. (1995). *Self control: Waiting until tomorrow for what you want today.* Englewood Cliffs, NJ: Prentice-Hall.

Logue, A. W. (1998). Self control. In W. O'Donohue (Ed.), *Learning and behavior therapy* (pp. 252–273). Boston: Allyn & Bacon.

Longstreth, L. E. (1971). A cognitive interpretation of secondary reinforcement. In J. K. Cole (Ed.), *Nebraska symposium on motivation* (pp. 33–80). Lincoln: University of Nebraska Press.

Lorenz, K. (1935). Der kumpen in der umwelt des vogels. *Journal of Ornithology, 83,* 137–213, 289–413.

Lorenz, K. (1952). The past twelve years in the comparative study of behavior. In C. H. Schiller (Ed.), *Instinctive behavior* (pp. 288–317). New York: International Universities Press.

Lorenz, K. (1966). *On aggression.* New York: Harcourt, Brace & World.

Lovaas, O. I., & Simmons, J. Q. (1969). Manipulation of self-destruction in three retarded children. *Journal of Applied Behavior Analysis, 2,* 143–157.

Lubow, R. E., & Moore, A. U. (1959). Latent inhibition: The effect of nonreinforced preexposure to the conditioned stimulus. *Journal of Comparative and Physiological Psychology, 52,* 415–419.

Lucas, G. A., & Timberlake, W. (1992). Negative anticipatory contrast and preference conditioning flavor cues support preference conditioning, and environmental cues support contrast. *Journal of Experimental Psychology: Animal Behavior Processes, 18*(1), 34–40.

Lutz, J., & Wuensch, K. L. (1989). Acoustic interference in a recognition task. *The Journal of General Psychology: Experimental, Physiological, and Comparative Psychology, 116*(4), 371–384.

Macfarlane, D. A., (1930). The role of kinesthesis in maze learning. *University of California Publications in Psychology, 4,* 277–305.

MacKay, D. G. (1973). Aspects of the theory of comprehension, memory, and attention. *Quarterly Journal of Experimental Psychology, 25,* 22–40.

Mackintosh, N. J. (1974). *The psychology of animal learning.* London: Academic Press.

Mackintosh, N. J. (1975). A theory of attention: Variations in associability of stimuli with reinforcement. *Psychological Review, 82,* 276–298.

Mackintosh, N. J., & Mackintosh, J. (1964). Performance of the octopus over a series of reversals of a simultaneous discrimination. *Animal Behaviour, 12,* 321–324.

Macphail, E. M. (1993). *The neuroscience of animal intelligence.* New York: Columbia University Press.

Madden, G. J., Petry, N. M., Badger, G. J., & Bickel, W. K. (1997). Impulsive and self-control choices in opioid-dependent patients and non-drug-using control participants: Drug and monetary rewards. *Experimental and Clinical Psychopharmacology, 5,* 256–262.

Maguire, E. A., Valentine, E. R., Wilding, J. M., & Kapur, N. (2003). Routes to remembering: The brains behind superior memory. *Nature Neuroscience, 6,* 90–95.

Maier, S. F., & Seligman, M. E. P. (1976). Learned helplessness: Theory and evidence. *Journal of Experimental Psychology: General, 105,* 3–46.

Maltzman, I., Weissbluth, S., & Wolff, C. (1978). Habituation of orienting reflexes in repeated GSR semantic conditioning sessions. *Journal of Experimental Psychology: General, 107,* 309–333.

Mandler, G. (1967). Organization and memory. In K. W. Spence & J. T Spence (Eds.), *The psychology of learning and motivation* (Vol. 1). Orlando, FL: Academic Press.

Mandler G., & Pearlstone, Z. (1966). Free and constrained concept learning and subsequent recall. *Journal of Verbal Learning and Verbal Behavior, 5,* 126–131.

Mandler, J. M. (1968). The effect of overtraining on the use of positive and negative stimuli in reversal and transfer. *Journal of Comparative and Physiological Psychology, 66,* 110–115.

Maricq, A. V., Roberts, S., & Church, R. M. (1981). Methamphetamine and time estimation. *Journal of Experimental Psychology: Animal Behavior Processes, 7,* 18–30.

Martin, E. (1965). Transfer of verbal paired associates. *Psychological Review, 72,* 327–343.

Matzel, L. D., Held, F. P., & Miller, R. R. (1988). Information and expression of simultaneous and backward associations: Implications for contiguity theory. *Learning and Motivation, 19*(4), 317–344.

Mayer, J. (1955). Regulation of energy intake and the body weight: The glucostatic theory and the lipostatic hypothesis. *Annals of the New York Academy of Science, 63,* Art. 1, 15–43.

Mazmanian, D. S., & Roberts, W. A. (1983). Spatial memory in rats under restricted viewing conditions. *Learning and Motivation, 12,* 261–281.

McCarthy, M. A., & Houston, J. P. (1980). *Fundamentals of early childhood education.* Cambridge, MA: Winthrop.

McClelland, J. L., & Rumelhart, D. E. (1988). *Explorations in parallel distributed processing: A handbook of models, programs, and exercises.* Cambridge: MIT Press.

McClosky, M., & Cohen, N. J. (1989). Catastrophic interference in connectionist networks: The sequential learning problem. *Psychology of Learning and Motivation, 24,* 109–165.

McDaniel, M. A., & Einstein, G. O. (1986). Bizarre imagery as an effective memory aid: The importance of distinctiveness. *Journal of Experimental Psychology: Learning, Memory, and Cognition, 12,* 54–65.

McGeoch, J. A. (1932). Forgetting and the law of disuse. *Psychological Review, 39,* 352–370.

McGeoch, J. A. (1942). *The psychology of human learning.* New York: Longmans, Green.

McHose, J. H., & Tauber, L. (1972). Changes in delay of reinforcement in simple instrumental conditioning. *Psychonomic Society, 27,* 291–292.

McIntosh, A. R., & Gonzalez, L. F. (1991). Structural modeling of functional neural pathways mapped with 2-deoxyglucose: Effects of acoustic startle habituation on the auditory system. *Brain Research, 547,* 295–302.

McLaughlin, B. (1965). "Intentional" and "incidental" learning in human subjects: The role of instructions to learn and motivation. *Psychological Bulletin, 63,* 359–376.

Meehl, P. E. (1950). On the circularity of the law of effect. *Psychological Bulletin, 47,* 52–75.

Melton, A. W. (1967). Repetition and retrieval from memory. *Science, 158,* 532.

Melton, A. W., & Irwin, J. M. (1940). The influence of degree of interpolated learning on retroactive inhibition and the overt transfer of specific responses. *American Journal of Psychology, 53,* 173–203.

Mewhort, D. J. K., Marchetti, F. M., Gurnsey, R., & Campbell, A. J. (1984). Information persistence: A dual buffer model for initial visual processing. In H. Bouma & D. G. Bouwhuis (Eds.), *Attention and performance. Control of language processes* (Vol. 10, pp. 287–298). Hillsdale, NJ: Lawrence Erlbaum.

Meyer, D. E., & Schvaneveldt, R. W. (1971). Facilitation in recognizing pairs of words: Evidence of a dependence between retrieval operations. *Journal of Experimental Psychology, 90,* 227–234.

Miczek, K. A., & Grossman, S. (1971). Positive conditioned suppression: Effects of CS duration. *Journal of Experimental Analysis of Behavior, 15,* 243–247.

Miller, G. A. (1956). The magical number seven, plus or minus two: Some limits on our capacity for processing information. *Psychology Review, 63,* 81–97.

Miller, N. E. (1948). Studies of fear as an acquirable drive: I. Fear as motivation and fear reduction as reinforcement in learning of new responses. *Journal of Experimental Psychology, 38,* 89–101.

Miller, N. E. (1958). Central stimulation and other new approaches to motivation and reward. *American Psychologist, 13,* 100–108.

Miller, N. E. (1960). Learning resistance to pain and fear: Effects of overlearning, exposure and rewarded exposure in context. *Journal of Experimental Psychology, 60,* 137–145.

Miller, N. E. (1961). Analytical studies of drive & reward. *American Psychologist, 16,* 739–754.

Miller, N. E. (1973). Interactions between learned and physical factors in mental illness. In D. Shapiro, T X. Barber, L. V. DiCara, J. Kamiya, N. E. Miller, & J. Stoyva (Eds.), *Biofeedback and self-control: 1972* (pp. 437–459). Chicago: Aldine.

Miller, N. E. (1978). Biofeedback and visceral learning. *Annual Review of Psychology, 29,* 373–404.

Miller, N. E., & DiCara, L. V. (1968). Instrumental learning of urine formation by rats: Changes in renal blood flow. *American Journal of Physiology, 215,* 677–683.

Miller, G. A., Galanter, E. H., & Pribram, K. H. (1960). *Plans and the structure of behavior.* New York: Holt, Rinehart & Winston.

Miller, N. E., & Kessen, M. L. (1952). Reward effects of food via stomach fistula compared with those of food via mouth. *Journal of Comparative and Physiological Psychology, 45,* 555–564.

Miller, R. R., & Barnet, R. C. (1993). The role of time in elementary associations. *Current Directions in Psychological Science, 2*(4), 106–111.

Milner, B. (1966). Amnesia following operation on the temporal lobes. In C. W. M. Witty & O. L. Zangwill (Eds.), *Amnesia.* London: Butterworths.

Milner, B. (1970). Memory and the medial temporal regions of the brain. In K. H. Pribram, & D. E. Broadbent (Eds.), *Biology of memory* (pp. 29–50). New York: Academic Press.

Mischel, W. (1966). Theory and research on the antecedents of self-imposed delay of reward. *Progress in Experimental Personality Research, 3,* 85–132.

Mischel, W. (1974). Processes in the delay of gratification. In L. Berkowitz (Ed.), *Advances in experimental social psychology* (Vol. 7). New York: Academic Press.

Mischel, W., Shoda, Y., & Rodriguez, M. (1989). Delay of gratification for children. *Science, 244,* 933–938.

Mischel, W., & Ebbesen, E. B. (1970). Attention in delay of gratification. *Journal of Personality and Social Psychology, 16,* 329–337.

Mischel, W., Ebbesen, E. B., & Zeiss, A. R. (1972). Cognitive and attentional mechanisms in delay of gratification. *Journal of Personality and Social Psychology, 21,* 204–218.

Moore, B. R. (1973). The role of directed Pavlovian reactions in simple instrumental learning in the pigeon. In R. A. Hinde & J. Stevenson-Hinde (Eds.), *Constraints on learning* (pp. 159–188). New York: Academic Press.

Morris, C. D., Bransford, J. D., & Franks, J. J. (1977). Levels of processing versus transfer-appropriate processing. *Journal of Verbal Learning and Verbal Behavior, 16,* 519–533.

Moscovitch, M., & Craik, F. I. M. (1976). Depth of processing, retrieval cues, and uniqueness of encoding as factors in recall. *Journal of Verbal Learning and Verbal Behavior, 15,* 447–458.

Mowrer, O. H. (1939). A stimulus-response analysis and its role as a reinforcing agent. *Psychological Review, 46,* 553–565.

Mowrer, O. H. (1947). On the dual nature of learning—A reinterpretation of "conditioning" and "problem solving." *Harvard Educational Review, 17,* 102–148.

Mowrer, O. H. (1960). *Learning theory and behavior.* New York: Wiley.

Mowrer, O. H., & Jones, H. M. (1945). Habit strength as a function of the pattern of reinforcement. *Journal of Experimental Psychology, 35,* 293–311.

Murdock, B. B., Jr. (1962). The serial position effect of free recall. *Journal of Experimental Psychology, 64,* 482–488.

Nairne, J. S. (2002). The myth of the encoding-retrieval match. *Memory, 10,* 389–395.

Neisser, U. (1967). *Cognitive psychology.* New York: Appleton-Century-Crofts.

Nelson, D. L. (1979). Remembering pictures and words: Appearance, significance, and name. In L. S. Cermak & F. I. M. Craik (Eds.), *Levels of processing in human memory.* Hillsdale, NJ: Lawrence Erlbaum.

Nelson, T. O., & Rothbart, R. (1972). Acoustic savings for items forgotten from long-term memory. *Journal of Experimental Psychology, 93,* 357–360.

Nevin, J. A. (1992). Behavioral contrast and behavioral momentum. *Journal of Experimental Psychology: Animal Behavior Processes, 18*(2), 126–133.

Nickerson, R. S., & Adams, M. J. (1979). Long-term memory for a common object. *Cognitive Psychology,* 287–307.

Noble, C. E. (1952). An analysis of meaning. *Psychological Review, 60,* 89–98.

Noble, C. E. (1963). Meaningfulness and familiarity. In C. N. Cofer & B. S. Musgrave (Eds.), *Verbal behavior and learning* (pp. 76–157). New York: McGraw-Hill.

O'Keefe, J., & Dostrovsky, J. (1971). The hippocampus as a spatial map: Preliminary evidence from unit activity in the freely moving rat. *Experimental Neurology, 51,* 78–109.

Olton, D. S. (1973). Shock-motivated avoidance and the analysis of behavior. *Psychological Bulletin, 79,* 243–251.

Olton, D. S. (1978). Characteristics of spatial memory. In S. H. Hulse, H. Fowler, and W. Honig (Eds.), *Cognitive processes in animal behavior.* Hillsdale, NJ: Erlbaum.

Olton, D. S., Collison, C., & Werz, M. A. (1977). Spatial memory and radial arm maze performance of rats. *Learning and Motivation, 8,* 289–314.

Orne, M. T. (1962). On the social psychology of the psychological experiment: With particular reference to demand characteristics and their implications. *American Psychologist, 17,* 776–783.

Ornstein, R. A., Naus, M. J., & Liberty, C. (1975). Rehearsal and organizational processes in children's memory. *Child Development, 46,* 818–830.

Ornstein, R. E. (1972). *The psychology of consciousness.* San Francisco: Freeman.

Osgood, C. E. (1949). The similarity paradox in human learning: A resolution. *Psychological Review, 56,* 132–143.

Osgood, C. E. (1954). Psycholinguistics: A survey of theory, and research problems. *Journal of Abnormal and Social Psychology, 4*(2, Supplement), 203.

Overmeier, J. B., & Seligman, M. E. P. (1967). Effects of inescapable shock upon subsequent escape and avoidance learning. *Journal of Comparative and Physiological Psychology, 63,* 28–33.

Paivio, A. (1971). *Imagery and verbal processes.* New York: Holt, Rinehart & Winston.

Paivio, A., Yuille, J. C., & Madigan, S. A. (1968). Concreteness, imagery, and meaningfulness values for 925 nouns. *Journal of Experimental Psychology Monograph Supplement, 76*(1, Pt. 2).

Paivio, A., Yuille, J. C., & Rogers, T. B. (1969). Noun imagery and meaningfulness in free and serial recall. *Journal of Experimental Psychology, 79,* 509–514.

Papini, M. R., & Bitterman, M. E. (1990). The role of contingency in classical conditioning. *Psychological Review, 97,* 396–403.

Parkin, A. J., & Streete, S. (1988). Implicit and explicit memory in young children and adults. *British Journal of Psychology, 79,* 361–369.

Pavlik, W. B., & Reynolds, W. F. (1963). Effects of deprivation schedule and reward magnitude on acquisition and extinction performance. *Journal of Comparative and Physiological Psychology, 56,* 452–455.

Pavlov, I. (1927). *Conditioned reflexes.* Oxford: Oxford University Press.

Pearce, J. M. (1987). A model of stimulus generalization for Pavlovian conditioning. *Psychological Review, 94,* 61–73.

Pearce, J. M. (1994). Similarity and discrimination: A selective review and a connectionist model. *Psychological Review, 101,* 587–607.

Pearce, J. M., & Bouton, M. E. (2001). Theories of associative learning in animals. *Annual Review of Psychology, 52,* 111–139.

Pearce, J. M., & Hall, G. (1980). A model for Pavlovian learning: Variations in the effectiveness of conditioned but not of unconditioned stimuli. *Psychological Review, 87,* 532–552.

Penfield, W. (1954). *Epilepsy and the functional anatomy of the human brain.* Boston: Little, Brown.

Perin, C. T. (1943). A quantitative investigation of the delay-of-reinforcement gradient. *Journal of Experimental Psychology, 32,* 37–51.

Perkins, C. C., & Weyant, R. G. (1958). The interval between training and test trials as a determiner of the slope of generalization gradients. *Journal of Comparative and Physiological Psychology, 51,* 596–600.

Peterson, L. R., & Peterson, M. J. (1959). Short term retention of individual verbal items. *Journal of Experimental Psychology, 53,* 193–198.

Peterson, N. (1962). Effect of monochromatic rearing on the control of responding by wavelength. *Science, 136,* 774–775.

Pinsker, H. M., Hening, W. A., Carew, T. J., & Kandel, E. R. (1973). Long-term sensitization of a defensive withdrawal reflex in *aplysia. Science, 182,* 1039–1042.

Postman, L. (1964). Short-term memory and incidental learning. In A. W. Melton (Ed.), *Categories of human learning.* New York: Academic Press.

Postman, L., & Schwartz, M. (1964). Studies of learning to learn: I. Transfer as a function of method of practice and class of verbal materials. *Journal of Verbal Learning and Verbal Behavior, 3,* 37–49.

Postman, L., & Stark, K. (1967). Studies of learning to learn: 4. Transfer from serial to paired-associates learning. *Journal of Verbal Learning and Verbal Behavior, 6,* 339–353.

Postman, L., Stark, K., & Fraser, J. (1968). Temporal changes in interference. *Journal of Verbal Learning and Verbal Behavior, 7,* 672–694.

Postman, L., Thompkins, S. A., & Gray, W. N. (1978). The interpretation of encoding effects in retention. *Journal of Verbal Learning and Verbal Behavior, 17,* 132–138.

Powley, R. L. (1977). The ventromedial hypothalamic syndrome, satiety, and a cephalic phase hypothesis. *Psychological Review, 84,* 89–126.

Premack, D. (1959). Toward empirical behavior laws: 1. Positive reinforcement. *Psychological Review, 66,* 219–233.

Premack, D. (1962). Reversibility of the reinforcement relation. *Science, 136,* 255–257.

Premack, D. (1965). Reinforcement theory. In D. Levine (Ed.), *Nebraska Symposium on Motivation* (pp. 123–180). Lincoln: University of Nebraska Press.

Premack, D. (1971). On the assessment of language competence and the chimpanzee. In A. M. Schrier & F. Stollnitz (Eds.), *Behaviour of nonhuman primates* (Vol. 4, pp. 185–228). New York: Academic Press.

Prokasy, W. F. (1984). Acquisition of skeletal conditioned responses in Pavlovian conditioning. *Psychophysiology, 21,* 1–13.

Prokasy, W. F., Grant, D. A., & Myers, N. A. (1956). Response shaping at long interstimulus intervals in classical eyelid conditioning. *Journal of Experimental Psychology, 66,* 138–141.

Pubols, B. H., Jr. (1960). Incentive magnitude, learning and performance in animals. *Psychological Bulletin, 51,* 89–115.

Quinn, W. G. (1984). Work in invertebrates on the mechanisms underlying learning. In P. Marler & H. S. Terrace (Eds.), *The biology of learning.* Berlin: Springer-Verlag.

Raaijmakers, J. G. W., & Shiffrin, R. M. (1992). Models for recall and recognition. *Annual Review of Psychology, 43,* 205–234.

Rachlin, H. C. (1969). Autoshaping of key pecking in pigeons with negative reinforcement. *Journal of the Experimental Analysis of Behavior, 12,* 521–531.

Rachlin, H. & Green, L. (1972). Commitment, choice, and self-control. *Journal of the Experimental Analysis of Behavior, 17,* 15–22.

Rachlin, H. C., & Herrnstein, R. L. (1969). Hedonism revisited: On the negative law of effect. In B. A. Campbell & R. M. Church (Eds.), *Punishment and aversive behavior.* New York: Appleton-Century-Crofts.

Randich, A. (1981). The US pre-exposure phenomenon in the conditioned suppression paradigm: A role for conditioned situational stimuli. *Learning and Motivation, 12,* 321–341.

Ratcliff, R. (1978). A theory of memory retrieval. *Psychological Review, 85,* 59–108.

Razran, G. (1965). Evolutionary psychology: Levels of learning and perception and thinking. In B. Wolman (Ed.), *Scientific psychology: Principles and approaches* (pp. 207–253). New York: Basic Books.

Razran, G. (1971). *Mind in evolution: An East-West synthesis of learned behaviour and cognition.* Boston: Houghton Mifflin.

Redhead, E. S., & Pearce, J. M. (1995). Similarity and discrimination learning. *Quarterly Journal of Experimental Psychology, 48B;* 46–66.

Reese, H. W., & Lipsett, L. P. (1970). *Experimental child psychology.* New York: Academic Press.

Reicher, G. (1969). Perceptual recognition as a function of meaningfulness of stimulus material. *Journal of Experimental Psychology, 81,* 275–280.

Reitman, J. S. (1974). Without surreptitious rehearsal, information in short-term memory decays. *Journal of Verbal Learning and Verbal Behavior, 13,* 365–377.

Rescorla, R. A. (1967). Pavlovian conditioning and its proper control procedures. *Psychological Review, 74,* 71–80.

Rescorla, R. A. (1968). Probability of shock in the presence and absence of CS in fear conditioning. *Journal of Comparative and Physiological Psychology, 66,* 1–5.

Rescorla, R. A. (1974). Effect of inflation of the unconditioned stimulus value following conditioning. *Journal of Comparative and Physiological Psychology, 86,* 101–106.

Rescorla, R. A. (1980). *Pavlovian second-order conditioning. Studies in associative learning.* Hillsdale, NJ: Lawrence Erlbaum.

Rescorla, R. A. (1982). Simultaneous second-order conditioning produces S–S learning in conditioned suppression. *Journal of Experimental Psychology: Animal Behavior Processes, 8,* 23–32.

Rescorla, R. A. (1987). A Pavlovian analysis of goal-directed behavior. *American Psychologist, 42,* 119–129.

Rescorla, R. A. (1988). Pavlovian conditioning: It's not what you think it is. *American Psychologist, 43,* 151–160.

Rescorla, R. A., & Holland, P. C. (1982). Behavioral studies of associative learning in animals. *Annual Review of Psychology, 33,* 265–308.

Rescorla, R. A., & Solomon, R. L. (1967). Two process learning theory: Relations between Pavlovian conditioning and instrumental learning. *Psychological Review, 74,* 151–182.

Rescorla, R. A., & Wagner, A. R. (1972). A theory of Pavlovian conditioning: Variations in the effectiveness of reinforcement and non-reinforcement. In A. H. Black & W. F. Prokasy (Eds.), *Classical conditioning II* (pp. 64–99). New York: Appleton-Century-Crofts.

Reynolds, G. A. (1961). Attention in the pigeon. *Journal of Experimental Analytic Behavior, 4,* 203–208.

Riley, D. A. (1968). *Discrimination learning.* Boston: Allyn & Bacon.

Rips, L. J., Shoben, E. J., & Smith, E. E. (1973). Semantic distance and the verification of semantic relations. *Journal of Verbal Learning and Verbal Behavior, 12,* 1–20.

Roberts, S. (1981). Isolation of an internal clock. *Journal of Experimental Psychology: Animal Behavior Processes, 7,* 242–268.

Roberts, W. A. (1969). Resistance to extinction following partial and consistent reinforcement with varying magnitudes of reward. *Journal of Comparative and Physiological Psychology, 67,* 395–400.

Robinson, K. J., & Roediger, H. L., III. (1997). Associative processes in false recall and false recognition. *Psychological Science, 8,* 231–237.

Robinson, R. S., & Brown, M. A. (1926). Effect of serial position upon memorization. *American Journal of Psychology, 37,* 538–552.

Roediger, H. L., III (1990). Implicit memory: Retention without remembering. *American Psychologist, 45,* 1043–1056.

Roediger, H. L., III, & Crowder, R. G. (1976). A serial position effect in the recall of U.S. presidents. *Bulletin of the Psychonomic Society, 8,* 275–278.

Roediger, H. L., & McDermott, K. B. (1995). Creating false memories: Remembering words not presented in lists. *Journal of Experimental Psychology: Learning, Memory, and Cognition, 21,* 803–814.

Rogers, T. B., Kuiper, N. A., & Kirker, W. A. (1977). Self-reference and the encoding of personal information. *Journal of Personality and Social Psychology, 35,* 677–688.

Rolls, E. T. (2000). Memory systems in the brain. *Annual Review of Psychology, 51,* 599–631. Palo Alto, CA: Annual Reviews.

Rosch, E. (1973). On the internal structure of perceptual and semantic categories. In T. E. Moore (Ed.), *Cognitive development and the acquisition of language* (pp. 111–114). New York: Academic.

Rosch, E. (1975). Cognitive representations of semantic categories. *Journal of Experimental Psychology: General, 104,* 192–253.

Rosch, E. H. (1977). Classification of real-world objects: Origins and representation in cognition. In P. N. Johnson-Laird & P. C. Wason (Eds.), *Thinking: Readings in cognitive science* (pp. 212–222). Cambridge: Cambridge University Press.

Rosch, E. H., & Mervis, C. B. (1975). Family resemblances: Studies in the internal structures of categories. *Cognitive Psychology, 7,* 573–605.

Roth, S., & Kubal, L. (1975). Effects of noncontingent reinforcement on tasks of differing importance: Facilitation and learned helplessness. *Journal of Personality and Social Psychology, 32,* 680–691.

Rozin, P., & Kalat, J. W. (1971). Specific hungers and poison avoidance as adaptive specializations of learning. *Psychological Review, 78,* 459–486.

Rudolph, R. L., & Honig, W. K. (1972). Effects of monochromatic rearing on the spectral discrimination learning and the peak shift in chicks. *Journal of Experimental Analysis of Behavior, 17,* 107.

Rumelhart, D. E., McClelland, J. L., & the PDP Research Group. (1986). *Parallel distributed processing* (Vols. 1 & 2). Cambridge: MIT Press.

Rumelhart, D. E., & McClelland, J. R. (1988). *Parallel distributed processing.* Cambridge: MIT Press.

Rundus, D. (1977). Maintenance rehearsal and single-level processing. *Journal of Verbal Learning and Verbal Behavior, 16,* 665–681.

Rundus, D. (1980). Maintenance rehearsal and long-term recency. *Memory and Cognition, 8,* 226–230.

Rundus, D., & Atkinson, R. C. (1970). Rehearsal processes in free recall: A procedure for direct observation. *Journal of Verbal Learning and Verbal Behavior, 9,* 99–105.

Runquist, W. N., & Spence, K. W. (1959). Performance in eyelid conditioning as a function of UCS duration. *Journal of Experimental Psychology, 55,* 613–616.

Schank, R. C., & Abelson, R. (1977). *Scripts, plans, goals and understanding.* Hillsdale, NJ: Lawrence Erlbaum.

Schneiderman, N. (1966). Interstimulus interval function of the nictitating membrane response of the rabbit under delay versus trace conditioning. *Journal of Comparative and Physiological Psychology, 62,* 397–402.

Schuster, R., & Rachlin, H. (1968). Indifference between punishment and free shock: Evidence for the negative law of effect. *Journal of the Experimental Analysis of Behavior, 11,* 777–786.

Schwartz, B. (1978). *Psychology of learning and behavior.* New York: Norton.

Schwartz, B., & Gamzu, E. (1977). Pavlovian control of operant behavior. In W. K. Honig & J. E. R. Staddon (Eds.), *Handbook of operant behavior* (pp. 53–97). Englewood Cliffs, NJ: Prentice-Hall.

Seligman, M. E. P. (1970). On the generality of laws of learning. *Psychological Review, 77,* 406–418.

Seligman, M. E. P. (1971). Phobias and preparedness. *Behavior Therapy, 2,* 307–320.

Seligman, M. E. P., & Groves, D. (1970). Nontransient learned helplessness. *Psychonomic Science, 19,* 191–192.

Seligman, M. E. P., & Hager, J. L. (1972). *Biological boundaries of learning.* New York: Appleton-Century-Crofts.

Seligman, M. E. P., & Johnston, J. C. (1973). A cognitive theory of avoidance learning. In F. J. McGuigan & D. B. Lumsden (Eds.), *Contemporary approaches to conditioning and learning* (pp. 69–110). Washington: Winston-Wiley.

Seligman, M. E. P., Maier, S., & Geer, J. (1968). The alleviation of learned helplessness in the dog. *Journal of Abnormal and Social Psychology, 73,* 256–262.

Seligman, M. E. P., Rosellini, R. A., & Kozak, M. (1975). Learned helplessness in the rat: Reversibility, time course, and immunization. *Journal of Comparative and Physiological Psychology, 88,* 542–547.

Shapiro, M. M. (1960). Respondent salivary conditioning during operant lever pressing in dogs. *Science, 132,* 619–620.

Shapiro, M. M. (1961). Salivary conditioning in dogs during fixed-interval reinforcement contingent upon lever pressing. *Journal of Experimental Analysis of Behavior, 4,* 361–364.

Shapiro, K. L., & LoLordo, V. M. (1982). Constraints on Pavlovian conditioning of the pigeon: Relative conditioned reinforcing effects of red-light and tone CSs paired with food. *Learning and Motivation, 13,* 68–80.

Sheffield, F. D. (1965). Relation between classical conditioning and instrumental learning. In W. F. Prokasy (Ed.), *Classical conditioning* (pp. 302–322). New York: Appleton-Century-Crofts.

Sheffield, F. D., & Roby, T. B. (1950). Reward value of a non-nutritive sweet taste. *Journal of Comparative and Physiological Psychology, 43,* 471–481.

Sheffield, F. D., Roby, T. B., & Campbell, B. A. (1954). Drive reduction versus consummatory behavior as determinants of reinforcement. *Journal of Comparative and Physiological Psychology, 47,* 349–354.

Shepard, R. N. (1967). Recognition memory for words, sentences, and pictures. *Journal of Verbal Learning and Verbal Behavior, 6,* 156–163.

Shepard, R. N. (1978). The mental image. *American Psychologist, 33,* 125–137.

Shepard, R. N., & Cermak, G. W. (1973). Perceptual-cognitive explorations of a toroidal set of free-form stimuli. *Cognitive Psychology, 4,* 351–377.

Shimamura, A. P. (1986). Priming effects in amnesia: Evidence for a dissociable memory function. *Quarterly Journal of Experimental Psychology, 38A,* 619–644.

Shull, R. L., & Pliskoff, S. S. (1967). Changeover delay and concurrent schedules: Some effects on relative performance. *Journal of the Experimental Analysis of Behavior,* 10, 517–527.

Shulman, H. G. (1971). Similarity effects in short-term memory. *Psychological Bulletin, 75,* 399–415.

Shulman, H. G. (1972). Semantic confusion errors in short-term memory. *Journal of Verbal Learning and Verbal Behavior, 11,* 221–227.

Sidman, M. (1961). *Tactics of scientific research.* New York: Basic Books.

Siegel, S. (1979). The role of conditioning in drug tolerance and addiction. In J. D. Keehn (Ed.), *Psychopathology in animals: Research and clinical implications* (pp. 143–168). New York: Academic.

Siegel, S., & Domjan, M. (1971). Backward conditioning as an inhibitory procedure. *Learning and Motivation, 2,* 1–11.

Skinner, B. F. (1938). *The behavior of organisms: An experimental analysis.* New York: Appleton-Century-Crofts.

Skinner, B. F. (1948). *Walden two.* New York: Macmillan.

Skinner, B. F. (1950). Are theories of learning necessary? *Psychological Review, 57,* 193–216.

Skinner, B. F. (1953). *Science and human behavior.* New York: Macmillan.

Skinner, B. F. (1956). A case history in scientific method. *American Psychologist, 11,* 221–233.

Skinner, B. F. (1961). *Cumulative record.* New York: Appleton-Century-Crofts.

Skinner, B. F. (1971). *Beyond freedom and dignity.* New York: Alfred A. Knopf.

Slamecka, N. J., & Graf, P. (1978). The generation effect: Delineation of a phenomenon. *Journal of Experimental Psychology: Learning, Memory, and Cognition, 4,* 592–604.

Smith, E. E., Shoben, E. J., & Rips, L. (1974). Structure and process in semantic memory: A featural model for semantic decisions. *Psychological Review, 81,* 214–241.

Smith, F. V. (1965). Instinct and learning in the attachment of lamb and ewe. *Animal Behavior, 13,* 84–88.

Smith, M. C., Coleman, S. R., & Gormezano, K. (1969). Classical conditioning of the rabbit's nictitating membrane response at backward, simultaneous, and forward CS-US intervals. *Journal of Comparative and Physiological Psychology, 69,* 226–231.

Sokolov, E. N. (1960). Neuronal models and the orienting reflex. In M. A. B. Brazier (Ed.), *The central nervous system and behaviour* (pp. 187–276). Madison, NJ: Madison Printing.

Solomon, P. R. (1977). Role of the hippocampus in blocking and conditioned inhibition of the rabbit's nictitating membrane response. *Journal of Comparative and Physiological Psychology, 91,* 407–417.

Solomon, R. L., & Corbit, J. D. (1974). An opponent process theory of motivation: Temporal dynamics of affect. *Psychological Review, 81,* 119–145.

Solomon, R. L., Kamin, L. J., & Wynne, L. C. (1953). Traumatic avoidance learning: The outcomes of several extinction procedures with dogs. *Journal of Abnormal Social Psychology, 48,* 291–302.

Solomon, R. L., & Turner, L. H. (1962). Discriminative classical conditioning in dogs paralyzed by curare can later control discriminative avoidance responses in the normal state. *Psychological Review, 69,* 202–219.

Solomon, R. L., & Wynne, L. C. (1953). Traumatic avoidance learning: Acquisition in normal dogs. *Psychological Monographs, 67* (Whole No. 354).

Spence, K. W. (1937). The differential response in animals to stimuli varying within a single dimension. *Psychological Review, 44,* 430–444.

Spence, K. W. (1947). The role of secondary reinforcement in delayed reward learning. *Psychological Review, 54,* 1–8.

Spence, K. W. (1956). *Behavior theory and conditioning.* New Haven, CT: Yale University.

Spence, K. W., & Ross, L. E. (1959). A methodological study of the form and latency of eyelid responses in conditioning. *Journal of Experimental Psychology, 58,* 376–381.

Sperling, G. (1960). The information available in brief visual presentations. *Psychological Monographs, 74* (Whole No. 498).

Spivey, J. E. (1967). Resistance to extinction as a function of number of N-R transitions and percentage of reinforcement. *Journal of Experimental Psychology, 15,* 43–48.

Squier, L. H. (1969). Autoshaping key responses with fish. *Psychonomic Science, 17,* 177–178.

Standing, L. (1973). Learning 10,000 pictures. *Quarterly Journal of Experimental Psychology, 25,* 207–222.

Standing, L., Conezio, J., & Haber, R. (1970). Perception and memory for pictures: Single-trial learning for 2,500 visual stimuli. *Psychonomic Science, 19,* 73–74.

Stein, B. S., & Bransford, J. D. (1979). Constraints on effective elaboration: Effects of precision and subject generation. *Journal of Verbal Learning and Verbal Behavior, 18,* 769–777.

Sternberg, S. (1966). High-speed scanning in human memory. *Science, 153,* 652–654.

Stillings, Neil A., Weisler, Steven W., Chase, Christopher H., Feinstein, Mark H., Garfield, Jay L., & Rissland, Edwina L. (1995). *Cognitive science: An introduction* (2nd Ed.). Cambridge: MIT Press.

Stuart, R. B. (1967). Behavioral control over eating. *Behavior Research and Therapy, 5,* 357–365.

Sutherland, N. S., & Mackintosh, N. J. (1971). *Mechanisms of animal discrimination learning.* New York: Academic Press.

Tarpy, R. M., & Sawabini, F. L. (1974). Reinforcement delay: A selective review of the last decade. *Psychological Bulletin, 81,* 984–987.

Tehan, G., & Lalor, D. M. (2000). Individual differences in memory span: The contribution of rehearsal, access to lexical memory, and output speed. *Quarterly Journal of Experimental Psychology, 53A*(4), 1012–1038.

Teitelbaum, P., & Epstein, A. N. (1962). The lateral hypothalamic syndrome: Recovery of feeding and drinking after lateral hypothalamic lesions. *Psychological Review, 69,* 74–90.

Teitelbaum, P., & Stellar, E. (1954). Recovery from failure to eat produced by hypothalamic lesions. *Science, 120,* 894–895.

Terrace, H. S. (1972). By-products of discrimination learning. In G. H. Bower (Ed.), *The psychology of learning and motivation* (Vol. 5, pp. 195–265). New York: Academic Press.

Thomas, D. R., Windell, B. J., Bakke, L., Kreye, J., Kimose, E., & Aposhyan, H. (1985). Long-term memory in pigeons. *Learning and Motivation, 16,* 464–477.

Thompson, L. T., & Best, P. J. (1990). Long term stability of the place-field activity of single units recorded from the dorsal hippocampus of freely behaving rats. *Brain Research, 509,* 299–308.

Thompson, R. F., & Spencer, W. A. (1966). Habituation: A model phenomenon for the study of neuronal substrates of behavior. *Psychological Review, 73,* 16–43.

Thorndike, E. L. (1898). Animal intelligence: An experimental study of the associative processes in animals. *Psychological Review,* Monograph 2, No. 8.

Thorndike, E. L. (1911). *Animal intelligence.* New York: Macmillan.

Thorndike, E. L. (1913). *Educational psychology, Vol. 2. The psychology of learning.* New York: Teachers College, Columbia University.

Thorndike, E. L. (1932). *Fundamentals of learning.* New York: Teachers College, Columbia University.

Thorndike, E. L., & Lorge, I. (1944). *The teacher's word book of 30,000.* New York: Teachers College, Columbia University.

Thorndyke, P. W., & Stasz, C. (1980). Individual differences in procedures for knowledge acquisition from maps. *Cognitive Psychology, 12,* 137–175.

Thune, L. E. (1951). Warm-up effect as a function of level of practice in verbal learning. *Journal of Experimental Psychology, 42,* 250–256.

Tierney, A. J. (1986). The evolution of learned and innate behavior: Contributions from genetics and neurobiology to a theory of behavioral evolution. *Animal Learning & Behavior, 14*(4), 339–348.

Timberlake, W., & Allison, J. (1974). Response deprivation: An empirical approach to instrumental performance. *Psychological Review, 81,* 146–164.

Tolman, E. C., & Honzik, C. H. (1930). Degrees of hunger, reward and nonreward, and maze learning in rats. *University of California Publications in Psychology, 62,* 676–687.

Townsend, J. T. (1971). Theoretical analysis of an alphabetic confusion matrix. *Perception & Psychophysics, 9,* 40–50.

Townsend, J. T. (1990). Serial vs. parallel processing: Sometimes they look like Tweedledum and Tweedledee but they can (and should) be distinguished. *Psychological Science, 1,* 46–54.

Tracy, W. K. (1970). Wavelength generalization and preference in monochromatically reared ducklings. *Journal of the Experimental Analysis of Behavior, 13,* 163–178.

Trapold, M. A., & Spence, K. W. (1960). Performance changes in eyelid conditioning as related to the motivational and reinforcing properties of the UCS. *Journal of Experimental Psychology, 59,* 209–213.

Treisman, A. M., and Gelade, G. (1980). A feature integration theory of attention. *Cognitive Psychology, 12,* 97–136.

Tulving, E. (1972). Episodic and semantic memory. In E. Tulving & W. Donaldson (Eds.), *Organization of memory* (pp. 381–403). New York: Academic Press.

Tulving, E., & Pearlstone, Z. (1966). Availability versus accessibility of information in memory for words. *Journal of Verbal Learning and Verbal Behavior, 5,* 381–391.

Turing, A. M. (1958). Computing machinery and intelligence. *Mind, 59,* 433–460.

Turner, L. H., & Solomon, R. L. (1962). Human traumatic avoidance learning: Theory and experiments on the operant-respondent distinction and failures to learn. *Psychological Monographs, General and Applied, 76*(40), 1–32.

Twedt, H. M., & Underwood, B. J. (1959). Mixed vs. unmixed lists in transfer studies. *Journal of Experimental Psychology, 58,* 111–116.

Underwood, B. J. (1945). The effect of successive interpolations on retroactive and proactive inhibition. *Psychological Monographs, 59* (Whole No. 273).

Usherwood, P. N. R. (1993). Memories are made of this. *Trends in Neuroscience, 16,* 427–429.

Van Houten, R. (1983). Punishment: From the animal laboratory to the applied setting. In S. Axelrod & J. Apsche (Eds.), *The effects of punishment on human behavior.* New York: Academic Press.

Vinogradova, O. S. (2001). Hippocampus as comparator: Role of the two input and two output systems of the hippocampus in selection and registration of information. *Hippocampus, 11*(5): 578–598.

von Restorff, H. (1933). Uber die wirking yon bereichsbildungen im spurenfeld. *Psychologie Forschung, 18,* 299–342.

Wagner, A. R., & Rescorla, R. A. (1972). Inhibition in Pavlovian conditioning: Application of a theory. In R. A. Boakes & M. S. Halliday (Eds.), *Inhibition and learning.* New York: Academic Press.

Wagner, A. R., Siegel, S., Thomas, E., & Ellison, G. D. (1964). Reinforcement history and the extinction of a conditioned salivary response. *Journal of Comparative and Physiological Psychology, 58,* 354–358.

Waiters, G. C., & Grusec, J. F. (1977). *Punishment.* San Francisco: Freeman.

Walker, C. M., & Bourne, L. E. (1961). Concept identification as a function of amounts of relevant and irrelevant information. *American Journal of Psychology, 74,* 410–417.

Walters, G. C., & Grusec, J. F. (1977). *Punishment.* San Francisco: Freeman.

Watkins, M. J. (1990). Mediationism and the obfuscation of memory. *American Psychologist, 44,* 328–335.

Watkins, M. J., & Peynircioglu, Z. H. (1983). Three recency effects at the same time. *Journal of Verbal Learning and Verbal Behavior, 22,* 375–384.

Watkins, M. J., & Watkins, O. C. (1974). Processing of recency items for free recall. *Journal of Experimental Psychology, 102,* 488–493.

Watson, J. B. (1919). *Psychology from the standpoint of a behaviorist.* Philadelphia: Lippincott.

Watson, J. B. (1924). *Behaviorism.* Chicago: University of Chicago Press.

Watson, J. B., & Rayner, R. (1920). Conditional emotional reactions. *Journal of Experimental Psychology, 3,* 1–14.

Waugh, N. C., & Norman, D. A. (1965). Primary memory. *Psychological Review, 72,* 89–104.

Wegner, N., & Zeaman, D. (1958). Strength of cardiac CRs with varying unconditioned stimulus durations. *Psychological Review, 65,* 238–246.

Weiner, H. (1969). Controlling human fixed-interval performance. *Journal of Experimental Analytic Behavior, 12,* 349–373.

Weiner, H. (1972). Controlling human fixed-interval performance with fixed-ratio responding or differential reinforcement of low-rate responding in mixed schedules. *Psychonomic Science, 26,* 191–192.

Weisman, R. G., & Palmer, J. A. (1969). Factors influencing inhibitory stimulus control: Discrimination training and prior nondifferential reinforcement. *Journal of the Experimental Analysis of Behavior, 12,* 229–237.

Weisman, R. G., & Premack, D. (1966). *Reinforcement and punishment produced by the same response depending upon the probability relation between the instrumental and contingent responses.* Paper presented at the meeting of the Psychonomic Society, St. Louis.

Weiss, J. M., Stone, E. A., & Harrel, N. (1970). Coping behavior and brain norepinephrine in rats. *Journal of Comparative and Physiological Psychology, 72,* 153–160.

Wickens, N. D., Born, D. G., & Allen, C. K. (1963). Proactive inhibition and item similarity in short-term memory. *Journal of Verbal Learning and Verbal Behavior, 2,* 440–445.

Wickens, D. D., & Harding, G. B. (1965). Effect of UCS strength on GSR conditioning: A within-subjects design. *Journal of Experimental Psychology, 70,* 151–153.

Wilcove, W. G., & Miller, J. C. (1974). CS-UCS presentations and a lever: Human autoshaping. *Journal of Experimental Psychology, 103,* 866–877.

Wilcoxon, H. C., Dragoin, W. B., & Kral, P. A. (1971). Illness-induced aversions in rat and quail: Relative salience of visual and gustatory cues. *Science, 7,* 489–493.

Williams, B. A. (1988). Reinforcement, choice, and response strength. In R. C. Atkinson, R. J. Herrnstein, G. Lindzey, & R. D. Luce (Eds.), *Stevens' handbook of experimental psychology* (Vol. 2, pp. 167–244). New York: Wiley.

Williams, D. A., & Hurlburt, J. L. (2000). Mechanisms of second-order conditioning with a backward conditioned stimulus. *Journal of Experimental Psychology: Animal Behavior Processes, 26,* 340–351.

Williams, D. R. (1965). Classical conditioning and incentive motivation. In W. F. Prokasy (Ed.), *Classical conditioning: A symposium* (pp. 340–357). New York: Appleton-Century-Crofts.

Williams, D. R., & Williams, H. (1969). Auto-maintenance in the pigeon: Sustained pecking despite contingent non-reinforcement. *Journal of the Experimental Analysis of Behavior, 12,* 511–520.

Wimer, R. (1964). Osgood's transfer surface: Extension and test. *Journal of Verbal Learning and Verbal Behavior, 3,* 274–279.

Wollen, K. A., Weber, A., & Lowry, D. (1972). Bizarreness versus interaction of mental images as determinants of learning. *Cognitive Psychology, 3,* 518–523.

Wolpe, J. (1958). *Psychotherapy by reciprocal inhibition.* Stanford, CA: Stanford University Press.

Yerkes, R. M., & Morgulis, S. (1909). The method of Pavlov in animal psychology. *Psychological Bulletin, 6,* 257–273.

Yuille, J. C., & Cutshall, J. L. (1986). A case study of eyewitness memory of a crime. *Journal of Applied Psychology, 71,* 291–301.

Zaragoza, M. S., McCloskey, M., & Jamis, M. (1987). Misleading postevent information and recall of the original event: Further evidence against the memory impairment hypothesis. *Journal of Experimental Psychology: Learning, Memory, and Cognition, 13,* 36–44.

Zeaman, D. (1949). Response latency as a function of the amount of reinforcement. *Journal of Experimental Psychology, 39,* 466–483.

Zeaman, D., & Wegner, N. (1956). Cardiac reflex to tones of threshold intensity. *Journal of Speech and Hearing Disorders, 21,* 71–75.

Zechmeister, E. B., & Nyberg, S. E. (1982). *Human memory: An introduction to research and theory.* Pacific Grove, CA: Brooks/Cole.

name index

subject
index